Praise for *Collapse of Dignity*

"*Collapse of Dignity* is about one man's quest to restore dignity in the mines of Mexico and in the minds of his fellow mineworkers. Napoleón Gómez's story captures the struggle of the human spirit and the fight for freedom in today's global economy."

—R. Thomas Buffenbarger,
International President of the International Association of Machinists
and Aerospace Workers

"A riveting story about standing up to big corporations, *Collapse of Dignity* delivers a message for us all: We the People must force the global corporatocracy to serve us, the workers and consumers. The contrast between Chile and Mexico is a striking call to action."

—John Perkins,
New York Times Bestselling Author
of *Confessions of an Economic Hit Man* and *Hoodwinked*

"*Collapse of Dignity* is an unblinking and unnerving look inside our world's labor struggle. Gómez's incredible account of the fight for justice in the face of seemingly insurmountable adversity is a warning, a lesson, and—ultimately—an impassioned call for international change. Essential reading for any working person."

—Thom Hartmann,
Author of *The Last Hours of Ancient Sunlight*

"Napoleón highlights the importance of continuing the fight against greed and corruption in the workplace, realizing that each worker deserves to be treated with respect and dignity, especially those in mining, as the sector is inherently dangerous. As a former mineworker and loyal member of the National Union of Mineworkers for close to thirty years, this book is a revelation in detailing the continued social injustices in this sector. This book encourages all union leaders and workers around the globe to stand up against exploitation, bad working conditions, and low wages given by the owners of capital."

—Frans Baleni
General Secretary of the National Union of Mineworkers
South Africa

"*Collapse of Dignity* is an extraordinary, personal, and essential dispatch from the brutal frontlines of workers' battle for rights in the face of corporate greed, government corruption, and the appalling neglect of the very lives and safety of Mexico's miners."

—CARNE ROSS,
Author of *The Leaderless Revolution: How Ordinary People
Will Take Power and Change Politics in the 21st Century*

"Gómez writes with passion, intelligence, and vision from his own extraordinary personal experience. His story of the brutal and deadly conditions of work in Mexico's mines and his sharp analysis of the global system that produces such inhumanity make this book essential for anyone who wants to understand how the global economy really works."

—JEFF FAUX,
Founder of the Economic Policy Institute
and Author of *The Servant Economy*

"*Collapse of Dignity* is a powerful testimony to the attack by corrupt politicians and cynical businessmen to silence a union and its leader. Napoleón Gómez, leader of the mining and metalworkers' union Los Mineros, gives a compelling account of the events that followed the industrial homicide at the Pasta de Conchos mine where sixty-five workers tragically lost their lives in February 2006. Gómez became the target of a vicious anti-union campaign in response to his loud and vocal demands for workers' rights, decent wages, and safe working conditions. *Collapse of Dignity* is also a story about heroic workers, men and women, who refused to give up the fight for dignity and social justice. Mexico, with its vast natural and human resources, could easily provide prosperity for all its 115 million citizens. Instead the rich elite collude with political leaders to abuse, distort, and corrupt Mexican society at the expense of human rights and economic development that could benefit all. The global trade union movement continues to support this courageous fight for free and independent unionism in Mexico, and for a better life for all workers and their families. This is what we remain deeply committed to doing by mobilizing our forces all over the world."

—JYRKI RAINA,
General Secretary of IndustriALL Global Union
Geneva, Switzerland

"Injustice never stops until one person summons the courage to become a hero. Inhuman conditions never end until many join that hero and say 'no more.' This is the story of such a hero and those who answered his call."

—KEN NEUMANN,
National Director for Canada of the United Steel Workers

"Napoleón is a hero, because every day he fights for the lives and welfare of the Mexican workers and their families."

"As a coal miner and a union leader, I found Napoleón's story of the Pasta de Conchos disaster both heartrending and infuriating. Everyone who cares about justice in the global economy should read this story about the heroic resistance of Mexican mineworkers."

—RICHARD TRUMKA,
President of the American Federation of Labor and Congress
of Industrial Relations
AFL-CIO

"Written with passion and honesty, Napoleón Gómez's memoir reveals a deeply personal story about the struggle of the Mexican National Union of Mine Workers. Theirs has been an epic battle for the safety and wellbeing of miners and their families, for their dignity, and for justice against callous mining corporations and corrupt politicians. This drama, filled with tragedy and inspiring resilience, is a poignant allegory of globalization and power that should be read by union leaders and activists around the world."

—DANIEL KATZ,
Dean of Labor Studies at the National Labor College
Washington, DC

"*Collapse of Dignity* is a story that had to be told. It's a story of corruption, greed, intimidation, death, and abuse of power, but it's also a story of courage, solidarity, and defying the odds. Napoleón Gómez is a patriot and his story is an inspiration to those fighting for a better, fairer world. Napoleón's leadership is a case study in what global solidarity can achieve through intelligence, honesty and integrity. In the global labour movement there have been heroes that we celebrate for their leadership. Napoleón Gómez is a hero and my friend and brother."

—STEPHEN HUNT,
Director of United Steelworkers District 3

"One of the most important tools in order to create a sustainable Democracy is the organization of trade unions and the respect for mankind, in every open society. In order to create a difference, we need to have the courage to stand up for what is right and wrong. Reasonable working conditions are a prerequisite to any development of a global world and a necessary pillar in Democracy and welfare state."

—CAROLINE EDELSTAM,
Co-Founder and Vice President of The Harald Edelstam Foundation
Stockholm, Sweden

COLLAPSE
OF
DIGNITY

The Story of a Mining Tragedy and the
Fight Against Greed and Corruption in Mexico

NAPOLEÓN GÓMEZ

BENBELLA BOOKS, INC.

Printed in the United States of America
10 9 8 7 6 5 4 3 2 1

Library of Congress Cataloging-in-Publication Data is available for this title.

ISBN 978-1-939529-22-0

BenBella Books, Inc., 10300 N. Central Expy, Ste 530, Dallas, TX 75231

Printed by Bang Printing

Distributed by Perseus Distribution
perseusdistribution.com

Jacket author's photograph by: Tom Hawkings

To the memory of Napoleón Gómez Sada, my father and inspiration; to my wife, Oralia, my partner and friend who stood with me unconditionally during this period of struggle; to my sons, for believing in me; to my brothers and sisters from labor unions around the world; to the brave and loyal members of our Union "Los Mineros;" to those who risk their lives working in unsafe conditions to provide for their families; and to all of those who stand for their beliefs.

CONTENTS

FOREWORD · XI

PROLOGUE · XVII

ACKNOWLEDGMENTS · XXIII

ONE · THE SUCCESSION · 1

TWO · A NEW LEADER · 21

THREE · TOMA DE NOTA · 39

FOUR · THE EXPLOSION · 51

FIVE · IN THE MINE · 75

SIX · DEPARTURE · 95

SEVEN · THE RESISTANCE · 113

EIGHT · A LEGAL FARCE · 125

NINE · A GLOBAL WAR · 141

TEN · DASHED HOPE · 157

ELEVEN · PROOF OF CONSPIRACY · 171

TWELVE · SLANDER AND REDEMPTION · 181

THIRTEEN · THREE STRIKES · 195

FOURTEEN · THE OFFER · 213

FIFTEEN · A FAULTY BRIDGE · 237

SIXTEEN · THE LARREA BROTHERS GO MISSING · 251

SEVENTEEN · A NEW CASUALTY · 267

EIGHTEEN · THE TRICK · 283

NINETEEN · THE EXILE · 297

EPILOGUE · 313

INDEX · 319

ABOUT THE AUTHOR · 344

FOREWORD

This is an extraordinary book by an extraordinary man.
—LEO W. GERARD

This is an extraordinary book by an extraordinary man. In its pages— part memoir, part history, part political critique—Napoleón Gómez Urrutia tells the story of the Mexican government's war against the National Union of Mine, Metal, and Steelworkers of the Mexican Republic (Los Mineros) and of the union's eight-year battle of resistance.

The story begins with a terrible disaster—an explosion at the underground coal mine at Pasta de Conchos on the morning of February 19, 2006 that killed sixty-five men. As the story unfolds, we learn that the miners' deaths were no accident, but rather the result of corruption and negligence on the part of the company, Grupo Mexico, and the government authorities. We see the events through the eyes of Mexican workers and their families as they confront the enormous power of the Mexican state at the service of a multinational mining company controlled by an avaricious billionaire.

But we soon learn that there is more to the story. The workers at Pasta de Conchos turn out to be pawns in an evil campaign by Mexico's ruling elite to destroy democratic labor unions in Mexico, starting with the Mineworkers led by Napoleón Gómez.

Since the 1970s, the PRI and later the PAN governments have systematically sought to weaken organized labor and reduce labor costs to maintain Mexico's low-wage, export-oriented economic model, enshrined in the North American Free Trade Agreement (NAFTA) in 1995. This policy has succeeded in increasing the wage gap between Mexico and the United States. Whereas in 1975 Mexican real wages of manufacturing workers stood at 23% of the US level, by 2007 they had dropped to 12%.

The government and employers control the majority of labor organizations through the system of "protection unions," which in Canada and the U.S. we call "company unions." However, a small number of democratic unions have continued to resist government control and to demand higher wages and better living standards for their members.

It is no accident that mineworkers would lead this resistance. Everywhere in the world—from the British miners' strike in the 1970s to the Pittston strike in the U.S. to the National Union of Mineworkers' leading the anti-apartheid struggle in South Africa to the Ontario nickel mines where my own family labored—the courage and determination of mineworkers has propelled them to the leadership of the labor movement. In Mexico, not only the labor movement but the Mexican Revolution itself began at the Cananea mine, which would again become a battleground in the first decade of the 21st century.

Los Mineros refused to bow to the elites. Instead, they demanded wage increases proportional to company profits, improved health and safety protections, and elimination of subcontracting. In 2005, the union struck the Las Truchas steel mill in Lázaro Cárdenas for forty-six days, winning an increase of 8% in wages and 34% in benefits, plus a 7,250 peso bonus and 100% back pay. Clearly this was a threat to the neoliberal model.

Napoleón tells us how President Vicente Fox and his advisers, working closely with giant mining companies, planned a coup against the democratically elected leadership of Los Mineros, including the de-recognition of the union leadership, criminal and civil charges against Gómez and other union leaders, a massive public relations campaign funded by the companies, the imposition of company unions in many workplaces and support for traitors within the union—all backed by the use of armed force. These attacks took a terrible toll on Los Mineros rank and file, including the loss of four more lives at the hands of police and company goons.

Yet despite this unprecedented attack by the entire might of the state and private capital, with their leader in forced exile in Canada, Los Mineros have not only survived but year after year have continued to win the highest wage increases of any union in Mexico (over 8% in average per year over the past seven years) and have organized thousands of new workers, while President Fox and his successor, Felipe Calderón, have landed in the rubbish bin of history. How is this possible?

I think there are three reasons. First and foremost is the courage and tenacity shown by the members of Los Mineros in the face of great and sometimes deadly adversity. It is the workers of Pasta de Conchos, of Lázaro Cárdenas, who won their strike after being strafed from helicopters by police who killed two workers and injured dozens more; the workers of Cananea who maintained their strike even against an onslaught of 4,000 police and goons. It is Los Mineros leaders who spent years in jail on trumped-up charges rather than betray their union. It is the tenacity of Napoleón Gómez himself, who has continued to stand tall despite many threats against himself and his family.

The second reason is the quality of the Mineros leadership. I have had the opportunity to spend a lot of time with Napoleón and the members of his Executive Committee over the past decade, and I can truly say that this is a band of visionaries. Los Mineros are not afraid to use the strike weapon. But unlike any other union in Mexico, they calibrate their wage demands to the company's profits, bargaining hard but always showing flexibility when a company is facing real difficulty. This is why—despite the ferocious attacks of the government and a few big mining companies— Los Mineros maintain good working relations with dozens of employers, both multinational and domestic. Los Mineros have also shown courage and creativity in launching campaigns to organize unorganized workers in mining and manufacturing, building alliances with rural communities and grassroots committees of industrial workers. They have challenged the government and Mexico's corporatist unions on wage policy, accountability and union democracy. The union's crack legal team has won battle after battle—most recently when the Mexican Supreme Court, in May 2012, ruled that the government's refusal to recognize the result of the union's elections was unconstitutional and violated Mexico's commitment to uphold the conventions of the International Labor Organization (ILO).

The third reason for the success of Los Mineros' resistance is global solidarity. From the beginning of his leadership, Napoleón showed a commitment to strengthening his union's international relationships and global trade union structures. This is why he pushed for affiliation to the International Metalworkers' Federation (IMF) and the International Federation of Chemical, Energy, Mine, and General Workers' Unions (ICEM), which merged in 2012 to become IndustriALL, a global union of 50 million industrial workers—with Napoleón elected to the Executive Committee. This is why the global trade union movement responded by organizing delegations, campaigns, and global days of action to expose the Mexican government's systematic violations of worker rights.

Most important to my union, the United Steelworkers, Napoleón understood from the beginning that industrial workers in North America, faced with the NAFTA regime that seeks to drive down wages everywhere, can only survive if we work together to build a single organization that can organize, bargain, and mobilize the political power of our members in Canada, Mexico and the United States. With this goal in mind, the USW and Los Mineros negotiated a strategic alliance in 2005, which was expanded and strengthened into a North American Solidarity Alliance in 2011. Today our organizations are engaged in continuous coordination in bargaining with common employers, organizing health and safety, education, economic policy and many other areas. Our members are meeting and marching and organizing and bargaining together in Michoacán and Indiana and Québec, Sonora and Arizona, Durango and Ontario, Hidalgo and Illinois, Coahuila and British Columbia. We are well on the way to our goal of a single organization harnessing the power of industrial workers throughout North America.

All of this is a collective story told by working people, but it is also, distinctly, Napoleón's story—the story of a genuinely modest man who did not seek power but, when the moment came, was determined to use all of his talent and capacity to exercise that power for the benefit of his members and workers everywhere. As well, it is the story of Napoleón's wife, Oralia Casso de Gómez, who has stood shoulder to shoulder with her husband on behalf of the members of Los Mineros and the Mexican people as their family has endured threats and forced dislocation as they all fought for justice and workers' rights.

It was my honor to be in the room with Oralia when the AFL-CIO Executive Committee in 2011 presented Napoleón with the Meany-Kirkland Human Rights Award "for his courageous commitment to defend the aspirations of Mexican workers to higher living standards, to democratize labor unions, to promote rule of law and a better future for their country…"

This is why Napoleón is, for me, a hero.

And this is why anyone who cares about the future of working people should read and study this book.

Leo W. Gerard
International President
United Steelworkers
Pittsburgh, November 2012

PROLOGUE

Deep in the unforgiving terrain of Chile's Atacama Desert, just north of the town of Copiapó, lies a small copper and gold mine. Now abandoned, the San José mine was the site of one of the most dramatic rescues in recent history. In October of 2010, the world watched as thirty-three Chilean miners, miraculously discovered alive seventeen days after a cave-in had trapped them underground, were brought to the surface one by one after a long and complicated rescue effort. Television stations and computer screens around the globe showed images of the grimy, weary-looking miners joyfully reunited with friends and family.

In the days after the collapse of the roof of the San José mine, on August 5, 2010, dozens of family members set themselves up near the mine's entrance, calling their encampment Camp Hope. Though they were originally told by the mine's operators that air and food in the mine would last only about forty-eight hours, the relatives of the miners nevertheless stayed at the mine, desperately hoping for good news. It came over two weeks later, when a drill that was breaking a borehole to the cavity where the miners were thought to be located came back up with a note attached to it. It read, in bright red letters, "Estamos bien en el refugio los 33"—*All 33 of us are well inside the shelter.*

Despite the elation of the moment, there was still no certainty of the miners' safe rescue. Some estimated it would take four months to drill a hole wide enough to pull the men up, and many were worried about the mental state of the miners if they had to stay underground much longer, as well as about the possibility of further collapse. Nevertheless, the rescue effort—nicknamed "Operation San Lorenzo" after the patron saint of miners—went forward, and less than two months later, drilling was complete. On Tuesday, October 12, the first rescue worker made the eighteen-minute descent in a one-person capsule, and over the next twenty-four hours, the miners made their way to the surface they hadn't seen in sixty-nine days.

It was a rousing victory, cheered on by the world. But for a group of people in Mexico who had witnessed a similar situation four years earlier, happiness for the Chilean miners and their families was tinged with pain. In 2006, thousands of miles to the north of the San José mine, a similar collapse had happened in a coal mine called Pasta de Conchos, near the town of Nueva Rosita in the northeastern Mexico state of Coahuila. In the early morning hours of February 19, a methane explosion caused a collapse that blocked off the sole entry to the mine. Two bodies were recovered a few months after the disaster, but sixty-three others remain on the other side of the cave-in, sealed within the mine's main tunnel.

Though the Pasta de Conchos miners were estimated to be about three hundred feet below the surface—less than a seventh of the 2,300-foot depth from which the Chilean miners would later be recovered—Grupo México, the company that operated the mine, was unable to mount an effective rescue effort. At the San José mine, caving to strong pressure from the families, the workers, the unions and their communities, the government and the company had stepped in reluctantly, spending millions of dollars and using state-of-the-art technology to penetrate the cavity that held the miners. President Sebastián Piñera, a conservative, had been at the site, along with a throng of reporters and family members, to greet each one of the miners.

But four years earlier at Pasta de Conchos, the people laboring to save the lost men were their fellow colleagues working with whatever tools they had, and Mexican president Vicente Fox never once visited the scene. Germán Feliciano Larrea, owner of Grupo México, also avoided the site. A few labor department officials and company officials did rush to Coahuila to be present at the scene, but it soon became clear that they were more interested in damage control and covering up their own starring role in the shameful series of events that led up to the explosion than in saving any lives. The landscape around Pasta de Conchos was smooth and flat, much more manageable than the rocky, mountainous terrain the Chilean rescuers would later face. Yet the sense of responsibility and ethical obligation wasn't there. After five days, the rescue effort was abandoned and the miners left to their fates, with no clear indication of whether they were alive or dead.

Some of these miners were members of the National Union of Mine, Metal, and Steel Workers of the Mexican Republic, an organization I had led for five years at the time of the explosion. In that span of time, I had seen firsthand the systemic abuse and exploitation of our members, at Pasta de Conchos and far beyond. Vicente Fox's National Action Party (PAN) had taken control in 2000, and his administration was characterized by its close ties to business interests, including many of the men who owned the mines and steel plants our union's workers labored in. There was constant pressure for the lowest wages possible, and an unmistakable favoritism shown toward these companies. The PAN government allowed them to take up huge concessions and run them with no regard for safety, fairness, or environmental impact.

Union members at Pasta de Conchos had repeatedly decried the conditions at the coal mine in the years before the collapse, realizing that it was a disaster waiting to happen. Their extensive reports did no good with Fox's fiercely antiunion labor department; the mine's operators simply prepared separate reports with government inspectors showing that there were no major safety concerns.

The Chilean miners, too, complained about the safety of the San José mine for years before the 2010 disaster. The mine had been the site of various deaths and dismemberments and had briefly been closed before being reopened—without the critical safety issues being addressed. Its operator, the San Esteban Mining Company, had also failed to equip the mine with safety ladders, which are supposed to be present in every mine in Chile. Had these been installed in the San José mine, the miners likely would have gained their freedom much more quickly.

Some criticized the Chilean government for turning the San José rescue into a self-promotional circus, but the wide attention the disaster received meant that important reforms were set in motion. President

Piñera fired some of the officials responsible for the oversight of the mine, and the San Esteban Mining Company is still on the verge of bankruptcy, facing huge repayments to the government and thirty-one lawsuits from the rescued miners. Several small mines in the Atacama desert were closed out of fear of a repeat.

The Mexican government and the operators of the Pasta de Conchos mine had known they would face a wave of criticism and reform were a rescue to drag on for too long and get too much attention. Two men were already confirmed dead at Pasta de Conchos, and there was a long, indisputable history of flagrant misconduct in the managing of the work site. Had any miners been rescued alive, surely they would have told the story of this misconduct in great detail, and the media would have listened. Thus, it was easier to close off the mine, throw a pittance of a few thousand dollars at each of the families, and move on. To help people forget about their arrogance and irresponsibility, they needed a diversion. I, leader of the Miners' Union, was quickly chosen to fill that need.

It was an obvious choice: I had been troublesome from the start, insisting as I did that our organization would not be one of the complacent and yielding unions of Mexico. Germán Larrea, owner of Grupo México, the company that operated Pasta de Conchos, and his good friends in the Fox administration immediately began publicizing a set of bogus charges against me and the union's national executive committee, peddling their lies to a corporate-controlled media. They thought we would immediately give in, but as you'll see in the following pages, we have matched every one of their underhanded tactics with honesty and commitment, and we are still fighting to this day.

I have never allowed—and never will—any offense or disrespect against any worker in our union, or to their families. That extends from the criminally low wages so many wealthy mining and metal magnates want to pay us, to the exploitation and inhuman conditions that have led to many of our colleagues' deaths, to the reprehensible insinuations of the smear campaign launched against the union's leadership. Each worker who helps to create the wealth of Mexico deserves respect and dignity, and I am uncompromising on that point. As you'll see, I've paid a high price for holding such a seemingly radical notion, but I would never have done it differently.

The seven years since Pasta de Conchos have seen a cowardly attack on our union and the Mexican working class at large, carried out by a wide cast of right-wing extremists from both the public and private sectors. Together, a group of businessmen and leaders in the rotted head of the Mexican government have sought at all costs to trample democratic trade unions, using unscrupulous individuals to do their bidding and help bring down the leadership of one of the most fiercely independent unions in Mexican history. The aggressors include Presidents Vicente Fox and Felipe Calderón, the former of whom said upon taking office that his government would be "of businessmen, by businessmen and for businessmen." He kept that promise, thereby betraying the citizens who voted for him in the hope of a financial recovery, development, expansion of opportunity, and the building of a better future for the whole country. His successor was no better. Calderón, a religious fundamentalist, likes to say that unions are like a cancer on society that should be removed immediately.

This book is my account of our struggle, which has now stretched on nearly seven years. It is a story of repression, arbitrary accusations and imprisonments, deep conspiracies, and of strikes, solidarity, and courage. It is the product of my own experiences, my own reflections, and the many long conversations I've had with the world's foremost labor leaders, my fellow Mexican workers, my wife, and the rest of my family. I hope to distill and record all that we have experienced in our battle and bring to light the extraordinary misdeeds of a few powerful individuals, actions that have for so long been absent from the large majority of the media's coverage of Pasta de Conchos, the union's ongoing strikes, and the criminal charges against me and my colleagues. This story has both innocent and guilty parties, and my hope is to give a new perspective on the conflict and to encourage those who may have unwittingly bought the lies from the top of Mexico's power structure to consider the mining conflict with a fresh, more objective viewpoint.

The aggression against the National Union of Mine, Metal, and Steel Workers and me is a vivid demonstration of how unbridled capitalism erodes the rights of workers, especially those of the most neglected social classes. Our fight has not been just to preserve one Mexican union. It has been a fight for human rights and human dignity. It has been a fight to show the world that we, the miners and steelworkers of Mexico, will not yield to my inconceivably powerful enemy, even with a deadly corporate mafia and the entire political apparatus against us. To do so would be to tarnish the legacy of the outstanding labor leaders like my father, who came before us, who fought and in many cases died for the rights of workers. We are proud of our wide base of international supporters—most of whom refer to us as simply "Los Mineros"—and of the great steps forward we have taken.

I have endured atrocities over the course of the seven-year conflict, as have many members of the union. We have faced appallingly unsafe work sites, physical abuse at the hands of police and government forces, threats of violence and job loss—and we have lost lives. Yet we continue on in our fight against the politicians and industrialists who want us to simply vanish, allowing them to continue at their game of squeezing every last drop of blood and profit from Mexico's workers and natural resources. We know that our cause is just. It would be unthinkable for us to not stand up to this exploitation. It would spell the end of one of the strongest unions in Mexican history, and represent a victory for the global effort to crush the labor movement.

This is the story of Los Mineros, and how we came together following a catastrophe to fight injustice harder than ever. Let our struggle be a warning to workers on any continent who face the same set of challenges we do. Let this conflict be a demonstration that, if we come together in defense of respect, dignity, and human rights, we can match our enemies, no matter how powerful they may seem, as the case of Los Mineros has shown. This is our message of hope, vision, and a better future for all.

Acknowledgments

I would like to express my sincere gratitude to the many people who saw me through this book and shared this journey with me. I appreciate the effort of every person who supported me with ideas, passion and creativity in the process of creating *Collapse of Dignity*. Thank you all for helping me to achieve my objective of sharing the truth about the plight of Los Mineros and their families´ ongoing struggle to defend labor and human rights in Mexico.

I also want to thank you, the readers, for spending time with this book and sharing its motivational message of truth and hope with others.

In unity, change is possible. Together we can make a difference.

ONE

THE SUCCESSION

Words are small, examples are huge.
—SWISS PROVERB

I spent my childhood in the city of Monterrey, Nuevo León, the second youngest of five children. From the day I first set foot in Nuevo León primary school, my parents drilled into us the importance of education. We knew from a very young age that it was our responsibility to gain as much knowledge as we could, as this would prepare us to be helpful, happy, contributing members of society. These were my first lessons from my charismatic father, Napoleón Gómez Sada, who during my early childhood labored as a unionized mine worker in Mexico.

My father started work as a smelter in the 1930s, at age eighteen, refining lead, zinc, silver, gold, and other precious metals in a facility in Monterrey. He was devoted to his work, and by the time I was a child, he was becoming increasingly involved in the National Union of Mine, Metal, and Steel Workers, an organization that had been founded in 1934. Its establishment came after decades of work on the part of the miners, including the 1906 strike at a mine in Cananea that served as a precursor to the Mexican Revolution of 1910, the first revolution of the twentieth century, which occurred even before the 1917 Russian Revolution. After twenty years of work, my father became the head of Local 64, the Monterrey section of the Miners' Union.

In his early years as a miner, my father had been working when an explosion in a furnace killed two of his colleagues. He was nearby and

1

sustained severe burns on both his legs. He spent six months recovering in the hospital, and afterward was transferred to the warehouse and storage department of the company, where he helped manage mining tools and the raw materials brought up from the mine. I have no doubt that this on-the-job brush with death was with my father in his later years, as he fought alongside his union colleagues for safety reforms.

As a large family led by a laborer, we had to make do on a modest income. I always attended public schools. My father and my mother, Eloisa (or "Lochis" as my father called her), took pains to see that we used our resources frugally in everything we did as they struggled to support the family. Rather than buying us things, my parents showed us that with knowledge, education, and culture, a person can better appreciate everything from history and art to an excellent meal, a good bottle of wine, or a thought-provoking film or play.

My father was a man who rejected luxury, who lived modestly and simply. He had good taste, but he exercised it with humility. His discreet elegance was born of an enjoyment of all the pleasures in life—in moderation. He didn't have the opportunity to go to college as my siblings and I did, but he was a voracious learner, reading and studying in his free time as much as he could. His personal library was full of books—ranging from histories of the Mexican Revolution and World War II to classic literature like *Don Quixote* and Dante's *Divine Comedy*—each with important passages underlined.

During the National Miners' Convention in May 1960, my father was elected general secretary of the Miners' Union, and my family moved from Monterrey to Mexico City. It was the beginning of a phase of my father's life that would solidify him as one of Mexico's most important union leaders. My three older siblings had left home by then, but my younger brother Roberto and I made the move with my father and mother. I was reluctant to leave school and my friends, but I understood what an honor this was for my father, and I'd soon realize that my educational opportunities were much greater in Mexico City.

My father turned out to be a natural union leader, and one of my heroes. He was sensitive to the social and economic needs of the workers and their families, and his strong, spontaneous personality and sense of determination won him a high opinion among the union's members. Though he had a great sense of humor, it was tempered by a certain discipline and firmness. Thus, he was well liked but also deeply respected by all the workers he represented.

After two years in Mexico City, my passion for economics—micro and macro—led me to enroll in the Faculty of Economics at the National Autonomous University of Mexico (UNAM). I thrived in the atmosphere of constant lively debate and analysis of the most important political, economic, and social questions of the day, including those surrounding the Cuban Revolution, the assassination of John F. Kennedy, French President Charles de Gaulle's visit to Mexico, and many other subjects related to the social struggle and the study of the impact of capitalism and socialism on the collective reality of Mexico, North America, Latin America, Africa, Europe, Asia, and the entire world.

Throughout my time at university, I retained my fascination with economics. I yearned to understand how economic fundamentals could make a positive difference in real life, whether in the case of a company, a country, or a continent. Despite the fact that accounting, statistics, and econometrics were not my strongest fields, I never failed a subject and graduated with honors and a high grade point average.

My career as an economist began in 1965, the fourth year I was at UNAM, when I was offered a position as an analyst at the Economic Studies Department of Banco de Mexico, the nation's central bank. The following year, my final year at the university, Horacio Flores de la Peña—one of my professors, who was also considered as one of the top five economists in Latin America—offered me a job as analyst and researcher for the Department of National Heritage, where he led the Department of Control of Decentralized Agencies and Government Companies Division of the Department of National Heritage. There, I analyzed the economic situation of state-owned companies, diagnosing problems and making strategic recommendations to increase the companies' efficiency and productivity.

I graduated from UNAM and continued working in the job Flores de la Peña had hired me for, but after a couple of years I found myself growing restless. The late sixties was a time of social upheaval. At universities in the United States, France, England, Germany, Italy, Mexico, and many other parts of the world, student movements were erupting against colonial wars, inequality, repression, and racial discrimination throughout the world. A few of my friends at UNAM left the country for the United States or France, and I was thrilled by the idea of going abroad at such an exciting and tumultuous time in history.

I started looking for opportunities to study abroad in the United States, England, and France, where most of my friends were headed. Flores de la Peña, after hearing about my interest in traveling abroad, called me to his office. In his paternal manner, he began making suggestions. "If you prefer to continue your studies in economics," he told me, "your first choice should be the L'Ecole des Hautes Études in Paris. As a second choice, you could go to England, to the London School of Economics or Oxford University. If you want to continue to learn more about economics go to England, but if you really want to consolidate your professional training and your studies, go to Oxford, where they study economic theory as well as development, public policy, and planning, subjects in which you have great interest. All the alternatives are very good, but the decision is yours alone."

I left his office with a spring in my step. On the trip back to my house I reviewed my conversation with this respected economist. How could I not follow his advice?

As soon as I got home to the small house I lived in by myself, I called up my girlfriend, Oralia, who was still finishing up art school back in Monterrey and I said, "We're going to get married and move to Oxford. Start looking for courses you can take!" I knew she'd want to study too—probably art or history—and could likely get a grant to do so.

Fortunately, Oralia was on board with the idea. I applied for a grant to continue my studies at Oxford, and the British Council awarded it soon thereafter. Oralia and I were married in Monterrey, our home town, and we were soon on our way across the Atlantic.

The first two years I lived in Oxford with my wife and life companion Oralia were among the greatest experiences of my life—academic and otherwise. In the first year I earned a diploma in Economic Development, and this course of study taught me much about how economics could transform countries, societies, and individuals. Once I'd finished that degree, I started working toward my master's in economics while Oralia studied for Oxford's three-year degree in drawing and fine arts. Upon our arrival in England, she had applied to Oxford's Ruskin School of Drawing and of Fine Arts, been accepted, and then received a grant from the Mexican Department of Education.

In 1970, we returned to Mexico, my grant from the British Council having expired after two years. We settled back in Mexico City, and I began work in the Faculty of Economics of UNAM as a full-time professor and coordinator of the Department of Seminars. During this time, our first son, Alejandro, was born. I crossed the Atlantic once again in 1972, when I was invited to a month-long seminar at the University of Economic Sciences in Berlin. On the way back, I stopped back in Oxford. Oralia and I had decided to see if we could continue our studies there, and on the visit I confirmed that we had received new grants and that I was enrolled to continue my doctorate studies beginning in the fall of 1972. UNAM, the Department of Public Education, and several other organizations had generously offered their support in the form of grants and supplementary payments to Oxford.

Our second stint at Oxford was just as fulfilling, and this time we had another major personal development. Already with little Alejandro in tow, we soon welcomed our second son, Ernesto, to whom Oralia gave birth in Oxford. With a toddler and a newborn, it was quite a task to care for the children and attend school, but we traded off duties so we both had time for our studies.

At the end of 1974, we decided to return to Mexico. My grant had run out before I was able to finish my thesis for a doctorate in economics. I wanted to stay in the academic world, and I hoped to teach full-time in the economics department of UNAM, wanting to pay back the university for all the financial support it had offered me. They didn't put me in the economics department, though; instead, I was offered a job in the government's Department of National Heritage, which was headed by my old mentor Horacio Flores de la Peña.

In December of 1976, José López Portillo began his term as Mexican president, and the new administration offered me the position of Assistant Director for Planning in the Department of Planning and Budget. I worked that job until July of 1978, when I was offered the role of Director of Planning and Development in a new public agency called Sidermex, a group that combined the three largest steelworking companies in Mexico—Altos Hornos de México, Fundidora Monterrey, and the Lázaro Cárdenas-Las Truchas (currently ArcelorMittal) Steelworks—and ninety-eight of these companies' subsidiaries.

I was now moving from macroeconomics into microeconomics, with an enormous interest in closing the circle and bringing my cumulative knowledge down to earth and putting theories of national economic activity into concrete practice at the company level. Both sides of this equation gave me a solid base for the position of union leadership I'd find myself in decades later.

In 1979, I got a call from David Ibarra Muñoz, Secretary of the Treasury and Public Credit. He explained that there was big trouble at Casa de Moneda de Mexico—the Mexican Mint. The previous director had allowed union and operations problems to get out of control, and they needed someone to help right the ship. (The previous director's inefficiency would later be rewarded with an appointment as undersecretary for tax inspection in the Department of the Treasury, and later with election as governor of the State of Veracruz. Sadly, that's how politics often work in Mexico.)

Ibarra Muñoz explained that they wanted me to take over as director— even if it was just for six months. If I did, I'd be rewarded with an even better position in the public sector. Though I was happy at Sidermex, I was eager to tackle what looked like a temporary—but significant— challenge. Thanks to the incredible work of my colleagues there—the board of directors, the engravers and artists, the securities and facilities agents, and every other worker—we succeeded in transforming Mexico's

Mint into one of the best in the world. The volume of coining went up, the quality of designs improved, the fidelity of the coins' mineral content was upgraded, and we exported more currency than any time in Mexico's history, producing the coins of more than twenty countries.

Despite my initial intention of having only a short tenure at the Mint, I ended up serving as general director for twelve years. I was delighted to bring a third son, Napoleón, into the world in 1987.

After I'd been at the Mint for nearly ten years, I had my first real brush with politics. I'd been invited to a conference in my home state, at the Autonomous University of Nuevo León (UANL), where I would speak to the crowd about the economic development of Mexico. After the conference, I was invited to a small gathering of students and professors at the home of a law student named Leonardo Limón, who was the president of the students' association of the Faculty of Law at UANL. I thought it was a social event, but it turned out to be more political in purpose.

Limón, his girlfriend, and a group of young professors from the university were looking for a fresh face to change up the stagnant political situation in the state of Nuevo Leon. At the gathering in Limón's home, they proposed a "Napoleón for Nuevo León" project: they wanted me to run for governor in the upcoming election. I would run as a member of the PRI—the center-liberal political party that had held power in Mexico since 1929—and they would form a committee to publicize my track record of democratic change and build support from unions, political groups, and voters.

They confirmed to me that the people of Nuevo León were disappointed in their leaders, who seemed unable to adequately represent the state and who many suspected were deeply corrupt. Opportunities and growth in the state were flagging, and the region seemed to get short shrift from the federal government. I nodded my head as they explained these political realities. I was no stranger to the situation, and I decided that day to accept the offer.

My commitment to the campaign was strengthened when I met with Luis Donaldo Colosio, president of the PRI party, about two weeks later to ask his opinion of me as governor of Nuevo León. I'd met Colosio before he became head of the PRI; he was a passionate man with a wide smile and big mustache, and he loved Mexico and its people. When I told him about the possibility of running for governor, he encouraged me to go through with the campaign in his encouraging, approachable manner and told me that if I succeeded, I would have established a democratic method of selecting candidates within the PRI—something that would be difficult under President Carlos Salinas, who simulated democracy while closely controlling those who obtained any sort of power in Mexico, including governors.

The "Napoleón for Nuevo León" group, made up of my colleagues and supporters, helped me schedule a tour of the state and set up many meetings. All of it would happen on weekends, so that I could retain my job at the Mint while campaigning. I would campaign on the importance of promoting investment and employment, and above all I would advocate the opening of new development opportunities that would benefit investors, workers, and the state as a whole.

Throughout 1990, we toured Nuevo León on weekends, meeting with mayors and *campesino* leaders as well as prominent agricultural, ranching, industrial, political, and student leaders, hoping to show them that I'd be an honest, fair friend to them if I was voted into the office of governor—unlike past governors who'd largely won elections by means of the president's influence. Most of these meetings were a success, and I was sure I could see the hope for true democratic change in the eyes of the people I hoped to represent. Through it all, I kept in touch with PRI president Colosio and kept him informed of our progress.

In the first days of 1991, I met with Pedro Aspe, who was treasury secretary and president of the board of governors of the Mint, to ask for an unpaid two-month leave to focus on my gubernatorial campaign. He said it wouldn't be a problem, but he added that he needed to check with President Salinas.

Behind Aspe's response I felt something deeper than the need to simply clear a leave with his superior. The president had a great interest in who became governor of Nuevo León, and Aspe could be making a huge political misstep by showing his support for me. Making matters worse, the president had a track record of swift punishment in response to such missteps while richly rewarding his unquestioning supporters with top-level government posts or fire-sale prices on the banks and companies that had previously belonged to the people of Mexico.

I knew full well that Salinas would never get behind my candidacy, but Aspe soon informed me that the president had cleared my leave from the Mint. After nearly a year of campaigning, I met with Salinas in his office at Los Pinos to reaffirm my intention of running. I knew Salinas from my days at UNAM, where he had studied in the economics department. He knew I'd been campaigning, and though it was to be a casual meeting between two acquaintances, I wanted him to formally hear from me that I had fleshed out a governing plan and wanted an opportunity to meet the challenge of serving my state. Salinas greeted me in his simply appointed office, offering me a cup of hot coffee and a seat on his office couch near a huge window that overlooked the gardens of Los Pinos. For about forty-five minutes, we chatted cordially about the general economic and political state of Mexico, and Salinas congratulated me on my work at the Mint. When we at last arrived at the final part of our conversation and I declared my intention of becoming Nuevo León's governor, Salinas's tone turned somewhat smug. He told me that I should continue my efforts and that he wouldn't meddle with the PRI's selection of its candidate. His speech was hard to listen to, since we both knew his hand controlled most of what happened within the party. He had no problem talking about democracy, but actually respecting it and allowing it to operate was another matter.

A few days later, Colosio invited me to dine with him at the PRI offices. With a tone of caution in his voice, he explained that the party had instituted a new method of selecting its candidate for governor: for the first time, the party would select its candidate after the five men who were interested in the position—"precandidates," he called us—completed a month-long campaign in Nuevo León. Each precandidate would get equal opportunity in terms of appearances and media exposure, and at the end of the campaign, the PRI's members would freely select the person they thought could win.

It sounded fine on its face. Typically, the party's gubernatorial candidates were selected by PRI officials, who didn't bother consulting with anyone about their selection and who took orders from the president. But as the group of five candidates listened to Colosio re-explain the democratic precandidate system in an official meeting the next week, most of us were skeptical. Colosio told us that if the system worked, it would set a the standard for a new, transparent process of selecting elected officials, but many of us cast glances toward one of our fellow precandidates: Socrates Rizzo, mayor of Monterrey. His close relationship with the president was well known, and we also knew how important it was that Salinas have a close ally in Nuevo León. Some of the president's family was from the state, and more importantly, he had close ties to many Nuevo León businessmen, including Roberto González Barrera, president of Grupo Maseca (a maker of flour and corn tortillas) and soon to be owner of Banorte, the massive Mexican bank. Barrera would make the purchase from the Salinas-led government in 1992. Rizzo seemed to be the man Salinas could rely on to oversee his interests in the state.

Before the precandidates officially registered, one of us dropped out—a "little bird" had told candidate Ricardo Canavati Tafich that the dice were loaded in favor of Rizzo. I had my doubts about the simulated "new democratic process of selection," too, especially when Salinas ordered that Canavati be replaced with Napoleón Cantú Serna, secretary general of government in Nuevo León. Now I had to not only overcome the president's preference for Socrates Rizzo; I also had to distinguish myself as one of two Napoleóns in the race.

I decided to register as a precandidate anyway. I had an excellent campaign team who truly believed that we could get the people of Nuevo León behind our plan for the state's development. Plus, Colosio—who I believe was sincere in his encouragement—convinced me that even if I wasn't selected, it would help me in the future if I used the campaign as a platform to publicize my ideas about the changes that needed to come not just to Nuevo León but to Mexico. Colosio had always been passionate about bringing equality and justice to his country.

You won't be surprised by who eventually won the PRI's nomination. As our precandidate campaigns continued, the hand of Salinas was felt by all of us. The media strongly favored Rizzo, despite the fact that he'd been absent from Nuevo León for more than twenty years. Many were unquestioning in their support of Rizzo, and the mayor's campaign materials advertised him as "Socrates Rizzo, Friend of Salinas." It became clear that through a series of privatizations of state-owned companies and banks, Salinas had bought the support of Nuevo León's businessmen for his friend.

About two weeks into the campaign, I told Colosio and a journalist that if they did not change the situation of favoring Rizzo I would renounce my position as a precandidate. I told the journalist about the clear bias toward Rizzo, and he printed it in his interview with me. But the only effect was an immediate call from Colosio, who told me not to pull out and that he'd do everything he could to make sure the PRI's new selection rules were adhered to. I knew his intentions were good, but I also knew that he was restricted by the abundant power wielded by the president. At the end of the campaign, Rizzo was selected as the PRI's nominee, and he went on to become governor of the state of Nuevo León.

If it mattered so much to Salinas that Socrates Rizzo become governor, why didn't he simply use his influence to pressure the PRI to select him, as past presidents did? The answer is that Salinas wanted his will to be imposed but with the appearance of its being the will of the people. The appearance of a democratic election would be maintained even as the president pulled the strings to make sure the PRI did exactly what he and his business partners wanted. It's a type of deception Salinas is no stranger to. After all, this is the man who habitually greeted citizens of Nuevo León with "*Hola, paisano!*" as if he were a man of the people, even though we all knew Salinas—born in the Federal District of Mexico City—was far from a humble peasant from our state.

There's no doubt that Rizzo needed the president's support to win the election, and this was shown further when Rizzo abandoned his governorship in 1996, two years before his term was up, a move that followed the end of President Salinas's term in 1994. Without support from the president's office in Los Pinos, the businessmen of Nuevo León had no faith in Rizzo's ability to serve their interests, and they pressured him to resign.

The experience of this campaign confirmed my suspicions that Salinas pulled the strings and much about how politicians and business-men behave in Mexico, and this type of collaboration to rack up benefits for the rich and powerful while selling off the property of the Mexican people was something I'd see plenty more of in my career.

Sadly, Luis Donaldo Colosio, the man who'd shown the most sup-port for fairness and transparency in the process of nominating the PRI's gubernatorial candidate, was assassinated on March 23, 1994. He'd been elected as one of the PRI's candidates for president of Mexico, but he was gunned down at point-blank range after a campaign rally in an impoverished neighborhood of Tijuana in the state of Baja California.

I returned to my job at the Mint for the remainder of 1991, but in 1992, I resigned, having completed a twelve-year cycle. The job had been more or less administrative in nature, and I felt I had achieved what I wanted to there. I'd served as president of the World Mint Direc-tors Organization for two years, from 1986 to 1988—I was the only Latin American to have ever been elected to that position—and had helped the Mint transform itself into the best it had been in decades. Upon my departure, I took a job as general director of the Autlán Mining Com-pany, which was still owned by the Mexican government, and its entire group of subsidiary companies. My stay there was short: after a year and a half, the company was privatized, and I resigned so that the new pri-vate owners could appoint their own leadership.

I didn't have a clear idea of what I wanted to do next, but my politi-cal passion had been awakened, and I knew I wanted to help Mexican democracy free itself from the grip of corruption. Toward that end, I began spending more time working with the miners' union my father led. After striking out on my own path into the world of academia and then public administration, I was now moving toward what would become my true vocation.

For years I'd helped my father where I could. He had grown into a widely revered figure in Mexico's labor movement and had served twice as senator and once as congressman in the Mexican government, all while holding the position of general secretary of the Miners' Union. He had also three times served as president of Mexico's Labor Congress, a federation of more than thirty labor unions. Helping my father in his capacity as general secretary of the Miners' Union was a rewarding task, though I was never paid for my services. I translated articles and passed along statistical information about markets, trends in metal prices, inflation projections, and changes in tax policy—information that helped the union negotiate wages and revisions to the workers' collective bargaining agreements. I also wrote, edited, and sometimes delivered speeches and presentations at national and international conferences on behalf of the union. Along with some of my colleagues from UNAM's economics department, I also helped design and publish the union's first official publication: *Minero* magazine, today called *Carta Minera* (Miners' Letter). Beginning with my studies and continuing through my time at the Mint, I acted as a consultant, active but in the background. I did this not just out of loyalty to my father but out of a deep and ever-growing respect for the dangerous work the miners of the union—Los Mineros—did every day, and a desire to fight for justice.

Most of the union members had known me since I was a child, first meeting me as I listened on the outskirts of the union meetings that would frequently take place in our home. Even before my father had been elected to lead Local 64 of the Miners' Union, he had organized a political group within local sector, and his comrades would often meet in our living room in the evenings, enjoying a beer or two and discussing how to create confidence and solidarity among the union's members. As

I continued doing unofficial consulting for the union in my adulthood, the members got to know me even better than they had when I was a child eavesdropping on the conversation of adults. As my respect for them increased, they came to trust me. My father tracked all of my work for the union with a vigilant and often critical eye. I know he was proud of the work I did, though he tended to keep his feelings to himself in our personal relationship. It was from others that I heard he was proud of me; he once told Oralia and his colleagues that I would do great things, and not just for Los Mineros. I would have preferred to hear it directly from him, of course, but he showed his respect in other ways—he consulted with me on nearly every important decision he made, even when it came time to look for his replacement as head of the union.

I didn't officially become a union member until 1995, when Grupo Peñoles, the second-largest mining company in Mexico, offered me a position with the administration, accounting, and operations of a project in a new mine opened in Santiago Papasquiaro, a town set in the valley below the Sierra Madre in the state of Durango. It was a post I could hold while maintaining my residence in Mexico City. The mine was called La Ciénega, and I took the job with the condition that all the workers at the mine be unionized—including me. The company agreed, and I began my official career as an active member of the Miners' Union. After a few months of work, the union named me Special Delegate to the National Executive Committee in Section 120 of La Cienega de Nuestra Señora.

The more involved I became in the Miners' Union, the more I felt as if I'd found my calling. Not only was I supporting and learning from my father, but I was putting my passion for economics to use to benefit the workers I respected so much. I had become more and more actively involved in the union's operations; I was now helping negotiate the workers' collective bargaining agreements, always looking for ways to protect the workers' dignity and maintain equilibrium between their rights and the goals of the company.

In 2000, my father's health began to decline. He was now eighty-six, and after a bout with pneumonia, doctors discovered that he was suffering from lung cancer. Though he had never been a smoker, he had spent years at the lead and zinc smelter. As his condition worsened, it became clear that the union would soon require a new general secretary. He began meeting with the individuals who hoped to take his place, among them Elías Morales, a member of the union's executive committee who would later earn the distinction of being one of the worst traitors to the labor cause in Mexico.

Morales was, like me, from the city of Monterrey, and he had earned a reputation among the workers as an opportunist who was driven by insatiable ambition. Using any means possible, including taking on a servile, sycophantic persona and accusing his fellow workers of crimes they didn't commit, he was bent on climbing the ladder and gaining more and more power. It was obvious to everyone that he wanted to take my father's place at the head of the union. Some workers even reported that, during one of my father's last workplace visits, to a steel facility in Lázaro Cárdenas in the state of Michoacán, Morales gave him a shove at the top of a steep staircase, hoping to disguise the fall as an accident. My father didn't fall, but Morales continued his efforts. Knowing my father was a diabetic, he continually offered him candy, rich desserts, and fatty foods. He even took on some of my father's mannerisms in an attempt to gain trust from the workers through mere imitation.

As he lay sick in bed, weakening by the day, my father met with members of the national executive committee of the union, and in those conversations, he detected the scent of betrayal. In private, my father confided to a few of his closest members of the executive committee that there were men in the union who'd grown inappropriately close to the companies. He was worried, and rightly so, that upon his death these men, Morales being foremost among them, would negotiate with the mining companies to their own benefit, and to the detriment of the workers. These colleagues shared my father's concerns with the union's leaders, and concern about who would serve as a trustworthy replacement spread. These concerns turned out to be well founded, as events years down the road would confirm.

At the time, no one had considered the possibility of me stepping in for my father—especially not me. I was excited about my family's plans. Oralia and I were already dreaming about our next adventure, hoping to take our sons abroad once again. We missed the rich culture of Europe, and hoped to educate our boys there. But as my father's time grew short, the executive committee began to view me as the safest option and proposed that I be appointed alternate general secretary under my father. They knew I would never betray the union or the workers. I was already their colleague, their brother, their friend. This was not the case with some union leaders at that time who aspired to replace him.

Though most of the workers seemed to like and respect me, my father insisted from the beginning that I not set my sights on taking his place permanently. From the time the subject first came up, he voiced his strong opposition. To me and to his colleagues he repeatedly said that it was inappropriate; that my serving as his successor would give the enemies of the union fuel for their attacks. He also told me what a difficult world it was—a world of treachery, with many powerful people and organizations fighting for their own interests. Being directly involved with union leadership would be a strain on my family, and he encouraged me to follow my own path.

At the time I completely agreed with him. I expected that before his term was up, a suitable replacement for my father would appear. I saw the position of alternate general secretary as temporary, an opportunity to help my father protect the union as he transitioned out of leadership and to protect it from those who might try to grab power for their own benefit. My plan was to serve in that capacity and then move on.

In early March of 2000, the executive committee of the union held a *pleno*, or formal meeting, in my father's office in the Mexico City headquarters of the Miners' Union. The majority of the thirteen assembled committee members wanted to name me as alternate general secretary, and I was ready to take on that responsibility. But also in attendance at the *pleno* were several traitors, including Elías

Morales, who was intent on securing his position as general secretary when my father died. The tension in the room was palpable. Over the course of the meeting, the committee members proposed that I be selected as alternate general secretary. As soon as the words were spoken, all eyes turned to Morales; everyone knew of his ambitions, and that he would see this as a huge blow to his chances. Seated directly under a deer's head that was mounted on the wall, Morales sat silently but turned a deep shade of red.

My father still wasn't fully on board with the idea of me becoming second in command, either. "Are you thinking clearly?" he said to the group, repeating his concerns. After we discussed the matter further, he eventually came to a grudging acceptance that this was best for the union. He knew that this was the only sure way to prevent the union from being compromised, but before he agreed, he took me aside to reiterate the heavy burden I would be taking on.

At last Constantino Romero, the union's Secretary of Acts, proposed that we raise our hands to vote on the matter, formalizing my selection as alternate general secretary according to the union's bylaws. Everyone raised a hand, even Morales, who grudgingly voted in my favor, too cowardly to even express his dismay.

When I got home after the meeting, I was overwhelmed with a feeling of responsibility and was excited to take on the challenge of meeting the high standards my father had set as general secretary of the union. Already I was mentally running through how I would build upon the foundation he had built, and transform the union into a modern, efficient organization that would continue to serve the workers. I told Oralia about what the union officials had proposed, and she was surprisingly enthusiastic about the potential change in plans. "I'm with you whatever you decide to do," she told me. "But how long would this be for?"

"Just a few years," I replied. "It would just be until I can help place someone at the head of the union whom the people can trust. Once we find the man who will really abide by the will of the people, I can move on."

I couldn't have known then about the dramatic events that would extend my tenure as general secretary of the Miners' Union, but I was pleased that I'd have the chance to help continue my father's legacy, especially if it meant saving the union from men who were more on the companies' side than on the workers'—men like Elías Morales and Raúl Hernández. I told the executive committee that I would accept the position. I gave up my responsibilities at the La Ciénega mine to focus on my new responsibilities in Mexico City. It was a difficult decision to make, but once I made it, I spent the next few months working closely with my father to prepare myself to carry out the duties of general secretary.

Morales, in the days after the *pleno* where I had been elected alternate general secretary, abruptly abandoned his duties as a member of the executive committee. He told everyone that his daughter was sick, but he was spotted at the offices of Grupo México—the foremost mining company in Mexico and employer of thousands of union members—and at the Mexican Department of Labor. It was clear what was going on: Morales, incensed at having been passed over, was now conspiring with the business interests who hoped to control the union. No doubt he thought he could gain their backing, take over the union, and then sell out the workers for his own personal gain.

At the national convention of the Miners' Union held in May 2000, Morales was expelled from the union along with two other traitors—Benito Ortiz Elizalde and Armando Martínez Molina—on proven charges of treason, corruption, and spying on behalf of the companies that employed the union's members. Unfortunately, that wasn't the end of Morales's involvement in the Miners' Union. The spurned traitor would be back.

My father passed away in the early morning hours of October 11, 2001. My sister had called my wife and me a few hours before to warn us that he was having trouble breathing. We rushed over, and he finally took his last breath, quietly and without distress.

That was on a Friday, and on the previous Monday he had told my sister that he'd seen my mother, who had died two years before. He said he saw her near the stairs, that he called to her. "Lochis!" he said. "How are you? I'm coming soon, but I have a few things to take care of." Over the following days, he made sure everything was in order, and by Friday night he was ready to go.

I had asked him whether he was afraid of death, and he said no. He told me he was satisfied with his life—he was proud of his family and of dedicating himself to serving others. He had once told me, as I sat with him in Taxco, a picturesque town outside of Mexico City, that he wondered if he had neglected his family by dedicating so much time to the workers of the union. He seemed upset about not leaving a fortune for his family.

I told him that day for the first time how proud I was of him. "I will always see your image in every mine worker," I said. "I will feel your presence, and I will always give my best to serve them and their families in the same way that you have done throughout your whole life, Dad. You can rest assured that you have been a great man and an extraordinary human being. You have been a very generous man, a great example, a great father."

As we all mourned the loss of Napoleón Gómez Sada in October 2001, the union held an extraordinary national convention, the union's highest authority, to address the successor. The delegates decided unanimously to elect me interim general secretary of the union until the next ordinary national convention, which would be held in May 2002. At that point, the union would elect its next leader.

Until that date, it was my responsibility to fight for the rights of the 250,000 members of the Miners' Union. I vowed to myself that I would keep my word to my father, and honor his memory with each of my actions.

TWO

A New Leader

Work must be given its dignity.
—JOSÉ MARTI

In my first days as head of the Miners' Union, my father's absence weighed heavily upon me. I felt grief at his death, and I felt the difficulty and importance of the job he'd done so well for forty years. I immediately set out to follow one of the many pieces of advice he'd given me: that the best way to understand the needs of workers is to talk to them face-to-face. I began arranging a tour of all the mines and steel plants in the country, hoping to hear what was important to the union's members and to build confidence in me as the new general secretary. My goal was to tour the whole country over the next year and visit each of the ninety or so union sections that existed at the time. I decided to begin with the sixteen sections in the state of Coahuila, which contains nearly 95 percent of Mexico's coal reserves and therefore has a high concentration of mines, as well as the biggest steel facility in the country, Altos Hornos de México.

Each week I would leave the union's headquarters in Mexico City for a few days to make these visits. As I toured work sites and held meetings and assemblies to hear the thoughts of the workers, nearly everyone I talked to expressed their appreciation for what my father had done during his life. They would tell me about sons and daughters who had been able to go to college because of a grant he won for them; about wives and parents who were still alive because my father had seen that they got

21

adequate medical services; and about the homes they still had because he had intervened and provided credit when they were in dire financial straits. At every turn, I heard about something my father had done for someone. I was humbled and overwhelmed. Since that tour, my father has been with me every day, serving as my role model and inspiration—as a man and as a union leader.

Though I felt that the workers—most of whom had known me since childhood—trusted me to continue my father's legacy as an honest leader, my appointment to general secretary of the union was not without some controversy. There were some—like Elías Morales and Benito Ortiz, who had been expelled from the union for their close relationship with the companies—who said I'd simply inherited my role from my father without earning it. Encouraged by companies like Grupo México and Grupo Villacero to challenge my leadership, these men and a small faction who took their side declared to the press that my election was somehow illegitimate. Not one of these traitors had the courage to tell me this to my face, but they were happy to please their corporate backers by spreading lies to reporters behind my back.

In their criticism of me, they spoke as if leadership of the union were an object—something that could be handed down from generation to generation. But the reality is that the union belongs to each one of its thousands of members, and these members freely elect their leader. I stepped into my father's shoes not because of a nepotistic advantage but because the members knew me, trusted me, and had seen the work I'd done for the union since I was in college. They had confidence in the knowledge I'd accumulated in my experiences with the union, in my academic career, in my time in public office, and as someone who grew up as the son of their well-respected leader. The members of the union's executive committee knew the dirty interests of Morales and the others who criticized the committee's decision to elect me general secretary. Everyone knew they were in it for themselves, not for the workers.

Despite these attacks, the fabric of the union—the rank and file—maintained its support for me, knowing that my intentions were good. As I spoke with workers across Mexico, I emphasized my willingness to fight for them—something many union leaders in Mexico don't do. The members soon saw that, like my father, I had the courage to confront the companies in negotiations, putting forth strategies and strong arguments, even when the government established roadblocks to increased salaries and benefits.

I took the responsibility of my new position very seriously. When I wasn't traveling, I was based in the union's headquarters in Mexico City. In my third-floor office, which overlooked busy Dr. José María Vértiz Street, I would meet with delegates from local sections of the union who were facing various problems and give them support in their efforts to negotiate collective bargaining agreements and improve working conditions for the members. I also met with government officials and delegates from the Labor Congress, always reinforcing our union's commitment to fighting for our members and their families. When I had time, I would read about the deep history of the labor movement in Mexico and in the world, in preparation for upcoming speeches and negotiations.

My days in Mexico City were quite structured and formal, a reflection of the union's tradition of discipline and respect for leaders. Each morning when I arrived at my office, the twelve members of the executive committee would meet for about an hour to advise me on the most critical issues of the day. When that meeting wrapped up, I would meet with my assistant and then begin my appointments with visitors, whether from companies, the government, or union sections. At the end of the day, the two lines would form again as I exited the building, with no one leaving the offices before I was officially seen off.

The confidence I built in the union members in my first months as general secretary allowed us to regain lost ground in collective bargaining agreement negotiations and wage discussions. We were able to make up wages lost during strikes—up to 100 percent—, and we significantly increased salaries and benefits in most cases, further building support for me among union members.

In all this, I worked closely with the other twelve members of the union's executive committee and was always there to address their concerns. I had total faith in most of them, but in the back of my mind, we all wondered if we were harboring another double-crosser like Elías Morales, someone looking for the opportunity to sell himself to the profit-hungry companies. We used to joke that we were like Jesus and the twelve disciples, and we were always on the lookout for our next Judas.

It certainly wasn't surprising to me, particularly after my experience with President Salinas and my own candidacy for governor, that my leadership of the Miners' Union brought me face-to-face with the increasingly strong ties between corporations and the government in Mexico. Back in 1988, the Mexican left had lost a huge opportunity to create real change in our country. It was in that year that a political alliance broke off from the PRI—the political party that had long been dominant in Mexico—and nominated Cuauhtémoc Cárdenas, a presidential candidate who would support true progressive ideals. This alliance would eventually break off to become the Partido de la Revolución Democrática, or Democratic Revolutionary Party (PRD), but in 1988 it failed to organize itself successfully. The battle between Cárdenas and the PRI's candidate, Carlos Salinas, was close, and though Salinas claimed victory, many claimed it was a fraud and that Cárdenas had actually won the election. But the PRD proved unable to adequately defend its candidate and claim his probable victory, trading committed political action for fruitless protests and sign-waving. Salinas was propelled to the top of government, and it was on his watch that the era of privatization began in earnest.

A dozen years later, in 2000, the political landscape changed again, with the advent of President Vicente Fox, who brought to power the aggressively conservative Partido Acción Nacional, or National Action Party (PAN). This has generated even greater social inequality, more corruption, and more repression against the working class of the country. Mexican society now bears witness to the fact that its populace struggles under the weight of a government that manages the nation's riches for a few.

Vicente Fox and his wife, Marta Sahagún, began taking advantage of support from the business sector to fuel his ascent to the presidency. In fact, the three presidents who preceded him had already begun imposing neoliberalism on the country. With the PAN in power, it was more of the same abuse, just with even less lip service to leftist ideals.

Among the corporate behemoths who benefited from a cozy relationship with the newly elected PAN administration were a handful of mining and steel companies who would continue with renewed vigor their attacks on the Miners' Union. Chief among these is Grupo México, the largest mining company in Mexico. It operates many mines in Mexico and the United States, including work sites where our miners labor. Its owner, Germán Feliciano Larrea Mota Velasco, is one of the five richest men in Mexico. He appears annually on the *Forbes* list of the richest people in the world, and sits on the board of directors of Banamex, a subsidiary of Citigroup.

In 1989 and 1990, Grupo México, at the time owned by Germán's father, Jorge Larrea Ortega, acquired two mining companies—Compañía Mexicana de Cobre and Compañía Mexicana de Cananea. They were put up for sale by President Salinas; previously, they had been the property of the Mexican state. Though they eventually bought them, Grupo México did not participate in the first round of bidding on these companies. In the case of Compañía Mexicana de Cananea, the winning bidder was Grupo Protexa of Monterrey, with an offer of $975 million. Another company, Grupo Peñoles, had been in second place with an offer of around $650 million. However, Grupo Protexa's tender was declared null and void when, fifteen days later, it was not able to produce the resources necessary to exercise its purchase option.

Instead of awarding the mining companies to the second-place bidder, the government decided to declare the tender vacated and call a second round of offers. In this second round, Grupo México won, with a proposal of $475 million—less than half of what Grupo Protexa had offered two months before. This amount was deemed sufficient, and Grupo México won the companies. No doubt there were behind-the-scenes deals taking place between Salinas' administration officials and Grupo México, resulting in this drastically reduced valuation of the companies up for bid. The fire-sale price was a big win for Grupo México, but a loss for the previous owners of the companies—the Mexican people.

During the process of the shady privatization of Compañía Mexicana de Cobre and Compañía Mexicana de Cananea, the union, under my father's leadership, negotiated an agreement with Grupo México and the Mexican government in which the company committed 5 percent of the shares of each company—valued at around $18.5 and $11.5 million respectively at the time, or $55 million in 2005 dollars—to a trust controlled by the Miners' Union, to be used in support of the social and educational programs designed by the union for its members. This was the company's way of preventing outraged protests at the Salinas administration's complicity in the privatizations.

When my father died, it had been almost twelve years since this agreement, and Grupo México, now under the leadership of Germán Larrea, had failed to deliver the shares. Securing those resources for our members was just one of the many tasks on my plate as incoming general secretary. I also knew it was my responsibility to expand and improve the programs my father had put in place for the workers.

"Educated Miner" was one of the first programs I implemented, and it immediately brought down on our heads the ire of Mexican businessmen. The program was an alliance between the union and the Monterrey Institute of Technology and Higher Education to authorize grants for mineworkers and their families in sixteen different professional careers, and in just the first year we enrolled a little more than seven hundred union members from all over the country. As the program flourished, I got a notice from Alberto Bailleres and Jaime Lomelín—chairman/non-executive director and CEO/executive director, respectively, of Grupo Peñoles, the second-largest mining company in Mexico. They urged me not educate the workers, since that would make them more expensive. Once they have educations, Bailleres and Lomelín explained, they will start demanding higher salaries and better benefits, and be more equipped to negotiate. They had meant to discourage the program, but I couldn't think of any better reason to continue it.

In a later meeting with Bailleres and Lomelín, they argued that if we kept educating miners, they would have more career options and would leave the mining industry. I told them that, first of all, the majority would not leave because most had deep family roots in the industry, but that even if they did, what was the problem? Either way, we were preparing more Mexican workers to be happier and more productive, and giving them new opportunities.

The condescending, classist attitude shown by the owners of Grupo Peñoles runs rampant in the top tiers of Mexican business and is shared by many of the highest PAN officials. We confronted it in nearly every struggle we had as a union, always having to prove that our miners deserved safety, fair compensation, and hope for a better future.

Despite the barrage of resistance, I built out several other programs in the first years of the twenty-first century: Miners' Insurance, which granted collective and individual life insurance on a voluntary basis for the mineworkers and their families, an essential benefit to workers in such a high-risk occupation; Miners with Homes, which provided decent housing for each mineworker, metalworker, and iron and steel worker in the country; and Healthy Miners, which supported safety and hygiene for members.

The Miners' Union also began to create opportunities for the members to participate in politics and democratic change. In the first years of my leadership, we created a national political organization called National Democratic Change ("Cambio Democratico Nacional" in Spanish, or CADENA), whose aim was and is to incorporate workers into political life and give them a chance for full political and social participation as citizens of the various regions and states.

All these programs were in addition to the benefits established in the workers' collective bargaining agreements. Many of our proposals were rejected, most companies preferring to keep the boot on the neck of the workers, but we made measurable progress. I knew my father would have been proud. In May of 2002, I was elected general secretary of the national Miners' Union, by the unanimous vote of the delegates to the Ordinary General Convention.

Part of what drove me in those years was the knowledge of how singular our union really was. Many unions in Mexico (and the world) are what we refer to as company unions: those that exist in name only, and actually generate benefits mostly for those who run the company and the so-called union leaders. (In Canada, they call them "yellow unions" or "rat unions.")

Particularly insidious is the use of "protection contracts"—agreements between the union's leaders and the company in which the union representative receives financial compensation for tamping down the workers' objections. If the workers demand a 6 percent raise but the company says it can afford only 4 percent, the spurious leader with the protection contract is obligated to convince workers that the company truly can't afford the increase. If we push the issue, the bought-and-paid-for union leader insists, we could all be out of a job. In exchange for arguing the company's side of the issue, the union leader is compensated, along with his personal staff and the union members who support his pro-company stances.

Workers who belong to one of these unions often don't even know that they have a union, let alone have the ability to read their contract or elect their representatives. Should they try to create or join an authentic union, they face the concerted opposition of the employer, the company union, and the labor authorities. Workers who fight for an independent union face harassment, firing, and often physical violence at the hands of goon squads.

The Miners' Union, on the other hand, signs only collective contracts with tangible benefits for its union members throughout the country. It's part of the reason we're seen as such a threat. The big mining conglomerates see us as a "bad example" for the other unions in the country that could follow our example of defending and protecting workers' rights and negotiating wages that provide a better standard of living for the workers.

That is the great difference and the true reason why we have achieved these wage and benefit increases over a decade, always above the inflation index and very high above the increases imposed by the government in other unions. I have negotiated for Los Mineros wage and benefit increases of 14 percent on average, year after year, versus the national average of 4 percent of other unions. This is the basis for the great support and loyalty for the Miners' leaders shown by the union members. In addition to defending the workers' rights and dignity, in many cases the members of our union have doubled their income in five years.

In the summer of 2003, Germán Larrea of Grupo México called my office to invite me to lunch. As the owner of the largest mining company in Mexico, he had met with me three or four times, and over the phone he said he wanted to talk about a few things that were bothering him. Though I knew Larrea to be bad-humored, egotistical, and unscrupulous, I agreed to have lunch with him, mainly because I wanted to personally chastise him for not turning over the shares he had committed to after the privatizations of the two mining companies back in 1990, and asked him to set the time and place.

We met a few days later in the restaurant of the Four Seasons Hotel in Mexico City. Larrea, a tall, stocky man with pale skin and light eyes, was seated at a table, wearing his typical gray suit and an arrogant expression. At the start of the meal, he asked if I would like some wine, and I said that sounded fine. He selected a bottle of Chateau Haut-Brion 1981, and I noticed with surprise the number of zeros in the price. It was nothing to Larrea, though: This is a man who owns, according to his collaborators, horses worth more than $50 million, and who's frequently seen at the Hipódromo de Las Américas, a racetrack in Mexico City, placing bets for staggering amounts of money. And that's just one example of the excesses of his lifestyle.

When the young French sommelier brought the wine, Larrea took it in hand and brusquely addressed our server. "It's very cold," he said. "Take it and put it in the microwave for twenty seconds—not a second more—or I won't pay." The man nervously went to the kitchen and returned a few minutes later, holding the bottle as if it were a newborn. Larrea took it again and said in a self-assured way, "OK, now it's OK.

Uncork the bottle and serve it." I privately wondered how that special wine had fared in the microwave, but I held my tongue.

Larrea made a little show of sampling the wine and then said, "Serve my guest a glass." After smelling the wine's bouquet and taking a small sip, I said, "This wine is excellent. It would be delicious at any temperature." Trying not to let too much sarcasm creep into my voice, I asked, "How do you know so much about wine temperatures? Do you have a built-in thermometer in your hands?"

Larrea began to give me a long explanation. Wines such as that one, according to the year, the region, and I don't know how many other things, must be served at 16 degrees centigrade and not at 14, the temperature of the bottle initially, he asserted. Again, I wondered briefly at how sensitive his hands must be, if he could measure a difference of only two degrees simply by holding the bottle. He went on to explain that his work and his position in Grupo México for many years was as chief of his father's wine cellar. His father was in the habit of giving entire cases of a good French wine at Christmas to his closest friends, many of them politicians.

We finished the meal, and the conversation, still civilized despite our differences, turned on my insistence that he acknowledge the debt he owed the union. I explained to him that it was better to acknowledge the debt and avoid having to obtain a legal decision, and I assured him that we would present a lawsuit against him. He haughtily answered that we could take any measures I wished, because he was not going to deliver the shares or pay a corresponding price because our rights had expired. It was a typical response from a man who believes that corruption is the normal state of society. Because it had no benefit to him personally, Larrea had absolutely no interest in fulfilling his moral and legal obligation to turn over the shares. We parted ways tensely, with no conclusion reached.

On the walk back to my office, I called a friend of mine who was a wine connoisseur to ask him if it was normal to microwave wine. I didn't explain who I had lunch with, but he told me immediately that of course that was not what one would do with a wine of that type and that the person who did it was naively trying to impress me. I have to admit having a small private laugh at Larrea's expense, thinking of all the eccentricities and errors committed every day by even those who feel the most powerful among us.

In January of 2005, over three years after my father's death, Grupo México at long last acknowledged its debt to the union, incurred during the privatization of Compañía Mexicana de Cobre and Compañía Mexicana de Cananea. That month, it turned over $55 million to the union, creating the Mining Trust that would support our members. In 2005, close to five thousand workers at Cananea and Nacozari mines received payments of $5,000 each on average, and as appropriate to seniority and salaries.

Forcing Grupo México to turn over this money to us was a victory that would have huge repercussions for me and the other leaders of the union in the ensuing five years, but at the time we celebrated. We were also making huge strides toward building alliances with other unions and union federations. In 2003 we joined the International Metalworkers' Federation (IMF), which has more than 25 million union members in over one hundred countries around the world. In 2005 at the World Congress of Vienna, Austria, I was elected as a member of its Global Executive Committee, for the period 2005 to 2009.

At the beginning of 2005, I had a meeting in Phoenix, Arizona, with Leo W. Gerard, International President of the United Steelworkers Union (USW), and some of his colleagues. I had talked to Gerard on the phone before and was impressed by his intelligence and fierce commitment to democracy, but this was the first time I'd met him in person. A tall, impressive presence, he spoke in our meeting like a true visionary of the global labor movement. After hours of discussion, we came to the conclusion that if we did not form a strategic international alliance in solidarity, and if we did nothing to stop the worldwide decline in union influence, the great pressure exerted against the worker movement from the large multinational companies and the conservative governments would result in the worldwide disappearance of trade unions in ten years at the most. We knew that, to be able to put up a fight, we would have to join our respective organizations in common purpose.

Later that year, the Miners' Union showed our solidarity with USW in a strike the steelworkers called in Arizona and Texas against the American Smelting and Refining Company (ASARCO), which at that time was a subsidiary of Grupo México. The strike, which lasted for four months, was called for the same reasons that characterized the company in our country: low wages; lack of safety in the mines, plants, and foundries; environmental damage; mistreatment of workers; and a despotic and arrogant attitude on the part of corporate ownership. We supported the U.S. strike with press conferences, reports, negotiations, and even political marches and rallies against the company in Mexico City, in Sonora, and on the U.S. border.

Following these collaborations, we signed an agreement that formed a Strategic Solidarity Alliance between the United Steelworkers and the Miners' Union in May 2005 at the International Steelworkers Convention in Las Vegas. That agreement stated that, faced with globalization and the common policies of transnational corporations, trade unions had to design and develop a comprehensive strategy, a new way to defend ourselves in a united way, without stopping at national borders. If multinational companies join forces, there is no reason for unions not to make a similar effort. This seems fundamentally obvious in an era when global trade unionism is enduring assaults and divisions by provocation across the globe.

At every chance, I tried to present to the union's opponents how important the labor movement is in Mexico. On September 13 of 2004, Oralia and I were invited to a private dinner held at Los Pinos, the official residence of the Mexican president, hosted by President Vicente Fox and his wife Marta Sahagún. Three other union leaders and their wives were to be in attendance. The Mexican secretary of labor, Carlos María Abascal, was also invited, as well as the president's chief economic advisor, Eduardo Sojo Aldape. Though I'd been in the presence of President Fox in larger political events, this would be the first time I dined with him in an intimate setting. There wasn't a set objective for the meeting; it was to be an open discussion, so that President Fox and his wife could get a closer look at the labor leaders' views on political matters.

Oralia and I arrived at Los Pinos and were ushered to a private dining room with a view of the gardens. Mexican art decorated the walls, and President Fox offered us a white-blue agave tequila from Jalisco that had been custom made for him. Labor Secretary Abascal, whom I'd met with several times at that point, seemed tense. Though he was conservative and an active opponent of the union cause, Abascal had a kind, soft manner and probably was nervous that the dinner would erupt into argument, given the wide divergence between my views and the president's. He knew there would be an inevitable disagreement when labor issues came up. I was committed to defending the dignity of the workers, while Fox was more interested in the interests of businessmen like Larrea, men whose money had put him in office. Abascal, like the president, looked at matters from the business perspective, but he always did his best to mediate—he likened himself to a marriage counselor, saying that he never failed to reconcile two parties. Germán Larrea and I, he insisted, weren't going to be his first defeat.

We were served a rich meal of pumpkin flower and corn soup, cactus salad, and beef tenderloin with guacamole and salsa. It was all delicious, but I couldn't help but have the thought that this would be a great opportunity for the president to poison several labor leaders at once. I hesitantly ate nevertheless and at one point made the comment that Mexico should review the models of advanced regions of the world, such as Scandinavia and many others. I said we should carefully analyze what we were able to learn from these countries that have achieved great progress in economic development and in their social policy in terms of education, productivity, efficiency, jobs, health, and housing.

I also mentioned the studies conducted by the International Labor Organization, the European Organization of Economic Development, the International Metalworkers Federation, and the International Federation of Chemical, Energy, Mine and General Workers' Unions that show high levels of honesty in these countries. I also pointed out that these are nations where the availability of resources is comparable to the distribution of wealth and they are all countries where union membership is the highest on the planet. "This leads me to conclude," I said, "that we could have governments that are honest and efficient and that show a high degree of unionization, between 80 and 95 percent of the workforce." Neither Fox nor the others made any comment, except Marta Sahagún, who said, "Well, they are very far away and they have different customs."

"That's true," I replied, "but they are examples of great success, and I am sure we can learn a lot of their experiences and policies."

The discussion ended there.

Though President Fox's wife had politely sidestepped the issues at the heart of what we at the Miners' Union work for every day, I knew that the government officials at that dinner held beliefs that ran counter to my wishes for Mexico to follow in the footsteps of countries with more progressive labor policies.

What I didn't know was how much of a threat the Miners' Union was becoming to both President Fox and the businessmen—German Larrea and the other metal magnates of Mexico—who supported the PAN party and the Fox presidency.

In June of 2005, Carlos María Abascal was promoted from labor secretary to secretary of the interior, a position similar to vice president in the United States. Abascal was an active opponent of the union cause and came from a conservative background—his father was one of the founders of the PAN and former leader of the Cristeros, the violent fundamentalist group that had killed enemies of the religious faith in the name of Jesus Christ the King in the 1920s and '30s. His whole career in government was something of a sham. He'd been fast-tracked into the position of labor secretary based on one credential: he had served as president of COPARMEX (Confederación Patronal Mexicana), the Mexican Employers' Association. In Fox's eyes, Abascal's time at the helm of a massive employers association—the antithesis of a labor union—qualified him overnight for the position of labor secretary. He had no knowledge of government or labor law, but he was firmly pro-business and antiunion, and that was enough.

Despite all this, Abascal and I had managed to maintain a cordial relationship at the time. We violently disagreed on almost everything, but we were still able to talk like two decent men. And apparently Abascal had enough respect for me to warn me of the coming storm.

On December 1, 2005, in Saltillo, Coahuila, Abascal was part of the presidential party attending the inauguration of the new governor, Humberto Moreira Valdés. He greeted me and steered me away from the other guests to make me some comments that he said he wanted to make personally.

After Abascal told me that the federal government was concerned about the growth of the national Miners' Union and how its growth was overtaking the others, he said that some employers were upset and angry about our struggle to organize and recruit more and more workers. They were particularly upset by such high increases in wages and benefits, upsetting the government's scheme to keep these costs at low levels that would allow, he said, competitiveness and rapid increase in business profits.

He also said that businessmen in the Chamber of Mines had also expressed their opposition to this strategy, to union wage demands, and to the further spread of our ideas and theories, which might complicate operations and future growth.

I stared at Abascal. "First of all, I'm an economist," I said. I told him I could prove that the companies were exaggerating the risks of our strategy regarding economic policy and controlling inflation, and all I wanted personally was to improve the welfare of workers and their families. I told him that increases in wages are not inflationary when linked to productivity and that, in contrast, they extend the purchasing power of people and thereby stimulate demand, thus strengthening the internal market. I told him that this strategy was appropriate and fair for all, and added that the productivity of the miners had grown tremendously over the past five years, so there was no excuse for not improving the welfare of workers.

Furthermore, the recovery in demand for metals and their high prices was historically unprecedented, allowing benefits to be shared with workers and their families without creating a mismatch or imbalance in the finances of companies. I told him this could all be proven.

I said the wage strategy of companies and the government was based on the absurd and unreasonable exploitation of labor and natural and financial resources that prevented these businessmen from seeing beyond immediate profits and interests.

If our social programs in education, training, health, housing, and life insurance were obstructing the companies' plans, I added, then I asked him to tell me what they wanted or what they were looking for to satisfy their ambition. I warned him that such wage-control policies were generally linked to abuse and that sooner or later these transform into pressures and conflicts that lead to social crises. I said that the government of Mexico should become allied with democratic, accountable, and modern unions to transform the entire society. I said that we were open to dialogue based on respect, justice, and equity.

Finally he asked if I had recently met with the businessmen Larrea, Bailleres, or Villarreal Guajardo, and I said no. Then he told me, "Look out for them because they have been meeting and have communicated to President Fox their anger and concern." I immediately questioned Fox's response to those negative comments from this group.

Abascal said, "You know that the president is very sympathetic and deferential because they have always supported him and his government, too."

"I suppose," I replied, "but in this case they are wrong and are distorting reality, because what they want to avoid is improving the welfare of workers and their families, preferring instead to keep the boot on the workers' neck and perpetuate the highest level of exploitation.

"You in the PAN government always talk about the 'common good' and the social equality that we should all have, but when it comes to the interests of workers, that concept seems to disappear," I said. I finally reminded Abascal that the Catholic church recognizes the value of work and the respect for those who provide labor, and that such value and respect must exist. Such a value is well above wealth, which is nothing more than an accumulation of material goods. I ended by telling him that it took more than crossing oneself every day, going to Mass and Communion every Sunday, then appearing at the office on Monday with the Bible and a rosary in the left hand to make a person righteous, especially if in his right hand he carried a stick to beat the working people, to suppress their fundamental rights and their chance for a better life.

We said good-bye but not before he insisted to me, "Search for them, meet with them, and find solutions before things get complicated." And in a tone of warning he added, "I know why I am telling you this." Then he left.

Of course I knew that as secretary of the interior he must be aware of all political issues in the country, since in Mexico this position is nearly equal in power to a vice president. Abascal at least made, at that time, a kind gesture to prevent a larger conflict that he saw coming.

THREE

TOMA DE NOTA

Man is the process of his actions.
—BENEDETTO CROCE

When President Fox removed Carlos María Abascal from the position of labor secretary and appointed him secretary of the interior, I was gravely concerned by the man Fox chose to take his place. Having dealt with Abascal before, I was familiar with his style and knew how to handle him, but that was not the case with Francisco Javier Salazar, whom Fox moved up from undersecretary of labor to take Abascal's place.

I'd met Salazar, a former chemical engineer, in Abascal's office during negotiations regarding the assets Grupo México owed the union, and he hadn't impressed me. He was a short, stout, shifty character from the conservative state of San Luis Potosí, and he rarely looked anyone in the eye—not someone who inspired confidence or trust. In our meetings, he acted like it was his job to defend the interests of Grupo México, neglecting his obligation to act as a government official who acts on behalf of the Mexican working class. I have little doubt that Grupo México and other actively companies supported his new appointment to the head of the labor department.

Salazar also had personal reasons for defending Germán Larrea and his company. The new labor secretary owned two companies—Latinoamericana de Productos Químicos and Productos Químicos de San Luis—that supplied raw chemicals to Grupo México. On top of that, Salazar is a religious fundamentalist and rumored to be a member of El

Yunque ("The Anvil"), a right-wing and virulently pro-Catholic secret society that grew out of the Cristeros movement of the 1920s. The group is violent and heavily armed and counts many high-level politicians in its ranks. Salazar's code name in El Yunque was supposedly "Capablanca"— "White Cape."

With this development, the Mexican people went from a labor secretary who was the former president of Mexico's staunchly pro-corporation employer's association and the relative of a right-wing militant—Abascal—and got in his place an antiunion religious funda-mentalist and active leader of a militant, ultra-right group. We shouldn't have been too surprised. What else would one expect of Fox, who dur-ing his a campaign rally in 2000 had flouted Mexican law by waving a banner depicting the Virgin of Guadalupe, the emblem of the Cristeros movement, and declaring her an inspiration for his political career?

About two and a half months after Abascal's warning at Governor Moreira's inauguration party, Mexico's labor leaders were scheduled to gather in the capital for a meeting of the Labor Congress, the leading federation of labor unions in Mexico. The Congress was founded in 1966 to give laborers a stronger voice in the political arena and help Mexi-can unions achieve their goals more efficiently. Over the years, though, it had become a supporter of the government's labor policies and had begun acting more like a corporation than an alliance of labor unions. The Congress had originally been closely tied to the PRI, but by 2006 it had aligned itself with the PAN government's political agenda, much to the detriment of workers' rights.

The occasion of the February 2006 meeting was to elect a new set of leaders to head up the Congress for the next year and also to hold a cele-bration of the organization's fortieth anniversary. Despite my misgivings about the Congress's recent cooperation with President Fox's reaction-ary agenda, I prepared for the meeting with hope. I was confident that my fellow labor leaders were also unhappy with the Congress's direction and would join me in making a democratic change.

When it was founded, the Congress elected a new president every six months, in order to give many union leaders the opportunity to serve and contribute their own ideas and experiences. As the organization matured, though, the president was elected for a one-year term with the possibility of reelection for a second year. The outgoing president was Victor Flores, head of the railway union, and he was at the end of his second term. I was glad that, according to the Congress's bylaws, he would have to be replaced; Flores himself was a big part of my dissatisfaction with the Labor Congress. As leader of the railway union, he had proven himself more loyal to the government and business interests than the workers he represented. He had cooperated with the government to sell state-owned Mexican railroads to foreign companies like Union Pacific and the Kansas City Southern Railways and to Mexico-based corporations like Grupo México and Grupo Peñoles. During those privatizations, 100,000 people lost their jobs, and Flores had willingly worked with the government to fire any remaining workers who protested the sales.

On Tuesday, February 14, 2006—Dia del Amor y la Amistad ("Friendship and Love Day") in Mexico, and Valentine's Day in the United States—I attended a meeting at the Melia Hotel with several members of the Miners' Union and other delegates from the Labor Congress to discuss who would take over Flores's presidency now that his time had run out. In attendance were Isaías González Cuevas, from the Revolutionary Confederation of Workers and Peasants (CROC); Cuauhtémoc Paleta, from the Regional Mexican Workers Confederation (CROM), Joel López Mayrén, from the Revolutionary Workers Confederation (COR); Mario Suárez from the Workers Revolutionary Confederation (CRT), and several others—all of whom were committed to democratically electing new individuals to the leadership of the Congress. At the breakfast, we planned to discuss our options for Flores's replacement and then make the decision final at an official meeting the following day. All members of the Labor Congress had been invited to the Melia that day, but we began noticing conspicuous absences: Victor Flores himself was missing, along with about half the delegates expected. We were missing delegates from the Confederation of Mexican Workers (CTM)—the largest federation of labor unions in Mexico—and several other smaller organizations. This was especially strange, given that they were the organizers of the election.

An explanation soon surfaced. Leaders of some of the smaller unions in the Congress reported that Flores and the others had the previous evening organized a secret meeting in Interior Secretary Abascal's office to reelect Flores, even though such an action violated the bylaws of the organization. They had agreed to reelect him, then gone straight to the Labor Secretary Salazar's office, where they were issued a *toma de nota*—the document through which the government officially recognizes a union leader as legitimate. Getting the *toma de nota* usually takes months, if not years, but coincidentally the document had already been prepared for Flores. He was immediately declared president of the Congress, with the full support of President Fox.

The union leaders who told us this had been caught in the middle of the break; Flores had tried to convince them to join his side, but they had refused. The breakfast table buzzed with the news, the excitement of a coming change in leadership turned to anger at Flores's betrayal.

On Wednesday, February 15, we reconvened at the Labor Congress headquarters, in a large complex many referred to as "the bunker." Reports had confirmed that Flores had been elected as president in Carlos Abascal's office and been issued the *toma de nota*. We also knew that the missing members of the Congress were hiding out in the Lepanto, a nearby hotel supposedly owned by Victor Flores, and wouldn't appear. Nevertheless, we waited for an hour to begin the meeting, full of disappointment.

At the time the session was scheduled to begin, we opened the meeting and formally decided that we would stand unified and, independently of the government's will, refuse to support Victor Flores's presidency. Instead, we would move forward with the legitimate elections, as we had planned from the beginning. That day, we elected Isaías González, leader of the Revolutionary Confederation of Workers and Peasants (CROC), as the new president of the Labor

Congress. I was voted first vice president, and Cuauhtémoc Paleta of the Regional Confederation of Mexican Workers (CROM) was voted second vice president.

It had been proposed that I serve as president of the Congress, but I ultimately decided to refuse that possibility. Abascal's warning rang in my ears: The Mexican government, along with several powerful companies, were highly displeased with the Miners' Union and the determination with which we fought for our rights, and I knew there was a strong possibility that outright aggression would begin soon. Having a president with that target on his back risked the integrity of the Labor Congress.

In the end, we stayed at the Labor Congress headquarters until that weekend. We organized a formal ceremony to commemorate the fortieth anniversary of its creation and held it in the courtyard of the building without Flores and the union leaders who had joined him. After that event, we returned to normal activities in our unions. We reaffirmed our commitment to preserve unity, and we called for the strengthening of it in partnership with other national organizations of workers, which we invited to join in this fight for union democracy and freedom. The adversity we were experiencing only reaffirmed our commitment to fight for the defense of the interests of workers. Our motto was, "An assault against a union is an aggression against everyone."

The government of Vicente Fox had succeeded in imposing Victor Flores on the Labor Congress without a democratic vote of all the organization's members. Flores had struck a deal with Abascal and Fox: He would remain as the head of the Labor Congress with official consent and presidential endorsement, and in exchange he would support Fox's labor reform project that the president had thus far been unsuccessful in getting past Congress and the Senate. Flores and his supporters seemed to have no concerns about the deep divide their actions would cause in the Labor Congress, and as I reviewed these developments in my mind, it occurred to me that perhaps that's exactly what Abascal had hoped to do. Divided and arguing amongst ourselves, the Labor Congress would be much easier for our external opponents to deal with.

The consequence of this mistake was the immediate splitting of the Labor Congress and the creation, at the initiative of several participants, of a broad coalition of unions and national confederations aimed at democratizing the leadership and the whole labor movement. The National Workers Union (UNT), the Mexican Electricians Union (SME), the Social Security Union (SNTSS), the National University Workers Unions (STUNAM) and many others—all of which had long fought for freedom and autonomy among workers—agreed to stop attending Labor Congress meetings and cut off contact with Flores and his followers. They had proven themselves servants of the government of President Vicente Fox.

By Friday afternoon, we had put together most of the details of the anniversary celebration that would take place the next day. Around 4:00 in the afternoon, some of my colleagues in the new union coalition and I held a press conference at the Marquis Reforma Hotel in Mexico City, where several of us gave speeches denouncing the reelection of Flores and questioning how he'd been able to secure a *toma de nota* so quickly. After we'd wrapped it up, I decided to head back to the Miners' Union headquarters with three of my colleagues. I needed to finish up some work and collect a few documents I planned to read over the weekend. On car ride over, at about 5:30 p.m., my cell phone rang. It was a member of the union, and he was frantic. He said that a group of over 300 thugs, assailants, and gangsters, armed with sticks, stones, knives, and firearms and led by a group of former miners, including Elías Morales— the man who had betrayed the union and vied to take my father's place— had assaulted the headquarters of the Miners' Union and were trying to take control of the building. Morales, the caller said, was declaring that he was now general secretary of the union. He was waving around a *toma de nota* that supposedly proved it, and accusing the union's leaders of misusing the $55 million Mining Trust we had won from Grupo México in 2005.

The caller told me that the small band of secretaries and union staff present at the building had been helpless to keep the attackers out. Morales and his band were stealing documents, destroying property, and physically intimidating the union workers. The police had arrived with a grand total of two patrol cars and left right away, saying that they would seek reinforcements. They hadn't returned.

I tried to calm the caller down, advising that they should not confront the gang, since they were armed, assuring them it wasn't worth it to risk anyone's life. Yet I could hardly believe what I was hearing. How could Morales, who'd been expelled from the union for years, have the nerve to say he was the true leader of the miners? How could anyone believe that the Mining Trust—handled with great care, in the interests of all the union's members—had been mishandled? There was only one way it was possible: He had to have powerful backing, from the government and from the reactionary mining companies that wanted me gone. I'd become too troublesome. I'd finally pushed too hard on labor rights, and now they were trying to break our union and remove me by force. Morales was an ideal replacement. Abascal was right—things had gotten complicated, but not out of control.

As we drove, I explained to my colleagues what was happening. I insisted that we get to the headquarters as soon as possible, but they wouldn't allow it, arguing that it was too dangerous. We changed course, heading toward my home. On the way, I was already lining up interviews with the press to denounce this unprecedented violation of our organization and defend the union's leaders against the spurious allegations of mishandling the Mining Trust.

We also called the fellow miners who were still gathered at the Labor Congress, asking them to return to union headquarters and help restore order. Word spread to Morales and the attackers that Los Mineros were on their way back to defend the building, and, less than an hour after descending on the building, they fled the scene. Defenseless female secretaries and other members of the administrative staff had been severely beaten, and important documents and many valuable items had been stolen. In the chaos, union members had managed to detain four of the assailants, whom they locked in the building and interrogated.

After intense questioning, the four detainees would say that they were hired in Iztapalapa in Mexico City for a fee of 300 pesos (approximately $30) and that they had been given their choice of cocaine, marijuana, amphetamines, and alcohol to help them muster the courage to carry out their assignment: steal valuable documents, take control of the offices, and impose Morales as the new general secretary. They could hardly articulate a word as a result of the drugs and alcohol they had consumed, and though they confessed who hired them, it had been done through several middlemen. It was clear to all of us that the AFI (Federal Investigation Agency, a creation with which Fox wanted to imitate the USA's FBI) and the secretary of the interior had knowledge and certainly planned this operation. The police response had been pathetic, and the tactic of using a gang of hired violent criminals was a classic trademark of the Mexican government. Most likely, they planned this attack to coincide with the meeting held on February 13 before the elections for president of the Labor Congress, with full endorsement of the government of Vicente Fox through Abascal and with the cooperation of antiunion companies and certain members of the Labor Congress.

Once again, Fox and Abascal displayed their double-talk and double standards. On the one hand, in their remarks they spoke of their respect for the autonomy of the unions, democracy, and freedom, and on the other they sent a crowd of thugs to ransack the Miners' Union. Theirs is a reactionary antiunion government that claims to champion the Christian faith and the Catholic Church, but which at the same time oppresses the disadvantaged.

That afternoon, I gave several interviews to the press in which I denounced the cowardly attack and pointed to Morales, the Fox government, and Grupo México as the responsible parties. Meanwhile, around 8:00 p.m., a group of union members, including part of our legal team, took the four men arrested for the assault on the union headquarters to the Eighth Delegation police headquarters to file a complaint and have them interrogated about who precisely had planned the assault. At the

station, the police took the complaint but didn't seem particularly interested in the case. When our members complained that the police had
left the scene of the attack after being called to the scene, they claimed
to have not been notified—even though union members had seen them
there. Once their statements had been taken, my colleagues and our
lawyers withdrew after midnight and left the four detainees in police
custody, expecting that the preliminary investigation would continue.

That night, after a long string of press interviews and one of the worst
afternoons since I took leadership of the union, I found it impossible to
rest, much less get any sleep. I was overwhelmed with anger and a feeling of impotence.

On Saturday morning, I got a call from one of the union's lawyers. The
police had released the four attackers, because Morales had shown up at
6:30 a.m. Saturday and presented a *toma de nota* designating him as the
leader of the Miners' Union. I knew it had to be forged—he would have
had to get the signatures of some members of the executive committee
in order to get a legitimate approval as general secretary. Morales had
withdrawn all charges against the four suspects and revoked the criminal
complaint filed by the union, arguing that he was now general secretary.
Shockingly, the district attorney's office acknowledged the withdrawal
of the complaint and left the gang's atrocious deeds unpunished, no
doubt because Morales had high-ranking men like Salazar and Abascal
at his back. By the time we heard what had happened, the attackers had
already been released. We filed another complaint against the four men,
with little hope that the police would proceed with a real investigation.

This attempted imposition was "black Mexico" in action—a land
where government and corporations work in tandem to achieve their
mutual goals. It's not a world we wanted to be part of. All I could do in
the moment was once again denounce this violation of the law in statements to the press. Morales had never cared about the union, nor had he
any conviction about defending the rights of workers.

From the moment I heard about the attack, I had little doubt that it
was a premeditated action, planned with the involvement of Fox's labor
department. The imposition of Morales and the freeing of the prisoners

confirmed my beliefs. Abascal's warning had come to fruition: in the darkness of the underground a major offensive had been brewing against the National Mineworkers Union.

Los Mineros had become the strongest democratic union opposing Fox's proposed changes in the labor laws, changes that would cripple the workers' freedom and human rights. They had come for me, precisely because I was making our union too strong. We were doing too good a job of making sure our miners were paid and treated fairly. The mining companies of Mexico, exasperated by having to spend a tiny fraction of their burgeoning profits on safety and compensation for the very laborers who'd made them rich, had decided to take the matter into their own hands. They felt so threatened by us that they had first openly lied and supposedly organized a sham election to unseat me and to set in my place this dark character who had been expelled by the Miners' Union when we discovered that he was privately negotiating with Grupo México, to the detriment of the mining workers. The express *toma de nota*, which Morales had secured on Friday morning, instituted an entirely new executive committee to lead the union. It was an infuriating development, but it would pale in comparison to the difficulties that were about to befall the union.

Undersecretary Emilio Gómez Vives and the general director of the Registry of Associations of the Labor Ministry, José Cervantes Calderón, put forth five documents with forged signatures in which they allegedly unseated me and the other members of the executive committee, sanctioning us for an alleged mishandling of the Mining Trust. These documents appointed in our place, with no election and no respect for the union's bylaws, Morales and a group of people under the direct control and financing of Grupo México—not one of them a current member of the union.

Morales, far from being a representative of Los Mineros, was simply a tool, of both the companies and the government. He was driven solely by personal resentment over his dismissal six years before. Even though he had never been a true unionist, he was ready to take this opportunity to have his revenge on the organization that had rightfully expelled him.

As this situation reveals, the *toma de nota* is an easily abused relic of fascist control of the people. The *toma de nota* is an instrument of political control invented and used by the fascist regimes of Benito Mussolini in Italy and Francisco Franco in Spain. The labor department of Mexico picked it up from them, and to this day uses the *toma de nota* as a means to exert political control over the labor unions at the behest of their corporate supporters. Since final recognition of all union leaders rests with the labor department, government officials can recognize the leaders they like—typically, the ones who they think will cause the least trouble—and reject or ignore those who are democratically elected. Acting as true authoritarians, they undermine the workers' ability to elect their own leaders, all the while claiming that the *toma de nota* is merely a tool for the government to validate the free and democratic election of labor leaders. Of course, little stands in their way if they decide to forge or falsify the document.

Toma de nota was abused during the decades the PRI was in power, but the situation got even worse in the PAN era. Mario Suárez, leader of the Workers Revolutionary Confederation and cofounder of the Labor Congress, struggled for five years to get the government to grant him recognition as leader of that organization, just as many other union leaders have been forced to fight for official recognition. The fact that the government has final say in who leads the union is absurd, and removing this obsolete instrument of oppression from Mexican labor law has been and is one of my primary objectives.

The workers affiliated with the union did not at any time accept the governmental and corporate imposition of Morales, who was universally loathed by Los Mineros. The fact that the government recognized persons who were appointed on the basis of forged documents did not at any time annul my real leadership. My fellow union members understood that a simple document does not make a difference, and my companions continued giving me support as general secretary. They knew that Morales was an imaginary creation, dreamed up by Fox to confuse the Mexican people and weaken the country's labor movement at its core. The union members were not as gullible as their enemies thought they would be: No one believed the lies. They immediately rejected Morales, condemning the government for slandering the true leaders of the union and attempting to replace them with a proven traitor.

On Saturday morning at 9:00 a.m., before the Labor Congress held its fortieth anniversary celebration, the union held an extraordinary meeting of the executive committee. We spent the whole morning discussing how we could strategically protect the union's headquarters from new attacks. Many of us felt the urge for revenge. It was tempting to look for ways to retaliate. But at that meeting I cautioned everyone that rash action could worsen the situation and expose the union to more risk. I told them that we had to act with more calm and intelligence than our criminal opponents had.

Later that day, two thousand workers assembled for the fortieth anniversary of the Labor Congress on Saturday. Given the events of the week, the atmosphere was charged, the crowd incensed by Flores's reelection and the attack on me and the Miners' Union. I was scheduled to speak at the event, and I condemned the previous day's events before the entire crowd. I publicly criticized our attackers and assured the assembled workers that we would not stand for these outrageous abuses of power. I wanted everyone who heard my words to understand that the actions of Fox's government and a cabal of cynical businessmen did not intimidate us but, instead, united us in a common defense of the rights of workers.

FOUR

THE EXPLOSION

There is no gold mine, not even the most valuable in the world, that can pay for the life of one worker.
—NAPOLEÓN GÓMEZ SADA

On Saturday night, I slept restlessly. I was exhausted from the anniversary celebration and all the work we'd done that day to prevent Morales and his band of traitors from taking over the union. It seemed unimaginable that Salazar and the labor department would so brazenly collaborate against us, compromising the democratic elections of both the Labor Congress and the union my father had left in our hands, but I knew better than to be too surprised.

After a few hours of sleep, I was jolted awake by the ringing of my phone. It was 5:00 a.m., and the caller was José Angel Hernández, the executive committee's delegate for the state of Coahuila. His grave tone immediately indicated that something was wrong. In a tense, shaky voice, he informed me that there had been an explosion in Mine 8 of the Pasta de Conchos Unit, a site owned by Grupo México in the municipality of San Juan de Sabinas. The accident had occurred at 2:20 in the morning, and there were many miners missing. There were still no reports of the magnitude of the disaster or of the exact number of miners dead or trapped in the mine, and José didn't know whether the affected men were contract workers or union members.

As I listened to the horrific news, I was immediately sure that Grupo México's negligence was to blame. I had visited Pasta de Conchos and knew it was a dangerous mine, poorly maintained by the company. I had demanded that Salazar conduct intensive inspections there, proposing that they stop work at the site altogether and pay the miners' salaries until it was decided whether the mine should continue to operate or be closed. There was no response, no action taken.

Now a catastrophe had actually happened.

"You tried to tell them," José Angel said before he hung up. "We all tried to force them to prevent something like this. But with the government on their side, they didn't think they had to."

Still trying to wrap my mind around the phone call, I woke Oralia to explain what had happened. Right away, she was up and ready to go. Her first thought was of the families of the miners; they would need comfort and support while they waited for news of the men. With total sincerity, she offered to go with me anywhere, anytime.

In the dead of night, I began calling the other members of the executive committee. I asked each of them to be at union headquarters on Sunday at 9:00 a.m. for a formal committee meeting and made arrangements for some of us to leave later that morning for Coahuila. It seemed unbelievable that this disaster would happen directly on the heels of the Labor Congress's sham election and Grupo México's attempt to place Elías Morales at the head of Los Mineros with the collusion of Vicente Fox's government. In the chaos of those early morning hours, I actually entertained the possibility that the Pasta de Conchos event had been a deliberate attack, a way for Grupo México and the labor department to divert public attention from the miners' widespread refusal to accept a puppet as their general secretary.

I made phone calls nonstop as the sun rose that Sunday morning, doing my best to stay calm as we arranged for a group of us to leave for San Juan de Sabinas. I also designated a few union men to stay and maintain surveillance of our headquarters in Mexico City, in case Morales and his gang of thugs decided to return for a second round.

My bags were already packed when I got a call from the union's secretary treasurer, Héctor Félix Estrella, and the secretary of the union's Security and Justice Council, Juan Linares Montúfar. Linares and Estrella had been discussing the wisdom of leaving for the site that morning, and they were now adamant that we delay our trip by a day in order to finish dealing with the damage done by Elías Morales and the thugs. At first I disagreed, insisting that we get to Pasta de Conchos as soon as possible to assess the situation and help save any lives we could. But as I listened to their argument, I began to see what they meant. If the entire leadership of the Miners' Union left Mexico City, we couldn't proceed with the complaint we'd filed against the four attackers who had been captured and then released. Even though we had been replaced in the eyes of the government, our lawyers' power of attorney was still valid, and we were determined to have the assailants of the union headquarters prosecuted.

On top of that, we would be financially strangled if we left right away: Morales and his crew had stolen huge stacks of checks and other bank documents during their assault, and we'd been forced to close our bank accounts on Saturday. We had to jointly sign for the opening of the new accounts, but we could only do that on Monday, the bank being closed on Sunday. (At this point, the banks were still cooperating with us, despite the government's decree that we were no longer the union's leaders. Soon enough, they would receive orders to act otherwise.)

Upon reflection, I had to accept that I must stay in Mexico City until the next day to avoid paralyzing the union, though this acceptance came with renewed outrage. I now saw that this was exactly what our enemies had intended when they sent Morales and his minions to vandalize our building. Although I now saw that they hadn't anticipated the Pasta de Conchos collapse, they had succeeded in throwing up roadblocks to keep us from operating effectively during the most trying time we'd faced under my leadership thus far. They had replaced our typically efficient mode of working with anger, confusion, and impotence.

That Sunday was one of the worst days of my life. As the day dragged on, heartbreaking details from Pasta de Conchos trickled in. It seemed that the number of men missing after the explosion was around sixty-five, but still no one could say exactly where they were in the mine or whether there was any chance that they were still alive. A good number of the men seemed to be union members, while the rest worked for the contractor General de Hulla, which Grupo México hired to operate the mine. My colleagues and I were in shock, wondering how something of this magnitude could have been allowed to happen, and we were all desperate for the details of the accident and the truth of what had happened.

For most of the day Sunday, I pictured how the miners must have felt at the moment of the explosion, and imagined the desperation any survivors must be feeling. Every coal miner understands the high risk that comes along with his profession, especially when he's working in a mine run by a miserly company that refuses to take safety precautions seriously. But now the worst possibility had come to pass. Our colleagues were either dead or trapped in the complete darkness of a collapsed mine, separated from sunlight and air by tons of rubble. I paced the living room, enraged and feeling absolutely helpless, cursing Germán Larrea and his reckless company. How many times had we told them that this type of accident was inevitable? The union's Joint Health and Safety Commission at Pasta de Conchos had insistently denounced the conditions at the mine, verbally and in writing, only to be threatened with the loss of their jobs.

I was on the phone all day Sunday, trying to find out whether any miners could have lived through the blast and working on a strategy to rescue them if it was a possibility. Knowing Grupo México, I was sure that bringing the men to safety wouldn't be their priority. I also got calls that day from several journalists who wanted my thoughts on the explosion, and I agreed to talk to one of them—a respected journalist named Miguel Ángel Granados Chapa—the following morning, after he finished his radio show.

Monday morning came at last, and my first appointment was with Granados. We met for breakfast at a café on Xola Street and discussed the previous week at length; we were both eager get to the bottom of the mine collapse as well as the labor department's outrageous support of both Elías Morales and Victor Flores. I explained to Granados precisely who was responsible for the attack on the union's headquarters, and I explained how the government had attempted to unlawfully oust me and put Morales and a group of expelled union members in charge of the union. Most importantly, I told him what I knew of the explosion at Pasta de Conchos, placing the disaster in the long history of shameless abuse and criminal greed, stupidity, and insensitivity shown by the operators of Mexico's mines. I told him bluntly that it was impossible to get companies like Grupo México to provide safe work conditions as required by the Mexican Constitution, Mexican labor law, the International Labor Organization, and the collective bargaining agreements they signed with the union—especially when these companies had the unconditional support of the Fox administration and were free to act as they pleased. The owners and operators of Mexico's mines hold profits above all else, I explained, and they routinely ignore their duty to provide adequate maintenance of the equipment and facilities. This was *industrial homicide*.

Granados took detailed notes while we talked, and he listened with a sympathetic ear. He hailed from Hidalgo, a state with many mines (and where the Miners' Union was founded on July 11, 1934), and understood Los Mineros's struggle to secure safe working conditions and a decent standard of living. I had hope that the truth of the matter would make it into Granados's radio show, or one of the columns he wrote for *Reforma* newspaper and *Proceso* magazine.

After the interview, I met Linares and Estrella, and we set about taking care of the Miners' Union business before our flight to Coahuila. We first went to the bank to confirm the cancelation of our old bank accounts, open new ones, and get provisional checkbooks. With that done, we regrouped at headquarters, where I gave instructions on how best to clean up and repair the damage from Friday's assault. I also made calls to my fellow labor leaders to explain the situation and ask for their assistance. I spoke with two of my colleagues and close friends from the United Steelworkers—Leo Gerard, international president, and Ken Neumann, national director for Canada—as well as several union leaders in Spain, asking that they send any rescue specialists, rescue equipment, or trained workers they could spare to Pasta de Conchos. Without even seeing the site yet, I was certain that Grupo México wasn't doing enough.

We managed to wrap up our business and collect our personal belongings by late morning, and we were on our way to the Mexico City airport by noon. Accompanying me on the trip were Oralia and three fellow members of the executive committee. Jorge Campos of Peru, the International Metalworkers' Federation's director for Latin America, and Jorge Almedia of Argentina, an assistant director in the IMF, had both taken flights to Coahuila as soon as they learned of the explosion.

Several hours later, we touched down in Múzquiz, a small town about an hour away from the mine, and transferred to a small caravan of vehicles. José Ángel Hernández, the committee's delegate from Coahuila, had met us at the airport with a group of our union colleagues, and as our SUV sped through the arid landscape of northern Mexico, José described the terrible events of the previous day. He had been down in the mine that morning, and he confirmed what I'd been told over the phone: The condition of the mine was catastrophic. The explosion was so powerful that most of its main tunnel had collapsed, and it was going to be very difficult to rescue our colleagues, if they were even still alive. Thirty-seven of the missing miners were contractors belonging to General de Hulla; three were employees of Grupo México, and the remaining twenty-five were unionized with Los Mineros. The families, José said, were gathered around the mine, deep in anguish, and neither Grupo México nor the government was giving them adequate information about what was going on.

When we pulled up to Pasta de Conchos at dusk, around 5:30 p.m., the gray, cloudy day had turned to night, and there was a chill in the air. A horde of grim-looking soldiers guarded the entrance to the mine. We got out of the SUV, and an army truck drove us around the site to a back entrance, since the soldiers had cordoned off the main entrance. There, more army guards were waiting to check our IDs to verify that we were affiliated with the union.

As we passed the guards, I saw close to a hundred journalists and other members of the media, along with a throng of volunteer workers, relatives of the miners, and Red Cross workers. Though they all looked somber, several reporters rushed up and asked me for a statement. I told them I had plenty to say but that I first needed to see the families and get a report on the latest developments.

We crossed the darkened work site to the company offices, which displayed a large sign reading "Industrial Minera México"—the name under which Grupo México operated the mine. Most of the family members were gathered in a large corridor, wrapped in silence and grief, with looks of profound desolation on their faces. Oralia and I began greeting each of them, one by one, hugging them and expressing our support and love. They said that the company hadn't notified any of them that there had been an accident in the mine. Instead, the news had spread through word of mouth, with some relatives hearing the first vague reports on the news.

By 8:00 in the morning on Monday, February 20, family and friends had begun arriving at the mine, only to find it already blocked by soldiers hired by Grupo México. The smell of burnt rubber was strong in the air. The mayor of Múzquiz was also there, and when he told the families that the mine had collapsed, they tore through the barrier in a wave.

Now, a day later, they were devastated by the lack of updates on the rescue, though they were still clinging to hope that a miracle would bring their trapped loved ones back to the light of day. Many were angry at the scattered, conflicting reports the company was giving about what happened inside the mine. At first they had been told that it was a small explosion at the mouth of the mine, but there was some confusion about whether it was an explosion, a collapse, or both. They had gone so long waiting outside the offices without an official update that they were ready to burst. I ensured them that I would speak with the company and share any new information I could get. I told them that I was going to do everything in my power to rescue our colleagues—that was my commitment.

At the end of the corridor was a set of closed doors that led to the company's main office. After spending some time with the families, I entered the office and found an assembly of directors, managers, and technicians from Grupo México and General de Hulla, the subcontractor who ran the mine. When I appeared in the doorway, a man named

Rivera—an engineer brought in from the steel company Altos Hornos de México—was speaking loudly and jovially, as if a tragedy hadn't occurred just outside the office. He cut off his sentence the second he saw me, the smile quickly falling from his face.

Labor Secretary Salazar, flanked by his personal secretary and other assistants, was also in the room, along with Xavier García de Quevedo, president of Industrial Minera and longtime member of Grupo México's board of directors. Spread on the table before them all was a map of the mine; it showed the depth of the different tunnels and described their interior. Except for the relaxed engineers from Altos Hornos de México, who didn't seem to understand the magnitude of what had happened, they all looked absolutely terrified, and they had reason to be. None of them would look me in the eye.

I demanded an explanation from Salazar and García de Quevedo. I told them we would settle for nothing less than a detailed and truthful description of the possibility of rescuing the miners. Many looks were traded before anyone spoke; no one wanted to speak a wrong word. They knew that outside the office, pressure from the families, the union, and the media was mounting.

At last, Grupo México's engineers spoke, explaining that there had been a huge explosion that caused several rock slides, or "falls," as they are known to miners—showers of coal and rocks that blocked and closed off access to the inside of the mine at certain points. They said that the blast generated temperatures exceeding 600° C (a body inciner-ates at around 400°) and, according to the technicians and experts, it generated an immediate reduction of oxygen to levels of 3 percent and a correspondingly high concentration of methane and carbon monoxide, which in some parts of the mine would have amounted to greater than 100 percent. They said they weren't sure whether anyone in the mine was alive, but judging from this report and the apparent lack of air below ground, it appeared that it would be difficult for our colleagues to sur-vive under those conditions.

I could sense the pessimism and despair in Grupo México's engineers as they explained the situation. It felt like they were already making a case for their being unable to rescue our colleagues, though they assured me that they were hard at work devising a strategy for bringing the men up. I demanded that they do everything humanly possible to rescue our colleagues, alive or dead, in the least possible period of time, and said that my colleagues and I, while not experts in rescue, would help in the rescue activities however we could.

I left Salazar, García de Quevedo, and the others holed up inside the Industrial Minera offices and followed several executive committee members to the mouth of the mine to hear a report from the rescue workers themselves. The volunteer workers were ready to continue their rescue operations, but with the succession of falls blocking their way into an unstable mine with no other points of entry, every course of action was complicated and perilous.

Earlier on Monday morning, some of our colleagues from the executive team had descended into the mine, before the rescue team had been assembled. What they saw didn't give them hope: they ran into the huge rockslide that prevented entrance into the body of the main tunnel. Later that day, the first rescue workers confirmed the poor state of the mine. They determined there was little possibility of finding the miners alive, plus high risks involved in treading any deeper into the cavity. The rescue party had progressed about one hundred feet into the tunnel but had slowed considerably once they encountered a thick wall of collapsed rock that blocked them from whatever lay deeper in the mine. Management of the rescue efforts, they told us, had been chaotic and disorganized from the start. No one from Grupo México, General de Hulla, or the labor department had any strategy for handling this deadly situation. Grupo México, finding itself short on men, borrowed workers from other companies to assist them, but they had no resources and no safeguards to protect the rescuers.

The company alone should have been responsible for the rescue— it should have sent in its own teams, along with inspectors from the labor department, but neither of those parties was present. Because we didn't trust Grupo México's ability to do the work or its willingness to give us honest reports, we knew that if we had any real chance of rescuing the trapped men, it would be up to us. Workers from other mines in Coahuila had come to Pasta de Conchos in solidarity with their endangered colleagues and their families, and the workers themselves, driven by the solidarity, began their rescue efforts with the complete support of the Miners' Union and its local branches in Coahuila. They created rescue squads made up of Pasta de Conchos miners who knew the mine's layout, and more experienced laborers from other mines in the area, the majority of them union members. With our own men involved, at least we knew we'd get a truthful report of how the mission was proceeding.

The rescuers told me that, progressing very slowly—frequently on all fours—and driven by the thought of their trapped colleagues, a team of about eight men had managed to break through the first coal slide. With no ventilation or electricity, and only their headlamps for light, they'd dug with their hands and rudimentary miners' tools until their bodies could fit through the hole. About fifty yards later, though, they ran into a second cave-in, and this one they were unable to break through. It seemed that the explosion had traveled along the floor of the mine over a distance of over one and a quarter miles, causing a series of these slides in a chain, and no one knew exactly where the group of miners had been at the moment of ignition.

After obtaining a report on the situation, we went to the mouth of the mine, where other technicians were coordinating the rescue efforts. I decided to go down into it myself, along with members of the union's executive committee and some rescue workers, to see the condition of the facilities for ourselves.

The mine's railway had been destroyed, so we descended into the sloped tunnel on foot, each of us wearing a miner's outfit and a helmet with a headlamp. One of us held the device that measured gas concentrations. The whole mine was filled with dust and a suffocating smoky smell, with no ventilation or electricity. We walked along in total silence, the narrow tunnel forcing us to walk two abreast. At a depth of about 400 feet, we reached the pitch-black chamber where the main tunnel began. It was cold and hushed inside; it was like walking into a tomb.

Dust and coal residue were piled all around us, and it was difficult to breathe. By the light of our lamps, we saw that the coal conveyer belts, which began in this chamber, and the cars that transported the miners were all destroyed. About 100 feet ahead, we encountered the first collapse. There was no getting through it without equipment. The reality was that we had to turn back.

The impasse conjured up deep sadness, frustration, and anger. They had been able to break through only one rockslide so far, and we felt powerless at not having been able to prevent the tragedy. We'd held strikes and loudly decried the safety conditions, but despite all the pressure we could bring to bear, the government had refused to compel Grupo México to meet even the most basic of safety requirements. The thought of it brought me close to physical illness.

When we got back to the surface, Salazar and García de Quevedo were finally ready to give the families their first report on the condition of the mine and the progress made by the rescue teams. Salazar looked shaky and nervous, and Quevedo went a pallid white as they fielded questions from the miners' relatives.

The two of them had apparently failed to hit upon any bright ideas for how to present the explosion. They said without much certainty that they had hopes of rescuing the trapped men, even as they were improvising rescue operations and sending men provided by other companies and equipped with hardly any equipment into the mine.

Rather than seeking the hard truth from García de Quevedo, as any upright labor secretary would have done, Salazar had cooperated with him and other company representatives to develop an explanation for the tragedy that downplayed their own involvement. In the report to the family, there was absolutely no mention of the underlying cause of the collapse or all the inspections Salazar's department had failed to carry out. As the private owner of two companies that are suppliers to Grupo México, and as the man responsible for ensuring proper inspection of Mexico's mining stations, Salazar had a doubly strong interest in seeing that the PR aspects of the situation were controlled as quickly as possible. As both a businessman and a public official, he was utterly committed to Grupo México.

After this pathetic briefing that brought no comfort to the families, I finally had a chance to talk to Governor Humberto Moreira, who had been at the site for most of the day. He was, of course, upset by the situation, but in our conversation he also seemed shocked by how Grupo México and Salazar were handling the catastrophe. He told me that the night before, on Sunday, at a private dinner in the guesthouse of Grupo México in Nueva Rosita, Coahuila, the main topic of conversation between Salazar and García de Quevedo was what my reaction would be when I arrived and how they could spin their story to the press and to the miners' families. Undoubtedly they knew that I wasn't afraid to place blame precisely where it belonged, and further, they knew Los Mineros were already inflamed from the attack on our union's headquarters and their plot to destroy its leadership. Despite the elaborate machinations that had led to Victor Flores's reelection, the attack on our headquarters, and the fast-tracking of Elías Morales's *toma de nota*, Grupo México and the Labor Secretary Salazar had no plan at all for handling the situation at Pasta de Conchos. Moreira confirmed for me that, privately, they were intent on not letting me publicize the full truth about why the mine had collapsed.

Around 11:00 p.m. on Monday, Oralia and I went over to thank the night-shift volunteers before we drove to a nearby motel to eat some food, discuss the rescue further, and get a few hours of rest before returning to the site early the next morning. On our way to the car, we were approached by Javier de la Fuente, CEO and a major shareholder of General de Hulla. He took me aside and anxiously asked that I not take legal action against him, arguing that he had a family and more than thirty years working in the mining sector. I was furious at his request. As head of General de Hulla, he was in charge of operating the mine and was therefore instrumental in making as much money as possible for García de Quevedo and Grupo México, even at the risk of the workers' lives. In fact, De la Fuente was one of the men the miners complained about most. He was a man who had repeatedly shown his carelessness and utter disrespect for the safety of his workers. Whenever any one of them would bring a work site hazard to his attention, his response was always the same: "If you don't like it, you can quit. When you work here, you do what I say."

Now de la Fuente was coming to me to ask for leniency, but I had no sympathy. How could he claim his family and his history in the mining industry for credit, when he had so callously put his fellow miners in danger every day? Didn't they have families too? Didn't they sacrifice far more than he ever had for their profession?

For me, de la Fuente's plea was an early acknowledgment of guilt. He knew full well that they had not heeded the repeated warnings of the Safety and Hygiene Commission. I could offer him no comfort. Before Oralia and I left for our motel, I told him simply that we would get to the bottom of who was responsible for the collapse.

The following day, my youngest son, Napoleón, and Oralia's sister, Darlinda, arrived in Coahuila, and we went with a few members of the executive committee to visit the workers who had been injured in the explosion. There were several miners in a nearby hospital, some with second- and third-degree burns. We talked with those who were able to speak to us, asking them to describe to us what occurred and to narrate their recollection of the tragedy.

One survivor we talked to had his hands and part of his face burned. Despite his injuries, he was able to speak, and he was very happy about having a visit from us. He told me that he escaped with his life because he was below, in the bottom of the mine, supervising the mobile belts that were transporting coal to the outside. Every twenty minutes he inspected the bands, ensuring that they were working properly and were free of faults and technical problems. He was stationed close the concrete slab in the subterranean vestibule of the mine, which sat at the bottom of the access tunnel that slanted up to the outside.

"I was there," he told us, "when suddenly I heard a sound like a roar, a loud boom. I didn't have time to react, because within a fraction of a second a strong blow hit me and threw me against the wall, with a force so brutal that I couldn't protect myself. I lost consciousness, but they said they found me facedown on the floor of the mine, near the entrance. Later, hours later, I sensed lights around me and saw that they were coming from the miners' helmets. They were rescue workers, and when they saw me they lifted me up and took me out of the mine."

This colleague assumed that his life was saved because, between the gas in the mine and the powder on the floor, there was a layer of oxygen approximately three feet high. "I breathed that oxygen," he said, "and I didn't suffocate on the methane gas or the smoke or the dust. That strip of oxygen was what allowed me to keep breathing."

For him the experience was indescribable: It had happened so fast that he couldn't estimate the size of the explosion. All he could tell us was that it was violent and monstrously hot. He said that, although he could not be certain, he doubted that his trapped colleagues could have survived the force and heat of the explosion.

In the face of this loss and the complete incompetence of Grupo México's rescue effort, the first thing I proposed was the rescue of our colleagues and a focus on supporting the families—morally and materially. Their lives had radically changed from this moment, and they needed to know that they could rely on the leaders of the Miners' Union.

Our second focus was on speaking the truth: explaining to the families, the workers, and the public what had caused this inexcusable loss of life. For a few gifts and the occasional fancy dinner given by Grupo México, the inspectors from the labor department had abandoned their responsibility to ensure that the Pasta de Conchos mine was safe. The inspectors, their higher-ups in the Fox administration, and the leaders of Grupo México had all let safety go by the wayside, ignoring our vociferous complaints about the mine and the complaints from the local union's Joint Health and Safety Commission. It was they who had set the cost of the lives of the workers.

Our trapped colleagues, despite being highly qualified and having vast experience, had been working in very dangerous conditions at Pasta de Conchos. Javier de la Fuente and General de Hulla constantly threatened them with dismissal if they voiced their concerns, and now the same companies were helping cover for Labor Secretary Salazar, who had failed to ensure the inspections that were and are required by law. The government never filed charges against Pedro Camarillo, Coahuila's delegate from the labor department, because he is Salazar's son-in-law. Now that their negligence had run its course, these companies were woefully incapable of handling anything. Had the company not received professional support from other companies' teams of technicians, Grupo México never would have been capable mounting even the smallest rescue effort.

For the sake of our trapped colleagues—and for the sake of all miners who every day faced working conditions similar to those at Pasta de Conchos—I knew we needed to reveal the reality of the situation. We didn't want anyone to think the collapse of the mine was an act of God or the result of the miners' own mistakes. This was a tragedy that could have been prevented. The lives of the lost men lay squarely on the shoulders of the leaders of Grupo México and their cronies in Fox's labor department. The company had, and still has, investments in mines, plants, and foundries in Peru and the United States where workers are treated the same and worse, and we knew this event needed to be seen as an international disgrace to a company that operates with no regard for anything but its own profits.

As Monday and Tuesday went by with no positive developments, Salazar and Grupo México officials became more defensive, seeming to strongly resent the presence of the families and the national and international communication media, who were constantly pressuring them for information about the rescue efforts. The company consistently refused to provide clear information, instead giving only evasive answers.

They held press conferences daily around 9:00 p.m., outside the gates of the Pasta de Conchos work site. The late hour allowed for a delay between their announcements and the reports the next day, and Salazar and Grupo México officials used that time to pressure reporters into editing their stories to hide the truth of what happened. They even prepared questions and gave them to reporters to ask in the press conferences. In their responses, Salazar, Quevedo, and Ruben Escudero, the mine's manager, were visibly scared, nervous, sweating, and often delivering their words in a broken, halting voice. Each event was completely disorganized, people shouting over each other and the officials giving poor, ambiguous information on their progress. The local reporters tended to be the most aggressive, shouting their questions over each other during the conferences.

Though Salazar hadn't directly confronted me about the situation with Elías Morales, he never referred to me in any of the press conferences as leader of Los Mineros. In the government's eyes—and their eyes alone—Morales held that position, though not once did he show his face at Pasta de Conchos, something even a poor leader would have done. When I addressed the media and the families, Salazar would simply turn around and retreat to Industrial Minera offices as if he didn't know who I was, too cowardly to even listen to Los Mineros' position.

As the days passed, Salazar and company officials grew more vexed by the search for answers, and their statements grew increasingly offensive. Juan Rebolledo Gout, Grupo México's official spokesman (and the former personal secretary of Carlos Salinas de Gortari in his last year as president), said on television that Grupo México always had adequate safety measures and worked within international guidelines, and that is why it had an outstanding position in the global market. This type of cynical, outright lie infuriated every union member who'd seen the company's negligence firsthand, and it was a slap in the face to the families of the trapped men, who at the time were consumed with sickening grief over the sudden loss of the miners.

They also began accusing the Miners' Union and its members of signing inspection certificates in which there was no report of serious safety conditions. At the same time they began to put forth the idea of possible human error, carelessness, lack of ability, or inexperience. Salazar, in ignorance of actual events, would later try to defend himself in televised interviews by saying that on February 7, two weeks before the explosion, the last inspection visit had taken place and that of thirty-four observations of safety concerns, twenty-eight were addressed and the other six were not, because they were in areas that were closed to the operation—a bold-faced lie. A little over a week after the collapse, Salazar told a *Televisa* reporter on national TV that the miners were on drugs and drinking alcohol before descending into the mine, to motivate themselves and provide "courage." Federal labor law clearly ascribes responsibility to the company for any accident, except under very specific circumstances, as when there is a conflict between workers or a worker is drunk. With his statement, Salazar proved himself willing to slander the name of our colleagues in order to save Germán Larrea and the other leaders of Grupo México from the consequences of their actions.

When Salazar came to Pasta de Conchos, it was not to begin rescue operations of the miners or to help the families. He was there on a mission to protect the interests of the Fox administration and Grupo México. His pronouncements became more and more negative, and it was clear to everyone that damage control was his priority, to the point that he was ready to close up and abandon the mine and the surrounding town as soon as possible. Everyone in the government simply wanted to forget that Pasta de Conchos ever existed. The miners were filled with anger; they understood that he had gone to Pasta de Conchos to finish off the job and bury alive any possible survivors, with the sole purpose of covering the criminal negligence of Grupo México.

The only thing that can be said for Salazar is that he had the courage to show his face at Pasta de Conchos. President Vicente Fox could not be troubled to make an appearance, much less the elusive coward Germán Larrea, whose own company was directly responsible for the catastrophe. Neither of them even expressed condolences to the family, and there were certainly no offers of material support.

Despite the appalling condition of the mine, the poorly organized rescue efforts, and the infuriating behavior of Salazar and the officials from Grupo México, we maintained hope of finding our trapped colleagues alive. The volunteer rescuers, though not trained for the work, put their hearts into the effort. César Humberto Calvillo Fernández, the local union section's social services secretary, joined one of the rescue teams on Wednesday; his brother was among the lost men.

We knew it was possible that they'd all died a sudden death, but we held out hope that we would encounter signs of life and find them hidden in a sheltered area of the coal mine. But with every day that passed without the results we longed for, despair grew among the families and colleagues of the trapped men. The rescuers, totaling about twenty-six, and going down in six-person shifts, succeeded in breaking through about one slide a day, but each time they didn't make it far before they encountered another slide that was equally or even more dramatic. They updated the families on their progress twice a day, but the long hours between updates were torturous.

Grupo México's entire approach to the rescue was wrong. Pasta de Conchos was not a complicated or especially deep mine; the company knew where the workers were when the explosion happened, and they could have expanded the six- to eight-inch respiration holes that ran about 400 feet from the surface and to the bottom of the mine. As we saw later in the Chilean miner rescue, these holes can be expanded to accommodate the passage of those trapped below. Trying to break through the rock slides one after the other was laborious and far more hazardous, but it was all the untrained rescue team could do.

We proposed again and again that they take the approach of widening the boreholes, but they showed no interest, falsely claiming that the drill could cause an explosion. For them, it was no problem to force the miners to use blowtorches in a highly explosive work site, but using a drill to expand the respiration holes was unthinkable. After the explosion, references to the boreholes would mysteriously disappear from inspection video footage.

Given the possibility of widening these holes to locate the miners and sustain them until they could be pulled out, why would Grupo México and the labor department not fully support the effort? In my mind, the answer is simple: With those miners, they would have retrieved sixty-five individual stories of the company's abuse, neglect, and greed. The media would explode with the story of the heroic miners, and the atrocious manner in which Grupo México operated would be exposed, along with the submissive, self-interested role played by labor department officials. And with the miners alive, it would be much easier to file criminal charges.

The company did use one of the respiration holes to lower a small camera into the mine, but the contents of that video were never officially released. On our third day there, a young engineer told Oralia that the camera had captured images of the miners' bodies—not torn apart or incinerated, but intact, seated or lying down in a circle. We couldn't verify this report—the following day the engineer disappeared from Pasta de Conchos—but the possibility that the miners did survive for a time underground haunted everyone.

After the third day at the mine, company and government officials had grown even more tight-lipped and reclusive. Though I was getting updates on the rescue from union members on the rescue team, they avoided me at all costs. The silence didn't bode well, but their next move shocked everyone.

On the fifth day, they gathered the families and, in a roundabout manner, explained that the condition of the mine would not allow for any further rescue activities. Without consulting the Miners' Union or the workers, Salazar and Grupo México officials said that they were suspending rescue efforts. The levels of toxic gas in the mine were too high, they said, and they could not continue to risk the lives of the rescuers. According to them, there had been no signs of life and the rescue had to be called off, despite the fact that the miners' colleagues were willing to continue their work in the reasonable hope that some of the miners, if not all, were still alive. The families, suddenly facing the reality that they would never see their brothers, fathers, and sons again, began shouting, many in tears.

Had there been political will or a sense of responsibility on the part of the operators of the mine, the bodies at least could have been retrieved. But since Grupo México closed the mine in a matter of days after the explosion, it left in place the well-founded suspicion that the company wanted to hide the true causes of the explosion: its own negligence and irresponsibility.

Our grief at the end of the rescue efforts was beyond words. These were men we all knew and respected, and now the high-rolling officials who had written their death sentence were turning their backs and leaving them underground as if they were no more than animals, and as if the mine were little more than a giant coffin. It was the first time since 1889 that workers had not been recovered, dead or alive, from the site of a mining accident in Mexico.

The day Salazar made the announcement, one former miner, consumed with rage, approached the labor secretary, grabbed him by the neck, and pushed him to the ground, screaming that the rescue couldn't stop. The man shouted that he had been fired a month earlier but that his brother was still trapped in the mine, and he wouldn't leave without his brother. The crowd roared in support, and a few people threw objects at Salazar. He quickly ran off, whisked away by security guards, but a cameraman caught the whole incident on film. I have no doubt that had this miner had a gun, Salazar would have been killed. Footage of the distraught brother attacking the labor secretary was run on television segments all over Mexico for the next several days, speaking for the fury every miner and every family member felt at the betrayal of their government.

President Fox himself could barely conceal his own guilt in the Pasta de Conchos disaster. Cameras were rolling after a stop on his tour of northern Mexico, when Fox, approaching the presidential fleet waiting to take him away, was asked by a young student why he hadn't traveled to Pasta de Conchos in the aftermath of the explosion. Fox, with a gesture of profound irritation, answered aggressively, stating that he was visiting an indigenous community in another part of northern Mexico. After his short, unconvincing excuse, he shouted "And did you go? Did you?" at the student and immediately turned his back.

After Grupo México abandoned Pasta de Conchos, it left behind soldiers to guard the mine. Despite the army and the official abandonment of Pasta de Conchos, a group of volunteers and union workers stayed at the site and continued their effort without help from Grupo México or the government. If there was a way to bring up the bodies of their colleagues, we were determined to find it.

Following the company's departure, I stayed at the mine to comfort the families and help mount whatever effort we could. It was an extremely tense time—violence bubbled over several times in conflicts between the army and the families, and the streets of the town were dark and deserted, like a ghost town. Plus, Oralia and I sensed coming danger: My pronouncements about Grupo México's abuses and the labor department's complicity had angered many powerful people. In press conferences at Pasta de Conchos, I had publicly accused the company and the government inspectors of *industrial homicide*—a term commonly used by the IMF and other labor organizations to describe death directly due to a company's negligence. (In Western nations, it is called "corporate murder.") Jorge Campos and Jorge Almeida, director and assistant, respectively, of the Latin American office of the IMF, confirmed the appropriateness of the use of this term; they said the explosion was clearly an industrial homicide.

Fortunately, Oralia and I had the support and protection of the miners and their families. In the days after Pasta de Conchos, they took us in their homes, hiding us from danger around the clock. President Fox and Germán Larrea were both undoubtedly eager to see me gone, and I felt we were in real danger. After she'd spent several days comforting the families, Oralia traveled to Monterrey at my request. There, in the city where I'd grown up, I felt she would be safer.

On February 28, 2006, barely eleven days after the explosion, and while I was still at the mine, Labor Secretary Salazar made an official public announcement that I had been removed by the government as general secretary of the Miners' Union. My replacement, of course, was Elías Morales. Like a coward, Salazar never once contacted me about this matter. He never mentioned it even when giving me updates during the few days he spent in Coahuila. He just sent a press release to all the major news outlets, and I first heard about the official announcement on a television news program. Despite Morales's expulsion six years before, despite the hatred of the workers toward him, and despite the lack of any election, the labor department was pleased to announce that it would help this traitor assume leadership of Los Mineros. Morales had no experience or courage, and no leadership ability, but he had one thing: a willingness to sell out each of the union members for his own gain.

The opening salvo in the violent campaign against me and Los Mineros had occurred a few days before the Pasta de Conchos tragedy, with the assault on the union's headquarters and the *toma de nota* passed to Morales. But now the explosion and my declaration of industrial homicide had rapidly heightened the aggression against us. I was prepared to reveal their blood-stained hands and publicize their unpardonable exploitation that had led to sixty-five deaths—and they needed me gone, fast. To them, it was no problem violating labor law, the union's autonomy, and basic morality to turn the miners and the general public against me. Obedient to Grupo México and the Fox administration, reporters printed lies and slander about me: It was my fault the mine had collapsed; I was a thief; I didn't care about the miners.

Salazar's granting of the *toma de nota* stripped Los Mineros of the powers guaranteed to them in law—specifically, their right to choose their own directors. Such power is enshrined in the General Constitution of the Republic and in the Federal Labor Law, in Agreement 87, signed by the government of Mexico in 1960 with the International Labor Organization, and in the bylaws of the Miners' Union itself. The only purpose of Salazar's declaration was to remove me—a leader disinclined to protect the interests of Grupo México—and in my place impose a person who was utterly in the company's service. Salazar acted as if he were the owner of the unions and not as if there were laws that he, as the supposed labor official, had to abide by and respect more than anyone.

Members of Los Mineros were furious about being told by a government official who their leader would be. They had elected someone whom they trusted to defend them; now they were trying to replace me with a proven traitor to the workers' cause. In the first days of March 2006, there were some isolated and loosely organized work stoppages at union sections throughout Mexico in protest of Salazar's announcement. But we planned to take it much further than that. The executive committee began planning a national extraordinary convention to take place in Monclova, Coahuila, in the middle of the month. There, we would decide exactly how Los Mineros as a whole would respond to the abuses and injustices that had taken place at Pasta de Conchos and beyond.

FIVE

IN THE MINE

Most of the things one imagines in hell are there in the coal mine—heat, noise, confusion, darkness, foul air, and, above all, unbearably cramped space.
—GEORGE ORWELL

I was sixteen years old the first time I set foot in a mine. My father, newly elected as leader of the Miners' Union, had asked me to come along on his visit to the Real del Monte y Pachuca silver and gold mine in the state of Hidalgo. It was one of the oldest mines in the country, and also one of the deepest and most massive, containing somewhere around three thousand miles of tunnels. When we arrived, my father chatted with the workers as I was equipped for our descent into the 3,000-foot-deep mine. It felt like a ritual, putting on the overalls and heavy, steel-toed boots; being fitted with a miner's helmet; strapping on the belt containing a first-aid kit and battery for the lamp; and putting on the harness and ropes that the workers relied on for survival.

As we went down into the mine in a very rudimentary elevator that was lowered by a winch, my father explained that in each mine there are levels, just like the floors of a building, although in the mines there are typically 125 or 150 feet between the levels. Moments after we'd started to descend, the whole elevator began to shake. I grabbed the side of the elevator, terrified, but my dad only laughed and shouted up to the surface. "Don't worry," he said, "the men just like to shake the winch to scare first-timers."

After about ten minutes, the elevator slowed and stopped at a level about 2,000 feet below the surface. We stepped off into the dark, hot, dusty chamber and visited briefly with a few miners. My nervousness started to wear off as I listened to them talk and saw how enthusiastic they were about talking with my father. Soon we were back on the elevator, on our way down to the very bottom level, about 3,000 feet deep.

My teenage mind was quite impressed by the working area at the mine's floor. It was sweltering, and the workers were clad in little more than loincloths, boots, and helmets. As they advanced ever deeper into small tunnels that followed the mineral vein, they were tethered by a rope at the waist to a safety cable along the wall. They sweated incessantly and profusely in the intense heat, their arms dirty from the powder that clogged the air in the mine tunnels. The only light came from the miners' lamps and occasionally from some rudimentary light fixtures in the bottoms of the tunnels.

I was struck by the fact that humans could work in the bottom of a mine and extract metals and minerals under such high-risk conditions. I was in awe of the sacrifice and effort involved in moving about the mine despite the lack of space, oxygen, and light, entrusting your life to your own skills, or perhaps the benevolence of a higher being.

My father observed the working conditions within Real del Monte y Pachuca. He shook hands with the miners and asked them how they were feeling, what work they were doing, how the company and supervisors were treating them. He asked them to tell him anything that was bothering them. My father was reinforcing to me the way he thought a union leader should work. He liked to hear from the workers themselves, and unlike most of the men who owned the mines, he wasn't afraid to go into the dark and dangerous places where they labored.

When we left for the surface after nearly three hours and once again saw the light of day and felt the fresh air, I was shocked by the blazing light of the sun. We were given dark glasses before exiting; after hours in the bottom of the dark tunnels, a person's vision becomes accustomed to the low light. We had spent a while in the mine, but I was amazed thinking about how most miners spent eight full hours or more a day in the depths of the earth.

It was the first of many trips I would make down into mines with my father. Later I accompanied my father to mines in Chihuahua and Coahuila. I went down into the San Francisco del Oro and Santa Barbara mines, both in Chihuahua and both very deep. The working conditions were risky in these sites, but seeing them with my own eyes made me understand the courage of the miners, whose labor brings the wealth of the earth to the surface, where it can be used to benefit the people of Mexico.

We often ate at the bottom of the mine during these tours, dining on food offered to us by the miners, typically meat empanadas, steak or chicken pies, or corn tortillas filled with eggs, beans, and salsa, served with water or coffee that had been prepared at the surface. Eating three thousand feet below the ground gives the person a temporary illusion that he is working at a normal activity on the surface. We would sit in caves that had been transformed into makeshift dining rooms, complete with tables and chairs, where the miners ate halfway through their workday. They get a half-hour or forty minutes to eat, as established in the collective bargaining agreements at each mine. If one of these dining areas was unsafe or unhealthy—if the ventilation was poor, or the concentrations of gas and debris too high—Don Napoleón would demand that the mine owners correct it. He firmly believed that these men, who couldn't even go to the surface for a proper meal, at least needed hygienic dining areas.

The memory of my early mine visits were vivid in my mind during the first days after the Pasta de Conchos collapse. I'd descended to the bottom of many coal mines, and I knew what it felt like down there. I remembered the feeling of being closed up inside the earth in tunnels brimming with throat-choking coal dust. I couldn't fathom what it would feel like to be trapped down there after such a collapse, with little or no hope of rescue.

The U.S. labor department has stated that since the beginning of mining, the extraction of coal and other ground minerals "has been considered one of the most dangerous occupations in the world." The state of

Coahuila produces the vast majority of Mexico's coal, and coal mines like the one at Pasta de Conchos are considered among the most dangerous and complicated of all mines, primarily because of the amount of methane gas and carbon monoxide associated with coal extraction. These gases are odorless and colorless and act very subtly when breathed in and circulated in the miner's body. One becomes drowsy, and once unconsciousness occurs death can come slowly as one falls into a sleep from which there is no awakening. Coal mining also generates vast amounts of coal dust, and the danger is directly proportional to the degree of ventilation at the level where the worker is occupied. The greater the distance and depth from the entrance, the greater the amount of methane gas, coal dust, smoke, and heat, and the more critical the need for adequate ventilation.

During the eighteenth and nineteenth centuries and the beginning of the twentieth, miners would protect themselves by bringing canary cages to the mines—the classic example of animals used as sentinels to ensure the safety of humans. If methane or carbon monoxide was present in dangerous quantities, the bird would die before the men felt the negative effects of the noxious gases, giving them time to escape the mine or put on gas masks.

The speed of the canary's death depended on the degree of concentration of the gas in the particular coal mine. When the percentage is below 0.09 percent, after being in the mine for an hour, the bird begins to feel initial pain. As the gas content increases to 0.15 percent, the canary begins to suffer weakness and general discomfort, and in eighteen minutes, the small bird falls from its perch. If the gas level increases to 0.20 percent, the pain is evident a minute and a half after exposure to the methane begins, and in less than five minutes the canary falls on the ground. Finally, with a degree of gas accumulation of 0.24 percent, the canary falls off its perch and dies in a short time: about two-and-a-half minutes.[1]

---

1   Data from the Mining Museum of Cumberland, Vancouver Island, British Columbia, Canada.

In those early days, workers were alerted by this primitive warning system and exited alive. It was unjust to the canary, of course, but it allowed many miners to escape from dangerous areas and preserve their health. It wasn't until the beginning of the twentieth century that gas meters were developed to measure gas concentrations, which, in addition to saving miners' lives, also prevented the deaths of many more canaries.

As technology has advanced and as the price of metals and minerals has skyrocketed in the past decade—resulting in unprecedented profits for the owners of the mines—one would think that conditions in coal mines would have become increasingly safer. But mines only become safer when the companies that control them are willing to invest in that safety and when the government carries out its duty to inspect these facilities and compel the companies to make improvements when necessary. In Mexico, workers like those who died in the Pasta de Conchos collapse are treated like little more than those sentinel canaries, sent down into the belly of the earth without any reliable safeguards against death.

Pasta de Conchos was one of the worst-maintained and most dangerous mining sites in Mexico at the time of the explosion. The situation inside the mine was terrible, and it is worth taking a look at the myriad ways Grupo México and General de Hulla—the contract company hired by Grupo México—repeatedly ignored warnings of the danger inside. These companies share responsibility for the loss of life, of both contractors and union members, when the explosion was touched off in Pasta de Conchos, but the final responsibility rests with Grupo México. Germán Larrea's company failed to oversee how its contractor was operating the mine, and the Mexican Constitution states that a company's responsibility for the safety of its facilities "continues even when the owner hires the worker through an intermediary."

To enter the Mine 8 at Pasta de Conchos, one must pass through an inclined tunnel, descending by a concrete stairway that ends about four hundred feet underground, opening onto a passage that continues a mile and a half horizontally. The only way in or out of the mine was through its single access tunnel, or *tiro*, which functioned as entrance and exit. Three tunnels begin at a vestibule at the bottom of the stairway, and each runs the length of the mine, connected at points by diagonal communication tunnels. These tunnels are approximately ten feet high and ten feet wide, no more. The workers would meet at the front vestibule, and a system of transport cars would carry them through the mine and let each worker off at the spot where he would be working that day. One of the three main tunnels contained coal transporter belts that extended to the exit, where there is a tower on the surface with a large hopper, from which the coal is transferred to the washing and coking plant on the outside. At the end of these tunnels there was a bigger vault where new coal deposits had been found, part of the constant search for more and better quality coal.

Pasta de Conchos is not a very deep mine, but its ventilation system was completely insufficient. A large fan installed in the main tunnel injected fresh air into the bottom of the mine, but the same air must return, now laden with gases and dust, out of the same passage. In a mine such as this, the miners are being poisoned, little by little. The deeper they go, the scarcer the oxygen becomes, and the more thick and toxic the air becomes. This one fan, in just one tunnel, was completely insufficient to freshen and oxygenate the air that the miners breathed as they moved away from the only entrance. To prevent suffocation, the workers use face masks, but the company frequently would not equip the masks with filters, rendering them useless. In these cases, the miners would simply go without them.

The gas meters that measured the concentration of methane gas were also defective and did not give accurate readings—and without those readings, all other safety precautions were useless. Many speculated that the methanometers used by the company were faulty, but access to them was tightly controlled. When miners asked to see the methane levels, they were shown broken meters or told that they'd already been checked. If the miners didn't believe the company, said the managers, they could quit. A rescue worker at Pasta de Conchos recorded gas levels between 95 and 103 percent after the explosion; normal conditions are 1.5 to 2 percent.

In addition to the poisonous gases that permeated the mine, in the farthest reaches of the mine's main tunnel the workers left behind a layer of coal dust a foot and a half high. As the coal was extracted, this remaining dust was concentrated until it formed a thick—and highly explosive—covering on the ground.

Lethal gas, excessive heat, and explosive coal dust are realities in any mine, but the operators of Pasta de Conchos took a perilous situation and turned it into a recipe for certain death. General de Hulla ordered miners to weld with a blowtorch in the depths of the mine, despite the abundant coal dust, which mimics gunpowder if ignited. Typically, the walls and partitions would be "powdered"—covered with inert powder to neutralize the coal's combustible nature, thus preventing explosions— at least once a month, but although this is a procedure fundamental to coal mining and had been recommended by Pasta de Conchos engineers, it had not been done. Had it been, at a monthly cost of around $10,000, the chain of coal detonations throughout the length of the mine would likely have been stopped. For Grupo México and its contractor, it was too high a price for the lives of its employees.

On top of this, the workers frequently wore shoes with holes in the soles as they walked on the sludge and accumulated dust. There were electrical faults in the transportation systems, in the cars that carried the miners to the bottom of the mine, and with the transporter belts that carried the minerals to the outside, toward the coal-processing plant. There were frequent discoveries of burned electrical cables with metal wires exposed, but instead of being repaired and insulated properly, they were haphazardly repaired with any tape that was available. This is especially risky in mines, since there are frequent water flows; such rudimentary installation of high-voltage electrical wires could allow dangerous electrical short-circuits and sparks that could cause a methane gas or coal dust explosion.

The support pillars in the facility were also found to be deficient. In any mine, as progress is made in extraction of the minerals, the miners attack the wall with pick and shovel or use a high-powered drill to bore into the deposits. As they do so, the cavity of the mine becomes deeper, wider, and higher, and each time they move forward they must continually reinforce the tunnel with posts—"monkeys," or "monos" in Spanish, as the miners call them—to support the ceiling and walls. There should also be steel plates at the bottom of the mine, to prevent cave-ins caused by any vibration or settling of the earth as it is being dug out.

As the miners of Pasta de Conchos advanced deeper into the coal seams, they were indeed setting up these monkeys to support the cave. It's a delicate and important procedure, and the monkeys should ideally be composed of steel or prefabricated concrete. Some mines use wood, though, and this was the case in Pasta de Conchos. When one of these wooden columns was too short to reach from floor to ceiling, the workers would cut a piece from another beam to achieve the right height. This was an improvised measure that severely compromised the stability of the mine. Columns that are broken and stacked or otherwise not in a single piece cannot maintain stability during any major shifting of the earth.

Why would the miners use this inadequate means of supporting the mine? First of all, many of them were not aware of the proper procedures, and there were no supervisory personnel present to correct their mistake. General de Hulla's supervisors were more than happy to have the workers cut up wooden beams and stack them—after all, that was a lot cheaper than buying new supports that would actually fit the mine. In other words, this was just another symptom of the company's obsessive drive for reduced costs and enhanced production and profit.

The disaster of February 19, 2006, was caused in no small part by the poor structure and support of the mine. The union members who were familiar with the state of the mine estimated that the explosion caused a total of fifteen slides throughout the length of the mine due to lack of proper reinforcement.

On top of all this, as I have said, there was no alternative exit tunnel in Mine 8; the company simply refused to build it, ignoring our demands. Even one additional tunnel at the bottom or halfway down the mine would have allowed much greater circulation of air and oxygen, providing better working conditions, greater degasification, and an emergency exit. In all likelihood, such a tunnel would have helped us rescue some or all of the men whose bodies to this day remain buried in the mine.

Grupo México wouldn't hear of building another exit, which would have cost them $1 million to $2 million, even though it had recently closed the mine briefly and spent between $10 million and $12 million to repair the coking ovens. Why would they do one and not the other? The short answer is that repair of the coking ovens increased the quality and purity of the coal produced at the mine, which in turn increased the price Grupo México could get for it. In other words, repairing the coking ovens had a direct impact on their already absurdly fat profits, but building extra access tunnels didn't. The only effect that would have had was on the safety of the miners, and thus Grupo México didn't care. Their insatiable greed for production drove them to refuse this small investment of $1 million to $2 million, in a year when their estimated profits exceeded $6 billion. The cozy friendship between corporation and government prevented this vital, and ultimately fatal, improvement to Mine 8. It's just one example of how easy it is for Mexico's ruling class to broker under-the-table deals.

It was in this hazardous and poorly maintained mine that the workers of Pasta de Conchos were forced to labor. The subcontractor, General de Hulla, which employed the majority of the miners, routinely threatened non-union workers with the loss of their jobs if they complained about their wages or the condition of the mine. Grupo México hired General de Hulla for its most dangerous and complicated jobs, and the contractor willingly offered cheap labor from men who were routinely put in harm's way. For $8 a day, the contract workers labored in Pasta de Conchos, while General de Hulla charged Grupo México $73 a day for each of the same workers. While its employer collected all the profits, these ununionized workers labored through ten- to twelve-hour days with no vacation. And of course, each time there were proposals to unionize them, the workers in question were threatened, fired, or relocated.

The miners regularly observed and reported many of the dangerous anomalies that existed at Pasta de Conchos. Had the system of routine inspections been enforced and responded to by Grupo México and the labor department, there is no question that Mine 8 of the Pasta de Conchos unit could have been made into a safe work environment. Yet Grupo México stubbornly fought off any efforts to improve the mine, their refusals invariably backed by officials from President Fox's labor department. Of all the companies the labor department should be monitoring, high-risk ones like Grupo México should be at the very top of the list. But officials in Mexico City ignore this obligation. They issue mining permits for locations thousands of miles away, with no oversight or understanding of the daily hazard faced by workers or the impact mining has in local communities. The citizens of Mexico have paid the salaries of government inspectors who repeatedly fail to do their jobs.

In a coal mine like Pasta de Conchos, inspections should take place at least every fifteen days. To represent the workers during these inspections, local branches of the Miners' Union select a Joint Health and Safety Commission at each work site. The size of the commission increases with the number of workers at a site, but for an average site the commission consists of about three or four union members. These commissions' basic role, according to Miners' Union bylaws and the collective bargaining agreements signed with each of the companies, is to make frequent visits to the mines and the work centers and detect defects in safety systems and equipment, making suggestions to immediately correct any problems they see. Reports from the Joint Health and Safety Commission typically fall into two categories: urgent reports, which warn that an accident could be imminent, and reports that recommend preventive maintenance or medium-term service for problems that affect production, operations, and maintenance of a production center.

As stipulated in the collective bargaining agreement between union members and company, these tours are to be conducted with a representative from the labor department and representatives from the company, and they should result in a jointly prepared report that carefully records every fault or problem observed. The report is then used as the basis for making demands of the company. The company must abide by the collective bargaining agreement, the Mexican Constitution, and the federal labor law to correct each irregularity in order to prevent accidents.

That's not how it worked at Pasta de Conchos. Labor department officials showed up for inspections only sporadically, and the resulting reports were often rigged. When inspectors did show up at the mine, instead of taking them down into the work site to perform their duties, company officials invited them to dine and chat with them. Grupo México prepared the reports and got them approved by the Department of Labor without input from the Joint Health and Safety Commission. (Naturally, this false certificate stated that everything was in order and within the appropriate safety standards and therefore there were no risks to fear.) In violation of law, officials then tried to get the workers who belonged to the Joint Health and Safety Commission to sign the falsified minutes. When the union members of the Joint Health and Safety Commission did not accept the minutes prepared by the company and supported by the complicit department of labor, they suffered threats of dismissal, either by losing their work altogether or having to relocate to areas that were more difficult and dangerous and where they would receive lower salaries and benefits. Thus, members of the Joint Health and Safety Commission who were supposed to make observations and propose urgent corrections were threatened with punishment or loss of their jobs. Officials would simply order that work proceed as if nothing were wrong. The contractors from General de Hulla and workers belonging to the Miners' Union were pressured into signing the minutes. They were routinely told not to worry, that the mine would "be okay." Javier Garcia, a contract worker who provided his services to General de Hulla, had persisted in reporting the deplorable conditions, and the company responded by firing him one month before the tragedy. Fortunately for him, being fired from his job saved his life.

Regardless of this deception and coercion on the part of the operators of the Pasta de Conchos facility, the workers would tour the mine on their own, prepare their own reports—some of which nearly reached book length—and save them, without the signature of Grupo México or labor department representatives. But the reports and complaints of the workers produced no results except silence from the mine's owners.

When it wasn't bullying the miners into acknowledging false inspection reports, Grupo México was giving the miners false hope about future improvements to the work site. According to the members of Union Section No. 13, the union branch at Pasta de Conchos, Sergio Rico, operations superintendent at the mine, assured workers that there were plans to improve Mine 8. The main part of the plan, in addition to correcting truly basic elements such as changing cables, replacing a recording box in the electrical control system, and correcting mechanical defects in the coal transport cars, was to build the desperately needed second access tunnel. The new entrance would be located at the end of the mine, with its own ventilation system. Supported by perforations to the surface to reduce interior gas concentrations, the new system would better circulate clean air throughout the mine. That, of course, never happened. Because it felt supported and protected by the Department of Labor, Grupo México did not consider the improvements necessary, although the company knew such negligence was totally illegal.

The last true inspection of the Pasta de Conchos mine took place in July 2004, a year and a half before the explosion. The report shows that forty-eight problems were detected, including problems with electrical systems, transportation, and gas concentrations. Severe situations were "fixed" with duct tape—not enough to prevent a spark and the ensuing explosion. The company never met with government inspectors, during or after their visit, and never met with the union members who belonged to the Joint Health and Safety Commission. The processes and rules for inspections and meetings of the commission—set forth in the union's collective bargaining agreements with Grupo México—were never taken into consideration. The labor department took a full year to even send the July 2004 inspection report to Grupo México.

In the aftermath of the explosion, Salazar stated that on February 7, 2006, two weeks before the explosion, an inspection had taken place and that of thirty-four observations, twenty-eight were addressed and the other six were not, because they were in areas that were closed to the operation. But the reality was that there was no such inspection, and the report didn't mention the still-uncorrected forty-eight irregularities from July 2004. The inspectors didn't even go down into the mine or tour the facilities on February 7. It was only a "verification" visit, as Salazar and Grupo México acknowledged much later, exclusively to check on the previously reported forty-two observations. If a true inspection had taken place, the inspectors would have seen that many of the forty-two anomalies from the visit in 2004 had still not been addressed—and had they any conscience, they would have closed the mine immediately. To inspect a coal mine on a yearly basis rather than biweekly one is nothing more than appalling irresponsibility.

It is equally appalling to note who was directly responsible for the governmental inspections of Pasta de Conchos. The labor department's delegate for the state of Coahuila is none other than Labor Secretary Salazar's son-in-law, Pedro Camarillo. Undoubtedly, Camarillo—even if he'd felt some need to honestly inspect and report on the conditions of Pasta de Conchos—would have felt extreme reluctance at opposing the wishes of his wife's father and the billionaire businessmen who supported him. (And of course, Salazar's own ownership of two direct suppliers to Grupo México constituted a major conflict of interest.) Yet Salazar and Grupo México representatives somehow managed to keep a straight face when they reported to the press that all necessary inspections had been done, and that Grupo México's operations were laudably safe.

On the night of Saturday, February 18, 2006, a few hours before the main tunnel of Mine 8 would become choked with tons of coal and rock, Francisco Perez was preparing to leave home for the third shift, which began at 11:00 p.m. It was his wife's birthday, and her party was just getting started. Francisco's family begged him to stay, arguing that he could always invent an excuse to justify his absence the next day, even if he just said he was sick. The miner reluctantly agreed—it was his wife's birthday, after all. It was a decision that saved his life.

Whether it was pure luck or some sort of premonition on the part of Francisco's family is impossible to say. But one thing is certain: The miners knew that their lives were at risk that night. Earlier on Saturday, the workers of the first and second shifts had decided to suspend work because of the miserable conditions they found in the mine: high concentrations of gas, dust, smoke, chemical substances, and materials that they felt in the atmosphere, getting denser all the time. It was apparent that the mine was ripe for a disaster. Some of the miners got together that day, and a colleague proposed that a formal work stoppage begin, starting officially after a meeting that would take place on the following Tuesday, February 21. Those present agreed that on the twenty-first, they would gather all the miners and vote on the strike, to establish the majority support that Mexican labor law requires before a stoppage begins. The law does allow for an emergency stoppage before the vote, but they wanted to follow the whole procedure before they officially walked off the job on Tuesday. They knew Salazar had it in for the union, and they thought it would be better to follow the most legally defensible path.

Most of these miners were probably working in the vault at the far end of the mine when the explosion occurred, and it is where any survivors were probably trapped. This is true despite the fact that, in a correctly overseen operation, the workers would have been spaced out and distributed throughout the length of the mine, some producing coal, some providing maintenance, and some monitoring production. But General de Hulla ordered all its non-union contractors to the back of the mine, where they were told to weld with a blowtorch, putting the workers at incredible risk. (It was routine for the company to give non-union workers the most dangerous jobs. It clearly felt not the slightest responsibility for their lives.) A single spark from an electrical failure or friction would immediately ignite the explosive methane gas and spread quickly to the coal dust piled along the mine's floor, which is precisely what happened at 2:20 a.m. on February 19, 2006.

There's no doubt that the explosion was large. In a fraction of a second, it raged through the mile and a half of the mine and burned like an underground wildfire. "I imagine it was like lighting a firework in a bottle," said Elias Aguilera, an employee of General de Hulla who survived that day. The explosion consumed all the air in the mine and weakened the tunnel's already weak construction. The impact of the blast reached the outside concentration plant and the coking ovens, quickly spreading from the four-hundred-foot depth to the surface. The large receiving hopper, which received the extracted coal, and the transporter belts were totally destroyed. A few men were saved by their close proximity to the inclined tunnel that led to the surface, though these survivors suffered serious burns.

In my visits with the nine hospitalized workers who survived the explosion, they told me that at 11:00 p.m. on Saturday, February 18, the workers were proceeding toward the bottom of the mine. It was the third shift (miners at Pasta de Conchos worked twenty-four hours a day in three shifts). As some of the survivors explained, each noise heard in the bottom of the mine as the workers advanced slowly, extracting the coal, filled some of them with fear, imagining that something very serious could happen that workday. The heat was increasingly intense inside the deeper they got.

According to what some of the survivors told me, the workers were walking slowly toward the mine's interior, worried the whole time by presentiments of danger for them and other colleagues. From here the descent toward the work areas at the bottom of the mine occurred slowly, in silence, as if they knew that they were walking to the last workday of their lives.

Of course, their concerns were well founded. To this day, no one knows exactly what befell the sixty-three unrecovered men in their final hours, and we don't know whether those final hours took place immediately after or days after the explosion itself. Rather than take responsibility for the tragedy and do their best to recover the men, Grupo México botched the recovery efforts and claimed its mines were safe. Indeed, the company and Labor Secretary Salazar blamed the victims themselves, claiming that they drank and did drugs before entering the mine, because they were scared to go inside.

This slander infuriated the families of the lost men and all their colleagues in the Miners' Union. Ignoring the litany of safety violations and the absurd lack of oversight from his own department, Labor Secretary Salazar insisted that the tragedy was due to the miners at Pasta de Conchos "screwing up" by taking drugs, smoking marijuana, or drinking alcohol before they entered the mine, to give themselves courage. All of this was filmed in a documentary called *The Fallen* that the union produced together with an independent filmmaker.

There's not a shred of proof that any of the miners were compromised in any way on the night of the explosion, and if they were scared, they certainly had a right to be. Germán Larrea himself refuses to enter his own mines, since, according to a comment he made in the mining industry press, he suffers from claustrophobia. The fault was with the owner and shareholders of Grupo México, who pressured public officials to ignore the blatant safety violations to satisfy their inordinate desire for profit—regardless of the cost to the miners.

It was based on this irrefutable negligence that I had accused Grupo México and the principal officials of the Department of Labor with industrial homicide, loudly pointing out their misdeeds to the families, volunteers, and reporters gathered at Pasta de Conchos. Grupo México did not respect standards or laws regarding safety. It violated the Collective Bargaining Agreement it had signed in 2005 with the Miners' Union, which in article 68, section 13, states the following: "The Company shall maintain the mines in a state that guarantees the highest degree of protection for the workers' life and health. For this purpose, all shafts shall have their corresponding returns, which must be wide enough to guarantee optimum ventilation of the mine and transit of the miners."

It also violated the Federal Labor Law, which in its article 132, Section XVII, requires that all companies, not just mining companies, "comply with the safety and hygiene provisions in laws and regulations to prevent accidents and illness in the work centers and generally in the places where the work must be performed, and make available at all times the medications and first-aid materials that are indispensible according to the instructions issued for the timely and efficient application of first aid; and the responsibility to notify the competent authority of each accident that occurs."

The corporation also violated Article 123 of the Political Constitution of the United Mexican States, which states in Section XIV that "companies shall be responsible for work accidents and workers' job-related illnesses, suffered because of or in the exercise of their profession or work; therefore, owners must make the corresponding payments as a consequence of the death or temporary or permanent disability of the workers, as determined by law. This responsibility shall apply even if the owner hires the worker through an intermediary."

It also violated Section XV of Constitutional Article 123, which states that "the owner must observe, according to the nature of the negotiation, legal precepts regarding hygiene and security in the facilities of his establishment, and adopt appropriate measures to prevent accidents in the use of machines, instruments, and work materials, as well as organize such that it provides the highest degree of protection for the health and life of the workers, and the unborn baby in the case of pregnant women. The laws shall contain the applicable penalties in each case."

The labor department has never, previously or now, even though informed and bound by this regulation, enforced the correction of Pasta de Conchos's safety deficiencies or punished Grupo México for the above violations. In fact, they rose to the company's defense, laying blame squarely on the shoulders of the very men who lost their lives deep in the Pasta de Conchos mine. But a special committee of the International Labor Organization (ILO), set up to investigate the explosion, concluded that "the Government of Mexico did not do all that was reasonably expected of it to avoid or minimize the effects of the Accident which had such devastating effects with the loss of life of as many as 65 miners."

In those first days after the explosion, Salazar was totally focused on the financial interests of Grupo México. We recall that when Fox assumed power he said that his government was "of businessmen, by businessmen, and for businessmen," thereby betraying the citizens who voted for him in the hope of a change to propel the financial recovery into development, expansion of opportunity, and the building of a better future for the whole country.

I'm sometimes asked whether it was up to the Miners' Union to prevent the tragedy of February 19, 2006. I believe the people who wonder whether we were partially to blame do not understand the reality of the irrational, irresponsible system we were up against. Disaster-prevention measures are part of our collective bargaining agreements, but if there is no government responsible for monitoring the fulfillment of these obligations, violations will continue, and more tragedies will take place.

To keep our workers safe in the Pasta de Conchos mine, we would have had to be on permanent strike, since despite Grupo México's high earnings—and the fact that their riches depended on the sacrifice and effort of the miners—the company invested hardly anything in the safety of its coal mines in Coahuila. Even though we faced a company that was firmly committed to not spending a penny on the safety of the mine and a right-wing government that gave its full support to businessmen of any kind, we did continually strike and raise concerns about the safety of many mines in Mexico. Each of our workers is instructed by the National Union, the National Executive Committee, and me personally that when the slightest risk is encountered in a mine, the worker should suspend activities until the defects are corrected or it is verified that the danger no longer exists. If the hazard persists, then the worker should demand the shutdown or closure of activity until the basic problem is corrected. But the miners of Mexico need work, and many are willing to risk their lives to support their families. "It's not safe," said Adrián Cárdenas Limón, a subcontractor with General de Hulla, "but we need the jobs. There's no way out."

The fault was not in our failure to call attention to the danger: Between 2002 and 2005, we called fourteen different strikes against Grupo México, primarily in protest of substandard working conditions in the mines they controlled. The honestly prepared reports written by the union's Joint Health and Safety Commission were going to be the basis for striking the Pasta de Conchos mine and charging Grupo México with violations of the collective bargaining agreement's provisions regarding health, safety, and hygiene, among other matters.

Because that strike happened too late, those documents now form the basis, along with the testimony of the rescuers, of the criminal complaint of industrial homicide that the Miners' Union has presented in Coahuila against Grupo México and its shareholders, in addition to Francisco Javier Salazar and the rest of the officials and inspectors from the department of labor. Sadly, our battle to hold the people responsible for the Pasta de Conchos tragedy still goes on, more than seven years since it occurred.

Of course, this unforeseen catastrophe presented a fresh opportunity for Fox's government and the mining companies to continue the attack on the Miners' Union that had begun in the days before the accident. Rather than face their own culpability, they decided to double their efforts to depose me as head of the Miners' Union. In their ignorance, they believed that their assault on the union and me personally would force us to come begging for peace or negotiation within a week or two. They were mistaken, and they will continue to be mistaken. We have never forgotten the bodies of sixty-three coworkers who have been abandoned some 370 feet below the earth's surface, still awaiting a proper burial, and we have never forgotten precisely who put them there.

SIX

DEPARTURE

*Only the misfortune of exile can provide the in-depth under-
standing and the overview into the realities of the world.*
—STEFAN ZWEIG

Once the rescue efforts at Pasta de Conchos had been called off,
Salazar turned his back and fled Coahuila and the angry families of the
miners, thereby issuing a death sentence for any men who may have
been buried alive in the bottom of the mine. Of course he had no interest in identifying the true cause of the disaster, knowing full well it was
the negligence and irresponsibility of himself and Grupo México. Xavier
García de Quevedo, along with the other managers and operators of
Grupo México, fled the scene as well.

A small volunteer rescue team remained behind, and I remained in
Coahuila as well, along with several of my colleagues from the executive committee. Meanwhile, in union sections across the country,
miners were holding assemblies in protest of Elías Morales's company-
backed takeover attempt and Grupo México's appalling mishandling of
Pasta de Conchos.

In the media, Grupo México and the Fox administration had launched
an all-out smear campaign against me, rooted in Morales's baseless
accusation that several members of the executive committee and I had
made inappropriate use of the $55 million Mining Trust. Morales him-
self arranged many interviews in which he elaborated on this supposed
fraud. Ruben Aguilar, President Fox's press secretary, appeared on

television calling us criminals, and saying that the government would investigate our misuse of the funds. Slanderous articles—undoubtedly paid for by Germán Larrea, who sits on the board of Televisa, the largest Spanish-language media company in the world—appeared in national newspapers and magazines with the intention of confusing the Mexican people and the workers of Los Mineros and convincing them that Morales was the "good guy" who would stand up for them. Every single day, some new piece of pro-Morales, anti-Napoleón propaganda appeared in the media.

Televisión Azteca, a company that previously belonged to the state under the name Instituto Mexicano de Televisión, Imevisión, and was privatized under Carlos Salinas, showed unequivocal aggression and perversity against the Miners' Union and me personally. During the Pasta de Conchos tragedy, Javier Alatorre, the news director of TV Azteca, interviewed me in the mine itself. We had a long and detailed interview in which I was able to explain openly the causes of the explosion. I mentioned the responsibility of Grupo México and its owner Germán Larrea: its criminal negligence and that of its board of directors, its management, and its shareholders. It was a wide-ranging interview that was never aired, not even a minute of it, neither on TV Azteca nor Televisa nor on any other communication linked to this company.

The fear and anger of antiunion businessmen and PAN politicians was such that their campaign against the union and me personally was as vicious as if we were a group of dangerous drug traffickers. They were infuriated by our accurate assignment of responsibility for the loss of life at Pasta de Conchos, and they were now more desperate than ever to discredit us and place Morales at the head of the union. There, he would destroy the autonomy of the Miners' Union and smash it into two pieces: one for mining and one for the iron and steel industry. Of course the union under Morales—whether in one or two pieces—would be purely for show. Every one of its actions would be in the service of companies like Grupo México and Grupo Villacero. This was their dream. The pressure Los Mineros exerted on mining and steel companies in defense of the workers would finally be at an end.

As the media campaign heated up in the week after Pasta de Conchos, unveiled threats began reaching me in Coahuila. I got death threats and anonymous calls saying that terrible things would happen to my family and me if I didn't end my accusations of industrial homicide. As soon as Oralia got to Monterrey, she too began receiving the same warnings through phone calls and emails. The phone would ring, and a voice, using vulgar, violent language, would tell her that if I didn't stop they would kill our children and cut her up into little pieces. She got email stating that they would use all their power to destroy our family. My youngest son, Napoleón, then a student at the University of Monterrey, UDEM, got out of class one day soon after the Pasta de Conchos tragedy and found a note and a bullet on his windshield that threatened the same thing: If I didn't shut my mouth about the government and Grupo México's lies and abuses, my family would pay with their lives. Phone calls to his cell phone, the phones of my other sons, and the union's headquarters in Mexico City reiterated the point.

These menacing messages came steadily, and the senders always knew where my family and I were located. They had access to our private numbers. It was clear that we were being spied upon by professionals—most likely by the government, through CISEN, its equivalent of the CIA.

The threat of death and bodily harm from our enemies was real, but there were also rumors swirling that members of the executive committee would soon be arrested in Coahuila based on Morales's false complaint against us. We stood firm in our innocence, but we knew not to underestimate the abuses of law that could be practiced in Mexico. Though no formal charge had been made against us, were a judge to issue an arrest warrant based on the false accusations, we could be thrown in jail with no way to defend ourselves. Presumption of innocence, a crucial principle in many countries, was and is not respected in Mexico, especially in cases like ours, cases of political persecution, where powerful interests have cause to keep an innocent person in jail. If they arrested us, we could be held for years with no bail and no access to a fair trial—or even worse. And with men like Germán Larrea and Francisco

Javier Salazar at his back, we had little doubt that Elías Morales would eventually procure such help from the justice system.

As the threatening phone calls, the rumors of arrest, and the national campaign of slander against the Miners' Union grew more intense, I and the seven of my colleagues who had remained in Coahuila decided it would be best to change the location where we spent each night. Starting about a week after the tragedy, we began moving around Coahuila, from San Juan de Sabinas to Múzquiz to Nueva Rosita to Allende to Nava and even up to Piedras Negras on the Texas border, in an attempt to stay close to the families of Pasta de Conchos but evade our persecutors and the spies who reported to them. We traveled from place to place in a two-car caravan, one car traveling about half a mile ahead of the other; if they spotted anything suspicious, the passengers of the first car would warn the trailing car by cell phone. For lodging, we stayed in small, run-down motels or relied on the hospitality of miner colleagues who welcomed us into their homes.

From Canada, Leo W. Gerard, president of the United Steelworkers, had been observing the escalation of the unfounded attack against me and the union in the wake of the mine collapse. He and the other senior leaders of the USW offered me full and unconditional support, inviting me and my family to come to the United States and stay with them as long as necessary. We had supported the USW in their previous strike against Grupo México, and they understood the lengths to which Germán Larrea would go to protect his profits. They knew, too, that Larrea had Salazar, Abascal, Fox, and Marta Sahagún in his back pocket. Gerard and his colleagues didn't hesitate to join with the Miners' Union in solidarity against this political persecution. In early March, following an executive board meeting on the matter, the leaders of USW sent a letter to President Fox on behalf of the organization's 850,000 members in the United States and Canada. "We call upon all labor organizations throughout the world to publicly condemn the actions of the Mexican government," it read in part, "and to take strong steps to get their countries' governments to put pressure on the Mexican government to reverse its illegal actions immediately."

Many others besides our friends at the USW had encouraged me to leave before I was either arrested or killed, yet the option of leaving Mexico did not appeal to me. My initial reaction was that I needed to stay in the country to continue the fight. I thought that the aggression would die down soon and that I could then return to Mexico City within a couple of months and continue my work as general secretary of Los Mineros from there.

Eventually, though, I began to be swayed by the argument. If Morales and his corporate sponsors did convince a court to begin action against us, I could end up a political prisoner. To both Grupo México and the Fox administration, it was highly undesirable to have me alive and free on Mexican soil. Dead or imprisoned, I would be of little use to Los Mineros. If I wanted to ensure the permanence of the organization and preserve its autonomy, I finally admitted to myself, I would have to leave my country.

About a week after the Pasta de Conchos accident, my colleagues and I were staying in a small, modest hotel in Piedras Negras, a border town about seventy miles from Pasta de Conchos. We were all anxious about the intensifying situation, and I was still wrestling with the question of whether it was best for me to leave for the United States. To relieve some stress, we decided to drive over to a nearby major-league baseball park owned by the union, one of its most important assets, thanks to its prime location near the border and next to a mall. The diversion would do us good, and we could check on the condition of the property.

Our hotel was famous for its breakfast dishes, and after a morning meal of barbacoa, eggs, fried beans, and handmade tortillas, we left for the park, which sits right by the border bridge. When we pulled up to the stadium, it was mid-afternoon, and the entire area was empty. We stepped out of the car and began walking around the deserted ballpark. We found all of its twelve square acres in great condition—the grass was lush and green, the stands were clean, and all the surfaces had been recently painted.

I found an abandoned baseball, and with a stick from the parking lot that functioned as a makeshift bat, my colleagues and I began hitting the ball around. As we played, memories from my childhood flooded back to me. In 1956, my hometown of Monterrey had hosted the first Little League tournament in all of Mexico. My father, at the time serving as the head of a local branch of the Miners' Union, worked for Grupo Peñoles, and I played first base for the Peñoles Miners. We were national champions for two consecutive years, and in 1957 and 1958—just after I'd become too old for Little League—our team from Monterrey won a worldwide championship in Williamsport, Pennsylvania, for the first time in the team's history.

My passion for baseball stems from my family's history. San Juan, Nuevo León, my father's hometown, is considered the birthplace of Mexican baseball, because it was there, in 1893, that a group of American workers, working with Mexican workers on a bridge over the San Juan River, introduced their fellow laborers to the game. It was that game that enabled me to play Little League baseball decades later. I cherish memories of accompanying my father and his brothers to Monterrey Sultans games, where we watched the game while enjoying soft drinks, hot dogs, hamburgers, and—for the adults—cold beer. My friends and I idolized professional ballplayers from Mexico and especially from the United States.

When my colleagues and I had grown tired and ended our impromptu game, I picked up the old baseball and wrote on it, "Piedras Negras, Coahuila, February 27, 2006." Knowing in my head that I would soon be leaving, I kept the baseball and vowed that I would one day return to that park, after the conflict was over.

Once I'd fully accepted that I needed to temporarily leave Mexico, I called Oralia and explained why we had to go. As always, she was fully supportive and ready to do whatever was necessary. I also called my three sons, all young adults by now, and explained to them, one by one, that it would be best if we left the country. I advised that each of them depart discreetly and as soon as possible. For tactical reasons, we decided that the family would be divided in groups to leave for the United States, and I recommended that no one ever travel alone. My sons were all reluctant to leave, especially our youngest son, Napoleón, who was very committed to continuing his studies at the university, but they nevertheless understood the severity of the situation. In preparation for my departure, I asked Napoleón to drive up from Monterrey with my visa and passport.

None of us was happy about leaving, but my family understood the threat of physical harm, not only to me but to them as well. By this time, we were living a nightmare: The threats were becoming increasingly aggressive, and some of our friends—people we thought were close to us—had turned their back on us. They didn't have the nerve to stand against the government's aggression with us. We felt alone, without anyone to turn to. The always-loyal mine, metal, and steelworkers, both of Mexico and the United States, were the exception. These steadfast workers had become like an extended family in our time of crisis. Our permanent gratitude to all of them.

On Friday, March 3, about two weeks after the explosion, I left Mexico in a black Suburban, escorted by staff and executive committee members Marcelo Familiar, José Angel Hernández Puente, and Héctor Rodarte. I departed my homeland with great anger and sadness, never intending to leave indefinitely. I hadn't even been able to go back to Mexico City, because of the aggressive attacks against the union. The Texas border was less than seventy miles from Pasta de Conchos, and we all decided that would be the simplest way to go. We left for the border town of Piedras Negras on Friday afternoon, crossed over into Eagle Pass around five o'clock, and made our way to San Antonio, where we spent our first night out of Mexico. We still weren't sure where our ultimate destination was, but at least San Antonio was familiar to me. Oralia has family there, and I'd visited many times.

The next day, we dove into a deep analysis of the strategy President Fox and the businessmen who wanted me out of power—Germán Larrea and the Villarreal Guajardo brothers, among others—were likely to use against us. We concluded that Grupo México, Grupo Villacero, President Fox, and key members of his cabinet, as well as the Mexican media, including Televisa and TV Azteca, were all colluding to drag my name through the dirt and, ultimately, compromise the democracy and autonomy of Los Mineros. The tragedy at Pasta de Conchos had begun to unmask part of this conspiracy, which had most likely been brewing for a very long time. These parties were now working even harder to defend themselves against our accusation of industrial homicide.

From San Antonio, we drove to Houston. Oralia and her sister, Darlinda, had headed there from Mexico; Oralia had a medical test coming up, and I wanted to be with her for it. When we arrived in Houston, Oralia told us about her and Darlinda's nocturnal departure from Monterrey. The two of them had left Monterrey together around 10:00 p.m. and crossed the Texas–Mexico border in the middle of the night. On the way out of town, they noticed a car tailing them, and they took many last-minute turns in an effort to lose them. They finally shook the followers—most likely state or federal police officers—about sixty miles out of Monterrey.

Our sons had left separately around the same time. Our youngest two sons were single at the time, but our oldest son, Alejandro, brought his wife and children with him to the United States. Despite the danger we faced, and despite having to uproot their lives in Mexico, my wife and sons showed incredible strength and solidarity, and they rose to the challenge in a way that heartened me more than I can say.

As I traveled through Texas, I remained in close contact with Leo Gerard and our friends at the USW, who had urged me to leave Mexico and continued to offer encouragement and aid on our trip. They suggested that we move on to Albuquerque, New Mexico, nearly 1,200 miles away, saying that they could accommodate us there and that we would be safer. Texas was President Bush's state, and they didn't trust him; plus, the USW had very little presence in that state.

After a few days in Houston, my wife and José Angel returned to San Antonio in the Suburban, while Hector, Marcelo, and I set off for the three-day drive to New Mexico in a rented silver Durango. From Houston we drove northeast to Dallas, and then continued toward Amarillo.

Once we left Amarillo, we were headed west along the path of what was once the mythic Route 66, the highway that once stretched from Chicago to Los Angeles. Called "the Mother Road" by John Steinbeck in *The Grapes of Wrath*, the route has come to symbolize the vastness of the American West and the adventurous spirit of those who traveled it.

Our drive along Route 66 was an unexpected gift—a time to reflect and renew our spirits. The landscape on the trip to Albuquerque was for the most part austere and desertic, interrupted by patches of farmland. For long stretches of highway, we were alone, passing only the occasional car or trailer. For all three days, the weather was overcast, and we went through a few storms. The tragedy of Pasta de Conchos was still fresh and painful. The whole trip still didn't feel real. I couldn't quite believe it was happening.

Small towns dotted our long, straight path, and driving through them reminded me of my high school days. There were little stores, restaurants, and coffee shops, some looking like they were straight out of the 1960s. I was flooded with memories of rock 'n' roll's heyday, of the music and films of that time—Janis Joplin, Elvis Presley, Bob Dylan, James Dean, Marlon Brando, Paul Newman. We stopped at one place for a burger, fries, and milkshake—it was like reliving the good old days, complete with a jukebox. Elsewhere, in small-town coffee shops and gas stations, we met kind locals. Their quiet rural existence seemed a world away from hectic Mexico City and the conspiracy we were now fleeing. Passing through one small town whose name I no longer recall, I saw a handsome little ballpark and immediately thought of my commitment to return to the union's park at Piedras Negras.

As my colleagues and I traveled along seemingly endless stretches of Texas highway, I gave many press interviews with the Mexican media, mainly by telephone, though it was at times difficult to find points with adequate cell phone reception. At times we had to stop so I could use phones in hotels and restaurants to make collect calls to reporters. In each interview, I explained the justice of our fight and defended our right to protect the welfare of Mexico's miners and steelworkers, even though some reporters seemed more interested in the superficial aspects of the story, like the spectacle of our journey, than in the underlying truth of the conflict. Some reporters were fair and seemed genuinely interested in my side of the story, while others peppered me with loaded questions designed to get the answers they wanted to hear. Regardless of their bias, all the reporters asked where I was. Many insisted I was on a private ranch somewhere in Coahuila, while others were sure I was in London or Madrid. My answer was always "Closer than you probably imagine." They pressed me, unsatisfied: "Where, exactly? Can we meet you for a face-to-face interview?"

From the road, I read reports in which press secretary Ruben Aguilar continued to speculate about whether I was in Coahuila, in my hometown of Monterrey, in San Antonio, in London, or in countless other places. (Aguilar, in addition to his own frequent mistakes, was famous for having to explain President Fox's erroneous and misleading statements. "What the president *meant* to say is . . ." was his constant refrain. Without exception, Aguilar said the fault was the media's, for distorting the president's words.) We also read and listened, with great disappointment, to the many biased reports that defamed my peers and me. They had succeeded in portraying the union's leadership as a group of self-serving frauds, though nothing could have been further from the truth.

On the road, I was also in frequent contact with my fellow union members as well as other labor leaders in the United States. I was pleased to find out how relatively easy it was to communicate and coordinate from afar with the use of a cell phone and email, and it gave me new hope that I could be an effective leader, even from afar.

During the trip to Albuquerque, I had time to reassess the life I was leading and the struggle the union was waging against powerful opponents. In the twelve-, fourteen-, and sometimes even sixteen-hour days I was putting in as leader of the union, I rarely paused to take a break and get perspective on the miners' ongoing struggle. Our trip along Route 66 allowed me to put some distance between myself and the daily grind of leading the union, and I found myself fleshing out new ideas for the modernization of the union. Surrounded by the desolate beauty of New Mexico and the deep history of the landmarks along Route 66, I saw more fully than ever before how the Miners' Union could be a key factor in transforming the economic, political, and social life of Mexico.

Now that I was away from the country of my birth, I began to see Mexico in a new light. I came to the conclusion that Mexico must stop being a country of injustice and exploitation. My passion for transforming Mexico into a modern, educated nation that embraces the majority of the population—including workers, women, and young people— grew stronger. Many Mexicans are eager to live in such a country, one that has transitioned from backwardness to modernity, and I realized that leaders who have an open and progressive mind can be the agents to bring this change, whether they are union leaders, politicians, or even business leaders. Mexico, like other nations, has an increasing need for radical changes and demands a governing class that is prepared to serve every part of the Mexican population. Though I was far from Mexico, I felt closer than ever to my people.

Of course, the trip also gave me time to think about how we could realistically defend ourselves against the constant stream of attacks coming from some of the most powerful men in Mexico. I saw that if we wanted to move our union forward and take the rest of the country with us, we needed to think about not just fighting off the attacks one by one, but about how we could survive in the medium and long term. In a strange way, I felt encouraged by the bull's-eye that had been placed on the Miners' Union. It meant that we were on the right track, and that our honest, committed leadership proved a real threat to the reactionary politicians and businessmen who were intent on raking in money at all costs.

All these travel meditations led me to one rock-solid conclusion: We could not allow Grupo México and its cronies in the PAN to get away with the irresponsibility that cost sixty-five miners their lives that day at Pasta de Conchos. We had to continue to demand the recovery of our sixty-five fellow miners who were still at the bottom of the mine and insist on punishment for those responsible for the explosion. On top of that, we had to keep demanding fair and adequate compensation for each of the victims' families, so they could rebuild their lives and move on without their husbands, brothers, fathers, or sons.

On the road to New Mexico, we got news from the volunteer rescuers who had stayed behind at Pasta de Conchos after Salazar and Grupo México had both departed. Weeks after the cave-in, bodies of two our colleagues were found in a diagonal communication tunnel close to the mouth of the mine. That left the number of dead or missing men at sixty-three. The two newly discovered bodies were intact and not damaged by the explosion, lending further credibility to those who believed that some of the miners could have survived the explosion. Even if the miners had initially been knocked unconscious, the layer of oxygen—topped by the lighter methane—could have kept them alive for some time, as it had the nine survivors of the accident.

That wasn't the only news we would receive on the road. On March 6, I got a call from Celso Nájera, a lawyer I knew personally, mainly because we were both from Monterrey. Nájera had agreed to represent the union once the accusation of fraud involving the Mining Trust had emerged. The union had many legal professionals who were experts in labor law, but none who had any experience with banking crimes or fraud; the union had never been in a situation like this. Over the phone, Nájera told me that Morales, along with two accomplices, Miguel Castilleja Mendiola and José Martín Perales, had done precisely what we expected them to, given all the lies they were spreading in the press. The three of them, supposedly on behalf of the union members, had officially presented a complaint with the federal district attorney's office against us, using the lawyers Antonio O'Farrill and his brother Patricio. The attorneys were borrowed from Julio Villarreal of Grupo Villacero, a massive steel company that was, like Grupo México, troubled by the strength and independence of Los Mineros. (Of course, Morales and his fellow traitors could never have afforded to hire a lawyer on their own; Grupo Villacero and Grupo México gave them unlimited resources to use in this new legal battle against us.)

Nájera explained that I, three other union leaders (Héctor Félix Estrella, Juan Linares Montúfar, and José Angel Rocha Pérez), and Gregorio Pérez Romo, a motorcycle courier who they claimed had been involved in making deliveries of illicit money, were accused of diverting funds from the $55 million Mining Trust. It was a banking law violation completely invented by Grupo México. The company had indeed agreed in 1990 to turn over 5 percent of the shares of each of those companies to a trust controlled by the union for its own social and educational programs, but it was only after years of struggle that we had finally forced them to honor their commitment and turn over the present value of the shares—$55 million—to the union in 2004. Now, we were accused at the federal level of illegally extinguishing the trust and making use of the funds derived from it, all under the false presumption that the "workers"—Elías Morales and his accomplices, who were not even union members—were the owners of the funds, and not the Miners' Union itself. The technical charge was "illegally disposing of the funds of a banking client," as referred to in Article 113 *bis* of the Mexican Credit Institutions Act. In fact, the trust had been legally extinguished; some funds were paid out to the workers of Cananea, some was used to pay legitimate union expenses, and the rest was in the union's rightful possession.

Also named in the complaint were about forty supposed accomplices, among them friends and family. They claimed we had given money to our friends, family, and several company presidents with whom Los Mineros had had good relations at the time, among them Sergio and Raúl Gutiérrez of the steel company Deacero and Alonso Ancira Elizondo of Altos Hornos de México (AHMSA), Mexico's largest steel producer. (Of course, it's no accident that these supposed accomplices head two of Grupo Villacero's biggest competitors.)

We have come to call this first spurious accusation the "mother criminal claim." For this type of banking charge, the attorney general's office is required to request a review from Mexico's National Banking and Securities Commission (CNBV) through official letter. The request was made on the very same day Morales and his cohort officially filed their complaint.

It took less than a week for the CNBV to come back with its technical opinion. By now we were in Albuquerque, having been warmly received by the representatives of the USW's District 12 section, including Terry Bonds, Robert LaVenture, and Manny Armenta. I was relieved to read the commission's finding: "From the official documents reviewed, and particularly as it refers to the cancellation of the aforementioned Trust agreement, and the transfer of the funds that formed part of the trust, no conduct is established that is consistent with any of the special criminal typical actions referred to in the Credit Institutions Act and specially, that which is referred to in Article 113 *Bis*, as stated by the party making the petition."

This response, issued by the highest banking authority of the country, categorically clears me and the other members of the executive committee of any wrongdoing. The CNBV also requested the opinion of Juan Velásquez, a respected attorney who acted as a counselor to that organization, and after having reviewed the documents pertaining to the extinction of the Mining Trust, he confirmed that no crime had been committed.

At the moment, it seemed that my name and those of my colleagues had been cleared. It seemed like a positive step toward officially stripping Elías Morales of his artificial title, and perhaps toward a return to Mexico. But for the time being, I was still being portrayed as a criminal in Mexican media, and it would take time to reverse the damage.

Fortunately, the USW were gracious and supportive hosts to me and to Oralia, who arrived in New Mexico soon after I did. Marcelo, Hector, and I worked from the District 12 offices in Albuquerque, New Mexico, every day, and I made calls to my union colleagues back in Mexico and made arrangements with Leo Gerard, Ken Neumann, Steve Hunt, and other leaders in the USW.

Oralia was devastated by the recent events, and I did my best to make life in New Mexico normal for us. The full extent of our situation was setting in, and I saw that we might not return to Mexico for some time. I was determined to not let our family fall apart. Terry Bonds, the USW's director for District 12, and his assistant director, Manny Armenta, took us out to play billiards, and Oralia and I took a quick trip to Santa Fe to have a break and see some of the beautiful Native American art. Even as I strove for normalcy during our time in Albuquerque, Los Mineros and their families were with me every minute. It was my constant priority that they keep their spirits up and continue insisting that Grupo México and the government be held responsible for Pasta de Conchos.

The union held its Extraordinary National Convention on March 16 and 17, 2006, in Monclova, Coahuila. I was able to attend the gathering by videoconference from the USW's District 12 offices, and I opened the initial ceremony and spoke again on the second day, to close the convention. Since the aggression began, the members of Los Mineros had expressed their full loyalty and solidarity toward me, so it never crossed my mind that they would believe the lies of Elías Morales and endorse him as general secretary. Indeed, during the convention the delegates unanimously agreed that I would continue in my role as general secretary of the union. They declared that they would not recognize the unlawful imposition of any other leader, including Morales, and that I would remain the head of the union's national leadership—the position to which they had elected me.

One other major resolution came out of that convention: We would publicly demand that the government immediately stop its aggression against the Miners' Union, and if the government did not respond immediately and grant full recognition to the union's true executive committee by April 3, 2006, we would call for a national forty-eight-hour strike that would shut down the country's entire mining and metalworking sector.

Our stay in Albuquerque was short. After three weeks, the Steel-
workers encouraged me to relocate once again—this time to Canada.
They were aware that the ultraconservative U.S. president George W.
Bush had no affinity whatsoever for the nation's labor unions and that
he had a close relationship with President Fox, to the point that Fox
had taken to dressing like his Texas counterpart. The two had had a
friendly meeting at Fox's ranch soon after they both took office, popu-
larly referred to as the "Boot Summit"; both men showed an affinity for
Western-style clothing. Given that closeness between them, the leaders of the USW lacked confidence in their ability to protect a politically
persecuted union leader in the United States, especially if the Mexican
government were to request my forced return.

Canada, a country much more sympathetic to the union cause than
its southern neighbors, seemed like the best option, though my family
and I received invitations to come and live in several other countries,
many of them in Latin America. Nestor Kirchner, president of Argentina, and his Minister of Labor Carlos Tomada, and Brazil's president,
Luiz Ignacio Lula da Silva, had both been following the developments in
Mexico and showed sympathy for our cause, offering us political asylum
in their countries. I am still grateful for their show of support. Lula de
Silva was particularly vocal in his encouragement, since he had started
his career as a leader of Brazil's metalworkers' union. Thus, the crisis had
given rise to new friendships, both within the union world in Mexico
and, now, with world leaders.

Before our departure to Canada, Oralia left for Texas, where she would
meet our eldest son, Alejandro. I then flew with Marcelo and Hector to
Portland, where we rented a car and drove to Seattle to meet my middle
son, Ernesto. From there, the four of us drove forth to Vancouver—our
new temporary home. We showed up in Vancouver on March 23, 2006,
in our rented Ford like a bunch of tourists, driving around downtown
and choosing a random hotel to stay at. Underneath the sadness of the
circumstances, I felt a growing sense of freedom and safety at being out
of reach of my enemies. I felt the beginning of something new—a time
for me to reassess and prepare new strategies to keep Los Mineros strong

and independent. I felt freshly inspired to strengthen the union against attacks, build international solidarity, and continue making our organization a vital part of the global labor movement.

Meanwhile, the members of the national executive committee made a decision to support all the legal, travel administrative, and maintenance expenses of my family and our colleagues, as long as the political persecution and the conflict lasted. Their resolution was confirmed unanimously during the next general convention of the Miners' Union.

A week later, Ernesto and I were at the Vancouver International Airport waiting for Oralia and Alejandro to arrive. Ernesto and I had found a furnished apartment and met with Steve Hunt, director of USW's District 3 in Vancouver, and his assistant director, Carol Landry, both of whom would become very close friends. At last we saw Oralia and Alejandro walking toward us through the terminal. We ran toward them, and tears welled in Oralia's eyes as the four of us embraced. It was a tremendous relief to be with them again, all together except our youngest son, Napoleón, who would be visiting soon.

That night, over Chinese takeout at the new, rented apartment, we stayed up late talking about our trips and the most recent developments in the campaign against Los Mineros. It pained me to see my family suffer, but at that moment, I felt our unity and commitment to the struggle grow stronger than ever. A week later, our son Napoleón would arrive to be with us in Vancouver, but he would soon decide to fly back to Mexico and continue his studies at the University of Monterrey. I worried about him but agreed that he should stay on at school if that's what he wanted.

The move to our new temporary home in Canada was a difficult transition for all of us, particularly Oralia, who'd had to leave her aging mother behind in Monterrey. Each of us was struggling with separation from the land we called home, from our friends and extended family. But we bonded together, committed to fighting a fight we knew was just—even if we had to do it from thousands of miles away.

SEVEN

THE RESISTANCE

The joy is in the struggle, in the effort, in the suffering
that accompanies the struggle.
—MAHATMA GANDHI

In the early 1990s, three brothers from the border town of Matamoros, Tamaulipas—Julio, Sergio, and Pablo Villarreal Guajardo— inherited a scrap steel business from their father. The operation made its profits by purchasing low-quality steel that had been discarded due to some defect and then reselling it. Jorge Leipen Garay shared the story of these three brothers with me, and it is well-known that as the brothers built up the company, which came to be known as Grupo Villacero, they developed relationships with crooked employees in the purchasing and sales divisions of two of its main suppliers: Fundidora Monterrey, a quasi-governmental iron and steel company, and Hylsa, a Mexican steel mill that today is called Ternium. The brothers pressured these employees into making superficial holes and tears at the heads or tails of the pristine rolled metal sheets, instantly converting high-quality steel to scrap. The Villarreals would then buy this lightly damaged metal for a vastly reduced amount and resell it at premium prices.

The brothers ran this scam on hundreds of thousands of tons of Fundidora Monterrey and Hylsa's metal, shamelessly amassing their ill-gotten gains in the coffers of Grupo Villacero. As the company grew, they began to regard themselves as masters of industry, but they were in reality little more than corrupt intermediaries and tawdry salesmen.

Their fraud played a large role in the eventual bankruptcy and dissolution of Fundidora Monterrey in 1986, though the brothers Villarreal proclaimed that it was the union's fault—according to them, it was the workers' demands for wage and benefit increases that had sent Fundidora under. Of course the true cause was the brothers' mafia-like style of business that had brought Fundidora Monterrey to bankruptcy. The company, which had previously belonged to the Mexican people, was sold off at ridiculously low prices. Fundidora's main subsidiary, Aceros Planos de Mexico, despite having the best and most modern sheet mill in Latin America, was auctioned off at an absurd price of less than $100 million.

In 1991, Grupo Villacero bought a company called Sicartsa from the government, during the presidency of Carlos Salinas, champion of privatization. Sicartsa, since its foundation in 1969, operated a steel mill complex in the industrial port of Lázaro Cárdenas, Michoacán, located on the Pacific coast of Mexico. (The port town was named after the Mexican president who in the 1930s had fought for workers' rights, nationalized the oil industry in 1938, and placed many of the country's resources back in the hands of the Mexican people.) Though the government had invested over $8 billion in Sicartsa over the years preceding the sale, Grupo Villacero picked it up for a mere $170 million, according to Jorge Leipen Garay, former undersecretary of Energy and Mines and former director of the government's steel holding company, Sidermex. Retaining the Sicartsa name, the Villarreal brothers set about ensuring the fattest profits possible at their new operation. By the time I became head of the union in 2002, they had about sixty subcontracting companies at the Sicartsa mill complex in Lázaro Cárdenas, fifty-seven of which were owned primarily by the Villarreal brothers themselves.

In Mexico, this is a common arrangement. A company is granted a concession, and it then hires contracting companies also owned by the company. The contract workers might make eighty pesos a day, while the contracting company charges the concession holder eight hundred pesos for the same job. It's a criminal arrangement by which companies like Grupo Villacero simultaneously steal Mexico's resources and get rich off the workers who labor in their facilities.

The leaders of Los Mineros, knowing the brothers hadn't changed since their steel-scamming days, had taken the incorporation papers of Grupo Villacero's contracting companies at the Sicartsa complex to Labor Secretary Abascal, demanding an investigation. Predictably, nothing was done. Adding to the atrocious situation at Lázaro Cárdenas, Grupo Villacero pretended that its contract workers had a union of their own, but no trace of this supposed union could be found. The "organization" wasn't registered, and it certainly didn't advocate for its members.

When open aggression toward Los Mineros began in February 2006, Grupo Villacero partnered with Grupo México and President Fox to carry out a wave of intimidation and repression. It was the Villarreals' lawyers, the scheming, discredited Patricio and Antonio O'Farrill brothers, who filed the "mother claim" on Elías Morales's behalf against me and my colleagues in March. Grupo Villacero had been more than willing to lend its help to Elías Morales as a way of weakening the union that troubled their operation at Lázaro Cárdenas.

As it turned out, the workers of Los Mineros were not prepared to accept these lies and welcome a backstabber like Morales as their leader. Union Local 271 from Lázaro Cárdenas would protest the attempted imposition most loudly of all, and in doing so would become the focus of the next major confrontation in the war against us.

Following the union's convention in March, we continued demanding that the government cease its attacks and hold Grupo México accountable for its fatal abuses at Pasta de Conchos. They utterly disregarded us. The lies and slander continued, legal action against me and my colleagues was continued, and Germán Larrea continued leading his destructive company with no repercussions for causing the death of sixty-five men. As agreed, we prepared for a national two-day strike in protest, to be held on April 3 and 4.

The members of the union's national executive committee developed a plan and arranged the massive strike. Meanwhile, I had started to grow accustomed to organizing and directing union business through email, phone calls, videoconferences, and frequent visits from my colleagues. In advance of the event, we elected a strike committee that would work with local union heads and the leaders of the executive committee on the logistics of each work site, as well as on how to handle negotiations.

Early on the morning of April 3, hundreds of thousands of workers around the country showed up at their plants and mines, preparing the picketing line and blocking the entrance and exit gates so company representatives couldn't get in. At each operation, workers organized into teams that worked in shifts to maintain the demonstration. The national strike was observed by all members in all the union locals, and because Los Mineros are such an integral part of the country's hundreds of thousands of mining and steel workers, the entire chain of production ground to a halt. Without the unionized workers, no one could work, regardless of whether they were part of Los Mineros.

The right to strike is guaranteed in the Mexican constitution as a last recourse for workers to defend themselves, and even in this time of aggression, Los Mineros exercised that right with respect and responsibility. Inside the facilities, we assigned teams where necessary to maintain blast furnaces, electrical systems, and anything else that could damage the work site if left unattended during a strike. The goal of a strike is never to damage the company's machinery or destroy its property; it is merely the best way to demonstrate our unwillingness to tolerate abuse, aggression, and disrespect for the needs and rights of workers. For two days, the strike paralyzed all work sites in Mexico's metal and steelworking sector.

After the stoppage, eight union sections around the country decided to continue the strike in protest of the government's violation of the union's autonomy. Many of those eight also had ongoing disputes with their employers regarding working conditions, wages, and respect for the union. The largest of these sections was Section 271, the Lázaro Cárdenas branch that had workers at the Sicartsa mill. In addition to their protest against the government's attempt to replace me with Morales, the five thousand steelworkers at the Sicartsa steel mill—3,500 union members, the rest contractors—had several other demands against Grupo Villacero and the exploitative Villarreal brothers. Rather than getting any significant share of profits, workers would get meaningless gifts—like key chains. With the full support of the executive committee, Section 271 decided it would continue the strike indefinitely, until their demands were met.

As the workers of Lázaro Cárdenas stayed off the job, and as they reached the end of the third week, Elías Morales and the Villarreal brothers asked that the labor department declare the strike illegal and petitioned for armed intervention to crush the striking workers. Morales, who purported to be on the workers' side, declared the workers of Lázaro Cárdenas "terrorists."

Sadly, President Vicente Fox, Labor Secretary Salazar, Interior Secretary Abascal, and Abascal's director of government—Arturo Chávez Chávez, who would later be appointed attorney general of Mexico with no qualifications except his pliancy in carrying out abuses ordered by those in power—eagerly complied with the request. Like Grupo México, Grupo Villacero had great influence with Fox's government. The federal government and the state government of Michoacán readied their forces to expel the strikers.

In Vancouver, on April 20, I was having a coffee at dawn with Oralia when one of my cell phones rang (at the time I had five to help me keep up with everyone—two Canadian, two U.S., and one Mexican). It was Mario García, the executive committee's delegate for Lázaro Cárdenas. With grief and anger in his voice, he told me that at about 6:00 a.m., federal and state police forces began arriving at the plant, completely unannounced. Huge navy ships carrying about one thousand heavily armed men pulled into the port where the steel mill was located. Each man looked like an individual Robocop—complete with shield, helmet, and R-15 rifle. The strikers, still at their posts, were bewildered but unwilling to cave. García told me that the unarmed workers were currently trying to hold their ground as best they could, but the scene was escalating rapidly.

I hung up with García and immediately began calling all the other members of the executive committee to request their support in Lázaro

Cárdenas. I called Leo Gerard and Ken Neumann to alert them to the attack. Committee members Juan Linares, José Angel Hernández, and José Barajas were in Vancouver at the time, and I called them too; they quickly showed up at the USW offices to help in any way they could. After his first call, I suggested that García keep in touch every fifteen minutes to give us updates.

The attack that day turned out to be one of the most violent repressions in recent memory. They took incredible measures against peaceful strikers and their families: the thousand men, primarily from the Federal Preventive Police and their tactical Special Operations Groups, carried rifles and high-powered machine guns, and they even sent in tanks with artillery. Several helicopters with snipers on board flew threateningly overhead. Worst of all, the armed forces descended on the strikers without any previous notification. Labor Secretary Salazar had declared the strike illegal only hours before the attack; there was no way the workers could have prepared themselves, and we had no time to fight Salazar's ruling legally.

The assault was bloody. Television cameras captured some of the violence of the security forces, who aggressively attacked the steelworkers despite initially saying it would be a "peaceful" eviction. Bullets rained down from the helicopters, hitting the union members and other people from the community. Though I was getting a steady stream of updates from Mario and other union colleagues in Michoacán, I felt outraged and impotent, being so far away and unable to defend the workers in person. Our strike was 100 percent legal, given the violation of our collective bargaining agreement. How was it possible that the government could resort to violence against workers in a completely legal strike?

The workers used the front blades of bulldozers to block the bullets being shot at them. Besides the tools they had around them, the striking steelworkers were defenseless. To help in the only way they could, the workers' family members and neighbors rallied around the strikers and began collecting rocks and even pieces of roofing for the men to hurl at their attackers. They were no match for their attackers, who shot into the crowd with no regard for women or children. The scene was chaos. Fires burned as the strikers tended to their wounded and bleeding friends.

Later that morning, García called with devastating news. Two of the striking workers had been killed—our colleagues Mario Alberto Castillo and Héctor Alvarez Gómez—and more than one hundred workers sustained gunfire injuries. García was distraught. I immediately asked him to go to each of the men's families at home to inform them of what had happened and console them as best as he could. Héctor Alvarez was married and had a young daughter, and Mario Alberto had lived with his parents. I asked Mario to call me from each of the residences so I could personally speak with the families.

I have never forgotten the conversations I had on the morning of April 20, 2006, two hours after the violent event, with the parents and the wife, respectively, of our colleagues Mario Alberto Castillo and Héctor Alvarez Gómez, who had been killed by the murderous bullets of the armed men sent to the Sicartsa mill by Morales and the Villarreal Guajardo brothers. Oralia and my son Ernesto were by my side, full of grief. Oralia was in tears.

The voice of the father of Mario Alberto Castillo was weighted with indescribable sadness. Indeed, I do not believe there is anything worse than losing a child, and the tragedy was even greater, since his son was murdered at the hands of politicians and businessmen. I called him from Canada and expressed my solidarity with him and his entire family on behalf of myself and all my colleagues. Mr. Castillo told me that his son struggled to defend his leaders and his colleagues against abuse and that he hoped that his death would not have been in vain.

I answered that his sacrifice for us, together with that of Héctor and the others, made him one of the true heroes of unionism, and that he would always be an example for us and an inspiration.

To speak with the widow of Héctor Alvarez Gómez, who also had a small daughter, was a terrible experience—heartrending beyond description. I almost could not bear to hear what had happened as, with an enormous sadness and with weeping that still rings in my ears, she thanked me for calling. Gaining a measure of emotional control, she told me she was very sad to know that her daughter would never see or live with her father. She said they were in a very bad financial situation, because they had just begun their married life and that she felt terribly alone in assuming the responsibility for guiding her daughter in her growth and moving forward. I expressed my admiration of Héctor for his heroism and said that we would always hold the image of the commitment of her husband. I promised that her daughter would know the story of her exemplary father and that we would not leave her or her daughter alone: that we would do everything to help them, as we have done and continue to do.

That night, my family, colleagues, and I watched the news reports from Lázaro Cárdenas with great sadness. Though more than one hundred strikers had been shot, many reports showed the default bias of the Mexican media and, unthinkably, portrayed the violence as the fault of the unarmed workers. "TV Azteca hasn't shown the workers' version," one Sicartsa worker would later say. "They only aired footage of the bad things. It isn't the truth."

In the end, the government's aggressive tactics at the Sicartsa steel mill on April 20, 2006, did not enable them to take control of the work center. They were repelled by the workers and their families. Faced with the prospect of having to murder more than a thousand men, women, and children to take control of the mill, they finally retreated.

The brutal attack occurred almost precisely one hundred years after the massacre and assassination of the striking copper miners at Cananea in 1906, an event that for many symbolizes the beginning of the Mexican Revolution and the labor movement in Mexico. Particularly disheartening was the involvement of the governor of Michoacán, Lázaro Cárdenas Batel, who bowed to the interests of President Fox and Grupo Villacero. A supposed leftist and member of the Democratic Revolutionary Party (PRD), he is the grandson of one of the greatest presidents in Mexican history, with whom he shares his name. His grandfather was president from 1934 to 1940 and had won the admiration of the Mexican people for promoting the creation of trade unions, supporting workers' strikes, distributing land to *campesinos,* and, as never before in history, developing a large-scale social policy that favored the workers. He also expropriated the oil industry in 1938, which up until then was in the hands of large international companies from Great Britain, the Netherlands, and the United States and which had rebelled against the government because they did not want to satisfy the fair union demands of petroleum workers. Regardless of this legacy, the younger Cárdenas was more than willing to send in troops to maim and kill the strikers of the town named for his grandfather.

I personally spoke from abroad to the governor of Michoacán, Lázaro Cárdenas Batel. In no uncertain terms, I protested these killings and the use of force to repress a legitimate strike, and I assigned blame to him and the Fox administration. I told him that he was shaming the PRD—the leftist party to which he belonged—and staining the image of his grandfather and his father, Cuauhtémoc Cárdenas Solórzano, a man who had also governed Michoacán and who had headed the struggle to democratize the PRI party. Cárdenas Batel begged my pardon, saying that Fox's government had deceived him. He claimed they told him there would be no violence during the eviction, but I didn't buy it. I knew he was submissive to Fox, and, like most politicians, opportunistic when it came to using circumstances to win favors from the powerful. He seemed frightened and actually asked me for help. I told him, full of anger, that the only advice I could give him was to demand that those responsible for this repression be punished.

I also demanded that Cárdenas Batel immediately compensate the families of the slain men and the more than one hundred injured workers. In addition, I requested that any remaining law enforcement personnel withdraw immediately from the area around the port of Lázaro Cárdenas and the total suspension of any other act of aggression against the workers and called for the investigation of the events and criminal punishment for the people who had made the decisions to use force and for all those responsible for the decision's implementation.

Sadly, Grupo Villacero had easily convinced Fox to send in troops—
Villacero was a generous contributor to his wife's foundation, Vamos
Mexico. Following the attack, Governor Cárdenas Batel, having already
capitulated to the demands of the federal government and the corporate
owners in the attack on the steelworkers, proved unwilling to conduct a
full investigation. How could he have, when he was one of the responsible parties? Not even the legacy of his respected father and grandfather
could persuade him to recognize the obvious: that the striking workers
were legally defending their freedom, their union's autonomy, and their
right to safe working conditions.

About a week after the attack, I found out that several days prior to the
invasion of the Lázaro Cárdenas complex, there had been a meeting of
Fox's security cabinet, with the president in attendance, and the group
had discussed whether to attack the facility with military force. A politician who was present at the meeting told me about it, and I later confirmed this report by looking at the president's published agenda. On
that day, it showed that Fox had attended a meeting of the national security team. Fox and the other attendees were frustrated that they hadn't
destroyed us in February and March of 2006 with their false accusations, and the Lázaro Cárdenas strike gave them a pretext to attack once
again. Some of those present at this meeting expressed doubt about the
effectiveness of sending armed forces in, questioning who would take
responsibility if things turned out badly.

Supposedly, Labor Secretary Salazar spoke up to address the concern. "When the miners see that our men are about to move against
them, they'll run like cowards," he said. Fox, along with the rest of his
security cabinet, believed the Yunquista Salazar's outrageous assertion,
and it was decided that they would invade the port. Had they known that
the miners would stand firm and repel the aggression with such courage
and dignity, I'm sure they would have made a different decision.

On April 17, three days before the attack, President Fox was on a tour
with Governor Cárdenas Batel in the city of Uruapan, about 125 miles from

Lázaro Cárdenas port. During a rally there, about twenty members of Los Mineros spoke up from the crowd and demanded to Fox's face that he immediately end the smear campaign against us and recognize me as the true leader of the union. They told him that they had expressed their desires in a free, democratic election, and that he was obligated to respect that.

Fox listened to their statement and, in front of Governor Batel, told them they should stop worrying—the whole conflict, he said, would be over in a few days. It was a perverted statement, and that was all he said. The steelworkers traveled back to Lázaro Cárdenas to prepare for the strike, and three days later found out exactly what Fox had meant with this cynical pronouncement. The president's intention was to end the conflict not through negotiation but through violent repression.

The workers at Sicartsa managed to keep control of the mine and plants for five months. The strike at Lázaro Cárdenas continued until September 15, 2006, nearly five more months, when there was a favorable agreement with the workers in which they received no less than a 42 percent increase in their wages, an unheard-of increase in Mexico and perhaps in the world. They also received 100 percent of the wages lost during the five and a half months the strike lasted. As part of the negotiations, in 2007, workers, some of whom had been with the company more than two decades, received a significant share of profits from the company.

This successful strike, conducted to defend the authentic election of its national leader, was the first of its kind. "Why would we want a government like this?" asked Olga Ospina P., a relative of one of the Sicartsa workers, after the attack. "Fox promised a change. Is this it? We are tired of the aggression against the workers. Why is it happening? Because they are fighting for their leader? What would Fox think if we took his wife—who is a rat—and gave him another one? He wouldn't like it. Let the workers choose who will be the one who speaks for them."

The ultimate victory of the Lázaro Cárdenas workers was a resounding defeat for the government, though it was paid for with the blood of two of our colleagues. The strike of our Section 271 colleagues was totally legal and there was no reason to use the armed forces against workers who were struggling for their labor rights and human rights, as firmly established in law. The terror and violence of the government had failed to end the strikes and work stoppages across Mexico.

Grupo Villacero didn't benefit from the brutal tactics, either. Its repressive activities and refusal to listen to the demands of the workers had cost it millions of dollars. At the end of 2006, the company was forced to sell its share of the Sicartsa complex to ArcelorMittal, currently the largest private steel-producing company in the world (and a model of efficiency in its collective bargaining agreements with unions in Mexico). Though we ultimately overcame the government's repression perpetrated on April 20, 2006, the memory of Héctor and Mario gave us fresh incentive to continue fighting with our utmost strength against the lies and slander of President Fox and his corporate supporters.

EIGHT

A LEGAL FARCE

Men without ethics are like wild beasts released in this world.
—ALBERT CAMUS

Two days before one thousand armed men descended on the workers of Lázaro Cárdenas, the enemies of Los Mineros had initiated a new phase in the legal persecution of our union. Elías Morales and his corporate backers had been blocked in their initial complaint by the CNBV's formal opinion, which deemed the extinction of the Mining Trust and the use of its assets completely legitimate and legal—the commission unequivocally stated that no banking crime had been committed. But Germán Feliciano Larrea of Grupo México and its collaborators weren't about to let that stop them from charging full speed ahead in their mission to see us discredited and distract attention from the sixty-five dead miners of Pasta de Conchos. They had asked themselves what they could possibly do to overcome this roadblock, enlisted the help of the attorney general, and hatched a new plan.

In Mexico, sadly, the office of the federal attorney general—the Procuraduría General de la República, or PGR—is often used by politicians and other powerful people to attack their enemies. Such was the case in the fight against Los Mineros. At the urging of Grupo México and Morales, the PGR decided to give it a fresh start at the *state* level. In early April, unbeknownst to us, the PGR had been casting about for state attorneys general—especially in states with many miners and steelworkers—who would move forward with the complaint against us.

On April 18, 2006, the PGR took its file from the mother claim, made copies, and sent each one to all the states, with special emphasis on Sonora, San Luis Potosí, and Nuevo León. Of course there was no mention of the CNBV ruling that had halted the case at the federal level (it would take us two years to even get our hands on a copy of this document). In these three states, they had found officials willing to go along with their plan, supposedly on behalf of the union members who lived there. Of course this was absurd; far from being the plaintiffs in a case against me, Los Mineros were actively protesting the attempt to remove me. There was no way of foreseeing this despicable plan, but we knew we were dealing with perverse characters. No action on their part would have surprised us.

As the failed mother claim spawned three identical sub-claims, aggression at the federal level was ongoing. Immediately following Morales's complaint in early March, the Mexican Mediation and Arbitration Board—the Junta Federal de Conciliación y Arbitraje, or JFCA—had ordered the seizure of all the union's bank accounts, including more than $20 million of the disputed $55 million. (The JFCA, the court that rules in all labor-related matters, is, absurdly, part of the executive branch even though it is a quasi-judicial entity. The arrangement leaves politicians an opening to meddle in matters of a purely legal nature.)

Personal bank accounts of all those charged in Morales's complaint were also frozen, in an attempt to financially strangle the union's leaders. The government's Financial Intelligence Unit made these unlawful seizures of personal assets notwithstanding the CNBV's report. (The CNBV, once it issues its opinion, has no authority to stop actions that are inconsistent with that opinion; thus, the banking commission did not impede seizures of union and personal assets and cooperated with the unit making them.) My family's home in Mexico City was seized, along with all its contents. The government even took possession of a house belonging to my wife's grandmother in Monterrey. Now abroad in Canada, all my family had were the few possessions we'd taken with us out of the country.

The fact that Grupo México encouraged the government to continue going after me and the other four men charged is not only absurd from a legal standpoint; it is also inconsistent with earlier statements made by its head, Germán Feliciano Larrea.

The entirety of the charges leveled at us is based on the $55 million that my father had won in negotiations with Grupo México in 1989 and 1990. Following the privatization of Mexicana de Cobre de Nacozari and Mexicana de Cananea, the government and Grupo México had made a clear commitment to take 5 percent of the stock of both companies and give it to a trust controlled by the Miners' Union, to be used for social, educational, and growth plans. The use of the money was to be entirely at the union's discretion. The arrangement was approved by the National Financial Authority, the government bank that facilitated the privatization of the two companies. After fighting tooth and nail against keeping their end of the bargain, and only after I initiated a long legal process against them, the company had finally paid the debt in 2005, placing $55 million into the Mining Trust. Subsequently, in 2005, the trustees voted to dissolve the trust and transfer its assets to the union.

Now, enraged by my accusation of industrial homicide at Pasta de Conchos, Grupo México (through its puppets like Morales) began to argue, just two years after finally honoring their obligation, that the simple act of dissolving the trust was a financial crime and that the union's leaders had nefariously used the money for its own purposes. The charge would have been funny had not so many officials—and the Mexican media—jumped on the bandwagon. The union kept meticulous records of each transaction involving the $55 million, and we could prove that a huge part of the assets, almost $22 million, had been paid out to workers who lost their jobs as a result of the privatizations at Canahen and Nacozari and to their families, while other smaller amounts went to legal and bank fees, publicity costs, real estate investments, and renovations—all expenses that served the union and all of its members.

Morales's claim, besides being utterly false, had its basis in the distinction between money belonging to the Miners' Union and money belonging to the *members* of the union as individuals. Morales and the other two argued that the workers, not the union, owned the assets. Yet, back in August of 1990, fresh from negotiations with my father about the 5 percent of privatization proceeds, Germán Larrea had personally disproven this claim. That month, Grupo México was undergoing bankruptcy, and during the proceedings, the First Court in Bankruptcy Matters in Mexico City mistakenly referred in writing to the 5 percent of shares of Mexicana de Cananea as belonging to the workers of the company, when in fact, as Larrea well knew, the shares had been explicitly negotiated to become the property of the Miners' Union itself.

Larrea, after spotting the error in the court's document, filed a petition requesting that the judge correct the mistake and clarify that the funds correspond exclusively to the union, not to the workers individually. The petition, which we have copies of, signed by Larrea in his capacity as legal representative of Mexicana de Cananea, contains this passage:

> As can be noted in the comment presented by His Honor in subsection C of point VIII previously transcribed, there is a mistake since it says that the company I represent offered to deliver 5 percent of its share capital to the workers of the bankrupted company, when in fact the company I represent declared to offer the said percentage to the Union of Miner, Steel and Related Workers of the Mexican Republic, as Trust Beneficiary of the Trust established on November 14, 1988, with Multibanco Comermex S.N.C.

In other words, Larrea himself said in August 1990 that the assets were the union's, directly contradicting the argument he would later use as the pretext for his persecution against me, some sixteen years later. Upon receiving Larrea's petition in that original matter, the judge issued an order modifying the sentence in the bankruptcy document to show that the assets belonged to the union, not to any particular group of workers:

As a background to the document presented by Germán Larrea MOTA VELASCO on behalf of Mexicana de Cananea, S.A. de C.V. Considering the reasons given by the petitioner and considering that the resolution issued by this Court on August twenty-four of this year, which accepted and approved the auction of the company mentioned above is imprecise, it is important to clarify point VIII subsection c) which refers to the allotting of five per cent of the share capital of MEXI-CANA DE CANANEA, S.A. DE C.V., in favor of the workers of the bankrupted company, should say the following; " . . .) MEXICANA DE CANANEA, S.A. DE C.V., offers to assign up to five per cent of its share capital . . . in favor of the Union of Miner, Steel and Related Workers of the Mexican Republic, as Trust Beneficiary of the Trust established on November 14 of one thousand nine hundred and eighty-eight with MULTI-BANCO COMERMEX, S.N.C. . . . which are the property of the said Union. In support of which we refer to Article 84 of the Code of Civil Procedures, applicable additionally, considering that this clarification is an integral part of the resolution issued on August twenty-four last.

From the moment the correction was made, it was crystal clear that the contents of the Mining Trust belonged to the union. In alignment with this and with our proof of having used the assets appropriately, the PGR had received a clear opinion from the CNBV that the union and its executive committee were innocent of any mishandling of the $55 million. Now, as 2006 progressed, the PGR and the labor department were ignoring the obvious truth and working together to widen and complicate the legal onslaught against us—all at the behest of Grupo México.

Germán Feliciano Larrea, aided by the Villarreal Brothers, was doing all he could to demonize me to the public and persuade public officials to persecute me on his behalf. We were told by a confidential source that he offered payments and gifts to Interior Secretary Abascal, Labor

Secretary Salazar, Attorney General Daniel Cabeza de Vaca, Secretary of Finance Francisco Gil Díaz, PAN senator Ramón Muñoz, and the presidential couple themselves, among many more, hoping to succeed in destroying the legitimate leadership of the Miners' Union. Larrea reportedly dangled a huge financial carrot in front of each one of these individuals, offering between $10 million and $30 million if they could help the government-corporate cabal reach its objective of destroying, at any cost, both my leadership and the Miners' Union itself.

At the beginning of 2007 in a private meeting between Germán Larrea and one of the vice presidents of Televisa, Alejandro Quintero, Larrea told Quintero that he would pay whatever it took to launch a smear media campaign in order to discredit me, the union, and my family. (Larrea is also a member of the board of directors and a shareholder of Televisa.) He told Quintero that he would risk his fortune just to break the union and break me too. In 2011, Xavier García de Quevedo, one of the closest accomplices of Larrea and a top official in Grupo México, made a public statement saying that the conflict with Los Mineros had cost them at that time more than $4 billion.

In Vancouver, I watched the conflict escalate in the spring of 2006 with a heavy heart. The bodies of sixty-three miners still lay buried at Pasta de Conchos. The failed eviction at Lázaro Cárdenas had proven the government's willingness to use lethal violence against us. My family had been forced into a strange land, with all our assets in the hands of the government. And it was looking more and more like our stay in Canada might last longer than we originally hoped. I was also getting discouraging calls urging me to step down as head of Los Mineros. Alonso Ancira and his advisor, Moises Kolteniuk—who supposedly had been a friend a long time before—both tried to convince me to surrender the fight and allow Salazar to impose Elías Morales on the workers. I was unwilling to even entertain the thought. Doing so would be tantamount to a confession, and it would be a betrayal of my fellow workers and my father's legacy.

Through it all, though, we had the stalwart support of our friends in the USW, and of the miners and steelworkers of Mexico. They refused to accept the lies of politicians, businessmen, and journalists. Upon hearing the full story, no one could believe that Morales was anything but a liar and traitor. He hadn't even troubled to show up at Pasta de Conchos. The only time he'd set foot in the union's headquarters in the past six years had been while trying to raid and destroy it with a band of intoxicated vandals. Since I'd left Mexico, he hadn't become involved in the union's work in any way, never negotiating a single issue on the workers' behalf. All Morales did was give libelous interviews in the media and attend official ceremonies where, in the presence of companies and government officials, he was presented as general secretary of the union.

The loyalty of Los Mineros, the USW, and the global labor community was unwavering in the wake of Pasta de Conchos, but securing legal help proved more difficult. In stark contrast to excellent lawyers like Nestor de Buen and his son Carlos, who worked on the labor side, and steadfast supporters like Marco del Toro, who would take on our case later, we would encounter our share of lawyers who let us down.

A matter of days after the explosion at Pasta de Conchos, a lawyer from Monterrey named Bernardo Canales had been referred to me by Celso Nájera. Canales offered me his professional services, and I was grateful for the potential help. Canales made a good first impression. He seemed like a hard worker, and I trusted that he had the union's best interests at heart, even though he was the cousin of Fernando Canales Clariond, a PAN member from Monterrey who had served as secretary of economy under President Fox. Throughout March of 2006, Canales provided legal defense services to the five of us who were charged, but at the beginning of April, he told me that his close friend, Guillermo Salinas Pliego, had invited him along on a motorcycle tour of Europe in the middle of the month to celebrate Holy Week. He told us he would call every day while he was gone and that he would have his cell phone by his side, day and night, in case of emergencies.

Canales's overly fervent assurances worried me slightly, as did the fact that Salinas Pliego, his traveling partner, was the brother of the president of TV Azteca—the multimedia conglomerate that had been particularly unfair toward Los Mineros since the conflict had begun. Salinas Pliego was a major TV Azteca shareholder himself. The two of them left Mexico in mid-April of 2006 and spent Holy Week motoring around Europe. The first few days he was gone, we didn't get the promised phone calls. Then emergency struck: the government authorized full searches of the union headquarters, the homes of my union colleagues Juan Linares and Félix Estrella, my home in Mexico City, and my home in Monterrey. In need of help to block these intrusions, we called Canales's phone over and over with no effect. At last he sent some colleagues from his firm to help us, but never once did he himself speak to one of us. He had been receiving our messages but simply refused to speak to us. We were left without defense in a moment of great aggression from the government.

When Canales got back, he ceased all communication with me or anyone from the union. Finally, a secretary from his legal firm called my office in Mexico City, saying that Mr. Canales was not going to continue with this case and that we should send someone to collect all the files from his office in Monterrey. A colleague called me at my Vancouver office with the news. That was it. Canales had collected more than $300,000 for doing absolutely nothing besides a few weeks of defense work. Like a coward, he made off with the workers' hard-earned money without personally calling me or any of my colleagues to say he was leaving the case.

When he took on the case, Canales never intimated that he was not able to carry out his work, that he was afraid, or that there was any other problem that would cause him to stop representing us. He took on our case without appreciating the magnitude of the aggression against the union, and then profited from the union's resources—heavily depleted from the government's arbitrary seizures—before realizing the enemy he was up against. We had trusted Canales and put all our confidence, and all our legal files, in his hands. The betrayal stung.

As we did our best to fend off searches, seizures, and threats, our efforts to prosecute Salazar and Morales for forgery was encountering frustrating setbacks. In order for the labor department to fast-track the approval of Morales as leader of the union in the days before Pasta de Conchos, Morales was required to submit certain documents to the labor department, and it was in these papers that they had forged the signature of union executive committee member Juan Luis Zúñiga Velázquez, who subsequently in 2010 betrayed the union. The false signature appeared on four different documents, all dated February 16, 2006. The first forged document was a union resolution sanctioning the five of us for the supposed banking fraud involving the $55 million. The second document informed Labor Secretary Salazar of the sanctioning. The third, which is addressed to both the union and the labor department, states that I have been removed as general secretary and expelled from the union. The fourth forged document is Zuñiga's supposed resignation from the union—as if he had coincidentally signed all these documents and resigned on the very same day.

These documents formed the cornerstone of our legal case against the labor department and the traitors headed up by Morales. As soon as he learned of the forgery, Zuñiga filed a criminal complaint. On February 28—the same day Salazar made the official declaration of the government's support of Morales—Zuñiga had personally alerted the labor secretary of the forgery and the fact that the false documents were being used to illicitly achieve the aims of Grupo México. Salazar was then obligated by law to inform the PGR of this crime, but of course he didn't; he was in on it.

Nevertheless, based on Zuñiga's criminal complaint, an investigation into the forgery moved forward. In late March, our conviction that the signatures had been forged was confirmed by a report from graphoscopy experts at the PGR. Though the attorney general's office had been instructed to press the campaign against us in every way possible, no one had been paying attention to the graphoscopy department—a technical team that was uninvolved in the PGR's overarching political machinations. The report, for us, was an exciting development. It was only after we went public with it that the PGR realized it had a problem.

Unbelievably, the attorney general's office announced in a brief public statement in mid-April that the false documents, along with the reports declaring their falsity, had been stolen from the PGR's Mexico City offices. Suddenly the most compelling hard evidence we had against Grupo México and the labor department was gone, without a trace. The PGR insisted on blaming low-level officers for the theft, failing to state why such officers would be motivated to take the documents. *La Jornada*—a daily paper that has done a better job than most at reporting honestly on the conflict—ran a story on the highly suspicious theft, along with several other major media outlets.

Once again, the economic power of Germán Feliciano Larrea had gotten him what he wanted. He'd managed to have evidence stolen while it was in the custody of the PGR itself. More than likely, he'd simply paid off someone in the attorney general's office to make the papers disappear.

As a result of this supposed theft, the falsification of the signatures remained unpunished, as it does to this day. In the coming years, we would continue to hold labor department officials responsible for the forgery. Marco del Toro, the criminal lawyer who would do so much for Los Mineros, presented several complaints on Zuñiga'a behalf. Incredibly, in 2010, Zuñiga would leave the union and publicly withdraw his complaint regarding the forgery, declaring that he no longer claimed any crime had been committed. He'd finally given in and been bought off by Grupo México, joining the side of the enemies of the union.

In May of 2006, a month after the PGR sent duplicated case files to San Luis Potosí, Nuevo León, and Sonora, each of those states issued arrest warrants for me as well as for my union colleagues Juan Linares Montúfar, Héctor Félix Estrella, José Angel Rocha Pérez, and Gregorio Pérez Romo (a courier who wasn't even a union member). The judge overseeing the complaint in the state of Nuevo León handled the warrant differently from the other two judges. Being slightly more principled, this judge saw that he clearly had no jurisdiction over the matter and said so—although all he did was wash his hands of the case, transferring it instead to the Court 32 of the Federal District in Mexico City.

Our defense had become triply difficult. Each one of those charged now had to fight off the same accusation in two different states and in Mexico City—a clear violation of double jeopardy. It was obvious to anyone who looked that the propagation of the rejected fraud charges to three separate states was an underhanded, unconstitutional move.

The plan was outrageous to begin with, but the carelessness with which Grupo México and the PGR tried to pull it off was truly astounding. While Marco del Toro was preparing our defense, he noticed that the warrants signed by the judges from Sonora and San Luis Potosí contained identical paragraphs—even to the point of repeating the same spelling mistakes. These officials simply approved the fully prepared warrants forwarded to them by the PGR, caving to pressure from Los Pinos and simultaneously staining their judicial careers. Rather than reviewing the case in good faith, these lackeys decided to move forward with their copy-paste version of justice.

We immediately went about preparing our defense with the lawyers Juan Rivero Legarreta and Marco del Toro, who had now officially taken over the case from our previous criminal defense lawyer, Mariano Albor. They began work on filing *amparos*[2] to move the warrants issued in San Luis Potosí and Sonora to the Federal District, where they would be consolidated with the warrant already transferred there by the judge from Nuevo León.

Initially, my colleagues and I were not as successful in the courts as another defendant in the case of the $55 million. When the judge from Sonora issued arrest warrants for my colleagues and me, he also issued

---

2 The concept of *amparo* (literally "protection" in Spanish) originated in Mexico and has since spread to many other countries. When a person appeals for a "writ of amparo," he or she is appealing for protection of his or her rights based on the Mexican constitution. One can appeal for a writ of amparo to protect human rights and personal freedom, to prompt a review of the legality of a judicial decision, and to challenge the constitutionality of a law or statute, in addition to several other protections. For the lawyers of Los Mineros, amparo trials would help us protest everything from rulings on the illegality of strikes to false charges like those against the executive committee.

a warrant for several Scotiabank executives who had acted on behalf of the Mining Trust. Their charges were identical to those made against us. The Scotiabank executives appealed for amparo against the warrant, and a federal court ruled on November 16, 2006, that the appeal was valid, *since the actions of which the trustees from Scotiabank were accused are not considered illegal.* The judge acquitted the Scotiabank employees of any wrongdoing, granting them the widest form of constitutional protection possible.

Two months later, the exact same Sonoran judge who oversaw the Scotiabank acquittal also ruled on the amparo presented on behalf of Juan Linares Montúfar, against the same warrant. Yet in that case, the judge decided that Linares would only receive limited protection. The warrant against him was valid, this judge said; it just contained a few formal errors made on the part of the prosecution. The case would move forward—quite a change from the day this same judge had declared that an identical warrant was completely invalid because no crime had been committed. Why the change? It can only be because the judge was biased against us, the individuals who so deeply threatened the entanglement of Mexican politicians and businessmen.

In the middle of these injustices, we learned that the PGR, through its organized-crime division (Subprocuraduría de Investigación Especializada en Delincuencia Organizada, or SIEDO), was charging me and the same four colleagues with a new crime at the federal level: *lavado de dinero*, or money laundering.

In Mexico, money laundering is defined as "operation with funds derived from illicit sources," and this new charge was based on the exact same facts that had originated the first federal banking fraud charge. SIEDO's thinking went like this: Since we had allegedly illegally extinguished the Mining Trust (an act that resulted in the banking charge), any use of the resultant funds constituted an operation with funds from an illicit source. Therefore, despite the fact that no crime had been committed, the money-laundering case aimed to take us down for using the money from the trust to compensate miners and their families and to cover union expenses. Because of the personal vendettas of a few immoral businessmen, SIEDO wasted its time and the taxpayers' money concocting these charges, when it could have devoted those resources to true criminals and real organized crime.

In the summer of 2006, we were relieved to hear that SIEDO's request for warrants on the money-laundering charges was denied—not once but twice. First, the Ninth District Court on Federal Criminal Procedures of the Federal District refused to issue the requested warrant, and then, on July 31, 2006, the Fifth Unitary Circuit Court in Criminal Matters of the First Circuit confirmed the refusal. In August, a federal judge confirmed the decision and revealed the fraudulent nature of the charges, saying, "Not only were there no indications of an illegal source of the assets, but there is clear proof of their legal origin," and "In any case...we can affirm that from the documents that the assets belong to the Union of Miner, Steel and Related Workers of the Mexican Republic." It was proof that even in a corruptible system, there were still some honest judges.

From Vancouver, I closely followed every step my defense team took as they fought the arrest warrants issued against the others and me. It was an enormous legal undertaking. Marco del Toro was working tirelessly on our defense, and the tax lawyers José Contreras and José Juan Janeiro and civil law specialists Juan Carlos Hernández and Jesús Hernández persevered in their assistance under very difficult conditions. As the legal battle grew more complicated after 2006, we had to adopt a different strategy, supported by diversifying our sources of income, ensuring international solidarity, and developing extraordinary loyalty, unity, and unprecedented internal cooperation. We devised a coordinated resistance action over more than five years, despite frozen bank accounts, and we continue to progress in the battle with no pause and no opportunity to rest.

Following my departure to Canada, Grupo México and its allies also worked hand in hand with the Departments of Labor, Economy, and the Interior in their efforts to destroy the leaders of Los Mineros. They even collaborated with the Department of Foreign Relations, exerting pressure on the Canadian ambassador to block the visa requests from our union leaders to travel to Vancouver. Fortunately, none of those attempts worked.

The PGR and the Department of Foreign Relations also worked together in the first months after my departure to have me either deported or extradited back to Mexico, where I would undoubtedly be imprisoned indefinitely. As Mexico tends to do, it pushed first on the migration side, hoping Canada would send me back the basis of purely on immigration law. No deportation was ever mentioned or attempted by Canadian officials.

Having failed there, Mexican authorities fabricated documents to use as the basis for extradition, begging Canada to send me back. Any person with the slightest familiarity with extradition processes would see that these accusations are unsupported. Accordingly, Canadian officials were not willing to play such games. They understood that this was a high-profile case that warranted further attention, and they spent time trying to get to the bottom of it.

How does the current Mexican government expect to retain any respect in the global community when it employs such dirty tactics and lies to foreign nations? Their actions should constitute an international scandal, and the truth of their deception and repression will emerge sooner or later.

With weeks turning to months in Canada, my family had begun to adapt to our new life, and the union had adjusted its operations to function with a leader who was permanently abroad. In the face of this separation, my colleagues and I have adopted the use of new forms of communication, and using modern technology I have been able to help organize the resistance and continually share my ideas and my moral support. Despite growing accustomed to the arrangement, I have been propelled in part by outrage at my forced exile. At times I have felt impotent, unable to be physically at my colleagues' sides at the forefront of the workers' defense, unable to be physically present as we fought for justice for the lost miners of Pasta de Conchos and their families. On more than one occasion I have tried to return to Mexico, against the advice of my lawyers and my fellow union leaders. The situation has filled me with profound anger at the government, headed by indecent people who would like to put an end to our organization, whatever the cost. The governments of Vicente Fox and Felipe Calderón are stained with miners' blood, and no one will forget this. No one will erase from the workers' minds what these unjust leaders did to protect immoral businessmen who, they knew, had committed criminal acts.

This forced exile has been a major commitment, a great challenge, and a stimulus for fighting harder than ever. When I was driven out of Mexico while my colleagues where in extreme danger, I was not about to abandon the mission or stop fulfilling my duties as general secretary. I committed to holding this role as long as I have the full support of the union's members.

NINE

A GLOBAL WAR

*The only one deserving freedom is the one who fights
for it every day.*
—JOHANN WOLFGANG VON GOETHE

In July of 2006, we got news that encouraged us that the rot of Fox's
labor department and the PGR had not penetrated to every branch of
the government. Following the Pasta de Conchos explosion, the Mexican
Congress had created a special commission to investigate the cause of the
explosion, and at the urging of these congressmen, the Mexican National
Commission on Human Rights undertook an extensive study of the background of the tragedy and how it was handled by Grupo México and the
labor department. On July 17, the Commission on Human Rights released
a report on its findings along with a press release. The commission unam-
biguously attributed the accident to deficient safety and hygiene conditions and laid the bulk of the responsibility on the public officials who
should have been inspecting and supervising the mine. It also holds Grupo
México and its subcontractor responsible, noting that the company operated the work site with extremely poor safety measures. Finally, it pointed
out the sloppy rescue work on Grupo México's part and detailed the errors
and omissions in how the tragedy was handled publicly.

My defense lawyers emailed me the report right away and brought
me a copy a few days later when they came to Canada. The commission
hadn't said anything that my union colleagues and I didn't already know,
but getting an official report that attributed the blame where it rightly

belonged was a significant step forward. That said, it wasn't enough. Nowhere did the report call for direct legal action against Germán Larrea, Labor Secretary Salazar, or any company managers or government inspectors, and for many of us the commission's findings renewed our anger at the entire situation. We were grateful for the truly amazing solidarity of labor leaders around the globe and for the honesty of the commission, but I knew the full story behind the report needed to be told. The families of the men who died—and the Mexican people as a whole—deserved to know the depth of the abuse and collaboration going on in the boardrooms of Grupo México, Grupo Villacero, Grupo Peñoles, and Altos Hornos de Mexico, as well as in the offices of their elected and appointed leaders in the government.

In December of 2006, Jeff Faux, author of *The Global Class War*, sent a copy of his book to me with an inspiring dedication regarding my fight for a better world. I didn't know Faux personally, but he has close connections with the leaders of the USW and AFL-CIO and had been following the story of Los Mineros. Faux had given the USW's Canada director, Ken Neumann, a copy of his book for me, and Ken passed it along at District 3's Christmas party, organized by my dear friend, Steve Hunt. I appreciated Faux's gift greatly and devoured it over the following week.

Reading that book was the stimulus I needed to tell my own story and the story behind the men lost at Pasta de Conchos. Like Faux, I wanted to fully flesh out the injustice. I'd given interview after interview to journalists, but only a paltry few were ever published and certainly not in widely read Mexican publications. The public had to know the truth about the people running their country.

This aggression against us must be a warning to all the labor movement's leaders, in Mexico and in the world. It must also be a warning to the Mexican people, showing them that they are actively threatened by wrongheaded economic policies, rampant corruption, and the desire of some business leaders to accumulate wealth at any cost. Yet our fight is also a warning to the companies in the world that think they can violate the rights of workers and get away with it.

Pure greed was the only reason Germán Larrea had refused to spend the $1 million on the *tiro* that would have prevented the Pasta de Conchos disaster—in a year when Grupo México pulled in $6 billion in profits. In exhibiting such callous avarice, they forget that Mexico's natural resources are not the personal riches of Mexican businessmen or whoever happens to be governing the country at a given time. According to the Mexican Constitution, subsoil mineral resources are the property of the nation, and they must be exploited reasonably through concessions that the government grants to companies or individuals, not doled out by politicians so that their friends can make exorbitant profits and keep the money for themselves. All the country's mineral products—the gas, oil, metals, and other resources obtained from the bowels of the earth— are part of the national heritage, and the profits they bring in should first ensure the well-being of the workers who risk their lives to bring these vital products to the earth's surface.

The current mineworkers' movement has deep roots in history. In the decades after 1940, Mexico experienced what is now known as a "stabilizer development," a period of economic growth and social peace that ended in the 1970s. In many ways, the demands and needs of mineworkers were served and the Miners' Union was highly respected during this time. The "stabilizer development" gradually but steadily ended as Mexico joined the global economy. From 1988 to the turn of the century, under the governments of Carlos Salinas de Gortari and Ernesto Zedillo, the country saw the privatizations of numerous state companies, among them numerous mining, metalworking, and steelworking companies, to the extent that currently there is not a single government-owned mining, metalworking, or steelworking company in Mexico. The state and quasi-governmental sector of the national economy was dismantled in all industries, thus cancelling the mixed-economy model—made up of the private economy working in tandem with the social economy and the state economy—that had prevailed and progressed since the government of Adolfo Lopez Mateos (1958–64). In the 1990s, the number of state companies plummeted from 1,155 to less than two hundred, with most being practically given away in sweetheart deals to investors. The

Mexican stock market boom of that decade was enjoyed only by these investors and businessmen; in a *USA Today* advertisement, the Mexican government admitted this disparity itself: "The number of citizens living below the poverty line has increased from 13 million in 1990 to 24 million in 1994." Today the estimates are close to 50 million.

The policy of privatization also caused a sharpening of the conditions of exploitation of miners' labor, as it did in other workers' sectors, until it exploded in 2006 in the mining conflict. There have been no solutions in sight since 2000, when the pro-business conservative governments took over, headed by Vicente Fox from 2000 to 2006 and by Felipe Calderón from 2006 to 2012. These governments, following the neoliberal route of Salinas and Zedillo, accent the private business side of the economy, to the extent that currently it is unclear who is governing: the government leaders formally elected by the people, or the unelected leaders of the private sector.

Over time, the granting of concessions to extract these resources has become characterized by complicity. In exchange for political and financial support, governing politicians betray the constitution and grant concessions under conditions favorable to private companies and a few individuals. They give the businesses unlimited permits to exploit natural resources, on top of tax allowances and authorization to dump toxic wastes and completely relocate indigenous communities. The companies then become monopolies, operating to generate profits at any cost. Meanwhile personal health and safety go out the window. All this is supported by the politicians, who continue granting the abusive companies more concessions.

Pasta de Conchos certainly did not give pause to any of the members of this ruling class—they have continued to shamelessly profit from these concessions. Until 2006, there had not been any concessions to any individual for exploitation of natural gas. But under Calderón and Salazar, shortly after the explosion at Pasta de Conchos, Germán Larrea lobbied the federal government and won the first natural gas concession, in violation of the Article 27 of the Mexican Constitution, which reserves the exploitation of hydrocarbons exclusively for the Mexican government. The company's argument for getting the concession, which represented an initial value of $600 million per year for the company, was that the Pasta de Conchos tragedy "left it no other choice" but to exploit methane gas rather than coal, to avoid future risk. The National Energy Regulatory Commission, the institution that grants private concessions—incidentally run by Salazar's son, Francisco Xavier Salazar Diez de Sollano—had no problem with delivering this prize to Grupo México. But before this company earns one more cent from any of its concessions, it should be stripped of all its holdings that violate constitutionality and compelled to recover the sixty-three bodies lying in the darkness of Pasta de Conchos that are still awaiting a dignified burial.

Since the Pasta de Conchos explosion, the government has presented Grupo México with more than six hundred new concessions for mining—about one hundred per year. Each mining concession represents thousands of acres of national territory to exploit, which Larrea and Grupo México have used to become one of the largest rights holders and speculators in the country, holding sway over enormous expanses of land. Today, more than 25 percent of the national territory has been given in concessions to private companies, domestic and foreign, according to different estimates. And Grupo México's new possessions aren't limited to mining projects; they have also collected railroads, seaport terminals, land and sea drilling projects, construction and engineering projects, beach resorts, golf courses, private residences, and farms. Despite the tragedy at Pasta de Conchos and the deaths of our comrades, Germán Larrea and Grupo México have gone on to create major new businesses—all under the protection of the government of Vicente Fox.

The privatizations—or "disincorporations"—started in the 1980s under Salinas, and Mexicana de Cobre and Mexicana de Cananea were among the early losses to the people of Mexico, with most of the wealth—except for the 5 percent the Miners' Union secured to fund its programs—transferred from national ownership to the Larrea family and their partners in Grupo México. Likewise, Altos Hornos de México (AHMSA) was subtracted from the national heritage and given to Alonso Ancira Elizondo and Xavier Autrey; the Las Truchas steel mill in Lázaro Cárdenas went to the Villarreal Guajardo brothers of Grupo Villacero; Aceros Planos de México (APM) was awarded to the PAN families Canales and Clariond; and many others could be named, besides.

Family relations and friendships have played a fundamental role in all the shady processes of privatization. Government officials have sold assets and reserves that were once part of the national heritage at ridiculously low prices—practically gifts—to family and friends. A good illustration of this is the relationship between Pedro Aspe, treasury secretary under President Salinas, and Alberto Bailleres, owner of holding company Grupo Bal, which controls Grupo Peñoles, the second-largest mining company in Mexico, the department store chain El Palacio del Hierro, and insurance company GNP. (Bailleres is also a member of the board of directors of Televisa, along with Germán Larrea.) The two men became family when Aspe's daughter married Bailleres's son, and gifts and concessions flowed freely from the government to Bailleres, enabling him to amass the second-largest fortune in Mexico. Aspe also oversaw, under the Salinas presidency, the privatization of the Nacozari and Cananea mines, sold for a pittance to Grupo México. Once he left office, Aspe used his connections from the treasury to begin amassing great troves of wealth for himself.

By throwing money at PAN officials, Germán Larrea and his ilk ensure that they continue to get top-dollar concessions—and they secure an unseen hand in the government's actions through controlled officials and direct appointments to office. Conflicts of interest are of no concern to men like Fox and Calderón, for whom a prior business interest in a related area is not a problem when making such appointments. In fact, coming from a business background is an advantage in their eyes. Corporations might as well send letters of recommendation for these individuals, who are uniformly unsuited to public service after a lifetime of capitalist greed.

Vicente Fox spent his entire term in the service of private companies that furthered his personal and ideological interests that financed his political campaign or that donated large sums of money to the Vamos Mexico Foundation run by his wife, Marta Sahagún. He forgot that he was just a manager of the country's riches, not the owner. As with so many others, power caused him to lose his mind.

The amount these individuals stand to make off Mexico's resources just keeps rising. When the mining conflict began seven years ago, the price of copper was around 75 cents per pound; the price of gold was around $300 per ounce; and silver was around $4.50 an ounce. Seven years later, we have witnessed a surge in demand and the speculative market mainly in China, Korea, India, and Japan, and prices have shot up dramatically: copper is about $4.40 per pound—600 percent higher than five years ago. Gold is above $1,650 per ounce, more than five times higher than five years ago. The price of silver is around $34, eight or nine times higher than five years ago. While these prices fluctuate, they are always on an upward trajectory.

Yet no one sees the benefit of these increases but the businessmen themselves. Their companies try to establish fixed costs of production and manual labor, ignoring or pretending not to know how much fatter their profit margin has become. The Miners' Union has been struggling for a long time for better wages and benefits, and we continue to do this because we know that the companies can afford the increases and because we also know that wages do not have a large impact on the ongoing profitability of these transnational giants.

In the comparison of wages between Mexican mine, metal, and steelworkers on one hand and those of the United States and Canada on the other, we find that wages in the two latter countries are fifteen times higher than in Mexico. A mineworker in Mexico can earn an average of $20 per day for eight hours' work, while a worker in the United States or Canada can earn $35 dollars *per hour*. This difference in wages is overwhelming. This comparative analysis does not fit the concept of economic justice and equity, much less respect toward the interests of Mexican workers and their families.

Mineworkers of Mexico, the United States, and Canada—and those of any other place in the world—perform the same type of activities, operating and producing the extraction of minerals and transforming them with the same equipment and technology in similar facilities. They produce the same materials and metals that are quoted in the international market, but the risks are much higher in a country like Mexico than in countries that have more advanced health and safety conditions, such as the United States and Canada.

Mexican mining, metalworking, and steelworking companies, and those of any other industrial sector, do not have the economic justification to explain the enormous disparities between the wages paid in Mexico and those paid in Canada, the United States, and many other developed nations. Mexican owners generally use the excuse that the cost of living is high in developed countries, thus justifying the higher wages, but if we measure real comparative costs, we can confirm that there is a difference that is at most double or perhaps a little more than in Mexico. It is not enough of a difference, however, to explain or justify the enormous difference in wages, fifteen times higher in the more advanced countries.

Exploitation and discrimination against Mexican manual labor is made even more unjustifiable by the fact that the finished products obtained from mining and steelworking are quoted in the international market at the same prices by the metals markets based in London, New York, Tokyo, or Hong Kong, established by buyers and importers from those countries. Thus, end prices are the same whether the minerals are extracted and mined in Mexico, Canada, or the United States, or produced or transformed in any of these countries. And no price differential or lack thereof, of course, can justify the gross levels of exploitation, abuse, and marginalization that exist and are tolerated, in complicity with the companies, by the Mexican government.

How can we explain, then, such profound differences in wages between the United States and Canada as opposed to Mexico? The only possible explanation is the difference in the degree of exploitation of the workers. If we produce the same product, with the same equipment and technology, in the same working conditions—actually, much worse conditions in Mexico—the result indicates the degree of exploitation of manual labor that the respective governments are willing to accept. In Mexico the governments allow very high degrees of exploitation of human labor, far above the levels permitted in the United States and Canada.

The case of Mexico illustrates the distortion brought about by an economic policy designed exclusively to benefit a single sector, as has become apparent in the past ten years. The first issue is misguided fiscal and tax policies that are designed to create incentives for large companies, such as granting voluminous exemptions in the payment of taxes. The majority of large companies, among them mining companies, owe the Mexican government many millions in taxes that they have not paid, or else the taxes are refunded or forgiven by the government. In the appendix, I have noted the relationships of some of these corporate "tax deadbeats": information that is very illustrative.

In January 2010, Carlos Fernández-Vega of *La Jornada* wrote a column that brought to light the enormous perversity of this situation. He revealed that since 2005 a group of forty-two companies has run up an unpaid tax bill of nearly 224 billion pesos (about 21 billion USD)—a number that is equal to a high percentage of federal public income for 2009.

This is just one of the many gains that Mexican companies have experienced under the neoliberal economic model, with its appropriation by individuals of public resources. To this cumulative and ongoing organic deficit in public finances that involves debts owed to the government, it is necessary to add what private companies have not paid to the Mexican treasury during the past twelve years of the PAN government—at a time when there has been greater pressure on individual taxpayers in the middle of the tax scale.

Although the figures are older, very recently the reality of these tax-avoidance schemes by large companies has been revealed. On February 26, 2011, *La Jornada* stated: "The Federation auditor general confirmed that the Tax Administration Service, SAT, failed in 2009 to collect 462 billion pesos [about 33.7 billion USD] in so-called 'tax expenditures,' in the majority extensions and subsidies."

This single amount represents a very large proportion of tax collections. And it is only the nonpayment from a single year, 2009. Imagine the unknown amounts from other years! And remember that this phenomenon has been occurring for many years, well before the PAN governments came to power. It has become worse during the two PAN presidential terms of Fox (2000–06) and the current Calderón administration (2006–12). The fact is that all companies in 2009 failed to pay a total of 462 billion pesos, and that the largest Mexican companies' debts to the Department of the Treasury account for roughly half of that (223.7 billion pesos, or a little over 16 billion USD).

The same *La Jornada* article reported that in 2010, capital flight from Mexico to foreign countries increased 79 percent, double the total amount of direct foreign investment, to a total 759.7 billion pesos (53.4 billion USD).

Thus, if we add what the tax authorities failed to collect in 2009 from many companies to the enormous amount of money that fled Mexico the following year, we can conclude that Mexico was brutally undercapitalized in just these two years. Capital that does not flow to the government through tax revenue is capital that does not increase the treasury's economic ability to invest in development. In addition, capital that leaves the country does not return to Mexico for reinvestment that could result in greater generation of stable jobs. What's more, the capital that left was transferred to foreign banks, mainly U.S. and European banks, and to tax havens, with which these corporations will actually finance the development of other countries, mainly our powerful neighbor to the north.

In summary, in addition to Mexico having a chronic capital deficit, and despite there not being sufficient resources from direct foreign investment, much Mexican capital is going abroad to finance programs and companies in other countries. It all indicates a scheme for dispossession of Mexican economic resources, a plan operated by private initiative that is not a bit nationalist, which does not invest capital in Mexico, and which seeks the protection of the United States and other nations to finance businesses there to the detriment of Mexican public and private finances. All this, of course, proceeds with the cover-up, if not the deliberate complicity, of the conservative PAN government.

As if all this weren't enough, current Mexican tax policy falls most heavily on the captive population, which already has a heavy burden. The government is always on the lookout for ways to increase value-added taxes (VATs) and direct or indirect taxes on public services, including electricity, natural gas, gasoline, and the prices of basic goods.

This situation, instead of creating stimuli in the economy, creates serious inequality, because it is privileging a few to the detriment of the vast majority. It cannot generate short-, medium- or long-term growth. It also does not develop solid, stable, equitable, and just growth. It merely favors those who have the most ability to pay at the expense of those who have the least ability.

The business sector's obsession with profits leads to problems beyond tax-avoidance schemes and an insistence on low wages. As we have seen, it also prevents many companies from investing in the most basic safety measures. In just the past five years, two hundred workers have been killed in accidents in Grupo México mines and plants. That record will certainly not improve if Germán Feliciano Larrea and others of his type are left to their own devices.

The situation that we miners have experienced in recent years has not just been another attack against a group of workers; it has been an all-out war against the free and democratic trade unionism of the people, an assault without precedent in our country. It certainly reflects the ambitions and appetites of unlimited power, the insensitivity of some groups who, by following globalization and international organization theories in addition to their own interests, seek to destroy the autonomy and freedom of workers and trade unionism itself.

The brutality with which this attack against Mexican miners and steel workers was orchestrated reflects how unbridled capitalism works against the fundamental rights of workers and the most neglected social classes. Above all, it is clear that exploitative systems have no principles, no ethics of any kind, not even the vision to realize that when the situation reverses in favor of the neglected and the oppressed, the reaction is much more violent.

Mexico does not need a new labor culture, but it urgently needs a new ownership culture—and governing culture—that would change the mentality of those insensitive and exploitative businessmen and authorities intent on maintaining the widest profit margins possible at the expense of basic safety and living standards for those whose labor generates the products they sell.

What these businessmen and politicians do not understand or accept because of their sick or selfish greedy mentality and lack of respect for human and labor rights, for safety and health—in a word, their lack of respect for human life—is that assuming their social responsibility and harboring a positive relationship with workers and their unions leads to benefits for all parties involved. Individuals like Germán Larrea and the officials in the labor department assume that unions are by nature destructive but fail to see that these organizations can actually be powerful allies. When worker and company share responsibility and are able to negotiate productively, they can progress toward increased production, job creation, efficiency, and competitiveness. When any company displays goodwill and respect toward its workers and keeps its commitments to them, efficiency and productivity are increased, and any disputes are resolved quickly and with the least amount of conflict and lost time. And these benefits for the company reach beyond its own walls; high production and a peaceful, content working class strengthen the country as a whole.

Yet under the difficult and violent conditions of contemporary Mexico, the importance and limits of union action have been reduced. These pro-business, right-wing Mexican governments applied a cynical and aggressive strategy to subjugate the unions to the imperious demands of the large companies and their voracious hunger for profits. Although they have not been completely successful, they have caused damage to the miners' movement. Some of this is associated with the political persecution launched against me personally as national leader and against the National Miners' Union, a struggle in which by no means will we let down our guard or fold our hands.

Never in the history of the union has there been any precedent for the magnitude of this aggression and repression that is so strong, perverse, and aggressive against the mineworkers, against our union and its leaders.

In response to the political persecution unleashed, the struggle of the mineworkers in the past five years constitutes a historic struggle that is, as I stated earlier, without precedent in the defense of union autonomy, liberty, and the basic human rights of workers. To a degree this has been a conflict and a movement that has inspired all unions, not just in Mexico, but all over the world. The great resistance and dignity with which we have defended these rights, principles, and fundamental values have been of sufficient interest to the unions, international federations, and organizations, who are well aware of the significance and transcendence of our effort, work, courage, and dedication to achieving great victory for workers and democracy in this universal struggle.

Since the invasion of neoliberal technocrats in the 1980s, most Mexican politicians have tried to ignore the reality of Mexico. They create an imaginary Mexico that reflects their desires and their demagoguery but that doesn't reflect what the people see around them every day. Whether out of convenience, conviction, or inability, they disregard the poverty that affects so many citizens. Were they to address this reality, their economic policies would have to change radically. They ignore the fact that Mexico is a country of workers—whether city dwellers, farmers, middle class, *campesino*, indigenous, or immigrant. To the PAN, Mexico is Fox's country that is, in the former president's words, "of businessmen, by businessmen, and for businessmen." This sentiment is a catastrophic mockery of the concept of a republic. They forget that labor laws were not created to cater to voracious private interests but to protect the interests of workers. People in the streets used to say that Fox's version of the country was "Foxiland" or "DisneyFox."

Right-wing politicians have lost their moral compass. The government has the ability to relieve many of the injuries it has caused; the legal, economic, and political structure of Mexico is fundamentally very solid. It has been dismantled and broken, but it is not destroyed. It will take a long time to repair the damage, but we must pick up the task urgently. The path of decay we are on can only lead to a profound national crisis.

Since Fox and the PAN took the helm of the country, our difficulties have increased exponentially. And Calderón, Fox's successor, has waged an ill-conceived war against organized crime that has seen the deaths or missing of more then 150,000 since 2006. Unemployment is rampant, and many young people without prospects for work or school are attracted to organized crime. Official figures show that seven million young people between the ages of seventeen and twenty-four lack education and jobs. Mexicans call them "NINI"—no education, no jobs—and they make up a huge potential market for organized crime. Unemployment among the total labor force of Mexico was estimated at 14 million in 2012. Capital has fled the country. Foreign and domestic debt is growing at an alarming rate. Prices, especially for consumer products, have spiked. There is corruption on all sides, in the legal system as well as in Los Pinos. The governing class has impunity with respect to nearly all its crimes. All these evils have reached insufferable levels, and the Mexican people are losing patience.

Yet our struggle has implications beyond the turmoil currently seen in Mexico. The principles we fight for are applicable to the struggles of our fellow unions in countries throughout the world. Multinational and global companies tend to exploit manual labor and natural resources— especially the nonrenewable, like minerals, oil, and gas—even more in less advanced countries, because these nations' governments allow them to. In the National Miners' Union we have insisted vigorously on fair treatment for laborers, and this has been the basis of one of my main conflicts with the government. The Mexican government should be more demanding with both Mexican and foreign investors regarding respect for working, health, and safety conditions as well as environmental contamination. Investors have a social and legal responsibility. They should not exploit natural resources indiscriminately, with no regulations, taking them out of the country and removing the profits from

Mexico. They should temper their focus on amassing profits even at the cost of leaving the soil and subsoil depleted.

The basic principles on which these companies operate must change. Working conditions in globalized companies tend to get worse all the time in terms of workers' interests, and at the same time we perceive a global policy focus on the defense of these companies' common interests. Therefore, we have proposed to other labor leaders around the world that, just as transnational companies globalize, unions and the union struggle needs to globalize. We can no longer afford to fight the battle for workers' rights one strike or even one nation at a time; we must expand the front to cover the whole world.

The global mining and metals sector now consists of huge multinational corporations implementing common strategies to defend their interests—companies like Grupo México; the British-Australian Rio Tinto and its Canadian subsidiary Rio Tinto Alcan; Brazil's Vale; and the British-Australian BHP Billiton. Equipped with advanced technologies and huge financial reserves, they cross borders and oceans in order to exploit natural resources and manual labor. In this environment, workers need a global strategy for the defense of their common interests more than ever. Working together will give workers and unions strength, and the ability to withstand the collaboration of corporations and public officials against them.

Fortunately, we have seen the response to these ideas. In June 2012, in a world congress of the three most important international labor federations celebrated in Copenhagen, Denmark, IndustriALL Global Union was created, a new federation representing more than fifty million members from 140 countries. I was honored to be unanimously elected by 1,400 delegates as a member of the new executive committee.

We must bring together members of the working class from far and wide, and from every industry. Without organizations to serve as a counterweight to the ambitions, greed, and massive exploitation of companies and governments that worship the free market, worldwide inequality will continue and worsen, sooner or later generating huge social and political crises across the globe. A country that protects the

individual interests of a few and exploits the manual labor of the majority is doomed to failure, when the ongoing frustration of the repressed
leads to widespread unrest and violence. Because unions supply the
counterweight to this inequality and exploitation, they are far from
becoming outdated or irrelevant. The opposite is true: They are needed
more than ever.

TEN

DASHED HOPE

Governments, like fish, begin to rot from the head.
—RUSSIAN PROVERB

In mid-November 2006, the International Metalworkers' Federation (IMF) held a press conference in the 11 de Julio theater next to Los Mineros' Mexico City headquarters. In the theater—named after the day the union was founded in 1934—and before a large delegation of union leaders who had traveled to Mexico from around the world, the IMF's general secretary, Marcello Malentacchi, announced a Day of Global Solidarity with the Miners' Union, to be held on December 11. Malentacchi had personally urged many congressman and senators to pressure the government to end its aggression against the union, and at the press conference that day, he encouraged workers to do the same on a global scale.

He announced that labor organizations around the world would be petitioning the Mexican embassies in their countries on December 11, protesting the Mexican government's collusion with the private sector and its efforts to strip the Miners' Union of its autonomy.

When December 11 arrived, I was ecstatic and honored by the international outpouring of solidarity for our cause. Union organizations in more than thirty countries on six continents—from Kenya to France to Japan—sent letters to their Mexican ambassadors, urging them to support respect for basic labor rights. Many of these organizations held marches and protests in front of the embassies and spoke to the press about the situation in Mexico and how the government's actions revealed a fundamental disrespect for workers. Up in Vancouver, I worked with the USW and several smaller unions to organize an event in front of the Mexican consulate there. I spoke to the crowd about the nearly one-year-old conflict, stressing the need to fight for the dignity and freedom of workers wherever it was threatened.

I felt optimistic that day, with so many showing their support for Los Mineros. In our battle against industrial titans, we would certainly need it. I was also pleased that the demonstrations would send a strong message to Mexico's new president, Felipe Calderón, who had taken over for Vicente Fox on December 1. It had been a hotly debated election that brought up many questions about the legality and transparency of the electoral process, but at least Fox was out of office. Through a request hand-delivered by Jack Layton, president of Canada's New Democratic Party (NDP), Los Mineros had requested an audience with Calderón. The prospect of a new president had awoken some hope in the members of the Miners' Union; we didn't think it could get much worse than President Fox and his wife, and Calderón seemed to be open to negotiating an end to the conflict. We were to be sorely disappointed.

At the end of 2006, two months before Vicente Fox's government left office, Interior Secretary Abascal sent me a message in which he told me it would be best to arrive at an arrangement with the outgoing administration rather than continue the call for recognition of the union's true leadership into the Calderón administration. Abascal insisted that it was better to seek an arrangement with President Fox before president-elect Calderón took up residence at Los Pinos. The incoming government was going to be, in Abascal's words, "much worse and more aggressive." The Calderón administration would never want to seek an arrangement with the union or me; on the contrary, they would push the confrontation to the point of destroying the Miners' Union, my family, and me. Abascal said that if I would resign, the Fox administration would cease its accusations against my union colleagues and me and end their campaign of slander before Calderón took office.

I didn't consider caving to this indecent proposal—this last pathetic attempt at extortion—for one second. There was no way I would validate their claims—or tacitly erase their hand in the Pasta de Conchos disaster—by acceding to their demand. Had I stepped down, I would have been implicitly admitting that the leaders of the Miners' Union had committed some kind of failure or abuse against the workers' interests, and there was no way I would help propagate that lie. My message in reply to Abascal was simple: "I am leader of the National Miners' Union based on the free and democratic decision of the workers, in which they voted unanimously. They are the only ones who can decide whether I should continue as head of the union. It is not a decision that the government can or should make, much less the companies who employ our members."

When Fox stepped down from the presidency, all the union's demands were still in place: that our autonomy be respected; that those responsible for Pasta de Conchos be held accountable; that the bodies of our colleagues be recovered; and that fair compensation be paid to the families immediately.

In the days after he became president, Felipe Calderón Hinojosa had his new and then-unknown secretary of labor, Javier Lozano Alarcón, set meetings with some of my colleagues from the executive committee and our labor counselors, Carlos and Nestor de Buen. In his initial communications with them, Labor Secretary Lozano expressed the administration's apparent intention of seeking a negotiated settlement to the strikes that were ongoing in some union sections and of determining the source of the aggression against the Miners' Union. He seemed to want a return to normalcy, and there were some indications that a favorable solution might be brewing.

Lozano said that Calderón had not created the conflict but had simply inherited it from the Fox administration, and that they wanted a resolution. Despite Abascal's warning, the new administration's intentions seemed good that December. One week before Christmas, Lozano told members of the union's executive committee and our labor attorneys that he had specific instructions from the president to terminate this conflict and to negotiate a solution consistent with the law and union autonomy. Lozano even said he was not going to leave for vacation yet, in the expectation that a solution would be reached soon. Of course it was a lie—with only fifteen days in office, we knew he had no such vacation planned.

Lozano's supposed intention to negotiate fairly with us did not translate into reality, and his promises quickly fell by the wayside. The year 2007 began with two meetings in the labor secretary's office, with several executive committee members and our labor counselors in attendance. Lozano made a point of never addressing me as general secretary. These loose, unstructured talks failed: Lozano said the incoming government was willing to end the conflict and halt the charges against us, but their first requirement was my resignation as general secretary, along with the resignation of the entire executive committee of the union. After two meetings, my colleagues got the feeling that the conflict wasn't going to be solved. They demanded that Lozano make the third meeting more formal, saying that he needed to send me a letter announcing the meeting and that it should address me as their general secretary. At that moment, Lozano said he would do it, but I never received anything from him. The third meeting never took place. It seemed nothing had changed since just a couple of months before, when we had been dealing with Fox and Salazar.

Calderón and Lozano's promised "solution" to the conflict—my resignation—disregarded entirely the views of the workers, our bylaws, the Mexican Constitution, and the country's federal labor law, in which it is established that the government must respect union autonomy. In addition, the Mexican government has ratified several agreements with the International Labor Organization over the past sixty years, including Agreement 87, which establishes freedom of association and gives the workers the right to create and join organizations of their own choosing and freely elect the leaders of those organizations, all without government intervention. No matter how many times it was suggested to us, my fellow leaders and I absolutely refused to give up the responsibility to which we had been democratically and legally elected by the worker base, much less yield to the whims of voracious corporations who had caused the deaths of sixty-five of our colleagues at Pasta de Conchos.

Beginning in April 2007, representatives of the Mexican government began traveling to Canada to meet with me about resolving the conflict, though we never received the direct audience with Calderón we had requested. Among those who came to Canada was the then undersecretary of the interior department, Abraham González Uyeda. González was a former engineer and owner of a large dairy business, and two years earlier, he had thrown a lavish birthday party for himself at Las Palmas, his dairy ranch in his home state of Jalisco. With many important PAN politicians in attendance, González got up and made the suggestion that Felipe Calderón run as the party's presidential candidate. This proposal quickly took on the nature of an official launch for Calderón's candidacy, and the media widely reported the story the next day. President Fox, who like all Mexican presidents maintained a tight grip on the workings of his party, was not pleased by this unofficial announcement—it was clearly outside the PAN's rules for selecting candidates. Calderón, then serving as Fox's secretary of energy, was quickly dismissed as punishment.

When González arrived in Canada in 2007 on behalf of the Mexican government, he carried the message that Calderón was looking for a solution to the conflict. González and I met in Toronto, but his proposal, like Lozano's, was unacceptable: Its first stipulation was that I resign as leader of the Miners' Union. Only then, González said, would they suspend the accusations against me and against the other union leaders. It was the same story, the same unlawful purpose, with false accusations invented by the government. There really was no possibility of finding a solution; they simply did not want to negotiate, preferring to impose their arbitrary decision.

Month after month went by without any solution in sight. On the contrary, the government's actions against the union were becoming even more radical. Calderón and his administration quickly came around to the old patterns of the Fox administration and began obeying the whims of Germán Larrea and the Villarreal brothers. Our initial misgivings had been confirmed. It seemed that Calderón had met with these businessmen and been convinced by their arguments for the destruction of the democratic and autonomous Miners' Union.

Meanwhile, the state-level banking charges against us were still dragging on. By 2007 we were making headway, though; Marco del Toro and his team had succeeded in convincing the federal judiciary that the arrest warrants issued in Sonora and in San Luis Potosí should be referred to the Federal District, since there was a clear lack of jurisdiction in both cases. That meant that the whole affair was now concentrated in Mexico City, in the Eighteenth Federal Court (corresponding to the warrant in San Luis Potosí), the Fifty-first Federal Court (corresponding to the warrant in Sonora) and the Thirty-second Federal Court (corresponding to the warrant in Nuevo León). We were expending vast amounts of energy and resources on fighting these charges, and Calderón and Lozano allowed it to go on, though they were fully aware that our supposed crimes were entirely fabricated.

I do not believe, observing the past six years in retrospect, that anyone in the Calderón administration ever had the sincere intention of seeking a solution through negotiation. It was nothing but a deceptive posture intended to distract and manipulate us. They tried to sound smooth and reasonable, so we would place our confidence in their black hands as they waited for the time to tighten the noose and unlawfully install a union leadership that would obey their whims. From 2006 to the present, we have continued to be subjected to the political persecution of the Calderón government, who simply inherited the Fox government's commitments to corporate ambition and continued support of Grupo México on one hand and Grupo Villacero on the other. And Calderón's unvarying support of business interests extends beyond the mining and metal sector; for example, he has actively protected the former head of Mexicana Airlines, Gastón Azcárraga, who bankrupted the company and caused the dismissal of most of its employees.

No doubt Calderón's myopia stems from the fact that he owes his elevation to the capital provided by businessmen who are determined to control him. Since his first day in office, they have extorted him with reminders of who placed him in Los Pinos; otherwise, there is no explanation of his obvious submission to their every wish. In practice, it seems that Germán Feliciano Larrea and his ilk—not President

Calderón—are the ones who lead Mexico. These fabulously wealthy tycoons have hijacked Felipe Calderón, just as they did with Vicente Fox before him.

Larrea, according *Forbes*'s latest ranking of the world's wealthiest individuals, stands at second place in the list of the super-rich in Mexico, with a net worth of $16 billion. Alberto Bailleres Gonzalez comes in at third place with a net worth of $11 billion. His holding company, Grupo Bal, controls Grupo Peñoles and the department store chain Palacio de Hierro; Grupo Peñoles, just like Grupo México, has set up mining work sites that resemble concentration camps, with extremely run-down and dangerous conditions. The same *Forbes* list is peppered with other enemies of the miners, including Ricardo Salinas Pliego of TV Azteca and Emilio Azcárraga of Televisa—both prominent persecutors of the union and friends of Vicente Fox, Marta Sahagún, and Germán Larrea.

A longer look at the *Forbes* list reveals that the combined fortunes of eleven Mexican businessmen amounts to $125 billion—which is equivalent to 12.4 percent of Mexico's yearly GDP and exceeds the country's international currency reserves of $121 billion. At the same time, about 50 million Mexicans, nearly half of the country's population, live in poverty, and we repeatedly hear that there is no money to help fund any level of public education or to meet the growing demand for health care, jobs, and infrastructure improvements. Of course, one of the main desires of these businessmen was that Calderón maintain his persecution of the Miners' Union and other independent, democratic trade unions in Mexico, such as the Electrical Workers' Union and the Aviation Workers' Union (representing pilots and baggage handlers), who have faced during the last three years struggles similar to ours.

So, in Calderón we got a man who was just as hostile to the Miners' Union as Fox, if not more so. Just as bad, Javier Lozano, like his predecessor, Salazar, showed great enmity toward the union. Lozano used a provocative anti-mining stance to stay on good terms with Germán

Larrea, Alonso Ancira, and the rest of Mexico's reactionary business leaders throughout the entire length of his term.

Both Salazar and Lozano significantly degraded this position of public trust and broke its tradition of respect. Earlier labor secretaries, though at times inclined toward business interests, knew how to reconcile these with the interests of workers. Adolfo Lopez Mateos, secretary of labor under President Adolfo Ruiz Cortines (1952–58), went on to win the presidency himself in 1958 and was one of Mexico's most important leaders of the twentieth century. Under Lopez's presidency, Salomón González Blanco served as secretary of labor and did outstanding work. Porfirio Muñoz Ledo, labor secretary in the era of Luis Echeverría (1970–76), was similarly perceptive and fair in the role. Salazar and Lozano shame the legacy of these conciliatory and constructive politicians. From the office of labor secretary, both have persecuted, attacked, insulted, and defamed the miners, metalworkers, and steelworkers of Mexico, and have done so with more barbarity than any other officials in the Calderón and Fox administrations—saturated as they were with individuals who have a true hatred of the working class.

As a young man, Javier Lozano attended the Escuela Libre de Derecho, where he first met Felipe Calderón. After graduation, he worked at the Bank of Mexico before starting work at Mexico's Department of the Treasury, where he held various positions, including controller of state-owned petroleum company Pemex. At this point in his career, Lozano was a member of the PRI. In 1998, President Ernesto Zedillo (1994–2000) named him director of COFETEL, Mexico's telecommunications regulator. (The commission was part of the Department of Communications and Transportation, which was headed by Carlos Ruiz Sacristán. In 2011, Ruiz would join Grupo México's board of directors.) From COFETEL, Lozano showed clear favoritism toward the Unefon telephone company, giving it two simultaneous extensions, both of them unlawful, by which the company saved hundreds of millions of pesos. In 1999, while a client of Lozano's consulting firm Javier Lozano & Associates, Ricardo Salinas Pliego—one of Lozano's cronies and head of TV Azteca—purchased 50 percent of Unefon. Even in the

1990s, Lozano was using his position as a public servant to win the favor of powerful businessmen.

In 1999, Lozano Alarcón, still a member of the PRI, was appointed Undersecretary for Social Communication for the Department of the Interior. He founded the Telecommunications Law Institute and continued to serve as a private consultant in this field with Javier Lozano & Associates. In March 2003, the PRI governor of Puebla, Melquíades Morales, appointed Lozano as representative of the Puebla government in Mexico City.

In 2005, Lozano resigned as Puebla representative to join the Felipe Calderón campaign full-time with its fundraising efforts. Lozano had been seeing a lot of Calderón's brother-in-law, Juan Ignacio Zavala, and it was Ignacio who brought Lozano into the future president's inner circle, reacquainting the two men who'd known each other in their law school days. On December 1, 2006, Calderón rewarded Lozano for his "efforts" by naming him Secretary of Labor and Social Services. Early in his term, Lozano would make an opportunistic flip, switching on June 30, 2007, from PRI member to PAN member. Dizzy with lust for power, he held out naive hopes of being a PAN candidate for the presidency all throughout Calderón's term. It would have been the peak of his miserable, unscrupulous life.

An intelligent journalist named José Sobrevilla has done extensive research on Lozano. After digging into the labor secretary's life and gaining access to many of Lozano's personal files, Sobrevilla reveals the following:

> Lozano has been characterized as a quarrelsome bully and many things by groups and organizations in various media; however, in edition 1740 of the magazine *Proceso* (March 9, 2010), the journalist Jesusa Cervantes stated that President Calderón and his cabinet, including Petróleos Mexicanos (Pemex) were informed that Gerardo, the brother of Javier Lozano, through his company Holland & Knight-Gallastegui & Lozano, SC, taking advantage of confidential information

provided by his brother Javier, obtained together with the company Intermix, located in the Cayman Islands, the trademark Pemex for Canada and the United States . . .

Various specialists have stated that this trademark could be revoked by the North American Free Trade Agreement. However, neither Pemex nor the Mexican government has taken any action in this regard. President Calderón and his entire cabinet received letters informing them of this process, the spokesman for Intermix told *Proceso*.

As labor secretary, Lozano was consistently incendiary and insensitive to nearly everyone around him. Marcelo Ebrard, elected governor of Mexico City in 2006, has been one of the prime targets of his hatred. Lozano publicly decried Ebrard's solidarity with protesters marching in the Federal District—to which Ebrard responded by suggesting that Lozano read the city's laws (*La Jornada*, June 15, 2007). And Lozano has also attacked the governor for arranging governmental aid to the state of Tabasco during a devastating flood.

Lozano was also notably aggressive toward magnate Carlos Slim, director and majority shareholder of Telmex, Mexico's massive, monopolistic telecommunications company. During his time in COFETEL, Lozano tried to open the telecommunications market to his friends at Televisa and TV Azteca—in other words, he wanted to break Telmex's monopoly by giving power to two companies that hold a monopoly over another sector: the media. Why? Purely because Lozano was friendly with a few businessmen at Televisa and TV Azteca. Later, in the run up to Calderón's presidency, Lozano expressed interest in serving as head of the Department of Communication and Transportation. But Slim—who was ranked by *Forbes* as the richest man in the world in 2010, 2011, and 2012—remembered Lozano's actions at COFETEL and his private interests in Televisa and TV Azteca. Exerting his significant power, Slim pressured Calderón to deny Lozano that position. But Calderón caved, and Lozano was appointed labor secretary instead.

Lozano would later help engineer the 2009 shutdown of Mexico's Central Light and Power company, a maneuver that resulted in the loss of 44,000 jobs in one day and was meant to destroy the Mexican Electricians' Union, one of the few democratic and independent Mexican unions like ours. And he also raised public suspicion due to his public defense of Jorge Mier y de la Barrera—a top official at the Department of Labor and an old colleague of Lozano's at COFETEL—when Mier was dismissed by the Judiciary Council for fraud and bribery.

But Lozano's most prominent scandal would occur in 2007. Zhenli Ye Gon was a Chinese entrepreneur and importer of pseudoephedrine who was accused by the Mexican government of drug dealing. In an interview with the Associated Press, Zhenli said that Lozano had asked him to store $205 million in cash at his home in Mexico—money that Zhenli claimed was to be used for Felipe Calderón's 2005 presidential campaign. According to Zhenli, Lozano had threatened to kill him if he didn't hide the money. "*Copelas o cuello*," Lozano had warned the Chinese drug dealer—"Cooperate or we cut your neck"—passing his hand over his throat as if his fingers were a knife. Lozano denied the accusations, and no legal action was taken against him. Calderón seemed to very quickly forget the incident ever happened, even though the Mexican people had seen the piles of money from the Zhenli's home on television news. After a while, the cash disappeared, never to be seen again.

In the first months of the Calderón administration, we witnessed Javier Lozano pick up the baton from Vicente Fox's labor department. As Calderón's labor secretary, he began to take a main role in the zealous defense of the interests of Grupo México. In doing so, he played a public role that in no way relates to his office. Lozano's undersecretary, Álvaro Castro Estrada, was no better: he seemed to be more of a Grupo México spokesperson than a public servant. Both made offers to stop the criminal charges against me and surrender the bank accounts if the miners ended all strikes against Grupo México and allowed the company to set up puppet unions.

Lozano Alarcón has been a resentful and obsessive persecutor of miners and of every other democratic and independent trade union in

Mexico. He has clashed most dramatically with the leadership of Los Mineros, but he has also antagonized the leaders of aviation union representatives, the widows of Pasta de Conchos, the National Workers' Union (UNT), and the workers of the Mexican Electricians' Union (SME), as well as prestigious legal defenders of labor, such as Nestor de Buen, Arturo Alcalde Justiniani, and Manuel Fuentes. These attorneys concluded that Lozano's decisions are clearly made for the benefit of the businessmen with whom he is complicit. Other labor lawyers who prefer anonymity, and some employees of the labor department themselves, have said the same thing.

As further proof, Germán Larrea frequently referred to Lozano—in front of business associates and to the labor secretary's face—as his "cat." Larrea's insulting nickname for the labor secretary was confirmed to me by several businessmen who made trips to Canada, as well as by a journalist close to Larrea's defense team. It's just like Larrea to openly brag in front of everyone that a high-ranking public servant is nothing but his toy. In 2005, Larrea had also told me that Vicente Fox was a *pendejo*—a fool, an asshole—and that he could easily convince the president to go along with his plans. No doubt he felt the same way about Calderón, as well as his new cat, Lozano. Unbelievably, Lozano was happy to play the role of servant to Larrea. Every day he spent in office, he displayed his loyalty to his new master.

A scene that took place at a major labor rally in 2007 is representative of his condescending, careless attitude. A group of workers from various unions, including the miners, held a protest outside the offices of the department of labor, demanding to meet with Lozano to discuss his support of the false allegations still being pressed by Elías Morales and Grupo México. The workers wanted to talk with him directly about the issue and force him to explain his support for this unlawful defamation. Yet all Lozano did was order that a large sign be placed on the railing of the building, bearing one provocative sentence: "Criminal cases are not handled in this Department." His complicit servitude to Germán Feliciano Larrea had been proven again.

Napoleón Gómez Sada at his first election as General Secretary of the National Union of Mine, Metal, and Steel Workers of the Mexican Republic with Mexican president Adolfo López Mateos during the 1960 National Convention. Napoleón Gómez Urrutia is behind, fourth person from right.

Oxford University: Napoleón Gómez with classmates at graduation.

Napoleón Gómez Sada during a mining tour in the north of Mexico.

Napoleón Gómez was General Director of Compañía Minera Autlán in 1992–1993. Here he speaks with a worker at the smelter facility in the town of Teziutlán, Puebla.

Napoleón Gómez was elected for the first time in 2001 General Secretary of the National Union of Mine, Metal, and Steel Workers of the Mexican Republic.

Napoleón Gómez with mineworkers in Hércules, an iron ore mine in the state of Coahuila.

In this image, photographer Peter Langer shows the intensity of the harsh working conditions found inside the mine.

Napoleón Gómez with mineworkers in the Mine of Fresnillo, in the state of Zacatecas—the largest silver mine in the world.

Napoleón Gómez inspecting safety and working conditions at Las Cuevas Mine in San Luis Potosi operated by Mexichem, one of the biggest fluorite producers in the world.

Javier Zúñiga, Secretary of Labor; Sergio Beltrán, Secretary of Interior; Napoleón Gómez, President; José Barajas, former Secretary Treasurer; and Juan Linares, Secretary of the The Justice and Surveillance Committee. Members of the National Executive Committee of the National Union of Mine, Metal, and Steel Workers of the Mexican Republic at Highland Valley Copper Mine (Kamloops, British Columbia).

Miners protesting the government of President Felipe Calderón and the aggressions of Germán Feliciano Larrea Mota-Velasco, CEO and major shareholder of Grupo Mexico.

Rescuers leaving the mine after the explosion at Pasta de Conchos on February 23, 2006.

This picture shows the horrible safety conditions in which Grupo Mexico operates in the copper mine of Cananea, Sonora, risking the lives and health of workers and violating human and labor rights.

At the headquarters of Grupo Mexico, protestors praise Napoleón Gómez and demand the recovery of the sixty-three miners who were abandoned to die in the Pasta de Conchos explosion.

Los Mineros protesting against Grupo Villacero and Julio Villarreal Guajardo, President of Grupo Villacero, for violating the collective bargaining agreement and basic labor and human rights in Lázaro Cárdenas, Michoacán.

Meeting of the Strategic Alliance Trinational Committee between Los Mineros and the United Steelworkers led by Napoleón Gómez and Leo W. Gerard in 2011.

Rally and meeting in solidarity with the USW during the strike against ALCAN Rio Tinto for injustices and violations committed in Alma, Quebec in March 2012.

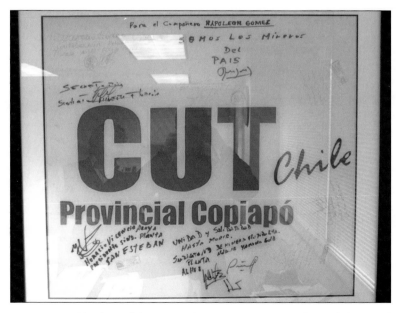

Survivors and leaders of the San José Copiapó mine tragedy in Chile signed a flag in appreciation for the solidarity received by Napoleón Gómez and Los Mineros from Mexico in 2010.

Napoleón Gómez visiting the monument of his father in Monterrey, Mexico, his home town.

Napoleón Gómez and his wife, Oralia Casso, at the 2009 National Convention of the NDP in Halifax, Nova Scotia.

Oralia Casso, on behalf of Napoleón Gómez, accepting the prestigious 2011 Meany-Kirkland Human Rights Award from Richard Trumka, president of the AFL-CIO, in Washington DC.

Napoleón Gómez and Ken Neumann with Jack Layton, former Leader of the New Democratic Party and the Official Opposition in 2011 at his office in Parliament.

From left to right: Ken Georgetti, President of The Canadian Labour of Congress, CLC; Steve Hunt, Director District 3 United Steelworkers, USW; Ken Neumann, National Director for Canada United Steelwokers, USW; Michel Arsenault, Président of the Fédération des Travailleurs du Québec, FTQ; Jim Sinclair, President of the BC Federation of Labour; and Napoleón Gómez, in Vancouver, BC, during the 2010 Second World Congress of the International Trade Union Confederation, ITUC.

Jyrki Raina, General Secretary of IndustriALL Global Union, and Napoleón Gómez in Montreal, Quebec, 2011.

Napoleón Gómez and Jack Layton, leader of the New Democratic Party, NDP.

Napoleón Gómez addressing over 100,000 workers in El Zócalo, the main square of Mexico City, on Labor Day (May 1, 2003 [top]; 2004 [bottom]).

Second World Congress of the International Trade Union Confederation, ITUC, Vancouver, BC, 2010.

Napoleón Gómez during his exile in Canada.

From left to right: Ken Neumann, National President for Canada of United Steelworkers; Hon. Darrell Dexter, Premier of the Province of Nova Scotia; Jack Layton, Leader of the Opposition; Napoleón Gómez Urrutia; and Gary Doer, Canada's Ambassador to the United States and Former Premier of the Province of Manitoba. National Convention of the NDP in Halifax, Nova Scotia, 2009.

Before leaving Mexico, Napoleón Gómez signed this baseball, promising to return.

Napoleón Gómez writing *Collapse of Dignity* on Vancouver Island.

Javier Lozano Alarcón, in addition to acting as a provocateur, did not know the labor laws or respect the rule of law. He was the worst secretary of labor in Mexico's history. He put his department wholly in the service of the darkest and most reactionary business interests. But worst of all, he tried to sell himself to the Mexican people as a man who respected workers. After Jack Layton, leader of Canada's New Democratic Party, traveled to Mexico and met with Lozano to demand that he cease the government's oppression of Los Mineros and the actions against me, Lozano put out a press release with a wildly inaccurate description of the meeting. Layton had harshly criticized the labor secretary and condemned his actions, but Lozano's press release portrayed Layton and himself as friends, and spun the meeting as a moment of agreement. Lozano cynically claimed he agreed with Layton's positions and that the labor department had been very respectful of union autonomy and freedom of association. Of course it was all lies, intended to do nothing but confuse the Mexican public. The aggression continued as before; bank accounts remained frozen, and Lozano continued to withhold official recognition of me as head of Los Mineros.

This man turned out to be no different from his predecessor, as did the new president. Our hope that things would change after Fox, Salazar, and Abascal left office has withered and died. Disappointed but resolute, Los Mineros prepared to soldier on and fight our way through yet another antiunion, pro-business PAN presidency.

ELEVEN

PROOF OF CONSPIRACY

The bureaucracy is a giant machine managed by pygmies.
—HONORE DE BALZAC

On February 19, 2007—on the first anniversary of the tragedy of the coal mine of Pasta de Conchos—Humberto Moreira, governor of Coahuila, made a stunning public allegation against the recently supplanted Vicente Fox. In a radio interview with veteran Mexican journalist Jacobo Zabludovsky, Moreira claimed that, a year earlier, President Fox had summoned him to Los Pinos to discuss the aftermath of the mining disaster, in a meeting also attended by Interior Secretary Abascal and Labor Secretary Salazar. Moreira stated that the four of them were in the president's office talking about how best to satisfy the demands of the miners' families when Fox suddenly interrupted to ask the governor whether there was any way he could find a charge to level against Napoleón Gómez, leader of the Miners' Union.

Of course, I had done nothing to warrant a charge in Coahuila, but the president was looking for the quickest way to cover up his administration's role in the negligence that led to the sixty-five deaths. He knew I would be the most vocal and visible of their accusers, and he needed a way to tarnish my reputation. In his mind, getting rid of a troublesome union leader was an added bonus. Moreira told the interviewer that he had informed Fox that I was innocent of any crime in his state, but the president had insisted that he invent a crime—anything they could accuse me of. Moreira repeated that I had committed no crimes in his state. They went round and round, the president encouraging the governor to make up crimes, and the governor protesting that he couldn't. Each time Moreira insisted he couldn't jail someone without a crime, the president would say, "I understand, but how would we do it?" Finally they parted, with President Fox telling Moreira to keep quiet about their discussion. "You never keep your mouth shut," Fox had told him.

"With all due respect," Moreira replied, "neither do you."

The governor's sensational story made national headlines. On February 20, 2007, *La Jornada* published a story under the headline "Moreira Is Willing to Remind Fox of His Proposal to Jail the Mining Leader":

> Humberto Moreira, governor of Coahuila, confirmed that he is willing to remind Vicente Fox that, after the tragedy at the Pasta de Conchos coal mine, the former president of Mexico proposed that he begin a criminal procedure against deposed union leader Napoleón Gómez Urrutia and send him to prison, in order to "distract attention."
>
> "The Secretary of the Interior and the Labor Secretary were there and were clearly his collaborators, but I am willing to face him and tell him directly," Moreira said to Zabludovsky.
>
> "You would say it to him?" asked the journalist.
>
> "That, and also how the conversation took place. He may have forgotten, given how many governors he holds conversations with, but a governor never forgets when he talks to the president," the governor responded.

The *La Jornada* story goes on to cover why the governor waited until a year after the tragedy to report this discussion. Moreira said that he came out with it then because of the PGR's intensifying focus on the fraud charges against me and the other members of the executive committee. Their diversion tactics, meant to confuse the citizens of Coahuila, were coming to a head, Moreira argued, so that was why he was speaking out to reveal the charges as just that: diversion.

He also claimed he did tell the media about Fox's statements at the time of the mine collapse and that he was the only one who told the media that the miners were dead, even as Salazar continued to say that they might still be alive. In reality, Moreira had only said that he would reveal the immoral propositions President Fox had made to him at the time. Not until a year later did he explain what those propositions had been.

What was the true cause of the delay? I believe that Felipe Calderón encouraged Moreira to make the statement. Fox, now out of office, had the annoying habit of making public statements as if he were still president. He acted as Calderón's shadow, angering the new president—particularly because Calderón was doing his best to look like a legitimate president even as the PRD's Andrés Manuel López Obrador made repeated claims that the election win was a fraud. By encouraging Moreira to go public, Calderón hoped to make Fox look bad and hopefully silence him for a while.

On the radio with Zabludovsky, Moreira insisted that he had acted purely out of his own conscience and that he wanted the people responsible for the tragedy to be punished. "I am interested in having those responsible punished, number one," he said. "Number two, I want the commitments to the widows to be complied with, and three, I want to see the necessary personnel and resources assigned in order to avoid more tragedies such as this in my state."

Regardless of his true motivation for making the statement when he did, Moreira had refused to comply with the whims of President Fox in the days after Pasta de Conchos and throw me in prison. No doubt Fox had made similar appeals to state officials in Sonora, San Luis Potosí, and Nuevo León—the three states who did move forward with the fabricated case against my colleagues and me when the PGR sent over its file.

As shocking as it was that a standing president would order the arrest of an innocent citizen, Moreira's story didn't surprise me when my lawyers called with news of the interview. It was just another piece of evidence that the campaign against us was not a lawful execution of justice but rather a calculated effort to silence a union leader who was giving private interests more trouble than they wanted. Fox was trying to recruit Moreira into the group that had been conspiring for the demise of the Miners' Union since long before Pasta de Conchos.

As my family and I approached the first anniversary of our departure from Mexico, it started to become clear just how calculated the conspirators' actions were. There was now a pile of evidence that the antiunion assault was the product of a coordinated plot conducted out of view of the Mexican people. The first sign of direct collusion in crippling our union had been Abascal's warning at Governor Moreira's inauguration in late 2005, when he'd told me that Larrea, Bailleres, and the Villarreal brothers were meeting with Fox about their displeasure over the power of the Miners' Union.

Another piece of evidence had come to light just after I left Mexico amidst the flurry of death threats and media slander. Halfway through March 2006, I called Roberto Madrazo, the PRI candidate for president of the republic (he would lose to Calderón later that year). I had talked with Madrazo, who served as president of the PRI from 2002 to 2005, numerous times since before he was nominated as a candidate for president. He once attended a dinner with members of the union's executive committee, and my colleagues asked that, were he to be the official presidential candidate of the PRI, he support me as a candidate for Senator of the Republic, representing my home state of Nuevo León. The Miners' Union in previous years had had two senators and ten federal deputies, and so it was logical to request the restoration of political commitments between the PRI and the miners—the majority of whom voted for PRI candidates and helped with their campaigns.

I hoped Madrazo would still honor his commitment to support my candidacy, but my main purpose in calling him that day was to ask for his intervention with the government of Vicente Fox; I hoped he could convince them to stop this absurd confrontation and show them it would lead to no good for anyone. When Madrazo answered the cell phone he greeted me warmly and asked me how and where I was. I gave him my customary answer—"Closer than you imagine"—and told him I was fine but disgusted with the political persecution headed up by Fox, Salazar, and Larrea, with its accompanying vicious smear campaign in the media, which by then had begun in earnest.

Roberto told me he would talk to Fox on my behalf and told me to call him again should I need anything, and he also assured me that the attack against us would not affect his support of my candidacy for the Mexican senate. But before we ended the conversation, Madrazo said, "Guess who came to see me a few days ago." I told him I couldn't imagine, since there must be thousands of people eager to say hello to a presidential candidate in Mexico. He told me that the group of businessmen headed by Larrea, Ancira, Bailleres, and Julio Villarreal came to his office to ask him not to support my run for the Senate because it would increase my power to a level they were uncomfortable with. If I won, I would be simultaneously a Senator of the Republic, the leader of the Miners' Union, and vice president of the Labor Congress (as voted in February 2006). That was a prospect that terrified them; they knew I would fight for the workers' interests and not blindly do as they wished.

"What did you tell them?" I asked.

"I told them to go to hell," said Madrazo, "because who I support for Senator is an internal decision of the party. I told them that you lead hundreds of thousands of workers, many of them activists and organizers who have the right to have their national leader represent them in the Senate." Madrazo's report of pressure from the business sector was utterly believable. I had no doubt that these reactionary businessmen were desperate to limit the power of the Miners' Union, and here was another story of them working behind the scenes to achieve their self-interested objectives.

The events that formed the backdrop of the entire conflict, by themselves, were plenty of evidence that there was an orchestrated conspiracy to eliminate my leadership and destroy Los Mineros. Three separate events had happened too close to one another to be any kind of coincidence—it is clear that important men had to be pulling strings behind the scenes. First, certain members of the Labor Congress, led by Victor Flores, had thrown their lot in with Fox and his PAN administration on February 15, 2006, renouncing democracy and trading support for Fox's labor reforms for their positions. Not two days later, the group of hired thugs descended on the Miners' Union headquarters. Fox and the rest knew we posed the biggest threat to derailing their scheme, so they resorted to physical violence and vandalism. And of course, the following day we discovered that Salazar had granted Elías Morales the *toma de nota*, acknowledging him as the leader of the Miners' Union—an event that had occurred two days prior but that we only discovered on February 16, 2006.

These near-simultaneous events had involved many different players and all but proved that Fox, Salazar, Abascal, and the business leaders who had them in their pockets had carefully designed this plan. How else had Victor Flores and Elías Morales come up with the *toma de nota* so quickly? And were we supposed to believe that a roving band of thugs had coincidentally attacked the union headquarters in the same week the conspirators tried to unlawfully remove me from the head of the union? At the time, though, thoughts of conspiracy were not at the front of our minds. With the tragedy occurring in Coahuila on the very same weekend, we were entirely focused on the rescue of our colleagues and on keeping our union alive so it could continue the fight on behalf of the miners.

I didn't fully understand just how far back this conspiracy stretched until April of 2007, when the head of one of the largest employers in the steel industry visited me in Vancouver. We had a busy day of meetings, discussing collective bargaining agreements and a new productivity agreement that we both hoped would bring benefits for both the company and the workers. After a long but fruitful day, we went to dinner. As we ordered our food and unwound, we were both relaxed and pleased with the outcome of our discussions.

Over dinner, I asked what he thought about the mining conflict. Though this employer had always had a strong relationship with the Miners' Union, I had little doubt that he knew quite a bit about how

Mexican businessmen operated behind closed doors. Right away, he began telling me that at the beginning of 2005, he had been invited to several meetings at the offices of the secretary of economy, Fernando Canales Clariond, and of the former labor secretary Carlos María Abascal. He had also received an invitation to a dinner at the Monterrey home of Julio Villarreal Guajardo, one of the three Villarreal brothers who led Grupo Villacero. The meetings were ostensibly to discuss the future of Mexico's mining and metal industry, and Los Mineros would have been a big obstacle in the future Clariond and Abascal saw for this sector. This business owner said he had declined these events, but that he had been told who attended them. The guest list he related to me was a Who's Who of the most vicious of the miners' enemies: the Villarreal brothers; Germán Larrea; Xavier García de Quevedo; Carlos María Abascal; Francisco Javier Salazar; labor department undersecretary Emilio Gómez Vives; Alberto Bailleres Gonzáles of Grupo Peñoles and his colleague Jaime Lomelín; Alonso Ancira Elizondo of Altos Hornos de México; Fernando Canales, Fox's secretary of the economy (and cousin to Bernardo Canales, our former lawyer who mounted a pathetic defense and made off with his fees); and Fernando's cousin, Santiago Clariond, president of a subsidiary of Grupo IMSA, a steel manufacturer owned by the Clariond family.

But there were two more attendees who signaled to me that this was no ordinary business dinner: none other than Elías Morales and his longtime collaborator in criminal activities, Benito Ortiz Elizalde. These were the two men who had been kicked out of the Miners' Union years before, in 2000, charged with proven treason, corruption, and spying for the businesses and government. Now this man was telling me they had been hobnobbing with the leaders of the coalition against us a full year before aggression broke out. There was no reason for those two to be there unless these businessmen and politicians hoped to use them as their traitorous pawns, which is indeed what happened. I now knew without a doubt that Morales and his coconspirators, lacking scruples and consumed by greed, had been working with Grupo México to plot our downfall since early 2005. (Of course, the union would still exist in name according to their plan, but it would be a puppet union in the hands of people like Morales—people who place their own ambition before the loyalty and honesty that characterize true leaders.) Those individuals, who were willing to sell out their fellow union members for their own gain, had been enlisted to spy on us, obtain any information they could, and create doubts and internal divisions wherever possible.

The man who told me about these secret meetings insisted that neither he nor any of his colleagues had attended them, much less participated in the conspiracy. His company was one of the few who saw the indecent nature of the actions against us and refused to be a part of it. He also told me that Vicente Fox and his wife were fully aware of the plot and supported its execution. The president's involvement in such a conspiracy is of course grounds for not only dismissal but for serious criminal charges. Sadly, Mexico is one of the countries where such abuses go unspoken of, concealed by an iron wall.

If this evidence doesn't amount to a proof of conspiracy, I don't know what does. A group of shameless individuals—businessmen, politicians, and union lackeys—had banded together in premeditated actions designed to destroy my colleagues, me, and the union we represent, merely because we were an obstacle to their perverted collective interests.

Although the tragedy at the mine took the company and the government of Vicente Fox completely by surprise, they did not hesitate to use it as an opportunity to accelerate a new phase of the conspiracy they had plotted in the presidential offices of Vicente Fox. They had been conspiring against us long before the mine collapse, but that event gave them all the more reason to work together for my downfall; if they didn't, they would be implicated in the deaths of the sixty-five men.

Once we made the public accusation of industrial homicide, their plans for persecution kicked into high gear, falling on us from the pinnacle of economic and political power in Mexico. Their attacks made use of the previously established relationships between Fox's labor department, the companies, and the media, and they were clearly coordinated and premeditated. These antisocial businessmen and ambitious politicians have long wanted to take advantage of the fact that the government consists of prominent individuals from the extreme, antiunion right.

Though we have been a primary target of this plot, it should not be seen as an isolated assault against the unionized miners, metalworkers, and steelworkers of Mexico. These businessmen and their attendant politicians are waging a general offensive against democratic and independent trade unionism; Fox, and Calderón after him, carried out aggressive actions against the Mexican Electricians Union, the Aviation Workers' Union, and others. The Miners' Union was merely the first on their long hit list of democratic and independent trade unions that they had prepared during their clumsy scheming in 2005.

Certain businessmen in Mexico hope to continue collaborating with right-wing politicians to effectively nullify all unions in the Mexican landscape. Since the PAN took power in 2000, we have experienced something like a lost decade: inequality has grown exponentially and abuse of power is rampant. Our main weapon in response is solidarity. Neither Mexico nor Mexicans deserve this intolerable situation. These individuals have created a bad image of our country abroad and have caused deep losses in Mexican society. For the future of our children and grandchildren, the situation has to change.

Following close on the heels of Moreira's accusation against Vicente Fox came an additional report that once again confirmed the presence of a direct conspiracy against the Miners' Union. Among the speakers at the opening ceremony of the Extraordinary General Convention of the Miners' Union in April 2007 was Francisco Hernández Juárez, head of the Telephone Workers' Union and president of the National Workers' Union (UNT). I knew Hernández only formally, through union business, but that day, as I watched his speech from Vancouver through a video conference, he dropped a compelling hint about the governments early intent to weaken Los Mineros.

During his speech he stated, to the surprise of more than nine hundred convention attendees, that at the beginning of 2005 Carlos María

Abascal, then serving as secretary of labor, had said to him personally "that they were coming for Napoleón Gómez Urrutia." This would have been a full year before Pasta de Conchos and the attempted imposition of Morales. It was further proof that they had been planning to remove me as general secretary of the union long before the official start of the conflict in February 2006.

Hernández Juárez repeated that same statement during the Ordinary General Miners' Convention in May 2008, to which he also was invited. His statement fell on us like a bucket of ice water. Abascal had given me a warning, but it came so close to the outbreak of aggression that we didn't have sufficient time to prepare a defense strategy and counterattack.

Though I felt great anger upon hearing Hernández statement, I knew we had to keep our focus on defending the union and finding justice for our lost colleagues. We were now over a year into the conflict, and we were still fighting the bank fraud charges and seeking justice for Pasta de Conchos. Yet we had just won a significant victory: In March 2007, shortly before our annual convention, the Fourth Collegiate Tribunal for Labor Matters of the First Circuit declared that I was the legitimate leader of the Miners' Union, and that the labor department had abused its authority and failed to follow correct procedures in its refusal to recognize me as such. According to the ruling, the government was obliged to officially recognize me as general secretary with a *toma de nota* within forty-eight hours. Lozano grudgingly complied. Elías Morales was at last stripped of the title he had held in name only.

Yet, rather than admit defeat, the forces allied against us were to show no signs of letting up. In fact, following my official reinstatement as general secretary, the conspirators ratcheted up their attacks. This time, they would throw all their efforts into the national media.

TWELVE

SLANDER AND REDEMPTION

The truth does not belong to the one who yells the most.
—RABINDRANATH TAGORE

In 2007, the union's lawyers presented a formal complaint before the PGR for the crimes committed at Pasta de Conchos. Our complaint, in accordance with the criminal code, was a charge of industrial homicide by intentional or malicious omission—also known as "corporate murder"—leveled against Germán Larrea, Grupo México's board of directors, Francisco Salazar, Labor Undersecretary Emilio Gómez Vives, and the rest of the officials and inspectors from the labor department. The case was presented before the Special Unit of Investigation for the Prosecution of Criminal Offenses Committed by Public Servants, under preliminary investigation number 4085/07/08.

In the more than five years since we made that complaint, the PGR has neglected to conduct even a preliminary investigation and has never looked into the facts we reported. Instead, it has frozen and attempted to drop our lawsuit completely. It has continued to try to lay blame for the disaster on the union itself, once again exposing its ongoing bias toward Grupo México. And it has continued to support Grupo México's efforts to prosecute me and my four colleagues for crimes we didn't commit, in an effort to distract attention from the real perpetrators of industrial homicide. Officials at the attorney general's office seem to have forgotten the sixty-five lives lost in February 2006 and the families who have been affected by these deaths. Perhaps unsurprisingly, they have shown no interest in exposing the wrongdoing of their powerful allies.

Yet, Los Mineros still held out hope of justice. Despite the fact that I'd been fully acting in the capacity of general secretary over the previous year, even from my station in Vancouver, the Supreme Court's official reinstatement of me as leader of the union gave us hope that the entire legal system hadn't been corrupted. We had received a just—if long delayed—ruling, and the labor department had been rightly criticized for its actions. At last, the workers' desire to rid themselves of the traitor Elías Morales had been respected.

The victory lifted the spirits of the entire organization, but for Grupo México and the labor department, it was a humiliation. Faced with this chastening from the Supreme Court and slow progress in their legal campaign against us—and still infuriated by our accusations of industrial homicide—the union's enemies began working on a new plan. Since the beginning of the conflict, Grupo México had held meetings every Wednesday specifically to discuss their efforts against Los Mineros. In attendance at these meetings were high-level Grupo México officials, the company's internal lawyers and its criminal lawyers, and former government officials who were on its payroll. They also invited publicists, psychologists, and consultants to advise them on the best way to carry out their attacks. In these meetings, they gave each party an assignment for the week—deciding who could best bribe whom, who could best pressure whom. Following the rebuke from the Supreme Court, this perverted mastermind group decided to shift its full focus to the national media. Their plan was to turn the general public against me in any way they could.

Though the media had been biased against us from the start, Grupo México now initiated an expensive paid publicity campaign against the leaders of the Miners' Union. It was a hatchet job unlike any other attack on a union leader in Mexican history. Beginning on April 20, they launched a campaign consisting of a series of slanderous TV advertisements that denounced me for supposed misuse of the $55 million Mining Trust. Over foreboding, dramatic music, a voiceover depicted me as a heartless criminal and portrayed the supposed "victims" of my crimes—the miners—as hoping to see me end up in jail. At the conclusion of the spot, the parties allegedly responsible for the spot are identified in small print: "Section XI of the Union of Miners of Santa Bárbara, Chihuahua, and Section VI Charcas, San Luis Potosí." In these sections, Grupo México had lied to, bribed, and threatened members of Los Mineros until they renounced the union. This unlawful coercion worked on a small minority of locals, and we lost a few union sections that had belonged to the organization for more than fifty years—though, of course, these union locals could never have afforded this kind of publicity. The truth is that this multimillion-dollar campaign was financed exclusively by Grupo México.

The ad was broadcast nationally on Televisa's Channel 2 (not coincidentally, both Germán Larrea and Alberto Bailleres sit on the board of Televisa and are supposedly shareholders). Another spot, broadcast nationally on Televisa's Channel 2 and on Televisión Azteca's Channel 13, made the same claim and again stated that the same union sections—both belonging to workers of Grupo México—had paid for it. For eight months, from April to December, the ads ran during peak times— during highly anticipated soccer games, for example—taking up the most desirable and high-dollar ad space. We estimated that in the end, these defamatory ads were run a total of about eight hundred times, all in prime "triple A" airtime.

Germán Larrea had plenty of money to put toward the cause, and, true to his cynical nature, he didn't care about the fact that everyone knew where the real backing for the ads came from. All in all, we have estimated, based on the cost of this premium media space, that Grupo México invested close to $200 million on the eight-month campaign. (The absurdity of this being nearly four times the entire amount of the Mining Trust was not lost on us.) In fact, Jaime Lomelín, CEO of Grupo Peñoles, the second-largest mining company in Mexico, told me that Larrea had been saying that he did not mind losing his fortune in his fight against the Miners' Union. I heard a similar story from one of our tax lawyers who has a connection with a member of Larrea's defense team. The company shamelessly threw money at their efforts to drag me through the mud and insert themselves into the union's operations. They hired more than thirty law firms to help them fight us, even as they made a big show of giving pitifully small amounts to the families of the men who died at Pasta de Conchos. The allocation of money to these two causes clearly reveals Germán Larrea's priorities.

What just country would allow TV ads to be bought and broadcast against an individual who should be presumed innocent until proven otherwise? What country would allow—and in fact support—such propaganda, which has the sole purpose of turning the public against a man who they all know is innocent? It seems that being on the board of Televisa, as is the case of Germán Larrea and Alberto Bailleres, has its advantages. No one intervened to stop the airing of these malicious ads, although we presented the request before several authorities. We presented a series of appeals to the media outlets airing slander against us and requested the legal right to a response. None of us were suing for a cent of damages, though the spots clearly justified that claim; we only wanted the right to reply when our accusers published articles or presented information that was false or slanderous. Each one of our appeals was ignored.

Because we didn't have the financial resources to mount a counterattack in the media (our accounts were still frozen by the government), the union members instead took their retaliation to the streets. In a national campaign, the miners spent their own time making huge posters and displaying them in public areas, particularly in the swanky neighborhoods where Larrea would be most ashamed. In large red lettering, the posters read "Larrea—Assassin of Miners" and "Grupo México Corrupt." Volunteers also printed many handouts and leaflets to give out, each of them showing the truth of the situation that was so egregiously distorted in the media and displaying a large photo of the reclusive Larrea. It wasn't as high-caliber as Larrea's multimillion-dollar national media blitz, but it was the best we could do to defend our honor and reveal Larrea and his cronies for what they are.

In its aim of co-opting the national press and discrediting me, Grupo México had hired García Puebla Consultores, a top publicity firm that has represented many politicians—and is owned by Eduardo García Puebla, a former PRI press secretary—on top of its stable of consultants, counselors, and psychologists. The company even directly hired mercenary media outlets to publish its words. One of our own publicists obtained a copy of an "order for publicity" through which García Puebla Consultores purchased a 10-by-15-inch space in the publication *Milenio* and provided the paper with the full text of an article to be published. The space purchased by Grupo México was in the paper's first section and included text and a photograph. The order for publicity is dated July 23, 2007, and indicates that the space is for publication on the following day. The title of the ordered article to be published is "Napistas [a term used to refer to followers of Napoleón] Continue to Take Advantage of the Pasta de Conchos Widows"; as the title suggests, it was a biased, fallacious story about how Los Mineros themselves were exploiting the widows of the lost miners for political reasons.

In the order for publicity, the publicist from García Puebla Consultores had the nerve to write the following: "Once the design of the page has been done please send it to the following email address: materialesgpa@yahoo.com." The request to approve an advertisement is common; the problem is that this was no regular advertisement. It appeared on an odd-numbered page (ads typically appear on even-numbered pages, on the left side of a spread), and it was laid out in *Milenio*'s typography, the type used for serious stories. There is absolutely no indication that the article was paid for, leading the reader to believe that this is a "news" article researched and reported by *Milenio* rather than PR for Grupo México.

This form of deception has been systematically employed throughout the conflict and up to the present day, using several different newspapers that allow this misleading practice. One newspaper, *El Universal*, one of the most widely read in Mexico, called a meeting with one of the union's lawyers and offered to publish articles favorable to me and the union—if we paid them. Over lunch in a bustling Mexico City mall, the *El Universal* representative told our lawyer that to make it believable, they'd have to start with small references to the conflict and short articles but then gradually move to longer articles giving the union's side. According to this man, Grupo México had paid them $800,000 for a year's worth of attacks against us, but that the agreement had been terminated and had not yet been renewed. Our lawyer was then told that for the same amount—and without the need for any kind of paperwork or receipt—they would publish articles in my favor, and they would also air stories that showed the union's side on the radio stations belonging to their group.

During this conversation, our lawyer noticed a small red dot of light hovering near their table, looking a lot like the laser sight of a gun. It soon disappeared without event, but after talking to a friend in the government, the lawyer realized it hadn't been a gun sight but a device for eavesdropping. That was the level of obsession the union's enemies had fallen to.

Before he refused *El Universal*'s offer (a given, since we would never resort to the same tactics employed by our enemies), our lawyer asked the paper's representative about Pedro Ferriz, a radio host under their corporate umbrella who systematically attacked me on his radio program while refusing to listen to my version of events. The man simply said that Ferriz was paid his professional fees and that he had to follow the politics of the company. Plus, one strict stipulation of the owners was that no hosts or guests could attack the president or any member of the clergy. Sadly, and to the detriment of the Mexican press in general, many other employees have similarly complied with immoral orders from their bosses.

We, of course, summarily turned down *El Universal*'s offer to sell us the "privilege" of fair reporting. Grupo México did however eventually renew its contract, and antiunion articles continued to run in the paper. In fact, *El Universal* may have solicited us for a deal only to wrest even higher payments from Grupo México. Surely Grupo México's arrangement with *El Universal* wasn't unique. We heard that the company had in fact paid an even larger sum to money and investing newspaper *El*

Financiero for positive coverage: $3,000,0000 per year. We have no doubt that they similarly contracted many other Mexican news outlets.

Adding to these attacks in major newspapers and TV stations, there were some new publications created solely for the purpose of attacking the Miners' Union. The most prominent of these was a magazine called *MX*, created jointly by Grupo México, PAN politicians, and President Fox himself. They tried to disguise the periodical as serious by including a handful of other features, but its main topic was always Los Mineros. Only five or six issues came out in 2006 before *MX* disappeared from the market, unable to sustain itself on lies alone.

During this time, the government, too, did its part to turn public opinion against the leaders of the Miners' Union. They sent out prejudiced press releases and distorted reports regarding the miners, many of which were prepared in the Department of Labor and in the office of President Calderón himself. From there, these reports went straight into the media, with all the government's false statements and errors duplicated. Their efforts were partially a success: slander against the Miners' Union and myself was apparent in nearly all the Mexican media's coverage of our conflict with Grupo México and the government.

The Mexican government's control over the communication media is nothing new. But today, with television stations privatized, many observers rightly point out that the reverse now seems to be true—the media outlets, now properties of corporate giants, dictate to politicians what their next move should be. Through the official news agency of the government, Notimex, the institutional leadership—backed by wealthy businessmen—disseminates information that is aimed at cultivating a very specific image. Notimex, in the hands of the right-wing government, has become a sectarian instrument to manipulate public opinion. Their obsessive reporting of distortions and half-truths harks back to the statement by Joseph Goebbels, Hitler's propagandist: "A lie repeated one hundred times becomes the truth for the masses."

At times, the television stations, the government, and the powerful companies of Mexico seem to make up one large criminal organization in charge of manipulating the "truth" that reaches the Mexican people. In the twenty-first century, television in Mexico has become the opium of the people. Ownership of the largest media properties in Mexico, including Televisa and TV Azteca, is concentrated in the hands of nine families. The Department of the Interior grants concessions to these families, and in exchange, the government gets the kind of glowing coverage it wants in the national media. They mobilized this abusive system to enhance their attack on the Miners' Union and to turn the public against us.

Is any of this reasonable and journalistically ethical? Of course not. But the "art" of manipulating public opinion through shameful financial agreements is allowed in the Mexican culture of deeply rooted political chicanery, to the detriment of the integrity of Mexican journalism. In our country, one can buy the conscience of many journalists, who are the main conduit for bringing information to the public at large. It's entirely possible to conduct a public lynching and print a barrage of deceptive slogans with impunity—as long as you have enough money.

From the start, many companies like Grupo México, Grupo Peñoles, and Altos Hornos de México regularly bribed communications professionals, paying many millions of dollars per year to ensure that they did not publish or broadcast a favorable word about the Miners' Union. They have imposed a news blackout, terrified that the public may one day hear the truth. Not even objective news that presents both sides of the conflict is allowed. The only choices are distorted stories or complete silence on the subject, with no mention of our progress in the battle to defend the rights of workers. The conspirators have created a wall that shields the truth of the conflict from public view. Every time we win a trial, the press simply does not mention it. But whenever one of their falsely founded arrest warrants is issued, the press gives them all the attention they desire.

I have given many long, thoughtful interviews to reporters on the subject of Pasta de Conchos and the mining conflict—interviews that were simply never published. It happened numerous times in the weeks following the disaster and continued to happen in the following years.

At the beginning of the rescue efforts at Pasta de Conchos, I denounced the atrocities and the deplorable safety conditions to many reporters—but in the end these reporters all transmitted their news as if they had never been informed of this. Not a word of my comments reached the public ear. Much later, in the fall of 2008 Javier Alatorre, the well-known journalist and news director of TV Azteca, came to Vancouver with a full team of technicians to interview me. He had also interviewed me the day after the explosion at Pasta de Conchos, but like all the others, the interview had never been published. I was still angry about that, but I attributed the omission not to Alatorre but to TV Azteca's owner, Ricardo Salinas Pliego, a close friend of Germán Larrea. At my second meeting with Alatorre, which took place as we walked down Burrard Street under a light Canadian drizzle, I gave an accurate picture of the conflict and expressed how I felt and how all of Los Mineros felt about the repression we had suffered. The result was a long and in-depth interview in which I challenged Secretary Javier Lozano to a public debate, by himself or with the businessmen who controlled him. Not a single fragment of the entire interview was ever broadcast, and Alatorre never sent me a copy of the article as he promised.

We have battled the media's malignance and lies every day for seven years, and we will continue to do so with complete faith that the truth will shine through sooner or later. The campaign against us created a widespread misunderstanding of the true nature of the conflict between our union and Grupo México, and many well-intentioned but poorly informed people are surprised when they learn the truth of the matter. Once they do, however, they are then quick to change their opinion.

In other countries, a campaign that distorted the truth so blatantly would be punished with all the weight of the law, but in Mexico the perpetrators of lies seem to have complete impunity. Of course, the government of Mexico as a whole should never have permitted this abuse by the communications media companies, since some of them—such as those employing the electrical workers—are state concessions that the owners have used for their own purposes. Administrators and politicians have allowed it, since the power of these groups has grown monstrously.

At the beginning of the conflict, our strategy was to answer and clarify all the accusations and lies. But the more we tried to defend ourselves, the deeper we seemed to fall into the trap that had been laid for us. The only way we could get the truth in front of the public was through paid announcements or reports, but these were extremely expensive; media outlets charged more when the announcement was political in nature. When such attacks originate with the presidency and multinational companies like Grupo México, it is very difficult to carry out a battle in the media. We simply couldn't afford the ruinous price of admission.

The playing field being far from level, we changed our strategy. We decided to strengthen our internal communication, to build unity and solidarity among our workers, and to at the same time improve our communication with other democratic unions, whether in Mexico or abroad. Through honesty, solidarity, and collaboration, we were confident we could convince people of the truth. I'm proud to say that the perverse, one-sided media campaigns only strengthened our resolve, and that none of the union's members—besides those in a small minority of union sections coerced into the opposition by Grupo México—bought the blatant lies propagated by bribable media professionals.

I must mention that even within this great scheme to twist the truth, there were a few notable exceptions in the media—there were some journalists who had the courage to report the truth. Some of these enjoy such prestige that, despite working for the same media companies that attacked us, they were able to publish interviews with me and to write honest columns about the conflict. Among these upstanding journalists are the late Miguel Ángel Granados Chapa of *Reforma* and *Proceso*; Carmen Aristegui from MVS Radio; Javier Solórzano, who publishes in various media, including his radio program; Jacobo and Abraham Zabludovsky and their respective radio programs; Marcela Gómez Zalce of *Milenio*; Ramón Alberto Garza of *Reporte Índigo*; Ricardo Rocha in his "Behind the News" broadcasts; Francisco Rodríguez, an independent journalist; Carmen Lira, Carlos Fernández Vega, and Miguel Ángel Rivera of *La Jornada*; José Gutiérrez Vivó, through his radio show; Juan Bustillos of *Impacto* magazine, and others, to varying degrees. Some labor lawyers, such as Néstor and Carlos de Buen and Arturo Alcalde Justiniani, have also written outstanding articles about the abuses of Grupo México and their corporate colleagues. These individuals have shown themselves to be true professionals by speaking truthfully about the conflict between the Miners' Union and the Fox and Calderón administrations. They have proven that all is not lost for Mexico.

Deserving of special mention is *La Jornada*, which has never abandoned objective reporting and the defense of the interests of the mineworkers. *La Jornada* has also been publicly confronting campaigns of denigration and hostility in other media, as well as the fallacious publicity campaigns carried out by the government. The magazine *Proceso* has at times also been bold in its exposure of the complicities and aggressions against the Miners' Union and its members.

These principled publications make up a sector of the media that is no less effective by virtue of being relatively small. Their readers are thoughtful, and their writers serve as a voice of caution and a breath of fresh air in a journalistic environment contaminated by private interests and the abusive power of the right wing. These voices appeal to the conscience of the citizens, entreating them to avoid the corruption that has sadly become a way of life in Mexico.

Without a doubt, it's no easy task for independent journalists to write objectively about these highly charged issues. Some journalists, initially swayed by the massive campaign of the PAN and its corporate backers, came to later realize the truth of the situation. I admire these writers who had the courage to refute the official lies in favor of the miners' struggle for justice. Luckily for Mexico and its democracy, despite the exorbitant financial resources mobilized against Los Mineros, and despite the government's control of the media, not all journalists are open to such influences.

In addition to the few courageous journalists who refused to take part in the war against the Miners' Union, we had the constant support of our friends in the labor movement. I was—and I am—constantly

In October 2007, I found out that Germán Larrea had even tried to insert himself in the independent audit we had conducted. Top managers at Horwath Berney had told the IMF's general secretary, Marcello Malentacchi, that Larrea sent them a friendly letter asking for certain documents regarding the audit commissioned in part by the IMF. Horwath Berney representatives had flatly refused Larrea, knowing his goal was likely to change the outcome of the audit. They turned the letter over to Malentacchi. Malentacchi then sent a letter to Larrea, stating that he had knowledge that Grupo México had requested these documents. "Instead of trying to contact Horwath Berney," Malentacchi wrote, "it would be better to have a direct meeting between IMF and Grupo México to seek a joint solution for the conflict affecting the members of the Miners' Union in the companies under the control of Grupo México."

In order to be as thorough and fair as possible, my defense lawyers also asked UNAM's Institute of Juridical Research and the law school at Ibero-American University to take a look at all the paperwork surrounding the termination of the Mining Trust and the handling of the assets it held. After an in-depth analysis, these scholars presented their reports in writing, and each one concluded that no assets belonging to the Mining Trust had been improperly diverted, confirming the Horwath Berney audit. In their expert opinions, the Mining Trust had been created, modified, and then terminated correctly—the exact opposite of the story Germán Larrea and his cohort were peddling to the citizens of Mexico.

It was sweet vindication, even if no Mexican officials paid much attention. We knew that the Miners' Union had always administered its assets with transparency and clarity. We were facing a storm in the press, but with the findings of Horwath Berney, we had yet another tool in our fight against the depravity of our enemy.

THIRTEEN

THREE STRIKES

When men are united, they lose the sense of weakness . . .
and gain the sense of strength.
—MONTESQUIEU

When Grupo México and its PAN backers mobilized to persecute
me and drive me out of the country, they had undoubtedly hoped that
the miners would believe all their lies. They hoped the workers would
blindly sign up for their useless company unions and stop causing so
much trouble. But even as the media disparaged us with great zeal in
2007, the members of Los Mineros held fast. They were more determined than ever to fight for respect, dignity, and freedom and to oppose
the oppressions of the corporations that were eager to exploit them.

At three separate Grupo México worksites, conditions had become
so bad that, by mid-2007, workers were prepared to go on strike once
again. All through the month of July, we worked on negotiating collective bargaining agreements with company officials. From Vancouver, I
was in frequent contact with the executive committee and the union's
bargaining commissions at these work sites: a silver mine in Taxco, Guerrero; a multi-mineral mine in Sombrerete, Zacatecas; and the famous
copper mine in Cananea, Sonora. Despite our best efforts at negotiation,
Grupo México was displaying its characteristic irresponsibility and arrogance. The company was offering a 3.5 percent wage increase, though
it could afford to pay more—a lot more—if it wanted to. The price of
metals was soaring; the market was excellent. We were demanding a

minimum increase of 8 percent, but then the company directors who'd been put in charge of negotiating with the union simply refused to compensate the miners fairly.

During this negotiation process, Grupo México also refused to review the safety conditions of the three mines. Working conditions in all three were more hazardous than ever—rivaling even Pasta de Conchos in the days before the blast. At the silver mine in Taxco, Union Section 17 explicitly drew the Pasta de Conchos comparison as they entreated company officials to do something about the atrocious condition of the mine. In this picturesque southern city of about 100,000 people, silver is a mainstay of the economy, and the workers who excavated it from under the earth were risking their lives daily. Machinery was broken down and badly in need of replacement. The electrical system was teetering on the edge of disaster, with cables intertwined dangerously with water lines. Rock slides were a constant threat.

At the mine in Sombrerete, Zacatecas, conditions were similar. The electrical system was just as bad as in Taxco, and the pairing of an abundance of silica dust and a badly insufficient air-filtration system in the mine brought to mind Pasta de Conchos, too. Silica dust, also present in abundance at the third site, the open-pit copper mine in Cananea, Sonora, is infamous for its detrimental effects on miners and stone-cutters; in addition to being carcinogenic, it leads to a severe condition called silicosis, in which the lungs are inflamed and scarred by the inhaled dust, causing irreversible damage.

The unacceptable working conditions at all three of these sites were not a new development, either. Back in 2005, the union's safety commissions had alerted the executive committee to the sorry state of the mines at Taxco and Sombrerete in particular. I visited them myself and saw the company's damage and neglect firsthand. Ever since then, we had been demanding that the problems be resolved, to no avail.

The pervasive disregard for safety was our most pressing concern during the July negotiations, but miners in Taxco, Sombrerete, and Cananea had other reasons to protest as well. There was the abundant environmental damage visited upon these towns by the irresponsible practices of Grupo México. Plus, the company was still hard at work to undermine the union's leadership, and their efforts weren't lost on these miners. And one final demand of the miners echoed the ongoing call from the union's national leadership: they, like all their comrades in the Miners' Union, insisted that the bodies left at Pasta de Conchos be recovered. But it was a condition Grupo México officials deemed "unacceptable."

The deadline for ending negotiations was July 30, 2007, and when that day arrived, Grupo México had made no effort to meet the needs and demands of workers. We were left with no choice but to raise the red and black flag—the traditional sign that a site is being struck—at all three mines. On that day, with the full support of the national union, workers from the three union sections corresponding to these three atrocious work sites walked off their jobs, refusing to return until their demands were met.

July 30 was a tense day for all of us, including for me in Vancouver. The three simultaneous strikes would put tremendous pressure on Grupo México, and company officials seemed sure that the miners wouldn't go through with it, especially at Cananea, Grupo México's largest and most important holding. Yet leaders of the union local in Cananea assured me that they were more than ready to stop work if an agreement with the company was not reached. I didn't relish the idea of a new conflict—and I knew that if we struck at Cananea there would be one—but standing up to Grupo México was the only dignified move we could make. After a day full of calls and conferences, I set about preparing a press release that would announce the three strikes to the world.

In the following weeks, Labor Secretary Lozano and Germán Larrea placed their attention mainly on the Cananea strike. The town of Cananea, home to 32,000 citizens, sits thirty miles south of the Mexico–Arizona border, and the copper mine on its outskirts is perhaps the richest copper deposit in Latin America. The mine was one of the Grupo México purchases that led to the creation of the Mining Trust in 1990. Back then, President Salinas had closed the Cananea mine, declared it bankrupt, and sent in federal troops to eject the workers. Three months later, the government sold the mine to the Larrea family for a pittance. As soon as Grupo México acquired the site, it began tearing apart the systems that had supported the miners. It immediately closed the Workers Clinic, a company-subsidized, union-run hospital that provided much-needed medical care to the Cananea miners and their families. That left only a small company-run healthcare facility open at the site, the Ronquillo Hospital. After the 1990 takeover, the company also went back on promises to provide the town with electricity and water, services the government had provided when it owned the mine. Instead, Grupo México hoarded the town's water and refused to pay for the residents' electricity. This forced many citizens to go without power and to rely on the badly contaminated Sonora River for drinking water.

Now, some seventeen years later, the 1,200 workers of Cananea were once again demanding their rights as employees and as humans, only to be met with threats and repression. Grupo México vigorously denounced the strike in the courts—as it did with the strikes in Taxco and Sombrerete. It's no wonder keeping Cananea open became Grupo México's number one priority: according to *La Jornada*, this one mine accounts for 64 percent of Grupo México's potential earnings, and if copper is excavated at the same rate it has been in previous years, experts predict that the deposits will last from thirty to eighty-two years.

Rather than negotiate a just solution to the Cananea strike, the company simply tried, with the support of Labor Secretary Lozano, to have the strikes declared illegal. On July 31, 2007, one day after the union initiated the strike, the Mexico's labor board, the JFCA, declared the work stoppage unlawful. With the strike officially seen as illegal by the government, workers could be compelled to return to work at the risk of losing their jobs. But the union immediately appealed for a writ of amparo that would grant constitutional protection against the JFCA's resolution; in the meantime, the strike could be legally continued. In October, we were granted protection by the courts. An ensuing appeal from Grupo México was denied, meaning that the miners of Cananea could continue their strike with full legal approval.

In the years leading up to the July 30 strike, conditions at the Cananea copper mine were notoriously poor. A joint inspection in 2005 between the company, the union, and the labor department had resulted in forty-eight complaints of negligence in working conditions, of which only nine were partially and incompletely remedied. In April of 2007, three months before the strike began, the labor department completed another inspection, finding seventy-two distinct issues in need of correction, many centered around faulty electrical systems and hazardous buildups of silica dust. Yet, by July, when the strike was declared, nothing had been done.

In October of 2007, with the strike in full swing, Cananea's Union Section 65 requested that the Maquiladora Health & Safety Support Network (MHSSN, mhssn.igc.org) undertake a study of the mine. The MHSSN is a volunteer network of four hundred occupational health and safety professionals who provide information and assistance on workplace hazards in the *maquiladoras*—foreign-owned factories where workers are traditionally paid very low wages—along the U.S.–Mexico border. The organization agreed to inspect the mine and subsequently found a mind-boggling level of negligence. The binational team working on the Cananea study was made up of occupational health professionals including three physicians, three industrial hygienists, a pulmonary technician, and a registered nurse. They inspected the facilities, interviewed workers, and administered lung-function tests to sixty-eight of the miners working in the copper mine and its related processing plants.

The resulting seventy-four-page report is an unconditional and extensively documented condemnation of Grupo México's handling of the facility, pointing to more than 220 serious health and safety problems at the Cananea facility. These were the first two bullet points in the MHSSN's list of major findings at the front of the report:

- "The conditions observed inside the mine and processing plants, and the work practices reported by the interviewed workers, paint a clear picture of a workplace being "deliberately run into the ground." A serious lack of preventive maintenance, failure to repair equipment and correct visible safety hazards, and a conspicuous lack of basic housekeeping have created a work site where workers have been exposed to high levels of toxic dusts and acid mists, operate malfunctioning and poorly maintained equipment, and work in simply dangerous surroundings."

- "The deliberate dismantling of dust collectors in the Concentrator area processing plants by Grupo México approximately two years ago means that workers in these areas have been subjected to high concentrations of dust containing 23 percent quartz silica, with 51 percent of sampled dust in the respirable particle size range, protected only by completely inadequate personal respirators. Occupational exposures to silica can lead to debilitating, fatal respiratory diseases including silicosis and lung cancer."

The MHSSN also reported that the Cananea mine operates under conditions that could lead to collapse due to high levels of toxic dust and acid gases, adding that it is not just the workers who are exposed to these risky contaminants but also their families and the residents of the town. The silicone content detected in workers' blood tests was at levels that lead to fatal respiratory illnesses like silicosis, whose symptoms appear only after years of exposure. In the enclosed processing buildings that are part of the complex, mine workers had exposures to very fine silica dust that registered at least ten times the government's legal limit.

Perhaps the most affecting part of the report is the collection of pictures the MHSSN used to back up its descriptions of the mine's deplorable condition. They show clear, full-color photos of silica dust mounded on top of machinery, pieces of disconnected ductwork that should be collecting the dust, and open holes in the floor surrounded by yet more piles of the dangerous silica powder. There are also photos of unguarded engine belts, steel corroded from acid mists, and open control panels where energized wires are coated in dust.

In addition to its report, on November 13, the MHSSN sent a message to Labor Secretary Lozano stating that "the industrial safety and hygiene conditions are deplorable in the mine at Cananea, Sonora, and that the same is true at the mines of Sombrerete, Zacatecas, and Taxco, Guerrero, all of which belong to Grupo México." They informed the labor secretary that they were conducting similar studies in Sombrerete and Taxco, free of charge. Based on their preliminary findings and on the union complaints dating back to 2005, they were confident they would find a level of danger in both mines similar to Cananea. In the letter, they invite Lozano "to visit the mines in question to personally corroborate the poor safety conditions," in order to "avoid continued risk to the lives of workers" of Union Sections 65, 201, and 17. They respectfully ask him to form a commission to check into the study's findings, with the participation of the Department of Health, the governments of the states of Sonora, Zacatecas, and Guerrero, the Miners' Union, the United Steelworkers, and the IMF.

But despite the findings of the MHSSN, Lozano and his labor department displayed their characteristic insensitivity and deceit. He sent a letter to the MHSSN and, through Labor Undersecretary Alvaro Castro, made public statements to the media containing the absurd statement that the study was not legally valid because it was not directed by the labor department itself and because it was completed while the mine was subjected to a strike. Unbelievably, the letter also described conditions in the mine as "optimal" and stated that the majority of problems found by the MHSSN were minor issues that the company had resolved, when in fact nothing had been done to correct them. Eduardo Bours, Sonora's governor, never made an inspection, but he defended Grupo México and the mine operation, and questioned the legality of the study.

Garret Brown, a certified industrial hygienist from California and the coordinator of the MHSSN study,* was pointed in his reply:

> Grupo México's response to our health and safety report at the Cananea mine deliberately misses the point and the facts of the case...Grupo México is deliberately misrepresenting our study, done by Mexican and US occupational health

*mhssn.igc.org/CananeaOHSReport.PDF

professionals who donated 100 percent of their time to complete it. In addition to the severe silica dust hazards, there are
literally dozens of other safety hazards on site—both in the
mine itself and in the processing plant... If Grupo México is
so proud of the conditions at the Cananea mine and its processing plants, then it should accept the proposal made on
November 13 to Mexico's Secretary of Labor, Javier Lozano
Alarcón, that the Secretary head a tripartite, fact-finding
commission to establish exactly what are working conditions
in the country's largest copper mine... The serious health
and safety hazards to the Cananea miners continue to exist,
regardless of the technicalities of the Labor Law, so we urge
the STPS [labor department] to fulfill its duties to protect the
health of Mexican workers in Cananea.

Brown's statement echoed the union's own press release, which we
had put out the day before, on November 14, 2007, and a series of ads we
placed in newspapers in Sonora and Mexico City. In them, we restated
the conclusions of the MHSSN and said that these "indicate that there are
serious health and safety hazards in the Cananea mine that require immediate long-term correction in order to protect workers from accidents and
chronic exposures leading to occupational illnesses." We detailed the steps
that Grupo México and the labor department needed to take to correct the
disastrous course Cananea was on. Predictably, we received no response.

In August 2007, labor-related violence broke out once again, this time
at La Caridad copper mine in Nacozari, Sonora—another one of the mines
whose privatization had contributed to the 1990 creation of the Mining
Trust. At La Caridad, the government had allowed Grupo México to unlawfully fire its whole workforce of nine hundred union members. The company then handpicked about seven hundred of those members to return to
their jobs (they had to be intimidated and threatened before they agreed)
and then brought in 1,200 additional workers from southern Mexico. To

combat this arbitrary firing, we won a legal injunction that compelled Grupo México to allow the dismissed workers to return to their jobs.

On August 11, 2007, the dismissed workers drove to the Nacozari facility to demand their reinstatement, in accordance with the judge's ruling. At 8:30 p.m., several buses belonging to Grupo México pulled up to the site and unloaded men who began attacking the assembled workers. Shots were fired, and the attackers began throwing union members forcefully into the buses. One group of three workers hid and subsequently got word that they should head to the foundry, close to the only exit of the Nacozari facility. They found the exit blocked by guards, and as the driver put the car in reverse, a bullet pierced the rear window, hitting the backseat passenger, miner Reynaldo Hernández González, in the head. The driver sped away, calling to Reynaldo from the front seat but receiving no answer. He stopped the car and, by the flame of his lighter, saw that his colleague was dead from the bullet wound.

That same night, company men seized, beat, and tortured the twenty union members who had been thrown into buses. Eventually, to stop the beatings, the workers falsely admitted that they had been the aggressors and had intended to forcibly seize the facility from Grupo México, when in reality all they had been doing was peacefully demanding their court-ordered reinstatement. The company also tried to get these workers to accuse the executive committee of the Miners' Union of having incited acts of violence. The men were then driven to the local jail, where they were detained for over a day. None of the armed attackers were questioned or taken into custody. An investigation by the Workers' Study and Action Center later found that relatives of the La Caridad miners called the police and begged them to come stop the violence but that the authorities refused to send patrols. One worker's wife actually went to the police station but was met with the same refusal. She said she overheard an officer say that there were company orders not to send patrols to the Nacozari mine, no matter what happened.

In the aftermath of Reynaldo Hernández's death at the La Caridad mine, Grupo México and the Sonoran government tried to cover up the true facts of what had happened. Hernández's body was never taken to the hospital but was instead driven to a morgue in Hermosillo, five hours away. The family was not permitted access to the body for four full days, and they received no reason for this delay. The most blatant attempt at concealment, though, came in the autopsy, which claimed that Reynaldo's death had come as the result of a blunt force trauma to the head, not a bullet wound. A blow to the head seemed much less calculated than a gunshot, Grupo México must have reasoned.

The company and Sonora governor Eduardo Bours Castelo both put forth the invented claim that the workers were going to take over the company's Nacozari facility by force and that the armed forces had been sent in to protect the workers while the company defended the facility. But in no way did the plotters of this carnage send armed public personnel to protect miners. The security forces were present, but they stood idly by, never once offering help while workers were beaten and shot. They were there only to make sure that the thugs hired by Grupo México carried out their violent repression.

Governor Bours lied constantly, saying that his government was going to conduct investigations to find the cause of Reynaldo Hernández's death. There was no investigation, nor have any of the authors of this violent repression been punished. Bours has never apologized to Hernández's family or any of the tortured workers. All his actions were meant to protect Grupo México. He proved himself to be one of the most "PAN-like" PRI members (we call these rightist PRI members *"emPANizado"*— "breaded"). A look at Bours's background reveals why he would act in such a way: He has a great personal stake in protecting business interests in Mexico. He is heir to Bachoco, an agro-industrial company created by his father, which primarily sells poultry and pork products. Although he has participated in numerous national and transnational businesses, Bachoco is his biggest endeavor, holding as it does a virtual monopoly over poultry products. Bours was also once a director of the Business Coordinating Council, a group of the richest businessmen in Mexico, and as governor he dedicated his time to defending these obscenely wealthy entrepreneurs. He entered politics not to serve the public interest but to serve businessmen, to build his own companies, and to satisfy his ambition. He is dedicated to covering for individuals such as Germán Feliciano Larrea. As governor of Sonora from 2003 to 2009, he ignored and disavowed the aggressions against mineworkers by Larrea's company, proving that all these business groups act as one large criminal organization. They are like a brotherhood or secret society, all protecting one another from the consequences of their criminal acts.

As repressions like these escalated, international support for Los Mineros continued. On August 14—days after the murder of Reynaldo Hernández—at the Regional Conference of the IMF of Latin America and the Caribbean, held in Montevideo, Uruguay, the assembly expressed its complete and absolute support for the Mexican miners in their struggle for dignity, autonomy, and liberty. The organization agreed to three global solidarity resolutions: (1) Recover the sixty-three bodies abandoned in Pasta de Conchos, treat the families fairly, and punish those responsible, both in the company and the government; (2) Find an immediate solution to the three strikes in Cananea, Sombrerete, and Taxco; (3) Immediately stop persecuting Napoleón Gómez Urrutia and the National Miners' Union.

Despite calls for an end to the persecution—from the IMF, Los Mineros ourselves, and many others—the attack on union democracy continued. Germán Larrea dearly wanted the strike in Cananea to end—along with those in Taxco and Sombrerete—and he knew that the only long-term solution to controlling the unrest of the workers was to have a union that served not to empower them, but to pacify and further subjugate them. To that end—and because their smear campaign hadn't convinced the union's members that I was a fraud—he and his band of fellow businessmen began directly intimidating workers, using outright threats and violence. The level of these assaults shot up in 2007, with me, my family, and a full ten members of the union's executive committee receiving death threats.

Mario Garcia Ortiz, the executive committee's delegate in the state of Michoacán (who was later elected as my alternate general secretary in the General Convention of May 2008), suffered extreme aggression at the hands of the government. Mario had always been a loyal advocate for Los

Mineros, and it was for that reason that they went after him. In February 2007, a group of men arrived at his house while his wife and son were there alone. His wife, María, heard the car pull up. Leaving the laundry she was doing, she walked to the front door to investigate. On the other side of the door, she found a group of strange men. "Are you the wife of Mario Garcia?" one asked. When she replied yes, she was grabbed by the hair and told she would be paying for her husband's actions. They dragged her by the hair to a waiting car, threw her on the back floorboard, and ordered her not to look at their faces. Before they left, they shot at the house and demanded that Mario's young son, Miguel, say where his father was. Miguel wouldn't say, even when they threatened him with the death of his father. Unable to get an answer, they drove off with María, leaving Miguel traumatized.

Witnesses to the abduction quickly identified the kidnappers as state policemen dressed as civilians; in a small town like Mario's, everyone knew everyone, and masquerading police were easy to spot. When Mario called me to tell me what was going on, he was in a rage, worried sick over his wife. He said that he and a few of his colleagues had decided to collect some collateral that would help them negotiate with her captors. They had followed a group of workers—traitors who were in the service of Grupo Villacero—to a water-bottling company, and then trapped the men inside. His plan was to kill the men one by one and then burn the building to the ground if María wasn't returned unharmed. It was the only way the distraught Mario could think of to pressure his wife's captors into letting her go.

I did my best to calm Mario over the phone, and I assured him that violence would not do anything to help the situation. Despite my great anger against the aggressors, I told him that we shouldn't make irrational decisions, that we should keep a cool head. If we lost our heads and acted rashly, I said, we would be acting like our enemies, and even more blood would be spilled as a result.

As soon as I was off the phone with Mario, I called Michoacán's governor, Lázaro Cárdenas Batel, and demanded that they release Mario Garcia's wife unharmed. I told him what Mario was threatening to do and insisted that María be returned right away. (We already knew

Cárdenas Batel to be a weak man who would not stand up to the union's abusers; he'd proven that excellently in his reaction to the attack against the Sicartsa mill the previous year.) The governor claimed not to know anything about the kidnapping, even though it was very clear that the perpetrators were disguised state police.

In the end, they held María for seven hours. She had been blindfolded, bound at the wrists and knees, and verbally abused for that entire time. Eventually, they set her outside and took off the blindfold and leg bindings. In an instant María was off and running.

None of us knew what prompted the policemen to release her then, or whether Cárdenas Batel or anyone else had spoken with them, but we were immensely relieved when she reappeared. Yet, it still gives me deep pain to consider the psychic harm inflicted on her and her adolescent son.

"I'm always thinking about that moment," María said later, "but I have to find the courage to continue. I love my husband and know he's working for a good cause. I know he must defend the rights of the union workers, and I will stand by him. When I sleep, I sleep dressed, just in case. And I send my boy to sleep across the street. I know he's been hurt by this, too, because now, whenever he hears something out in the street, he always stands up to see what's happening outside. I want to take him to a doctor but he won't go. He says he'll get over it." Miguel was so disturbed by the threats and seeing his mother assaulted in such a way that he lost his ability to speak for quite a while.

"I'd given up my wife for dead," Mario told me. "And if she was dead, those fifteen cowards and traitors that we had in custody were going to go with her. We were getting ready to act if they didn't release her soon, because that was the decision of all the workers in Section 271 of the National Union." To this day, I am grateful that such terrible events did not come to pass.

On top of brutal intimidation tactics like these, Grupo México also launched broader and more systematic efforts to undermine the union organization. In late 2006, a new labor union purporting to represent Mexico's metalworkers had appeared and applied for *registro*—governmental recognition—from the labor department. Called the "National Union of Workers in the Exploration, Exploitation, and Benefit of Mines" (SUTEEBM), it had been established with the direct involvement of Grupo México. It was a Germán Larrea project, a union set up by a company to put on a front of worker representation while in reality further suppressing the workers. SUTEEBM was headed by Francisco Hernández Gámez, a former Cananea miner who had been expelled from the union in 2006 after attempting to set up his own subcontracting business in the mine. SUTEEBM had received its *registro* from the Calderón government so easily and quickly that it was hard to take the organization seriously. Clearly, Larrea's influence—along with that of Alberto Bailleres and Alonso Ancira—put the *registro* on a fast track through the bureaucracy, just as it had done with Elías Morales's *toma de nota* in February 2006. Labor Secretary Lozano, of course, lent his aid.

In September 2007, the JFCA called for a decision from the miners on which union they preferred—SUTEEBM or Los Mineros. It announced a series of elections to be held at eight Grupo México work sites in the states of San Luis Potosí, Chihuahua, and Coahuila (the sections in Taxco, Sombrerete, and Cananea were not included, since they were already on strike). Leaders of the Miners' Union were given less than two days' notice that the elections would take place. Once they were over, Los Mineros—a seventy-year-old organization—had lost several of its sections to an upstart puppet union controlled by Germán Larrea.

In execution, the elections were little more than campaigns to coerce members of Los Mineros into signing up for the new SUTEEBM. The IMF, the Center for Labor Action and Reflection, and many human rights activists have voiced their opinion that the election was rigged in favor of Grupo México's union. The irregularities were numerous. Our labor lawyers and executive committee members present at the worksites recorded the efforts used to intimidate the workers.

First of all, many work sites held the elections in company offices, in the presence of supervisors and the company union. Moreover, the polling stations were surrounded by armed federal, state, and municipal forces sent by Lozano to oversee the election. There were even members of the Mexican army at some stations, brandishing their weapons in front of the workers. Supposedly their mission was to ensure "peaceful elections," but the polling stations looked like they were in a state of siege.

Furthering the intimidation, there were two ballot boxes at each station, each clearly marked—one with SUTEEBM's logo and the other with the logo of Los Mineros. Everyone in the room—including the hovering company men, labor department officials, and the armed troops—could see which box each miner put his ballot into. At the time this was permitted by Mexican labor law—not until the following year would the Supreme Court require secret ballot votes in union elections. The result was a climate of intimidation that made it impossible for workers to freely choose their union, as ILO Convention 87—ratified by Mexico—requires.

The governor of San Luis Potosí, PAN member Marcelo de los Santos, was especially active in the threats against the miners, and his influence was a big factor in their outcome. De los Santos put his law enforcement resources at the disposal of Grupo México—which has a predominant interest in his metal-rich state. The company used these forces to kidnap several miners before the election so they couldn't vote. Fifteen other workers in San Luis Potosí were fired just before the vote, both to prevent those fifteen from participating and to intimidate their colleagues.

During polling at the La Caridad mine in Nacozari, where Reynaldo Hernández had been murdered, the nine hundred recently fired workers were prevented from voting. The new workers brought in to replace them were directly threatened into voting for the puppet union; company officials told them that they would be fired and deported back to southern Mexico if the puppet union didn't take the election. And just before the election in Nueva Rosita, Coahuila—a few miles away from Pasta de Conchos—several workers were locked in a mine so they couldn't get to the polls in time. In other cases, the company tried bribes rather than threats; several workers received payments of between $150 and $350 in exchange for supporting SUTEEBM.

Once this forced voting was done and these sections had "decided" to leave Los Mineros for SUTEEMB, the Department of Labor issued an official news bulletin celebrating the supposedly free decision of the workers to join the new union.

Grupo México and the JFCA broke the law by holding these sham elections, and they also violated the workers' universal right to freedom of association. Now, as members of SUTEEBM, many of our former colleagues were entirely at the mercy of the company's whims. Following the instatement of Larrea's puppet union, Grupo México increased the Nacozari miners' workday from eight hours to twelve. This change—supported by SUTEEBM—meant more exploitation and more potential for tragic events like Pasta de Conchos. Today, nearly three-fourths of Nacozari workers are employed by contractors. They don't even have the benefit of belonging to a company union, much less a free, democratic one.

Despite this bullying, our former colleagues in the sections that lost to SUTEEBM have expressed their desire to rejoin the union. We are confident that they will do so when conditions are right.

After the election, the union's dialogue with the government broke down completely. Labor Secretary Lozano was openly displaying his complete servility to Grupo México through his opposition to the Cananea strike and his help in setting up SUTEEBM. He seemed proud to be Larrea's "cat," acting more like a lawyer for the man's company than a servant of the Mexican people. Our only hope was that we would win a judgment against him soon; we had demanded before the Chamber of Deputies that he be removed from office and barred from ever returning. We also demanded that he be investigated for unlawful gains, obstruction of justice, and abuses of power. Though the Mexican Constitution states that the mines are a state concession, not private property, Lozano—like his predecessor—never compelled Grupo México to honor and respect the law while operating these sites.

Through all the abuse, we maintained a fierce defense of our right to strike, fighting hard to keep the Taxco, Sombrerete, and Cananea strikes going. We refused to allow the company, through underhanded legal maneuvering, to have them declared illegal—though they tried hard, and in some cases succeeded.

On January 11, 2008, the JFCA issued a second resolution against the workers at Cananea, once again declaring the now nearly six-month-long strike illegal. According to the ruling, the workers would have twenty-four hours to return to their jobs before any punitive action would be taken. Yet just a little more than *one hour* after the union was notified of the ruling, armed state and federal forces numbering around seven hundred descended on the Cananea mine in a caravan of eighty vehicles. They fired rubber bullets and released tear gas, injuring twenty to forty miners. Larrea was again making use of the public forces that were always at his disposal (even though those forces are paid for by the Mexican people—and even though Grupo México doesn't pay taxes). The supportive PAN government gladly sent the troops to help this businessman protect his greed-fueled exploitation of Mexico's largest source of copper.

The workers of Cananea showed the bold resistance of their forefathers, repelling the government forces and hanging on to the facility as best they could. A group of strikers also gathered in front of the mayor's office, calling for Bours to order the attackers off the work site. The miners called a special assembly the following day, and I spoke to them via videoconference—as I had done about once a month since the strike began. I heard their stories and felt their anger, and then gave a speech encouraging them to take back the facility, to fight hard, out of pride and dignity. Though they were furious at the company's acts of repression, I ensured them that I, personally, as well as all the members of the executive committee, was with them to the end. That same day, in response to an amparo filed by the union's defense team, the court changed its ruling and again recognized the strike, forcing Grupo México to withdraw its forces.

A month later, Grupo México and the PGR filed an appeal against the court's decision to recognize the strike, but the following month a judge confirmed the constitutional protection granted to the union. Then, on April 23, 2008, the JFCA issued a third decision, fully overruling its earlier position and declaring the strike legal, probably in order to avoid responsibility for violating the previous amparo granted in favor of the union. But our struggle continued: On May 19, 2008, Grupo México filed yet another amparo against the JFCA's decision. On July 3, 2008, the Fourth District Court in Labor Matters of Mexico City denied the company's amparo, meaning that the strike would continue with the approval of the courts.

We had won a battle at Cananea, but there were many more coming. This mine had become the centerpiece in our battle against Grupo México. It was the company's most important Mexican asset, but it was also a holy ground for union members—in declaring and defending their strike, the Cananea miners were upholding the legacy of their ancestors. Over a century before, in 1906, workers at the very same mine had sacrificed greatly for worker's rights. During the dictatorial regime of Porfirio Díaz, conditions in the mine were terrible, and the Mexican workers there were making three and a half pesos per day, while the American workers at the same mine were making five pesos. The Cananea miners went on strike, demanding an end to discrimination against Mexican workers in addition to an eight-hour workday, minimum wage, prohibition of child labor, and several other demands. President Díaz called in the Arizona Rangers and local Sonora forces to crush the uprising, leaving twenty-two miners dead, twenty-seven injured, and fifty arrested. The strike ended with this violence, but with the triumph of the Mexican Revolution that began in 1910, the Cananea strikers' demands were incorporated into the 1917 Constitution as fundamental rights of all workers. It is that heritage that the strikers in modern-day Cananea hoped to uphold as they fought the ongoing aggression of Grupo México.

FOURTEEN

THE OFFER

To fall is allowed, to get up is required!
—RUSSIAN PROVERB

Since the beginning of the conflict, the union and its executive committee had relied heavily on the aid of our legal advisors. In Mexico, a complicated situation like ours can involve the filing of amparo after amparo: by 2008, in the more than two years that had passed since the Pasta de Conchos tragedy, the courts had gone back and forth on the legality of the Cananea strike, the recognition of me as union leader, and the legitimacy of the fraud charges against me and my colleagues. Although we had received favorable rulings on all these state-level fraud charges, the legal situation remained complicated and painfully sluggish, with the PGR appealing every decision the courts made in our favor.

Fortunately, since 2006, we'd had the aid of our incredible defense lawyer, Marco del Toro, who to this day is a crucial ally to me and Los Mineros. But del Toro's partner, Juan Rivero Legarreta, proved himself less of an asset to the union.

I'd first been put in touch with Rivero by Alonso Ancira of Altos Hornos de Mexico, soon after the conflict began. At the time I was still on fairly good terms with Ancira, and I took his recommendation. In the first stages of the partnership between Rivero and the union, it didn't seem like a bad decision; with Rivero came his partner, Marco del Toro, and the two won some important victories for the workers and the members of the executive committee. The Supreme Court had forced the labor department to grant me recognition, and, though the state-level banking charges were still in play, they had gotten them consolidated in three courts in Mexico City. Rivero and del Toro had also helped us win amparo trials to keep the Cananea strike legal and ongoing.

From the start, Rivero had been something of a character. A tall, loud, flashy guy, he came across as someone in love with the high life. When he came to Vancouver, he was always dressed in the most fashionable clothes, and he would stay in the most upscale hotels he could find. Most of these expenses he paid with a corporate credit card given to him by Alonso Ancira. He loved the spotlight, too. Whenever Rivero got a chance to appear on radio or television, he took it. Interviewers usually found it difficult to wrest the microphone from his grip.

But this somewhat ostentatious demeanor was coupled with increasingly unsettling actions on Rivero's part. The union's relationship with Ancira had deteriorated rapidly—the steel magnate had become increasingly close to the business coalition aligned against the union—and Rivero's close relationship with him was troublesome. Several of the union's executive committee members complained about Rivero's manner, as did a few of the Steelworkers who had worked with him. Once, my wife asked him what he thought the time frame would be for our family's return to Mexico. "I'm not a magician!" he responded, telling her rudely that he didn't know how much longer it would take before he could straighten out the criminal charges. (Since that incident, all of us in Canada called him "the Magician.") Another time, he told Oralia that she should just divorce me, because the persecution would never end. A few months later, he told her it was a shame she would never leave me. But despite these unseemly actions, we kept Rivero on, mainly because he was willing to work without much up-front pay. He always told us not to worry about the fees, that his price would be determined by the results he obtained. The union's accounts still being frozen, we had little choice but to continue using his services.

Eventually, though, we were pushed to a breaking point. All through 2007, I talked to him nearly every day on the phone, and he visited

Vancouver every month, but he was becoming very tight-lipped. He would gloss over important points in our discussions. It almost seemed like he wasn't trying anymore. At one point he assured me that he had been able to secure my home in Mexico City, but we later found out that he had done no such thing—it was still seized by the government.

Though he'd been brought on as a criminal defense lawyer, Rivero had also begun inserting himself in the labor side of the union's business. While he should have been working with Marco del Toro on having arrest warrants struck down, he was busy trying to gently talk me into stepping down as general secretary. At one point, he even advised me that if I didn't relent and give up my leadership, the government would frontally attack the union and harm my family. I was stunned to hear him saying such things after we had placed so much confidence in him. I had trusted him greatly, but now he was acting suspiciously like a double agent. Sometime later, Rivero came to me and proposed a solution that he claimed would end the conflict once and for all. He said he had set up a meeting between himself, a representative of Grupo México, and Labor Secretary Lozano—to take place in Lozano's office. The three of them, Rivero assured me, would resolve the conflict "freely and without interference"—and without the presence of members of the union. I'm not sure how naïve he thought we were, but with this suggestion it was now fully evident that our own defense lawyer was acting in the service of the union's prime enemies, Germán Larrea and Javier Lozano. Our response to this "solution" was that we would gladly accept a meeting in Lozano's office about a resolution to the conflict, but that there would need to be three representatives present from the union's executive committee, plus our labor lawyer, Nestor de Buen. Naturally, our suggestion was answered with silence.

The final straw came when several members of the executive committee came to me absolutely enraged over a series of meetings they had had with Rivero over the previous months. In the presence of Labor Secretary Lozano, Rivero had repeatedly tried to convince them to be more acquiescent to the demands of Grupo México and told them that they should stop pushing so hard for wage and benefit increases and accept more of the company's terms. He had told my colleagues that they needed to be more flexible, and that they should accept that I wasn't present and feel comfortable making decisions in my absence. Rivero, my colleagues told me, had also adopted a completely submissive attitude to the labor secretary—and none of them liked that dynamic one bit. In fact, he was acting as if he were me. He called the members of Los Mineros *his* colleagues, *his* workers, acting as if he had taken on the responsibility of being my personal spokesperson. From the things Rivero had been saying, several leaders within the union were convinced that his goal was to take over control of the union from me and become general secretary himself.

It was a troubling report, but it fit with my growing doubts about Rivero. I now suspected that his true clients were not the union but Alonso Ancira, Germán Larrea, and Javier Lozano. No doubt someone, most likely Lozano, made Rivero believe that if he could get me to step down, he would be appointed as head of Los Mineros—as long as he kept the workers subjugated, of course. The thought of this lawyer as leader of a union is absurd: first of all, the workers would never accept him (he was not even a member of the union) and second, Rivero was absolutely ignorant of our organization's procedures, its bylaws, its internal regulations, and the practice of true union democracy. He took Lozano's bait but fell in the trap of his own unbridled ambition.

Now that we'd seen through Rivero's game, we knew we couldn't let him do any more damage to the organization. Already, he was trying to win the loyalty of some executive committee members, and his actions were provoking internal confrontations. In February of 2008, Rivero made a trip to Vancouver, and I told him bluntly that I didn't like the way he was acting and that he was in no way authorized to make decisions on my behalf or on the behalf of anyone in the union. I told him it was not his job to be involved with the labor negotiations; he had been hired as a criminal defense lawyer, and his job was to vigorously fight to clear the names of those falsely accused. He thanked me for relieving him of involvement in those meetings and said he would start concentrating more on the criminal side. We said good-bye without event.

I suspect that he left that meeting and immediately called up Lozano and Ancira to tell them what had happened. With no involvement in the labor negotiations, Rivero would be useless to them. When the lawyer got back to Mexico City, and without speaking to me, he made a public announcement claiming that I had fired him as defense lawyer, and he complained that the union and I had treated him unfairly. The media, being sponsored by Larrea, Lozano, and Ancira, picked up the story, portraying Rivero in a sympathetic light.

It was absolutely infuriating, but at least we had expelled an internal enemy. Unfortunately, it wasn't the last we would see of Rivero.

In May of 2008, the union held its biannual convention in Mexico City, in the union's 11 de Julio hall. Once again, I opened the ceremony via videoconference, giving the more than one thousand assembled members of Los Mineros an overview of the past two years and entreating them to hold fast. Miners at Taxco, Sombrerete, and Cananea were now in their tenth month of striking; the banking fraud charges against me and the others were still on their seemingly endless journey through the Mexican legal system; and we had lost several union sections to the threats and harassment of Lozano and Grupo México in the last year. Yet the vast majority of the union's rank and file remained energized and steadfast in their belief in the union's purpose. Over the course of that convention, I was once again reelected unanimously as general secretary of Los Mineros. It was the third time I'd been unanimously elected to lead the union, and I had now been in Canada for over two years. There was no end to my exile in sight.

It was at this 2008 convention that Francisco Hernández Juárez, head of the Telephone Workers' Union and president of the National Workers' Union, repeated his claim about the long-brewing conspiracy against the union, stating that Carlos María Abascal had told him back in 2005 that "they were coming to get" me. The 2008 convention also marked our final decision to officially leave Mexico's Labor Congress—the umbrella organization made up of mainly PRI-associated unions. In the two years since Pasta de Conchos, it had become clear that our dire struggle for democracy and the rights of workers threatened the Congress's comfortable relationship with the administrations of Fox and then Calderón. Though we'd received enthusiastic support from around the globe, the Labor Congress never once expressed a single word of solidarity or encouragement. We knew why: the Labor Congress depended on the existing power structure for its own power, and thus it did not matter to them that the Miners' Union was one of its founding members, nor that I had served as president of different commissions of the Congress in the past—it had to preserve the status quo at all costs. The Congress had shown clearly that its loyalty lay with the government, whatever its ideology was, not with the workers whose rights it was established to protect.

In the days after the convention, we gathered the paperwork regarding my reelection and sent it off to the labor department; Labor Secretary Lozano would then have sixty days to either present me with the *toma de nota* that would officially recognize my leadership of the union or deny it to me. Given that the courts had, just a little more than a year before, forced Lozano to recognize me, one would think he would do the right thing and honor the miners' democratic choice. But in the final week of June 2008, Lozano called a press conference and, to a crowd of reporters, announced that the labor department was denying Napoleón Gómez Urrutia the *toma de nota*. The announcement was broadcast live on Televisa and TV Azteca, as well as on several radio stations. NOTI-MEX, the government news agency carried the story as well, without finding any problem in Lozano's announcement. Not one story pointed out that his denial of the *toma de nota* was a flagrant violation of both labor law and the principles set forth by the International Labor Organization, an agency of the United Nations that deals with international labor standards. The ILO's Convention 87 clearly establishes the right of workers to freely elect their union representatives, and furthermore, its Committee on Freedom of Association has stated in its "Digest of Decisions" that "in order to avoid the danger of serious limitation on the right of workers to elect their representatives in full freedom, complaints brought before labor courts by an administrative authority challenging the results of trade union elections should not—pending the final outcome of the judicial proceedings—have the effect of suspending the validity of such elections."

Following Lozano's press conference, I was flooded with calls from our lawyers and my executive committee colleagues. Lozano's denial was blatantly abusive, but in truth, we'd seen it coming. The labor secretary was Larrea's "cat," after all. He was Calderón's reward to that businessman for all the financial support that had put him in Los Pinos. We were too used to Lozano's rabidly antiunion obsessions to be surprised.

Regardless of the denial of *toma de nota*, the union continued working as it had before, with me performing all the duties of general secretary. Los Mineros had decided that I would continue in that capacity whether we had Calderón's meaningless stamp of approval or not. My fellow union members have understood from the start that a simple document does not make any difference on whom they elected, and they unwaveringly supported me as general secretary.

A couple of months after the announcement, the Miners' Union went on to press criminal charges against Lozano and his undersecretary, Castro Estrada, for this blatant of abuse of authority. In interviews on national radio and television programs, Lozano said that the accusation made him laugh. What he wasn't taking into account was that, even though he had used his influences to shelve the charge, we have won all the amparo trials thus far, and the complaint was in effect once he leaves his appointment. Once he no longer has the privileges that come with being labor secretary, he will stop laughing.

Indeed, any impartial organization that examines our case is quick to condemn the government's action. At the beginning of June 2008, the IMF and the Miners' Union presented a complaint to the Committee on Freedom of Association of the International Labor Organization (ILO). Our complaint, which the ILO classified as Case 2478, details all the aggressions of the Mexican government against the union and its leaders, collecting all the maneuvers, aggressions, and violations of the law that had been perpetrated thus far: the withdrawal of the *toma de nota*, the freezing of the bank accounts, the violent repression and murder of striking workers, death threats, the establishment of a company union, the detention and torture of union members, and all the rest.

On June 12, our colleague Marcello Malentacchi, general secretary of the IMF, spoke at an ILO conference in Geneva and gave a passionate denunciation of the political persecution that we have suffered since 2006. After detailing all the episodes that have made up the mining conflict since its beginnings in February 2006, he ended his speech by saying:

> We call on the government of Mexico to:
>
> lift all pending charges against Napoleón Gómez and other members of the Mexican Miners' Union;
>
> process immediately and transparently in a court all those responsible for the corruption of documents and events;
>
> recover the sixty-three bodies from the Pasta de Conchos mine and investigate and bring to justice those responsible;
>
> investigate the involvement of Grupo México in the murder of Reynaldo Hernández González and in the detention and torture of twenty members of the Union in Nacozari, Sonora; and
>
> release all Union funds, which are illegally embargoed by the government.
>
> The Mexican Miners' Union has actively promoted a democratic and independent labor movement in Mexico. The Union has obtained important benefits for its members and has assumed a posture of speaking openly against negative labor reforms in Mexico. This Union deserves the backing of the international community and I urge every one of the delegates to this Conference to support the Mexican Miners' Union in the struggle for union independence in Mexico.

The ILO committee, after reviewing Case 2478, issued a statement on June 22, 2008, ordering the government of Mexico to respond to the accusations made by the Miners' Union and the IMF. The committee also directly criticized the actions of the Mexican government, saying the ILO "considers that the labor authorities engaged in conduct that is incompatible with Article 3 of Convention No. 87, which establishes the right of workers to elect their representatives in full freedom." In addition, it demanded that the government quickly resolve the mining conflict, a demand the Mexican government is required by law to follow.

I was immensely grateful for this vindication from the International Labor Organization, but I didn't hold out much hope that it would change the Mexican government's approach to the conflict. Calderón, like Fox before him, displayed a pervasive and complete disregard for justice. Indeed, the contrast between the current government of my homeland and the government of Canada—the first largely corrupt, the second free and democratic—was stark.

The government of Mexico had attempted to use the Canadian government to make my situation abroad quite difficult and complex, publicly stating that they had repeatedly requested my deportation and then extradition, demonizing me the whole time. But the truth is that the Mexican government had never requested my extradition; they would only do this later, when I decided, with the advice of my legal counselors, to submit a lawsuit against the Mexican government to formally request my extradition. I knew that if Canada accepted the extradition request, it would be reviewed by the courts in Canada, not in Mexico, where I could win the case and make a shame of Calderón and the Mexican government for their lack of grounds and the conspiracy of the Mexican judiciary system. Thankfully, the Canadian government refused both measures. The first step in the extradition process would have been for Canada to review the case and find that it had merit—but, Canadian officials being honest and seeing the truth, it never passed this first stage. Canada is not willing to tolerate the transfer of Mexican misconduct to its own legal system, and officials rebuffed pressure to pervert the rule of law and help persecute me for a crime I did not commit. We worked hard to communicate clearly and often with Canadian officials about the progress of the case. Every time we received a favorable ruling, Marco del Toro would draft a report explaining the new developments and send official translated documents showing the court proceedings. Even when we were denied amparo now and then, his reports would explain that we were appealing and were confident that we'd win in the next round.

So, as the attack on the union and my leadership continued in earnest during 2008, we were glad to have in Vancouver something of a safe haven. From Mexico, though, we were still receiving threats from politicians and businessmen. Anonymous email, letters, and phone calls came to our home, all warning me to step down from the union and stop fighting Grupo México.

The government was still using unlawful tactics against us too, for no reason other than punishment for my standing up to them. In one of its most cowardly moves, the PGR seized a real estate property belonging to my son Ernesto that had been acquired long before the conflict began. We filed an amparo in a federal court against the confiscation of Ernesto's home, and when my defense lawyers consulted the file, they found a page that had by mistake not been removed at court. The top of the page read

> . . . FEDERAL JUDICIARY POWER
> Indirect Constitutional Rights Protection Trial 410/2007
> **SON OF NAPOLEÓN GÓMEZ URRUTIA . . ."**

They hadn't even bothered to use the actual name of my son, the owner of the property! It was a clear confirmation that the confiscation was about one thing only: putting pressure on me and threatening me into giving up leadership of the union. There is no reason I should've been mentioned in that file. The legal action was against my son and supposedly had nothing to do with me, but when Ernesto went to court to defend himself against this arbitrary seizure, he was seen only as a relative of the political enemy.

My own home in Mexico City was still seized as well, though Rivero had been lying to us and saying that he was making progress on it. But in the hands of Rivero's former partner, Marco del Toro, we did eventually get a ruling from a judge declaring that the home was no longer in the government's control. When the PGR first took the property over in April of 2006, it had sent heavily armed men to surround it, and the government had called in news crews to cover the scandalous story. Now, years later, when Marco went to take back the house pursuant to the judge's ruling, the PGR was ready to put on another show of intimidation. As Marco pulled up to the house with the court order in hand and a notary public in the passenger's seat, he saw a car full of armed police forces (who'd been sent by the PGR) waiting for him. As he exited his car, they got out of theirs as well, looking stern and displaying their weapons. Marco charged toward the house anyway, shouting for the notary to make an official record of the police intimidation.

More threats were to come. October 2008 brought their most dire move up to that point, according to retired military general Arturo Acosta Chaparro. He said that in that month, a group of government officials and retired military officers had held a meeting in Mexico City. Some of the attendees were participants in the massacre of peasants in Aguas Blancas, Guerrero, in June 1995. PAN senator Ulises Ramírez—former mayor of Tlalnepantla, chief of staff of Interior Secretary Juan Camilo Mouriño, and according to many books, an El Yunque member—was at the meeting along with Mouriño himself. Ramírez offered General Acosta millions of dollars to travel to Canada and perform a "dirty job": that is, kidnap me, take me to a private place, and make me disappear. The offer was made on behalf of—who else?—the Department of the Interior and Grupo México. General Acosta had a controversial background; in addition to spending six years in military prison for alleged ties to a drug cartel, he was known for his involvement in the Dirty War of the late 1960s and 1970s, during which the ruling PRI government sought to suppress the left-wing student movement and bands of associated rebels. Over a period of nearly eighteen years, the government tortured and killed untold numbers of suspected rebels. General Acosta was rumored to

have been among the most ruthless of the leftists' persecutors, kidnapping and murdering hundreds of dissidents in the state of Guerrero. In
La Jornada, Andrés Nájera—president of the Eureka Committee, an
organization dedicated to finding justice for the detainees and casualties
of the Dirty War—attributed a full 30 percent of the deaths to Acosta.
Needless to say, hearing that such a man was out of prison and being
enticed to come after me was unsettling.

Julio Pomar, head of the union's press department, had heard the
story straight from General Acosta's mouth, at a breakfast meeting of
around ten people. Acosta told the group that he'd refused the assignment and advised Mouriño and Ramirez that he considered it extremely
dangerous and difficult to perform such an operation in Canada, a country that has very advanced security systems, particularly after September 11, 2001. After the terrorist attack, the governments of Canada and
the United States had decided tighten controls on people coming into
the country, and their security measures were now beefed up and intertwined. It would take considerable effort for the general to pull off the
proposed mission.

Pomar told General Acosta after that breakfast meeting that he was
going to tell me this story. The general said that was fine—all of it was
true. (Further, General Acosta didn't care about angering the current
administration; apparently Calderón had promised him an appointment
to a high-level position but hadn't kept his word.) As soon as Pomar's
tale got back to us, the lawyers drafted an affidavit describing the incident. We presented it before a Canada's Minister of Justice as evidence
of the ongoing institutional persecution against me and my family.

The Canadian government reacted immediately. From the beginning, my family had received help from a sergeant from the intelligence
unit of the Royal Canadian Mounted Police; this sergeant had a strong
relationship with several members of the USW, and he'd been extremely
kind and supportive in the many meetings we'd had since my arrival in
Vancouver. Now that federal officials had seen the affidavit regarding
the hit man who was almost sent to kill me, they arranged a meeting
between me and an RCMP special detective from the Royal Canadian

Mounted Police. The detective told me that the safety of me and my family was a priority for him, and he helped set up alerts in my home, on my office telephones, and in my vehicles that I could use to rapidly call authorities should any of us encounter trouble. To this day, my family enjoys the added security of these measures, and we deeply appreciate the Canadian government's actions in this regard.

Yet the Canadian police couldn't stop all the abuses. It is sad, to say the least, but I, my family, my lawyers, and many of our colleagues had become used to the fact that our every communication is being listened to, primarily through phone taps. Since I'd been elected general secretary in 2002, I'd suspected that my phones had been tapped and that government officials made a habit of listening in to union business. But after Pasta de Conchos and my departure from Mexico, I became absolutely certain of it. The union's legal team, some of whom had connections in the PGR and in the Department of the Interior, assured me that politicians were capable of phone tapping—unlawful, of course—and employed it routinely. My response to this criminal eavesdropping is simple: they should feel free to listen, listen, and keep on listening. The invasion of our privacy is inexcusable, but I have absolutely nothing to hide.

The year 2008 brought more threats against my family and an assassination plot, but it also brought other forms of pressure for me to step down—gentler methods of persuasion, but no less infuriating. From the start, businessmen, politicians, and union leaders had made the trip from Mexico to Canada to visit me, including Alonso Ancira and Graco Ramírez, a former PRD senator and a friend of mine (he would be elected governor of the state of Morelos in July 2012). I had telephone conversations with Manlio Fabio Beltrones, a PRI senator, former governor of Sonora, and current leader of the Mexican Congress, with PRI congressman Emilio Gamboa Patrón, who is today the leader of the Mexican Senate; and with many others. All these visitors declared the same intention: they wanted to help negotiate a solution to the conflict. However, none of their proposals for mediation were serious. Each encouraged me in his own way to give up my position; none of them had an authentic desire to resolve the conflict legally and with respect for union autonomy and freedom of association. It seemed that for many of them the union was merchandise to be traded, and their only solutions were based on destroying the organization. For my colleagues and me, who remember the sacrifices of those who came before us, that solution was unacceptable in every respect.

Two of my colleagues in the labor movement—Elba Esther Gordillo and Carlos Romero Deschamps, national leaders of the Teachers' and Petroleum Workers' Unions, respectively—made the trip to Canada as well. They too said their intent was to intercede and negotiate. Yet when we began discussing a solution, they had the same solution as everyone else: They hoped to convince me to step down. These two union leaders both told me this would allow Calderón and Lozano to appoint a new person at the head of Los Mineros; that way, all the fabricated accusations would be dropped and I could return to Mexico with my family. They were convinced that things would calm down eventually, probably not until the PAN government ended, but that I could then return to my position in the union. It was the same argument I had heard from crooked businessman and power-obsessed politicians. They wanted me to lay down my arms and abandon my colleagues.

I consulted many times with my colleagues on this matter. The answer from the workers was always unanimous: *Napoleón Gómez Urrutia is the one we elected and, with toma de nota or without toma de nota, he will continue to be our leader.* To accept their proposal would be to acknowledge that we had done something wrong. As I repeated to anyone who made the suggestion that I simply leave the union: The workers are my bosses, not the companies or any politician.

Of all the parties interested in seeing me step down, it was the mining and steel companies of Mexico who had the most to gain. Without any truly democratic unions in their sector, they would reign supreme. Unchecked, they would continue to rake in profits and manipulate politicians. Thus, it was the businessmen of Mexico who made the most strenuous efforts to end my leadership, and they were willing to pay me handsomely to get out of their way. The most remarkable of these bribery attempts came from Alonso Ancira himself.

At the beginning of the administration of Carlos Salinas, Ancira's company, Altos Hornos de México, had been owned by the Mexican government. During his privatization spree, Salinas sold the company—which was and is Mexico's largest steel producer—to the Ancira Elizondo brothers. Alonso Ancira, being a close friend of Salinas, became the largest shareholder and stepped into the role of chairman and CEO. As in most of Salinas's privatization deals, the new owners got the company practically for free. Altos Hornos de México had a value estimated by its own governmental technicians and bureaucrats at more than $4 billion. The government sold it to the Ancira brothers for less than $150 million. The inventory the company had in warehouses at the time of the sale was by itself worth more than the purchase price.

Ancira—just like Germán Larrea, the Villarreal brothers, and Alberto Bailleres—is an active opponent of the workers who were the lifeblood of his own business. He's also a deeply narcissistic person. A portly man, he seems locked in a perpetual struggle to lose weight, and as he aged, he's had several surgeries to make himself look younger and slimmer. Wherever he goes, he's surrounded by at least one or two young, beautiful assistants, typically girls around twenty years old, whom he pays large sums of money to accompany him on trips. He's also constantly trying to play himself off as some kind of academic or legal expert, though he often exposes his own lack of knowledge. At his core, he is not scholar but a businessman.

One of Ancira's favorite tricks was to prop up union leaders who served his interests and then begin persecuting them—often by throwing them in jail—when they ceased to be useful or opposed him. And he resented any progress made by the workers of Mexico; he could not stand to see any of his employees become educated, out of fear that it would reflect badly on his own lack of a college education. He even prevented the upper echelons of his company's staff—the managers and directors—from living comfortable lives. If they did, Ancira reasoned, they would be equal to him, the all-powerful businessman. He also thought he was so important that no rules or laws applied to him; for years, he hid in Israel, refusing to pay off massive debts to his creditors, including a huge tax debt to the Mexican government.

Like most heads of Mexican mining and steel companies, Ancira was closely tied to the conservative PAN governments of Fox and Calderón, including having donated huge sums to Marta Sahagún's Vamos Mexico Foundation. Ancira's powerful influence had even swayed Coahuila governor Humberto Moreira to allow suppression of the workers in his state. In 2008, workers from union sections in Monclova, Piedras Negras, and Nava—the three most important sections in Coahuila—planned a meeting to report on a recent review of local workers' collective bargaining contracts. The night before the meeting was to be held, Ancira sent more than five hundred thugs—mainly drunks and drug addicts from the poor areas of the state—to attack and set fire to the meeting rooms of Sections 288 and 147 of Monclova and 293 of Nava in order to prevent the members from meeting and expressing their opinions about the agreements. Ancira could not have perpetrated this action without Moreira's tolerance and help in covering it up after the fact.

The governor's complicity with Ancira is shameful and disappointing—especially considering that Moreira had been a unionist as a member of the National Teachers' Union, and considering the fact that he had previously asked for and received support from the union in his 2005 bid for governor. (And of course, he previously publicly denounced Vicente Fox for trying to have me unlawfully imprisoned.) Sadly, Moreira had begun associating with Ancira, and the businessman had persuaded him to renege on his union past and sign off on further persecution of the miners. Ancira, like Larrea, Bailleres, and the Villarreal brothers, was intent on his mission to disband the union and set up a company union in its stead.

On three occasions Ancira had visited me in Canada to try and convince me to abandon the union's leadership. Each time he came to Vancouver—first in 2006, then in 2007, and again in early 2008—he had offered many personal benefits in exchange for a resignation, and the "benefits package" increased every time we met. In October 2006, after the first months of aggression and threats from the government, Ancira had offered me $10 million. His next two offers were for $20 million.

These meetings ended in failure, of course—he should have known I wouldn't take a bribe. But in June 2008, I got another call from Ancira. He said he was on a business trip in the United States and wanted to fly in from New York to meet with me on June 23. I told him I had to refuse because it was my wife's birthday and I had promised to dedicate the day to her. Oralia and I had planned to do something special that day, hoping to forget for a short time the aggression that had now lasted over two years.

Ancira insisted. I have no doubt that he knew the date's significance and arranged his trip accordingly—it's a prime example of how he and his ilk express their perversity, even in the smallest of ways. This fourth meeting was crucial, Ancira said. This time he had a clear proposal to end the conflict, one that would be suitable for everyone.

I finally agreed—albeit unhappily—to meet for a brief one-on-one breakfast at 9:00 a.m. at the Fairmont Waterfront Hotel in Vancouver. The restaurant was crowded when I arrived, but we were seated at a private table tucked away from most of the commotion. Ancira's demeanor was chilly; neither of us trusted the other.

He quickly told me that he had a new offer—this one much more appealing than those of previous years. He told me that some high government officials, headed by Labor Secretary Lozano, had met with a group of businessmen who belonged to the Chamber of Mining, including Germán Larrea, Alberto Bailleres, and the Villarreal brothers. Lozano had pressured all of them into pooling funds to offer me a payment in exchange for stepping down. Lozano told the group that they had provoked the situation, and that, with the prices of metals back up to sky-high levels, the Miners' Union under my leadership was a significant threat to their ever-fattening profit. If they wanted to keep the cost of labor down, Lozano told the assembled businessmen, this was the easiest way to do it.

Together they put together a sum of $100 million. The amount was nothing compared to the money they would save with the obstacle of Los Mineros removed. Now Ancira had come to offer the money to me on the condition that I resign immediately as general secretary of the Miners' Union. As part of the deal, I would also allow them to impose a new person at the head of the organization—without consulting the workers, of course. Finally, I would stay outside Mexico for three years, until the end of the Calderón administration in 2012. I would then be able to return to my home country without any problem, and they would immediately cancel and withdraw all false accusations they had leveled against me.

As he explained the deal, Ancira made sure to not include himself as one of this group of conspirators; he spun himself as the "negotiator," and acted like he was ever respectful of my leadership. At times he mentioned the concepts of loyalty and friendship—two things he obviously does not understand. At last he looked me directly in the eyes and said, "So, what do you think? A hundred million dollars is nothing to sneeze at. You and your family will have a comfortable life, tranquil, with no worries. You will live in peace and you could dedicate yourself to traveling, reading, writing, and giving conferences—anything you want."

Ancira had an answer immediately. "Napoleón Gómez Urrutia," I told him, "is not for sale. Neither is the Miners' Union." I told him that if he and his cronies truly want to resolve the conflict they had created, they needed to sit down and negotiate with respect, and immediately end the aggression. It's thanks to the workers' effort, commitment, and sacrifices that these businessmen are making the biggest profits in their companies' history, I pointed out. The miners deserve fair compensation as part of the huge profits they were generating. I then told him it would be better if they took the $100 million and distributed it among the workers and their families, or used it to develop new plans for education, health, housing, and life insurance.

Ancira listened to my speech but told me right away that I should think about it, that I should talk with my wife and family. He told me it would be a mistake not to accept the offer and its conditions.

I told him no amount of consideration would ever change my mind. If they didn't like the conflict, they shouldn't have started it. It was their ignorance, arrogance, lack of vision, and insensitivity that had put them where they were. The only way forward, I said, was for company and union to develop mutual respect. I told Ancira that we would be more than happy to discuss ways to cooperate and increase productivity in a manner that aligned with our collective bargaining agreements.

"Napoleón," Ancira replied, "that kind of cooperation is a serious threat to these guys, and to the president they stand behind. You have a big problem—you came twenty-five years before your time. Your ideas scare them, all this training and education for workers, all this modernization and progression toward a new future for workers. Plus, Mexico's just not ready for a union leader with graduate and postgraduate degrees in economics, who speaks multiple languages, who has international relationships. And Germán Larrea hates you, more deeply than any of the others. He's insane. He'll break any law if he has to in order to see you fall."

Of course I knew Larrea hated me, but I didn't think the rest of Ancira's argument made sense. Union leaders with backgrounds in economics have found success in other countries, including the general secretary of Germany's Volkswagen Workers Union, who previously served as the country's minister of the economy. And it wasn't Mexico that was resistant to these changes—it was this cabal of greedy, amoral businessmen and politicians who were unwilling to move forward.

By now, Ancira could see that I wasn't going to accept the offer, but he wasn't ready to end breakfast yet. I took the opportunity to get some more information out of him. "Why," I now asked, "did President Calderón decide to continue all this? It started under Fox's watch, and at first he acted like he didn't want it to be his problem. Why keep it alive?"

"I think you know the answer to that question," Ancira said. "Germán Larrea, Alberto Bailleres, the Villarreals—they all donated enormous sums of money to Calderón's campaign, just like they did for Fox. In exchange, Calderón gave them Lozano." I recognized this as the truth, even coming from a man who had no scruples. Lozano had been at these businessmen's beck and call from the beginning. "It's to these business-men that he owes his position—not the population at large, much less the working class," Ancira said.

That was true, I replied, but once the president of Mexico assumes his duties, he has all the legal power to become a statesman, a king, or a dictator. Calderón could have begun his administration by looking for a true solution to the conflict. He could have behaved like a great negotia-tor who faces and resolves challenges and problems as they arise.

"You expected that of a short, ugly, conflicted person who had no personality?" Ancira replied, in his typically offensive manner. "All he does is yell and bang his hands on tables. He makes terrible rash deci-sions just for the sake of feeling like he's the president. Add to that the fact that he drinks a lot while he's making these decisions, and you'll see why his choices have been poor."

Ancira's characterization of Felipe Calderón immediately reminded me of how Germán Larrea had always referred to Vicente Fox as stu-pid and ignorant, and of Larrea's insulting nicknames for Lozano. I couldn't imagine what Larrea now called Calderón behind his back. It's a shame that men like Calderón exist, but it's even worse is that there are those—like Ancira and Larrea—who recognize the faults and fail-ings of these government officials and yet cynically protect and defend them as if they were close friends.

"Calderón won't end the conflict on his own." Ancira continued. "That's why I strongly recommend that you accept their offer. If you don't"—and here came the threat—"things are going to get worse. They are going to attack you, invent things, and slander you, your wife, your children, and your colleagues. You know they can get the media to print whatever they tell them to. And," he added with an unmistakable air of complacency, "that's just the way Mexico is: the corruption, the illegal-ity, the abuses of authority; they can apply or interpret the laws any way they feel like it." The people, he told me, are asleep, stultified by the propaganda that's all over TV, newspapers, and radio. "The Mexicans are afraid. They live in terror, and that culture was created intentionally, to control their businesses, the economy, and the political environment.

"You broke from that system," Ancira continued, "and you became a danger to it, an obstacle. And besides, you have education and intelligence that many of us don't. The extreme right is in power, and to these PAN politicians, social and union leaders like you are enemies of God and the Church. To them, unions are like a cancer on society and have to be removed. Calderón told us he feels precisely that way many times during the campaign."

I had to agree with Ancira on this last point. It had been two or three decades since Mexico had seen such vitriolic hatred toward the lower and working classes. The PAN government had brought these extreme violations back, fueled by arrogance and unbridled ambition.

"That is why," Ancira insisted, "you should accept the offer. If you don't, things are going to get worse for you, your family, and the union. Think about it. You can take the money, free and clear, then just walk away."

I refused once again.

Ancira insisted on giving me his numbers and told me to think about it. "If you don't accept this, you'll be making a mistake, and you will come to regret it."

"Is that a threat?" I asked. "Are you trying to intimidate me? My colleagues and union friends in Mexico and all over the world are prepared to deal with whatever happens. They haven't deserted me so far, and they never will."

By then, the meeting had lasted more than four hours; it was now past one in the afternoon. I finally told Ancira I'd had enough, that I had to get back to Oralia. Before I left, I once more gave him a clear and emphatic answer. I then stood up from the table and walked out of the hotel restaurant without looking back.

That night I went out to dinner with Oralia to celebrate her birthday. After a while, I told her I had just rejected a very important offer, but that I felt good about having made the decision. "They offered me $100 million, Oralia," I said.

"In exchange for what?" she asked, unperturbed.

After I recounted the whole conversation, she said, "You know what? You made the right decision. You are like your father—a man of integrity, honesty, and courage. I know you would never lower yourself to their level. It would torment you forever. You know that the whole family is with you, and that we'll keep supporting you until the truth is known. Things seem to be getting worse sometimes, but the time will come when that will change.

"The repression, corruption, and irresponsibility of a few do not represent the vast majority of Mexicans," Oralia continued. "When the transformation begins, you will be there. Men of courage, decent men with ability and knowledge, consistent and honest men who love their country and are ready to commit everything to her are very rare. You are among this small group, and that is why you are and you will be the best example for me, for our children, for the whole family. You are a great inspiration for the workers of the world. They have been and will continue to be with us through this struggle."

Oralia's words had touched me deeply, and we enjoyed the rest of our dinner quietly. I had never been happier to celebrate another year of having this generous and marvelous woman by my side.

Ancira's visit had been a straightforward attempt at bribery. I have never believed—and still don't—that a union should be treated as a business, subject to bribes and personal interest, and I do not say this romantically or idealistically but with all the realism and toughness of character of which I am capable.

Many have asked why we continue the struggle. What's the point in so stubbornly maintaining our position? My answer is that we are not the stubborn ones. We have been willing to discuss the problems at the root of the conflict. Ours is not a personal dispute with one or more businessmen or politicians. Our fight is for the noble values in which we believe. It is for justice, respect, dignity, and equality—values that no one should throw overboard in exchange for a comfortable position or a fat check.

I was never tempted to accept any bribe, yet the dream of returning home is always with me. Without question, we have had painful times due to our separation from our beloved Mexico. In 2009, in the midst of a long illness, my wife's mother had a long period of physical incapacity. She always said that she was going to wait until this conflict ended and we returned to be together again, and we were in constant communication with her by telephone and videoconference. However, that was no substitute for personal, caring contact. When my mother-in-law eventually passed away, she hadn't fulfilled her dream of having us back in Mexico. For all of us, but especially for my wife, it was extremely painful to not to be able to caress her or kiss her in her final moments. It was one of the incredibly high costs we had to pay to maintain our integrity— but better to pay that price than to lose ourselves, to buy our return to Mexico by selling out the miners of Mexico. As painful as it was to be separated from our homeland, that betrayal was an impossibility.

FIFTEEN

A Faulty Bridge

Violence solves no social problems; it merely creates
new and more complicated ones.
—DR. MARTIN LUTHER KING JR.

On November 4, 2008, Juan Camilo Mouriño, Felipe Calderón's secretary of the interior, was flying into Mexico City in a Learjet that had departed from a small airport in San Luis Potosí. In the plane with Mouriño was security advisor and former federal prosecutor José Luis Santiago Vasconcelos as well as several other officials. As they approached the heart of Mexico City, the pilot suddenly lost control, and the craft plummeted toward the earth. The jet slammed into rush-hour traffic on a street in the middle of Mexico City, less than a mile from Los Pinos. It burst into flames on impact, killing all eight people on board, in addition to six people on the ground.

Though the cause of the crash was eventually determined to be pilot error, there was wide speculation of a terrorist attack perpetrated by one of Mexico's powerful drug cartels, particularly in light of the fact that Vasconcelos and, to a lesser extent, Interior Secretary Mouriño had been key figures in Calderón's war on drugs. By November 2008, that war had already cost thousands of lives, and violence against government officials was rising. But regardless of the cause of the crash, Mexico was in shock at the loss of Mouriño, the country's second-most-important public official. (In Mexico, the office of interior secretary is much like the vice president's in the United States.)

Mouriño had been a controversial figure and certainly no friend of the miners—in fact, he'd allegedly been instrumental in recruiting General Arturo Acosta, killer of leftists, to come to Vancouver and assassinate me. Mouriño had taken over the job of interior secretary the previous January, when Calderón fired Francisco Javier Ramírez Acuña, a provincial and repressive official who did nothing to resolve the mining conflict but instead threw up roadblocks all along the way. Some groups had called for Mouriño's resignation immediately after his appointment, saying that he had rewarded his father's company with government contracts while holding the office of undersecretary of energy. But Calderón supported his appointee, and Mouriño kept his job. The underhanded dealings of which he was accused were, after all, commonplace in the administration. During his tenure as interior secretary, Mouriño had done nothing to resolve the problems the union faced, besides a few just-for-show meetings (and of course, the effort to—according to General Acosta—send a hit man after me).

The day Mouriño's jet went down, the United States held its presidential election, and the people selected Barack Obama as their first nonwhite president. This development built great hope in our American colleagues, including the AFL-CIO, the USW, the UAW, and many others, all of whom had contributed thousands of organizers in support of Obama's campaign. It sparked hope in me, too, and the other members of Los Mineros. With a more liberal president who respected workers' rights, we hoped the United States would join with Canada to exert pressure on President Calderón to end the aggression and political persecution against us and the ongoing lack of respect for human rights. After all, the Mexican government's actions clearly violate the parts of NAFTA that cover labor rights and freedom of association.

As harmful as Mouriño had been to our cause, when I got news a few days after the plane crash of whom Calderón had appointed as his successor, I was sure we had moved from bad to worse. Calderón's pick was a man named Fernando Gómez Mont. Like so many appointees in the last two PAN cabinets, Gómez Mont was by profession a corporate lawyer. But it got *a lot* worse: This man—as part of the law firm

Esponda, Zinser, and Gómez Mont—had for years been retained as a criminal attorney by none other than Grupo México itself. Up to the very day he took public office, Gómez Mont had been Germán Larrea's professional defender.

The entire mining union was distraught. We couldn't believe that the legal counsel of our number-one enemy, with no political experience at all, had been given the enormous responsibility of conducting Mexico's interior policy. We saw nothing but sharpened persecution in our future. Earlier in 2008, several of my colleagues on the national executive committee had been in a meeting in Javier Lozano's office along with Gómez Mont and another Grupo México lawyer. The group had been very close to reaching an agreement that would end the conflict—and they might have done so had not Gómez Mont strongly opposed one of the conditions. The business lawyer, with an arrogant and insensitive attitude, insisted that the false accusations against me and my colleagues remain in place. Gómez Mont's opposition ended the meeting, and no agreement was reached.

Days after Gómez Mont took on his new role in the interior department, our defense lawyer, Marco del Toro, got a flurry of phone calls from him. Gómez Mont called Marco repeatedly and left insistent voicemails asking if the two of them could meet. It was strange: Typically one doesn't have the second-highest government official in the land beating down your door for a meeting. Curious, Marco called Gómez Mont back and agreed to meet with him and Alberto Zinser, one of Gómez Mont's colleagues in his law firm. (Esponda, the third lawyer in the firm, had been best friends with Calderón in law school.)

The meeting was held in a Mexico City hotel on a Sunday morning, even though Marco knew that Gómez Mont rarely (if ever) worked early or on weekends. Gómez Mont and Alberto Zinser arrived via helicopter. During the meeting, Marco was surprised to see before him a person whose attitude toward Los Mineros seemed to have changed dramatically. "Listen," Gómez Mont told Marco, "now that I've been appointed as interior secretary, I'm no longer on Grupo México's side. I'm not going to even pursue the case anymore. I'm not even going to follow it. I won't go against you or Napoleón in any way—I just want to help find a solution."

Gómez Mont adamantly assured Marco that he had freed himself from his previous job as Grupo México's lawyer, and that his relationship with Larrea might actually help Los Mineros: He told Marco that he wanted to be a "communication bridge" between Grupo México and the Miners' Union. He claimed he wanted to help solve the ongoing strikes at Cananea, Taxco, and Sombrerete. Marco thanked him, the meeting ended, and the new interior secretary was whisked back to his helicopter.

Not being born yesterday, we had trouble believing Gómez Mont's claims. In fact, when Marco told me about the meeting, we agreed on his true motive: he simply wanted to get to us before we went to the media and publicized his direct connection with Grupo México. That explained the rush to meet, and his insistence that we would see a new, fairer Gómez Mont in office. He didn't want to help. He just didn't want us pointing out in public how outrageous Calderón's appointment was.

Gómez Mont immediately validated our doubts. In the following weeks, he called several union leaders from the Cananea copper mine to his office to discuss the continuing strike, but each time, he made them enter through a secret door, saying he wanted to "avoid creating false expectations." He knew full well he wasn't about to negotiate fairly with us. Nevertheless, our colleagues attended the meetings in the spirit of wanting to give him a chance. Gómez Mont also pointedly excluded members of the national union's executive committee from these meetings—a gesture meant to show his solidarity with Lozano's recent denial of *toma de nota* and with the calls for me and for the rest of the committee to resign. Meeting with any member of the executive committee would be a tacit acknowledgment of my leadership, and Gómez Mont refused to cross that line.

But the new interior secretary's antiunion actions weren't limited to ignoring the democratically elected leadership. In fact, he was about to perpetrate some of the worst direct aggression we had seen from the government in a while.

In the Federal District courts where our defense lawyers had consolidated the state-level banking charges against us, Elías Morales's accusations were beginning to fail. Though the PGR always appealed rulings in
our favor, it was becoming clear that, ultimately, the nearly three-year-
old charges wouldn't stick. This was infuriating for our enemies.

So, Grupo México's mastermind group got together once again and
came up with a new offensive. They would start back at the original
banking-fraud investigation, they decided—the one that the Mexican
banking commission (CNBV) had declared without basis. But, since the
charges were exactly the same as they were in 2006, what would make
the outcome different this time? In a country like Mexico, the answer
was simple: They decided to simply skip the CNBV, even though the
commission's review is required by law. In late 2008, the PGR sent the
old criminal file straight back to federal court. The plaintiffs were
the same—Grupo México lackeys Elías Morales, Martín Perales, and
Miguel Castilleja. The three spuriously claimed to be representing
"thousands" of workers. The defendants were also the same: me, Héctor
Félix, José Angel, and Juan Linares (although this time they left out Gregorio Pérez, the courier who had been charged in the first case, and who
had already ended up spending a good deal of time in jail). The CNBV
report from 2006, which stated that the case could not proceed because
no crime had been committed, was left out. The judge at the First District Court in Criminal Procedures, unaware of the CNBV report, issued
all four warrants without hesitation.

Now it was time for our "communication bridge" to get involved.
Mere weeks after his appointment, Gómez Mont ordered that all the
union's bank accounts and all my family's accounts be re-seized based
on the new charges. Our defense team had fought long and hard after
the 2006 bank account sequestrations and had recently regained control
of most of our assets, but now we were back at square one. Obeying
Gómez Mont, SIEDO, the PGR's organized-crime division, again froze
my personal account as well as those of my wife, my three sons, and my
sister in Monterrey. Once again, we were relying fully on the solidarity
and support of Los Mineros and the USW. The accounts of all twelve

members of the executive committee were also refrozen, along with all the national union's accounts and those of all union sections in the country. We immediately filed an amparo against all of the freezes, but we knew it would be just the beginning of a long fight. Once again, they were out to financially asphyxiate us and reduce our ability to fight back, especially at Cananea, Taxco, and Sombrerete, which were by now in their sixteenth month of striking.

These seizures were the first actions of our new mediator, the supposed "communication bridge" between Grupo México and the Miners' Union. Next on his agenda was to follow Germán Larrea's request for the physical capture of the executive committee's most prominent members.

In Mexico, there are two types of offenses: "serious" and "not serious." The only difference between the two is that for a "serious" offense (a *delito grave* in Spanish), the accused person can be held without bail and is not eligible for a stay of legal punishment while the validity of an amparo filing is with a judge. Thus, many people accused of a "serious" crime are imprisoned with no bail regardless of an ongoing amparo proceeding—not because they are a flight risk or a danger to society, but because the crime they are charged with happens to be in a catalog of offenses the Mexican legal system has deemed "serious." The arrangement creates a fertile climate for political persecution.

The banking fraud charges were categorized as serious, and that's a big part of why I had to leave the country; had they managed to apprehend me, they could have held me indefinitely without having to prove anything. From the beginning, Juan Linares, secretary of the union's Safety and Justice Council, had been named in the case brought by Elías Morales. Thanks to the amparos filed by our defense team, Juan had managed to stay out of jail while continuing to play an active role in Los Mineros. But when the PGR refiled the federal case in late 2008 and convinced judges to order new arrest warrants, Juan knew it was time to move.

In November, Juan left Mexico City for Michoacán, hoping to stay out of sight until the union's defense team could file for protection. The union's enemies knew, as did I, that Juan was one of the most valuable members of the executive committee. I'd known him for over twenty years at this point. He was a kind man with a white beard. Many years before, my father had designated him as the committee's delegate for the state of Sonora, a position he retained after I was elected. During my first four years as general secretary, I had made many trips to Sonora and seen Juan in action as delegate. On one occasion, we had organized a strike in La Caridad outside Nacozari, but some of the workers were more obedient to Grupo México than to their own interests, and the company was starting to make threats about calling in the army to evict the strikers. In this highly tense situation, I saw Juan's ability to lead firsthand; he spoke to the workers and to company officials with equal amounts of conviction and without any fear. He refused to let anyone intimidate him or corrupt him, though many tried. Juan called for solidarity from every worker at La Caridad, asking in strong, eloquent language for their commitment to the cause of Los Mineros. In short, Juan was one of the pillars of the union's executive committee, and that made him a prime target of the PGR.

It didn't take long for federal forces to find him in Michoacán, as they'd been ordered to do by Gómez Mont. On the afternoon of December 3, Juan was playing soccer with some union colleagues near his home. Suddenly a group of policemen interrupted the game and seized him on the field. He'd been easy to spot: large letters on his jersey read "LOS MINEROS." Though he was innocent of any crime, it would be Juan's last day of freedom for two years, two months, and twenty days. He was promptly taken to Mexico City's North Prison and locked up with no bail set. He was now officially a political prisoner of Felipe Calderón.

The very next day, they nabbed another union member who was key to us at that time. This time it was Carlos Pavón, executive committee member and the union's secretary of political affairs. Pavón hadn't been named in Morales's case, but Alonso Ancira had stepped in with a completely new charge intended to further confuse the situation and create more internal divisions in Los Mineros. Weeks before Pavón's arrest, Ancira had filed a complaint against him, Juan Linares, and executive committee member José Barajas, who had served as secretary treasurer since May 2006 and was also charged along with Juan and me in the federal fraud case. Ancira's charges were filed in the state of Coahuila, and a judge in the town of Monclova—who happened to be a friend of Ancira's—issued an arrest warrant for the three men.

Linares, Pavón, and Barajas were targeted in this new case precisely because Ancira knew they were some of the most important figures in the executive committee. With me out of the country and these three out of commission, the union's day-to-day operations would be severely compromised. As justification for the arrests, Ancira claimed that these three were responsible for a multimillion-dollar fraud against Altos Hornos de México. The accusation was completely false and easily disproven and, at its core, resembled the federal charges against us. Ancira's complaint said that Altos Hornos had given the union one thousand pesos for every active worker in its operations but that the union's leadership had kept these funds for themselves. They twisted it to make it sound like the Pavón, Linares, and Barajas had hoarded the workers' money, which wasn't the case at all. The complaint failed to mention that the money was meant for the continuation of social programs for the miners, which is precisely what it had been used for. That purpose was clearly stated in the collective bargaining agreement signed by Ancira himself. His complaint was nothing but a malicious scheme to further slander these three men, imprison them if possible, and keep them locked up until they became traitors to Los Mineros.

On December 4, personnel from the federal Department of Public Security burst into Pavón's home in Mexico City to carry out the arrest warrant based on Ancira's charges. They dragged him away with ridiculously excessive security measures—it was as if he were a notorious drug lord. He was taken to the airport, where he would be flown back to Monclova, Coahuila. Even though the warrant had been issued by a state judge, a jet owned by the federal government was waiting to take him away.

From the PGR's hangar in the Mexico City airport, Pavón called Marco del Toro. (Curiously, the arresting agents hadn't yet taken his cell phone.) Pavón was distraught, and he begged Marco to send help. After that, he called me too, and he sounded absolutely paralyzed with fear. We assured him we would help him fight the arrest, and within the hour, Luis Chavez, a lawyer from Marco's firm, was on a flight to Coahuila to meet him. Marco had had to rent a plane to get Chavez there in time, but it was a necessity: if someone wasn't there to represent Pavón, he would likely be appointed a public defender instead.

The following morning, Pavón appeared in court to make a statement to the judge who had ordered his arrest. The courtroom was crawling with news reporters who had been sent by Alonso Ancira. Because of the way Mexican courts operated, there typically wouldn't be much to see: court cases are conducted mostly in writing, and judges typically sit in their offices for the majority of the day while clerks attend hearings and take notes for them. But in Pavón's case, Ancira wanted a show. Not only did the judge personally appear to listen to Pavón's statement, but she also agreed to take an interview with a group of reporters as soon as she left the courtroom, which was an unusual move. In this interview, she warned that if a provisional release were requested for Pavón, the bail amount would be close to ten million pesos. With our accounts freshly frozen by Gómez Mont, there was no way we could bail Pavón out at that price.

Later that day, Pavón was on the verge of a breakdown. He met again with Marco's associate Luis Chávez and was in tears. Luis told him not to worry—he and Marco had come up with an idea. Their plan was to request Pavón's provisional release not through the presiding judge but from an amparo judge. No one would expect the move, and they had a hunch that they could convince the amparo court to drastically lower the bail amount to something the union could afford. (For Ancira's charge, bail was possible; the supposed crime was not on the list of "serious" offenses.)

During the nine days Pavón was in jail, we began to see signs of great timorousness in him. In the telephone calls they allowed him, he tearfully reported to Luis Chávez that the union's enemies—including business associates of Alonso Ancira—had been visiting him in jail. He said they had offered him freedom and a large sum of money, in exchange for a denouncement of the union's executive committee. He said he turned down the bribe, but he yelled and wept, in a cowardly and stupid manner, accusing us of having abandoned him. He said he was deathly sick, that jail was going to kill him. And he showed no appreciation for our strenuous efforts to raise the money needed to get him out of jail. By the end of Pavón's stay in jail, Luis was at his wits' end listening to the man's complaints.

Nevertheless, Marco's plan to request bail from an amparo judge ended up working. Pavón was granted provisional release with a lowered bail amount of about five and half million pesos. It was still a steep price, but we thought we could come up with it, and we were confident we would be reimbursed after we won the case in court. To make the payment, we had to pull from one of our last remaining assets—a striking fund that was used to support the workers at Taxco, Sombrerete, and Cananea, as well as the families of the men lost at Pasta de Conchos.

Once Pavón was released, he asked to be relieved of his duties for a week so he could visit his family in Zacatecas. When he got back to Mexico City, though, he was a different person than the man who had been arrested. He seemed nervous and shifty all the time, and his contributions to the executive committee meetings were scattered and confused. The illness he was supposedly dying of in prison had mysteriously vanished. A few weeks after his release, he flew to Vancouver to meet with me, and I noticed this change in demeanor firsthand. I was shocked to hear him personally blame our colleagues in the executive committee for leaving him in jail so long—a baseless and unfair accusation. We had gone to great lengths to get him out. Before his arrest, Pavón had been a key spokesperson for the union and one of the most visible defenders of the cause of Los Mineros. He'd loudly criticized the conspiracy against the union, and had even called Labor Secretary Lozano an "asshole" in public. Now he was the opposite: a weak, complaining mess.

Nevertheless, the union's legal team continued the amparo case in his defense and made significant progress toward having him acquitted.

Over the following months, it became apparent that Pavón hadn't told us the full truth about what had happened in prison. He had in fact accepted the bribes offered to him, and every day since his release, he had been working against the union from the inside. He was now following the marching orders of Javier Lozano, Germán Larrea, Alberto Bailleres, and of Alonso Ancira—the very man whose false accusations had put him in jail. In the spring of 2009, we found that Pavón had been trying to cut deals with Grupo Peñoles, to the detriment of the workers, and that he'd been actively promoting internal divisions. We had no choice but to expel him, which we did in May of 2009.

All pretense of support for the miners fell away after that. He suddenly reversed sides and became openly treacherous. He claimed that I was a burden on the union, that I had left him in jail without legal support, and that I had stolen the $55 million all along. He even stated that I was encouraging the strikes in Taxco, Sombrerete, and Cananea just to pressure the government and the companies into dropping the charges against me. He seemed to develop an addiction to appearing in the media for the sole purpose of spreading lies and bashing me and his former colleagues. Never once, however, did he give an explanation of why, if he believed this, he had spent so much time defending the union's leadership.

Pavón was quickly taken under the wing of Alberto Bailleres of Grupo Peñoles, who had great business interests in Pavón's home state of Zacatecas. Bailleres gave Pavón complete legal support and helped him set up a company union that, like Grupo México's SUTEEBM, would compete with Los Mineros. Pavón even had the gall to use my father's name in the title of this new organization. His betrayal was among the worst we had experienced thus far.

Unfortunately, the defense team had already completed work on Pavón's defense in Coahuila, and he had been acquitted of the fraud against Altos Hornos de México. But when we contacted the court about the huge sum of money we'd put up for Pavón's conditional release, we found that the court no longer had possession of the funds. Right after his charges were dismissed, Pavón had traveled to Monclova, presented himself in court, said it was he who had put up the bail money, and collected over five million pesos. It was money that was supposed to support striking miners and the widows of Pasta de Conchos, but now it was in the hands of this vulgar turncoat.

Once we were aware of this robbery, we filed charges against Pavón. Curiously, Pavón suddenly had a new legal team to defend him, and it happened to be paid for by Grupo Peñoles. He claimed he had given the money to the treasurer of the union section in Zacatecas—a total lie. Our case against him is still pending.

Meanwhile, Juan Linares was still languishing in jail for his "serious" crimes. But unlike Pavón, Juan had shown great strength and loyalty. Despite the pitiful conditions he was living in—the cell was rude and bare, and his diet consisted of cold food out of cans—Linares was in good spirits, committed to holding fast until his accusers could be proven wrong. A couple of weeks after Linares's December arrest, Marco del Toro visited him in his cell. After the two of them discussed the case for a while, Linares—with his full white beard and large frame—said, "You know, Marco, this year, Christmas isn't coming."

"Why's that?" asked Marco.

Linares smiled. "Because Santa Claus is in jail."

Clearly, the appointment of our supposed "communication bridge" hadn't solved anything. One day Gómez Mont was assuring us he would end the conflict, the next he was stripping us of our resources and having us arrested. Though he was, like Javier Lozano, a lawyer by trade, he seemed to delight in perverting the law. The position of interior secretary demands that a person have stature, ability, and integrity—Gómez Mont had none.

Not for a moment had he stopped acting as attorney on behalf of his former client. He staunchly defended Grupo México and its leaders, the only change being that he now had use of the public power that came with his new position. He had broken his promise of acting impartially in his role as interior secretary—not that we ever expected him to overnight be transformed from a vigorous defender of Grupo México into an angelic and honest mediator.

In the years after his appointment, Gómez Mont would develop a close partnership with Lozano, through which the two pressured federal judges and even Supreme Court justices to impose the whims of Grupo México at any cost. Their shameless fight against workers' rights would continue throughout the remainder of the Calderón administration. In 2009, they would together engineer the demise of Luz y Fuerza del Centro (Central Power and Light), a state company. When Felipe Calderón announced the end of the company, more than 44,000 workers lost their jobs in one day, but it was all a maneuver to destroy the Mexican Electricians' Union, one of the three or so democratic and independent unions in Mexico.

The people whom Gómez Mont associates with are yet another indicator of his character as a politician—or lack thereof. Roberto Correa, a former government official who today is a casino businessman, has deep connections with Gómez Mont and the law firm to which he belonged. Correa, who served as Director of Gaming and Raffles in the Calderón's interior department, was investigated for granting forty-one expansion permits to gaming company Atracciones y Emociones Vallarta just twenty-four hours before resigning from his position. Like many Mexican regulators, he helped companies develop workarounds for federal antigambling laws, in one instance allowing betting on poker games only allowing players to collect their winnings only after taking a trivia quiz.

A 2011 story in *El Universal* outlined the connections between Correa Méndez, his associate Juan Iván Peña, and the Esponda, Zinser, and Gómez Mont law firm. According to the article, both men "boasted of their close connections with politicians and lawyers such as Julio Esponda, who is a partner of Alberto Zinser and Fernando Gómez Mont, the ex-secretary of the interior." Correa Méndez and Peña Neder, who was also a former official of the interior department, operate the companies Juegos de Entretenimiento y Video de Cadereyta, and Ferrocarril

Endige and, according to *El Universal*, "through them sell documents, some of them false, used to install and operate casinos in various states."

None of the lawyers of Esponda, Zinser, and Gómez Mont refuted the accusation that they were linked to these unscrupulous casino owners. Even when they take on the guise of public servants, these lawyers remain staunch servants of big business, to the detriment of their own names and their professions.

SIXTEEN

THE LARREA BROTHERS
GO MISSING

*Three things cannot be long hidden: the sun, the
moon, and the truth.*

—BUDDHA

Juan Linares rang in the year 2009 in his cramped cell in Mexico
City North Prison. Like Carlos Pavón, he had been offered his freedom
several times. The price was always the same: betrayal of Los Mineros.
"I could walk out of this jail tomorrow if I were willing to betray my
union," Juan told family and friends who visited him, "but that's something I could never do."

It was tremendously painful to see one of our colleagues locked up like
a criminal when he was totally innocent. But because his crime was "serious," and because he was jailed on orders of Grupo México, no bail was
set. We could do little but press forward with his legal defense. Along with
Pavón, we had acquitted Linares of Ancira's charges in Coahuila—his arrest
warrant in that matter had been nullified. But the charges regarding the
Mining Trust were still in play, so in jail he stayed. (José Barajas, the third
defendant in Ancira's case, had avoided capture long enough that our legal
team was able to block his arrest completely; he was allowed to merely sign
in monthly before the courts in Monclova rather than stay in jail.)

Our defense team had had great success in fending off the lingering
2006 state-level charges against Linares. We had long before appealed

the warrant against him that originated in the state of Sonora, and a year and a half before his arrest, in June of 2007, the First Collegiate Tribunal for Criminal Administrative Matters in Hermosillo had upheld the appeal, stating that there was no illegal conduct. On December 14, less than two weeks after he was taken into custody, the Eighteenth Criminal Court of the Federal District, which had inherited a warrant for the same charges from San Luis Potosí, also declared Juan innocent and ordered his release, saying that there was no evidence of a crime. (The PGR appealed this ruling but was later denied in May of 2009.)

When we began our vigorous fight against the renewed federal charges in early 2009, we started with the premise that since the state charges against Juan had been thrown out by the courts, the renewed federal charges should also be dismissed, since they were based on the exact same accusation. We also argued that the three accusers—Elías Morales, Miguel Castillejas, and Martín Perales—had no right to press charges for the full $55 million. First of all, they had no proof that any crime had been committed. Second, although they claimed to be fighting on behalf of thousands of miners who made up a cooperative of ex-union members called Veta de Plata, we knew that wasn't the case. In reality, Morales, Castilleja, and Perales were the only true plaintiffs; therefore, they could claim only the small share of the trust they argued was theirs personally.

But the judge presiding over Linares's case rejected these requests. We therefore began calling witnesses to testify before the court, as did the opposition. Starting in early 2009, dozens of hearings were undertaken regarding the federal charges. All these took place at the Mexico City North Prison, in the open courthouse attached by a long tunnel to the bank of cells that held Juan. For extended stretches of time—sometimes more than fifteen hours in a row—the court held interrogations that lasted at least several hours per witness. The proceedings generated a file of seventy volumes. From Vancouver, I followed every step of the case, communicating with Marco del Toro daily via cell phone and two-way radio.

The court had at first appointed a judge named Silvia Carrasco to the case, but after hearings were already under way, it decided to transfer the case to Judge José Miguel Trujillo of the First District Court. Judge Trujillo had ruled in some of our amparo trials before—including the seizure of my son's home—and we thought this move was unfair, especially since it took place after the trial had begun. We filed an amparo against the switch, but it was denied.

Though judges in Mexico typically do not attend hearings themselves, Judge Trujillo was present for most of the proceedings in Linares's trial. The main reason for his presence was that arguments would frequently break out in the courtroom between Marco del Toro and the lawyer representing Elías Morales and his fellow traitors. This attorney was a man named Agustín Acosta Azcón, a man whose shady past I was very familiar with. His father, Agustín Acosta Lagunes, had been general director of the Mexican Mint for years when I took over that role in 1989. Through his dictatorial management style, the elder Acosta had prompted the Mint workers' union to strike several times. After he left the Mint, he would use his connections with President José Lopez Portillo to become treasury undersecretary and, later, governor of the state of Veracruz. In these two roles, Acosta Lagunes would use his power to repress peasants and leftist groups.

Over the course of our legal battle with Grupo México, we came to find that Acosta's son, Agustín Acosta Azcón, was hardly better. The younger Acosta had gotten his career off to an inauspicious start. A few days after Calderón took office, the new president had appointed him director of financial intelligence for the Treasury Department, but Acosta Lagunes soon ran into scandal. One of his clients was René Bejarano, a high-ranking member of the Mexico City legislature, and mere weeks after Acosta began his new job, a video surfaced of Bejarano taking a bribe from a well-known businessman. The grainy footage, which originally aired on a popular news program, hosted by Brozo the Clown (Victor Alberto Trujillo Matamoros in real life), showed Acosta's client taking stacks of money from the businessman and thrusting them into a briefcase, a plastic bag, and his pockets. For weeks, the video was a staple of Brozo's show. The scandal ruined Bejarano's career and got Acosta kicked out of the Treasury Department. Thanks to the misdeeds of his client, Acosta had set a new record for shortest tenure in an appointed government position, with four weeks in office.

Next Acosta became a mercenary lawyer for Grupo México— though to best serve their purposes, he acted as if he were an independent attorney. Since early 2007, just after his dismissal from Calderón's cabinet, Acosta had served Grupo México. The company had recruited him specifically to take on the case of Morales, Castilleja, and Perales and lead the charge in the case against me and my colleagues. Though judges had blocked arrest warrant after arrest warrant, Acosta kept on pushing. It should have been obvious that Germán Larrea was footing the bill for his fees; Morales and the others never could have afforded this lawyer and a drawn-out legal battle on their own salaries. Acosta's services would have cost many times more than the three accusers' annual pay combined. (The protracted legal battle was a financial drain on the union, too, of course—one of the most important lawyers from Grupo México, Salvador Rocha, approached Marco del Toro in a restaurant and cynically said, "Keep filing those amparos, Marco. You're making me rich!")

In every media appearance, Agustín Acosta behaved like a Grupo México spokesperson, publicly insulting the union's executive committee as though he himself were a party in the conflict. He acted as if he were defending thousands of righteously angry miners rather than three tools of a morally bankrupt corporation. Acosta, through Grupo México, also enjoyed cozy relationships with many judges, court officials, and the PGR, and he often got word of resolutions in the case before they were officially announced. He would often share verdicts with reporters before they were formally issued—at a time when only the judge himself could have legally known the outcome. When making these "predictions" to the media, he acted as though he were some sort of soothsayer.

During Linares's trial, Acosta didn't make a single move without consulting Grupo México's primary legal firm: Zinser, Esponda, and Gómez Mont. Acosta constantly denied any connection to the firm, but the truth proved difficult to hide. One of the younger attorneys at that firm, a man named Roberto García, was given the assignment of coaching

Acosta through the Linares case. García would show up at every one of the hearings in the Linares case and sit very near the front. Naturally, the judge did not allow García to participate, since he was not a party in the trial and was not representing anyone involved. Yet at almost every public hearing, there he was, sitting in right at the front of the courtroom. Marco del Toro, fully aware of the relationship between García and Acosta, would each time ask the judge to have him move further to the back, declaring that García had been sent by Grupo México to support Acosta. After each time this happened, García would move to the back of the room but then slowly and surreptitiously make his way back up to the front, closer to Acosta, as the day progressed.

One day, Marco turned around during a hearing to see García handing Acosta a small yellow slip of paper. Marco immediately shouted for the judge's attention. Judge Silvia Carrasco, like a schoolteacher reprimanding children for passing notes, ordered that Acosta hand over the paper. Clearly embarrassed, Acosta obeyed. It turned out to be a Post-it, on which García had written a series of questions for Acosta to ask the person being cross-examined that day. At Marco's request, the court certified that this transaction between García and Acosta had occurred, and the Post-it was added to the case file as evidence. There it remains as irrefutable proof that Grupo México is the driving force behind the persecution of Juan Linares, and by extension, all of Los Mineros.

Over the course of Linares's defense, the judge heard many statements that confirmed Juan's innocence. The executives of Scotiabank themselves—the former trustees of the Mining Trust—were once again very clear in saying that the union's finances had been managed honestly, and the same was said by accounting experts, both the officially appointed ones and the one acting on behalf of the defense.

But there was one witness Marco wanted above all others. There was one person who deeply understood the conflict that had led to Juan's arrest, a man who had been involved for decades, and who had been instrumental

in setting up the very Mining Trust that was being disputed. More than anything, Marco del Toro wanted to get Germán Larrea in the courtroom. On
January 9, 2009, before Judge Trujillo had taken over the case from Judge
Carrasco, Marco entered testimony from Germán Feliciano Larrea and his
brother Genaro as evidence in the case. (Genaro has held several top positions within Grupo México and was familiar with the case as well.) This
move on Marco's part meant that the two Larrea brothers were going to
be required to make a formal declaration about the circumstances behind
the fraud accusation—specifically against Linares, but they were the same
charges as those against me and the others. We were extremely curious about
what Larrea would say under Marco's cross-examination, since Germán
himself had in 1990 signed a document clearly stating that the $55 million
was for the union, not for the individual workers (and that distinction was
the basis of Morales's claim). Calling Germán and Genaro as witnesses was
a simple development, but it would change the course of the entire trial.

As soon as he heard he was going to be summoned to testify before
Judge Trujillo, Germán Larrea told his counselors to prevent his appearance at all costs. He is a famously secretive man who has never given an
interview and rarely appears at public social events. Indeed, few people
had even seen a picture of him until the Miners' Union obtained one (we
would later legally acquire a copy of his driver's license and passport) and
distributed it. Though Larrea is listed as the second-wealthiest person in
Mexico, he lives such a hermetic, introverted, anonymous life that taking
pictures of or with him is strictly prohibited. Nowhere—on the Internet or
in any of the company's materials—are there photographs of him.

On January 14, the court sent a clerk to Grupo México's headquarters in Mexico City to deliver the official legal summons. The clerk was
received at the building by a secretary, who said that the Larreas did
indeed work on the fourth floor. She told the clerk that neither man
was there at the moment, but that she would deliver the documents to
them when they returned. Two days later, however, she sent the summons back to the court with a note claiming that the Larreas did not in
fact work at the building in question. As we expected, Germán wasn't
going to make this easy.

About a month later, Marco del Toro had done some research into the woman who'd received the clerk. Her name was Marisol Barragán, and not only did she work for Grupo México, but she was actually one of the company's internal lawyers. Marco petitioned the judge to summon her to the court and, unlike her bosses, she did appear. However, under cross-examination, she refused to cooperate and wouldn't explain why she had covered for the brothers Germán and Genaro. Finally, Marco stood up and declared to the judge that Barragán was lying to the court. That was a crime, Marco announced, so he would be pressing charges against her. Barragán's face went white as a sheet, and she reluctantly admitted that she did in fact serve as internal counsel for Grupo México.

We'd caught Barragán in a lie, but we still didn't have the brothers. The two of them would entirely disregard a series of judicial orders over the following months, flouting the law shamelessly. When Germán was summoned to appear in U.S. courts, as he had been recently in a case in Texas involving Grupo México subsidiary ASARCO, he did obey the judge's order to appear. But in Mexico, Germán thought he could get away with nearly anything.

Throughout our attempts to get Larrea into court, the PGR itself got involved. Bizarrely, its efforts were not on behalf of the court but on behalf of the resisting witnesses. Rather than ensuring Juan Linares's right to a fair trial, the attorney general's office filed a series of amparos against the admission of the Larreas' testimony in the case. Not once did it explain what conceivable reason it had for such an action. (Of course, we knew the real story—that the PGR was, as usual, defending powerful business interests.)

Fortunately, the PGR's attempts to have Larrea's testimony thrown out were denied, and the Sixth Unitary Court in Criminal Matters of the First Circuit confirmed our right to interrogate the Larreas. But the brothers still wouldn't cooperate. On a total of nineteen occasions, they failed to comply with the court summons.

The Larreas' lawyers at Zinser, Esponda, and Gómez Mont had also gotten involved; they too had begun filing amparos against the summons. These lawyers used every legal ruse they could think of to keep the brothers out of court, but Marco argued successfully against them, and amparo was denied. The Larreas were now racking up fines for their refusal to appear, and by March, Marco requested that the court order a three-day arrest of both brothers.

On March 24, 2009, the newspaper *Milenio* published the following story:

> The First District Court in Federal Criminal Procedures ordered the administrative arrest for 36 hours of the owner of Grupo México, Germán Larrea Mota Velasco, and of the [supposed] former union leader, Elías Morales Chávez, due to being in contempt of a judicial order.
>
> According to Marco Antonio del Toro, legal representative of the Miners' Union, the judge ordered that both men present themselves to give testimony in regards to the mining trust, and the alleged misuse of $55 million at the North Prison of Mexico City, Federal District.
>
> "Employees of Grupo México have attempted to hide Germán Larrea, and this has been proven before the Federal Court, and it is for such reason that we requested he be taken by the Federal Police and compelled to appear before the court," he stated.

As soon as the story ran, Agustín Acosta began calling the paper and denying what had been stated in *Milenio*, again acting as if he were a Grupo México spokesperson. The journalist who wrote the story, Blanca Valadez, got in touch with Marco del Toro—she was concerned she may have inadvertently published something inaccurate in her article. Carlos Marín, editorial director of Grupo Milenio, had apparently scolded her about the story, since he had received many phone calls, from Acosta and others, claiming that there was no arrest warrant for Germán Larrea. Marco assured her that indeed there was, and Valadez asked him if he could provide proof that backed up her story.

Marco promptly sent her a copy of the judicial decision, which explicitly confirmed the truth of the article she'd written. Seeing the proof, both Marín and Valadez thanked us for setting the record clear, relieved that the paper had not published any false information.

Yet, on the following day, *Milenio* published another story about the Larrea summons that, strangely, hardly mentioned the document we'd sent them. Instead, the article dedicates most of its space to Acosta and is presented with a headline that quotes his blatant lie: "Larrea 'did not receive an arrest warrant.'"

Valadez writes in the second article:

> Attorney Agustín Acosta denied that there was any warning and even less an administrative arrest warrant for 36 hours against the businessman and owner of Grupo México, Germán Larrea Mota Velasco, as the Miners' Union stated last Monday.
>
> Acosta said that Silvia Carrasco, judge of the First District Court in Federal Criminal Matters, only issued a summons and that this procedure had been definitively suspended due to the fact that the Federal Judicial Council had determined to send the entire file regarding the investigation into the alleged embezzlement of $55 million to Judge José Miguel Trujillo Salcedo.
>
> Acosta added that Judge Trujillo, to whose docket the file was sent, said that he was "prevented by law from having knowledge of the case and had suspended all hearings, everything. There are no summons, well, there are even no copies. The procedure is suspended."
>
> The new judge declared himself legally incapacitated to handle the case, as he had previously decided on some amparos, precisely, from persons of the Miners' Union.
>
> Therefore, the attorney indicated, there is no summons and no judicial decision issued against Germán Larrea.

However, Marco Antonio del Toro, attorney of Napoleón
Gómez Urrutia, leader of the Miners' Union, presented as evidence file 140/2008, which orders an arrest due to the fact that
the court had been unable to successfully summon the men.

This is a shocking example of how wealthy individuals can directly
sway the supposedly unbiased press. Apparently a few phone calls from
Grupo México's people were sufficient to relegate our hard evidence to
the tail end of the article. To blur the truth, they gave us only a small
paragraph and didn't even clearly explain the incontrovertible proof we
supplied. This was on top of the fact that Acosta once again had no reason to defend Larrea, since he stated repeatedly that Larrea and Grupo
México were not his clients and were not involved in his efforts on
behalf of Morales, Castilleja, and Perales. All throughout this drama, we
released press releases about Germán Larrea's unconscionable avoidance, doing our best to present the truth that wasn't being shown in the
mainstream media.

Nearly six months after our original request for the Larreas' testimony,
we still hadn't laid eyes on Germán or his brother. In accordance with the
court's ruling that we had a right to such testimony, the PGR was required
to make every effort to produce these witnesses. In the fulfillment of that
task, it should have made full use of the Agencia Federal de Investigacion
(AFI)—a federal agency similar to the FBI—over which the PGR exerts
control. Yet given the PGR's attitude on the matter thus far, we doubted
they were trying very hard to bring Germán and Genaro in.

In mid-June, AFI agent Mario Martínez was brought into court to
explain his agency's efforts to find and arrest the brothers. After hearing about the completely ineffective methods employed by the AFI
thus far, Judge Trujillo ruled that the agency had not done professional
work. Their attempts were half-baked and not serious. Before Martínez
left the courtroom, he was ordered to bring in both Larreas to be cross-
examined by July 27, 2009. The judge told him that this time he needed
to use professionals to do it and to use local authorities as necessary. He
made it clear that there would be no excuses for not finding them by the

deadline. That order was given on June 15, giving the AFI forty-three days to investigate the Larreas' whereabouts and bring them in.

When July 27 rolled around, the judge was presented not with the Larreas but with a document signed by two AFI agents from the judicial-orders unit and their subcommander. This report was a chronicle of laziness and stupidity that was hard to take seriously. Over the previous months, Marco and his team had requested possible addresses for the Larreas from every state in the country; we had gathered data from the Internet; we had even obtained copies of both men's passports and gotten confirmation of a good address from Grupo México CEO Xavier García de Quevedo. There was no shortage of information. Yet the two AFI agents assigned to the case had massively bungled their task—probably on orders from above.

First, the document stated that the PGR had located an address in its database registered as belonging to Genaro Larrea. The agents reported that they undertook surveillance of the building every day between June 16 and June 22 and never once saw either of the Larreas. Then, on June 23, they interrogated a person who came in and out of the building frequently. This person ended up being an attorney who was the owner of the building, which is used as offices for his practice. In other words, it took these brilliant agents a full eight days to realize that the building was not a home but the offices of a law firm.

After this failed attempt, the agents continued their search at another address in the database, this time for an apartment in a twelve-story building in another part of Mexico City. On June 29, they began surveillance of the complex and continued it until July 6. Again, there was no sign of either Larrea brother. On July 7, they spoke with the receptionist at the front desk of the apartment building, who informed them that for the past five years unit 1202 had been inhabited by a person who rented the apartment from Germán Larrea, and that Larrea lived in the United States. The agents knocked on the door of unit 1202 repeatedly to confirm the story, but there was no response. The agents had spent another eight days to find out that Larrea had not lived in the building for five years.

Their next stop was at an address in the Roma neighborhood of Mexico City, where they interrogated the receptionist of a third address connected to the Larreas. This person told them that the building did indeed belong to Grupo México but had been vacated over a year before. The receptionist also said that he thought the Larrea brothers now lived in the United States.

Next, the AFI agents were off to the Mexico City airport to see if they could find evidence of either Larrea leaving the country. They claim to have spoken with representatives from nine different airlines, all of whom denied them the information they were looking for. They had to have known this would happen going in; such information could have been given to a public prosecutor, perhaps, but certainly not an investigating agent. The agents make no mention of the time periods of the records they asked for or why they had requested this data only verbally. They also fail to address why they asked only nine airlines of the twenty-four that operate at the airport, or why those nine were chosen.

The final conclusion of the two agents was so stupid that there was no doubt they were trying to mislead us and waste our time. "There's a chance that the way to find the Larreas," the report stated, "is to travel to Phoenix, Arizona." No reason was given for why the Larreas might be in Phoenix. We knew that the offices of Asarco, a copper-mining company controlled by Grupo México, are located in Arizona, but it's unlikely the agents even knew that much—they were likely just told what to say.

This pathetic, scattershot investigation confirmed to us that the PGR was again covering for Grupo México and making a mockery of the court. Our legal team asked to interrogate the AFI agents about the deficient investigation they undertook. Our request was denied.

After the Larreas had missed their final deadline twenty times, Judge Trujillo issued a writ to the attorneys of both sides, asking for their formal responses to the AFI's failed search. Agustín Acosta called up Marco to ask if he'd received the writ, and Marco told him yes. Acosta then asked Marco to email over his response. Marco agreed and asked Acosta to send his as well. Marco received a rather routine statement and forwarded it on to my son, who was closely following the case.

Shortly thereafter, Marco got a reply from Alejandro. "Did you see the email below?" my son asked. Scrolling down, Marco now saw that when Acosta had forwarded his response to the judge's writ, he had also included several emails below it, one of which was to Roberto García, one of the attorneys of Grupo México. From the email chain, Marco saw that Acosta had also sent his response to the writ to García, and García had given him feedback and made a few changes. When García emailed it back, he copied Armando Ortega, legal director for Grupo México. So much for Acosta being totally independent of the company's legal team.

Here is the email from García that Acosta accidentally sent to us:

From: Roberto García González
Sent on: Friday, July 31, 2009 07:04 p.m.
To: Armando Ortega; Agustín Acosta
Subject: GM – COMMENTS REPORT AFI

Thank you, Agustín, I made a couple of suggestions. We shall see what they think about them.

I understand that our opportunity to comment on their remarks ends next Tuesday. The public prosecutor asked me to do it on Tuesday and said that he preferred to make his on Monday.

I am still wondering whether we should include the question regarding the legal assistance, considering the previous criticisms that have been made implying that you are just another lawyer for the witness.

We have from now until Tuesday. Have a good weekend.
Regards,
RG

First of all, this email further proves that Acosta takes his orders from Grupo México and its lawyers. But it also reveals the relationship between García and the public prosecutor from the PGR. Because the company has no part in the matter—the Larreas were called as witnesses only—its lawyers have no right to communicate with the PGR's office about the case. In the last part of the email, García is doubtful about whether Acosta should intervene on the matter of the Larreas' testimony, considering that Marco was constantly criticizing him for acting as just another defense attorney for the Larreas (which he, in fact, is). Acosta's role has always been that of Larrea's defender. We always knew it, but the email proved it irrefutably.

A while after the failed AFI search and after they had escaped testifying in court close to twenty times, we finally got word that Genaro Larrea had surfaced and would appear in court. Sure enough, he showed up at the North Prison courthouse with a whole battalion of lawyers headed by Roberto García (who now, for once, had an actual reason to be present in the hearing). Once Genaro and his team had arrived, Marco del Toro stood and made an announcement that stunned everyone: "We're not going to cross-examine Mr. Genaro Larrea." The room erupted in gasps and shouts. "We asked for testimony from both brothers," Marco argued. "If I cross-examine this man, he will immediately run to his brother and tell him all the questions he will be asked. We're not going to cross-examine him!" Marco had a point, and his argument held up in front of the judge. Germán was the one we really needed to talk to, and we wouldn't accept just his brother. As Genaro left the courthouse surrounded by his legal team, he shook his head and said ruefully, "I don't understand Mexico."

Soon after all this, Judge Trujillo, despite issuing the arrest warrant for the Larrea brothers in the first place—and notwithstanding their lack of compliance with such order—reduced their penalty from a three-day arrest to a fine. In other words, Trujillo was refusing to make any further move to physically take the brothers into custody to appear in Linares's trial. It was a decision that blatantly favored the plaintiffs and put Juan Linares at a severe disadvantage. In October 2010, based on this biased action, we filed a criminal complaint against Judge Trujillo for crimes against the administration of justice.

Judge Trujillo immediately recused himself from the case. In order to justify dropping Linares's case from his docket, he presented a copy of the criminal complaint we filed, even though under the law he should not have had access to the document. As Judge Trujillo should well know, the secrecy of every criminal investigation is crucial, and his knowledge of our filing constituted a crime. Nonetheless, he argued that due to the complaint, he now felt enmity against Juan Linares and should not preside in the case. Juan would just have to wait, unjustly imprisoned, while the case was transferred to a different judge.

SEVENTEEN

A New Casualty

He knows not his own strength that hath not met adversity.
—BEN JONSON

Grupo Peñoles was perhaps the only one of the country's metal companies that did not directly participate in the shady privatization boom of the 1980s and '90s. However, Peñoles does have a history of staunchly opposing unionism. In 2009, as we fought against the arrest warrants for me, Linares, and the others, the company's current president, Alberto Bailleres, joined in the outright aggression against the Miners' Union. He took up Carlos Pavón as his pawn, using him much as Germán Larrea was using Elías Morales.

Bailleres's father, Raul, hadn't gotten Grupo Peñoles off to a good start. The late Jorge Leipen Garay—director of Sidermex, the government holding company that had controlled several companies, including Altos Hornos de México (AHMSA), before privatization—told me on a trip to Vancouver about Raul's shady dealings. According to Leipen Garay, the elder Bailleres had made his fortune shortly before and during the global conflagration of World War II. Although Mexico was aligned with the Allies, Raul mined mercury in Huitzuco, Guerrero, and secretly sold it to the Japanese, who used it to make powerful chemical weapons for the Axis powers. The mercury was transported to the port of Acapulco in small to medium-size trucks and then carried by boat fifteen or twenty miles offshore. There, Japanese ships would be waiting to purchase the mercury at dramatically inflated prices. Thanks to Raul

Bailleres's clandestine trafficking, the Axis powers got their hands on precious—and dangerous—Mexican resources. Leipen Garay also gave me a copy of Juan Alberto Cedillo's *The Nazis in Mexico*, and although the book doesn't name Raul Bailleres specifically, it gives a general picture of how he and other Nazi sympathizers in the mining and steel sector created a whole line of business selling minerals to Mexico's enemies.

According to Leipen, Raul's son Alberto inherited his father's habit of disloyalty. Many Mexican businessmen have repeated one particular story of his unethical business dealings. It is said that Alberto was once dining with his friend Carlos Trouyet, the most prominent Mexican businessman of the 1960s, '70s, '80s, when Trouyet told him that he planned to buy El Palacio de Hierro, a chain of department stores, from García Cisneros Group, a large Spanish holding company. Bailleres, upon learning of his friend's intent to purchase the chain, immediately sent one of his partners to Spain to meet with the García Cisneros Group, instructing him to offer slightly more money than Trouyet had. Bailleres, taking advantage of his friend's confidence, won the department store chain for himself.

After Carlos Pavón was released from prison and made off with the union's bail money, Alberto Bailleres used the traitor to actively promote dissidence among the union's members. Bailleres set up the now openly treacherous Pavón in Fresnillo, Zacatecas, just southeast of the striking workers at Grupo México's mine in Sombrerete. The Fresnillo worksite, where Section 62 of the Miners' Union was set up, boasted the largest silver mine in the country, run by Grupo Peñoles subsidiary Fresnillo PLC. The workers at the site had temporarily suspended work when they heard news of the unlawful arrests of Pavón and Linares back in December 2008. Now the man they had gone on strike for had returned, but he was singing a new song. He now took every chance to appear in the media and slander my name and disparage Los Mineros.

Pavón quickly set about establishing a useless company union in Fresnillo at the behest of Grupo Peñoles and Calderón's labor department. To aid him in this villainous effort, Grupo Peñoles did its best to divide the forces loyal to the Miners' Union at the silver mine; the company handed out illicit money to workers and threatened them with violence and job termination if they didn't side with Pavón.

The workers of Union Section 62 and the leaders of the national union were outraged by these threats and bribes, though a minority, including local head David Navarro, caved in to the pressure and sided with Pavón's new company union. In response, a group of loyal union members from around the country requested a meeting on June 10, 2009, to reveal Pavón and the other traitors at Fresnillo as violators of the union's unity and democracy. At the meeting, they hoped to reestablish the section's solidarity with the executive committee of Los Mineros and show that Pavón was a tool of Bailleres.

Grupo Peñoles's reaction to this attempt at peaceful dialogue inside the union was to put together a group of armed paramilitaries backed by a gang of civilian drug addicts and thugs to suppress the workers loyal to Los Mineros. Led by Pavón, Pavón's brother Héctor, and David Navarro, these attack forces were sent to meet the group that had traveled to the Fresnillo mine to discuss Pavón's new union. At 7:00 a.m. on June 10, the armed men began a surprise attack in a parking lot outside the mine.

To disguise the attack, the assailants used posts, baseball bats, stones, and metal tubes to beat the Miners' Union members—high-powered firearms would have indicated federal police and the army, which would have led observers back to the true source of the aggression: the government and Grupo Peñoles. The attackers did have firearms, but they simply flashed them and shot them off into the air to intimidate the union members.

During this aggression, the buses that brought the union members to Fresnillo were burned, and the representatives of Los Mineros were savagely assaulted. Ten union members received severe injuries, and our colleague Juventino Flores Salas was beaten on the head by the men hired by Grupo Peñoles so badly that he died at the scene. Another man, Alejandro Vega Morales, was stuck so violently that he today still suffers from brain damage. With this terror and abuse, the leaders of Grupo Peñoles warned Los Mineros that coming back to the silver mine at Fresnillo would be a bad idea.

It was clear to everyone present that this aggression was premeditated and that the assault groups had been prepared inside the company: the pipes and sticks with which Pavón's supporters were armed were all identical, and the attack was too coordinated to be spontaneous. And as we tried in the days and weeks following the attack to prosecute those responsible for the death of Juventino Flores, it also became clear that, once again, this aggression was fully supported by the government.

When they heard about the death caused by Pavón and his cronies, union sections throughout the county protested loudly. The members of the national executive committee went straight to Amalia García Medina, governor of the state of Zacatecas, to demand the prosecution of those responsible for this aggression, with criminal charges brought against the men who did the killing. García, a member of the Democratic Revolutionary Party (PRD) and thus presumably a leftist, began an investigation at the insistence of our workers, calling witnesses to present testimony and evidence in order to assign criminal responsibility for the murder. And there was plenty of evidence that pointed to the responsible parties, including statements from eyewitnesses, expert testimony, photographs, and news accounts. At least initially, Governor García seemed committed to completing an investigation so that, as the governor said, "justice will fall where it may."

But García broke her word and did absolutely nothing to bring Juventino's killers to justice. Months passed, with no action being taken against Pavón and the other traitors. By the fall of 2009, it had been several months since the attack, and we were becoming impatient. In a meeting of delegates from all the union sections in the country, both the executive committee and the union's Safety and Justice Council agreed that a delegation of union members would travel to Zacatecas's capital city (also called Zacatecas) to demand that the state government meet its responsibility to apply justice.

On November 25, 2009, more than four hundred workers began a bus trip to protest the aggression against Los Mineros and the death of Juventino Salas. When they reached the border of the city of Zacatecas, however, they were intercepted by a heavily armed group of federal and state police who told them they could not enter. The union members were treated like criminals who were on a mission to assault the city, not like workers exercising their constitutional right to free association and freedom of movement.

For hours, the authorities blocked the exits from the buses and would not allow anyone off, denying the riders food, water, and the ability to relieve themselves. It was an outright act of repression; photographs taken that day have been seen throughout the country and around the world. Only after fifteen miserable hours would the supposedly leftist governor send word that the delegates were allowed to enter the city, but only on the condition that they leave Zacatecas the following day. The next day, the delegates met some of their colleagues who were demonstrating in the main plaza outside the state capitol, increasing the size and visibility of the protest significantly.

I personally spoke with Governor García Medina a couple of times after the outrageous mistreatment of the union members who were seeking justice for Juventino. I demanded justice and respectful treatment of our colleagues. I told her that we were not going to allow such shameful repression to occur with impunity. She agreed with me, in word anyway, that justice would prevail, but said that she did not want any violence. I assured her that our colleagues were on a mission of peace, expressing solidarity with the victims of the June 10 attack. She again promised to abide by the law and apply justice.

But yet again, the governor of Zacatecas did not honor any of her promises or meet any of the dates agreed upon to arrive at a resolution against the aggressors. There was no justice. And so our worker colleagues, once they were in the main plaza, decided to stay there in a permanent sit-in, during which they held daily demonstrations, distributed leaflets, denounced the arbitrary acts committed against the colleagues under attack, and decried the complicity of the government of Zacatecas with Grupo Peñoles.

The mineworkers stayed for fifteen days in Zacatecas, demonstrating peacefully. Since it was close to Christmas, the governor asked them if they could end the sit-in, promising that before Christmas justice would be done. The members of the executive committee trusted her word and agreed to vacate the portion of the plaza the demonstrators had occupied. The governor reassured us that with this action they were agreeing to her offer and that there would be legal measures before the holiday.

Christmas went by and nothing happened. New Year's passed with similar results. In the first week of 2010, the government of Zacatecas, through a judge, decided to deny the arrest orders that had already been issued based on the complaint against Carlos Pavón, his brother Héctor, and David Navarro, as well as seven more thugs responsible for the killing of Juventino Flores.

The judge also denied that there were material damages, even though the evidence presented in videos, photographs, and oral and written testimony indicated the contrary. Evidently Governor García was afraid of angering Alberto Bailleres and decided to protect these criminal thugs from the law. In doing so, she proved herself to be among several Mexican governors who refused to show any decency in the face of the attacks on the Miners' Union. Had these governors had the strength and integrity to stand up to the aggressors, much of the repression we experienced would not have been possible.

The situation at the Fresnillo silver mine, which continued under Pavón's gangs and his puppet union, deteriorated from there. The work site, without a powerful union to protect it, became something equal to or worse than a concentration camp. Jaime Lomelín, CEO of Grupo Peñoles subsidiary Fresnillo PLC, oversaw an operation marked by virtual slavery and frequent instances of torture, with full support of the "new union." In this mine, they punished the noncompliant by exposing them naked to the inclement cold of the nights and forcing them on their knees in front of their comrades as a "lesson" for their rebellion. In 2011, the Miners' Union would file an official complaint regarding the degraded state of the Fresnillo mine, but it would pass to federal and state authorities without prompting a response of any kind.

Although Juan Linares remained unjustly jailed, Carlos Pavón's betrayal stung, and Grupo México, Grupo Peñoles, and Altos Hornos de México continued their aggression, the Miners' Union kept up negotiations with the other seventy companies with which it had contracts, obtaining the highest wage increases in the entire country, with 14 percent raises per year for its workers on average. (In 2012, we would receive increases at this level for the seventh consecutive year.) We also kept up the centerpiece of our fight against corporate corruption and governmental complicity: the ongoing strike at the open copper pit in Cananea. At this mine—the birthplace of the modern Mexican labor movement and the place where our forebears in 1906 had fought to establish the eight-hour day, to defend respect for collective bargaining agreements, and to stop the exploitation of children in the mines—the majority of workers continued their work stoppage faithfully, even in the face of continued belligerence from Grupo México and continuing declarations from the JFCA that the strike was illegal.

From the day we declared the strike, on July 30, 2007, everything about it was legal. When unionized workers begin negotiations with any company, they draft a list of demands. That document always states that, according to the collective bargaining agreement, the workers are entitled to strike if an agreement isn't reached by a certain date. If the date arrives and the company has refused to negotiate, we file the strike with the JFCA. We followed the rules and had extremely good reason to strike at Cananea. It was, in the words of many miners, a "Pasta de Conchos waiting to happen."

Regardless of our adherence to procedure, Grupo México did everything it could to have the strike declared illegal. It provided the JFCA with false documents claiming that we hadn't started the strike on time. According to Mexican labor law, strikes must start at the declared time, and a public notary must observe and record this. We had followed this policy precisely, but the company simply lied to the labor court and said we hadn't. We also ran into complications because of my lack of *toma de nota*. After Lozano denied me recognition in June 2008, Grupo México could easily criticize the strike's legitimacy by saying that I had no legal authority to approve it. To get around this, we always had one of our labor lawyers or an executive committee member who did have *toma de nota* sign the documents that called for the strike. Loyal union members Javier Zuñiga and Sergio Beltrán did have official recognition, so they handled a lot of the Cananea paperwork.

Every time Grupo México presented false evidence, the JFCA would buy the company's lies and declare the strike illegal. Just as quickly, our lawyers would file amparo against the decision. On and on it went.

In January 2008, federal forces took over the mine and tried to evict the Cananea miners by force, but we quickly filed an amparo and were allowed to stay while the outcome was decided; the government had to withdraw its troops. But a few months later, in May 2008, as the strike continued, Grupo México representatives violated the collective bargaining agreement with the union by calling a meeting with the personnel of the Ronquillo hospital and announcing that the facility would be closed, meaning that the community would lose its only remaining healthcare facility available to the workers of Cananea. (Grupo México had shut down the union-run Workers' Clinic in the 1990s—unilaterally, without the union's approval.) The move left ten thousand miners and family members without medical care. Many of them suffered from severe sickness and disability, including cancer and silicosis, much of it directly related to their work in the poorly maintained copper mine. Under their collective bargaining agreements with the company, the union's members were entitled to medical care as a condition of their employment. Grupo México didn't care. The company refused to transport the sick—even those in need of dialysis—to the nearest hospital, in Hermosillo, several hours away. Patients in need of immediate care were forced to hitchhike. It was yet another burden piled on the backs of the workers of Cananea and their families, who were already suffering from the company's decision to cut gas, electricity, education, and potable water services.

Nevertheless, in early July we had won a court ruling that officially reversed the JFCA's second denial of the strike. Grupo México wasn't about to let that stand, though. On July 30, 2008, on the one-year anniversary of the strike's declaration, the company appealed the court's decision, and two months later, the Sixth Collegiate Tribunal in Labor Matters of the First Circuit—led by Judges Genaro Rivera, Carolina Pichardo, and Marco Antonio Bello—revoked the decision issued by the Fourth District Judge and provided amparo to the company. Now, the JFCA would be required to hear Grupo México's arguments against the strike for a third time. After a hearing, the JFCA, unbelievably, declared the strike nonexistent for the third time. In the ensuing months, we went through the now-familiar process: We appealed for amparo and were granted it by the courts in January 2009. The JFCA's third attempt to end the strike was ruled without force.

The union's labor attorneys, led by Nestor and Carlos de Buen, had won each of these trials in a systematic manner, showing each time that the strike was indeed both warranted and legal. Despite Germán Larrea's powerful friends in the departments of labor and the economy, he was unable to completely manipulate the legal system and win control of Cananea. The judges consistently saw through the manipulations of Larrea and his lawyers. De Buen had given the company's lawyers a lesson in how to practice law.

Grupo México had now run out of pretexts to declare the strike illegitimate. Germán Larrea, however, is a man of perverse creativity. With the help of his "cat" Lozano Alarcón in the labor department, he concocted a new strategy. In March of 2009, the company requested that Mexico's General Mines Director, from the department of the economy, inspect the Cananea facilities. The company claimed that there was "destruction, deterioration, robbery, and vandalism in the facilities and special equipments of the mine, of such dimensions, that they made its functioning impossible." According to the company, it was the workers who had done all this damage during the strike, even though we never destroyed any company property; it was the company's own negligence that had left the facilities in such a sorry state. Nevertheless, Grupo México now argued that this damage constituted a *force majeure*—the contractual clause that would have freed the company from liability in the case of a weather disaster, war, flood, or earthquake. Based on this,

the company said, sarcastically, that after almost three years of the workers' legal strike, it could no longer continue production in the copper
mine. The employment agreement with the miners, they argued, would
therefore have to be canceled.

The simple fact is that under the federal labor law, *force majeure* does
not apply when a company has let its own greed and neglect deterio-
rate an operation. It was a fraudulent, unprecedented move, concocted
merely to end the strike. Now that the courts had upheld the strike three
times, it was their only recourse.

The General Mines Director, a person I had never met or had contact
with, complied with Grupo México's request and ordered the inspection
of the Cananea facilities. Then, on March 20, 2009, he hurriedly issued a
resolution stating that, based on reports from the inspectors and statements and documents from Grupo México, he concluded that the damage to the facility had indeed prevented Grupo México from carrying
out the mining concession granted to them at Cananea. It was a fabrication, though; the inspections never happened. The resolution claimed
that the damage to the facility and its equipment was "of such a serious
nature that it makes it impossible to undertake the work in the terms set
forth in the Mining Act." He concluded that the damage was caused by
"third parties," which supposedly constituted *force majeure* according to
Article 70, section IV, of the Regulation to the Mining Act. Not only does
Article 70 not apply to the situation at Cananea, but the General Mines
Director's findings were a total fabrication. All the paperwork relating to
the supposed inspection had been prepared in Grupo México's offices.

That same day, Grupo México initiated a special proceeding before
the JFCA in order to request termination of the employment relationship with Los Mineros and all its members at Cananea based on *force
majeure*. After a hearing in which the company repeated its false claim
that the workers had vandalized and destroyed the mine's equipment
and facilities, the court stated that the result of this evidence would
be the immediate termination of the union's labor contracts. In one
fell swoop, the workers were fired, and Grupo México began gathering workers who were not "contaminated" by unionism. Right away,

the company began hiring hundreds of contract workers from different regions of the country, even from several Central American countries, all of whom lacked sufficient training, and started up production with them. So much for Grupo México's claim that the mine was inoperable. As usual, the company didn't show any shame about exposing its own deceit. (The company had performed a similar maneuver as it fought the strike in Taxco: Larrea presented the Mexican Stock Exchange with reports saying that the silver mine had proven mineral reserves for forty years, but in the labor courts, he was simultaneously claiming that the reserves had been exhausted and that he would therefore have to terminate the miners' employment agreements.)

The nine hundred Cananea miners had been displaced, but they were determined to continue the strike. Following the JFCA's approval of the termination, we filed an amparo to have the workers reinstated. Unfortunately, the case would be held up in the courts for nearly a year. When the Second Collegiate Tribunal finally made its ruling on February 11, 2010, it announced its decision: The judge had taken Grupo México's side, and we were denied amparo. In the eyes of the court, the workers' agreement with the company had ended, meaning the strike had ended too.

But we weren't ready to give up. We appealed the decision to the Supreme Court and got another blow: On March 17, 2010, a year after Grupo México's dishonest *force majeure* maneuver, our appeal was denied. It was now looking like Grupo México would bring in federal forces to evict us from Cananea.

Mexico's Political Coordination Board—a governing body of the Chamber of Deputies—saw that this was a possibility and made an effort to prevent the powder keg of Cananea from exploding. In April, the board formally urged the government to avoid using force to remove the strikers, and it even asked the government to consider ending Grupo México's concession. The company, the board argued, clearly was incapable of exercising competent stewardship over this resource. The board called for a thirty-day break followed by renewed negotiations between the workers and Grupo México.

Shortly afterward, the International Tribunal on Trade Union Rights completed a yearlong study of the situation at Cananea and announced its opinion. It called into question the court ruling that had approved the termination of the miners' contracts and noted the government's pervasive bias toward Grupo México.

We knew, however, that Calderón, Lozano, and Gómez Mont would never listen to such reasoning. The company was loudly complaining about the strike, claiming that the conflict had so far cost the company over $4 billion. Interior Secretary Gómez Mont, in particular, was eager to help his former legal client recoup these costs, and he helped the company organize a forceful attack. On June 6, 2010, nearly four thousand heavily armed forces from the federal government and the state government of Sonora invaded the Cananea mine. They forced workers out of the mine, chased them to the union hall, and then tear-gassed the people who had taken shelter inside, including women and children.

It's remarkable that no one was killed in the violence. I made a call to our Cananea brothers that day and urged them not to confront their attackers or give in to their provocation, since the miners were outnumbered four to one. But the miners of Cananea did not give up without a fight. They did their best to resist nonviolently, and many were wounded. At the end of the vicious assault, the workers and their families had been terrorized and ejected from the mine facilities. Five miners were badly beaten, and twenty-two miners suspected of being leaders within the union local were arrested. The armed forces were receiving orders from top government officials, including President Calderón himself. They had never obeyed the rule of law, and they clearly lack human principles and morals.

The captured miners were subsequently released in the absence of a legal basis for the charges, although one of them, Martín Fernando Salazar, who at the time was dealing with a family medical situation in Hermosillo, is still detained in a prison in Agua Prieta, Sonora. The company pressed criminal charges against several more.

Following the full Grupo México takeover, the company brought in thousands more scabs and signed them up to a useless company union.

The town of Cananea now resembled a military outpost, as hundreds of armed forces stationed themselves around the mine to keep the strikers out.

With Los Mineros out of the mine, Grupo México announced that it would invest $120 million to improve and enlarge the Cananea copper mine, while the state of Sonora would invest $440 million of its own funds in the town of Cananea.

It seemed like a final defeat in our struggle for Cananea, but in no way were we prepared to give up fighting against the abuses of Germán Larrea. The vast majority of union members held firm, refusing any severance pay or offers to come back to their jobs under the company union. On August 11, 2010, two months after the invasion, the Ninth District Judge in Sonora—Víctor Aucencio Romero Hernández—ruled that the strike could continue. Though we had been forced out, our strike was still legally recognized, even if the government wasn't prepared to enforce the court's ruling.

In August of 2010, while we were still dealing with the aftermath of the Cananea assault, I got a call from a fellow labor leader in Chile. He told me that an explosion in the San José de Atacama mine, near Copiapó, had trapped thirty-three miners more than 2,300 feet below the surface. No one knew whether they were alive or dead. I immediately expressed the solidarity of Los Mineros, and soon read the reports in the national media. We watched the situation with great concern, finding it nearly impossible not to draw parallels to Pasta de Conchos.

Though Chile also has a conservative government like Mexico's, there was an intense effort to determine the fate of the trapped miners, and all thirty-three were found alive seventeen days after the rescue began. For more than two months the whole country devoted their faith and resources to saving the miners—including the mineworkers' unions; the communities and families; the directors of Minera San Esteban Primera, the company that owned the mine; the provincial authorities in Atacama; and even President Sebastian Pinera.

The rescue of the thirty-three Chilean miners put into stark relief the enormous guilt that Mexican businessmen and governing politicians bear on their conscience for the industrial homicide that occurred on February 19, 2006, in the Pasta de Conchos mine in Coahuila. Sixty-three miners are today still abandoned at the bottom of the mine, at less than four hundred feet of depth, on land that is smoother than the mountainous, rocky landscape of Chile. In Chile, a concerted effort was sustained for more than two months after the accident, while in Pasta de Conchos Grupo México, directed by Germán Larrea and his accomplice Xavier García de Quevedo, as well as the concealing and enabling government of Vicente Fox, closed the mine and suspended rescue operations just five days after the explosion, condemning to death the miners who might have still been alive.

And the differences continue: In Chile the rescued workers were offered payments on the order of one million dollars each, while in Mexico the relatives from Pasta de Conchos were offered miserly payments equal to only seven thousand dollars for each family of the deceased miners. This was in 2006, a year in which the income of Grupo México was on the unprecedented order of $6 billion.

When twenty-nine workers died in a tragic accident at a coal mine in West Virginia in April 2010, President Barack Obama himself went to the site of the accident on two different occasions. He ordered an investigation into who was at fault for the accident, but he also immediately pushed through reforms aimed at preventing other industrial homicides in the mines throughout the country. In the end, payments of three million dollars were ordered for each family of the miners killed.

The outcomes of these mining tragedies in other countries puts Mexican government leaders and the owners of the mining companies in a very poor light. Neither President Vicente Fox nor Germán Larrea ever visited the relatives, either to express their condolences or to offer technical, financial, or material help that would have enabled the rescue to continue. President Felipe Calderón also has not visited in the more than seven years since the Pasta de Conchos disaster and continues to ignore his responsibility in this matter.

The insensitive and egotistical attitude has continued in Mexico, since Calderón has not taken a single step to rescue the sixty-three bodies that remain abandoned in Pasta de Conchos. He also has done nothing to help the families or to make fair and respectable payments, much less to criminally prosecute those responsible for the catastrophe. Of course, neither Grupo México nor the governments of Fox and Calderón have ever wanted to know the true causes of the explosion, because that would display for all to see the irresponsibility, abuses, and criminal negligence of Larrea, his board of directors, and his management staff, exposing them to criminal prosecution.

Thus, we celebrated the rescue of our mining comrades in Chile with the rest of the world, but not without a heaviness of heart. It was impossible not to speculate what the outcome would have been had the labor department forced Grupo México to carry on its rescue efforts for even as little as seventeen days, rather than the mere five allowed. Because it is a question we will never know the answer to, all we can do is fight tirelessly, day to day, as hard as we can, to bring to justice the criminals responsible for the deaths and to ensure that corporate greed and governmental deceit do not take the lives of any more of our colleagues and friends.

EIGHTEEN

THE TRICK

It is strange how casually the wicked believe
everything will turn out well.
—VICTOR HUGO

On September 24, 2009, Felipe Calderón appointed a new attorney general to head up the PGR. His pick was a close friend of his, Arturo Chávez Chávez, a former director of government in Abascal's interior department. Chávez lacked the ability or experience for the job of attorney general, and he had taken part in authorizing the deployment of armed forces against the striking workers at the Sicartsa mill at Lazaro Cárdenas in 2006. He was also widely criticized in the press for mishandling the investigation of mass murders of women in Ciudad Juarez. A cable leaked by Wikileaks in 2011 would later reveal the United States' opinion that Chávez's appointment was "totally unexpected and inexplicable." To us, the appointment was absurd, but not inexplicable: Chávez was supported by Grupo México. Even though Calderón knew his friend wasn't qualified for the position of attorney general, the company had forced him to appoint Chávez. As usual, it was as if Grupo México held the president hostage, and it succeeded in getting a new PGR head who would protect its interests.

Despite the ongoing appointment of antiunion officials to top government positions, the injustices at Cananea, and the imprisonment of Juan Linares, the justice system—with all its flaws—had helped us resist the attacks of reactionary corporations and politicians. I am proud to say that there *are* judges in Mexico who act independently of individuals like Germán Larrea and Javier Lozano, and who work to maintain the unbiased administration of justice. Finding this justice in a country like Mexico is a slow, grueling process, but in the end, truth prevails. In 2009 and 2010, we began to see some of the long-awaited rewards of our legal struggle.

On March 13, 2009, the Eighteenth Court in Criminal Matters of the Federal District, which had inherited the banking fraud charges from state officials in San Luis Potosí, refused to issue an arrest warrant against me, citing the fact that there was no evidence of any illegal activity. The PGR appealed the cancellation of the arrest warrant, but three judges from the Second Criminal Court of the Supreme Court of Justice confirmed the decision in my favor that September. The file was then referred to the PGR, who at last approved the proposal to cancel the prosecution of the alleged crime. That was one of the three state charges down, thanks to the excellent work of Marco del Toro and the rest of his team.

The Fifty-first Court of the Federal District, which had inherited its charges from the state of Sonora, refused our request that it terminate criminal action against me. However, we appealed this decision and got a favorable outcome: The court passed a sentence of acquittal, and that judgment is still in effect. On January 6, 2010, the judges of the Ninth Criminal Chamber of the High Court of Justice of the Federal District determined in a firm resolution that my defense was well founded. In light of this, it terminated the criminal action and ordered the revocation of the arrest warrant. Once again I was acquitted and declared absolutely innocent.

The result in the Thirty-second Court in the Federal District was similar. We requested termination of the criminal action that had begun in Nuevo León and a cancellation of the arrest warrant. An honest judge declared my arguments valid and complied, ending the charges against me. The PGR, of course, appealed the ruling but was denied, and my acquittal was officially confirmed in July of 2010.

Thus, all the arrest warrants that had originated in the states of San Luis Potosí, Sonora, and Nuevo León were invalidated. At long last, the courts had firmly declared in all three cases that there were no crimes, no damages, and no victims—and that those who presented themselves as victims (Morales and the others) did not fulfill the necessary requirements to be considered as such. It had taken us over three years of tireless effort, but we had finally been exonerated of all banking fraud charges at the state level.

We had also managed to make progress in the matter of the union's sequestered bank accounts, which had been seized right after Pasta de Conchos and again by SIEDO at Gómez Mont's request in December of 2008. (The personal accounts have proved a more difficult matter; they remain frozen to this day.) Immediately after the second sequestration, the union presented an amparo against SIEDO's unlawful action before the Fifth District Amparo Court in Criminal Matters of the Federal District. Due to the painful slowness of the judicial system, the judge did not pass sentence on this appeal until May 13, 2009. We were disheartened to find out that he had dismissed it.

Of course we appealed the sentence, and on August 13, 2009, the judges issued another ruling, this time in our favor. The court granted the amparo we had requested against the sequestration. From that moment on, the PGR, through SIEDO, was under the obligation to obey the ruling and unfreeze the accounts. Sadly, things don't work that way in Mexico, especially when powerful individuals don't want it to.

On August 25, 2009, SIEDO did comply with the ruling regarding the sequestration, but that same day it issued a new sequestration order, allegedly for reasons different from those that had justified the first sequestration. We presented a complaint, and in October 2009, the amparo court requested that SIEDO obey the original ruling. The second sequestration, said the judges, lacked sufficient grounds, just as the first had. As if it were nothing but a game, SIEDO issued yet another sequestration order a few days later. We filed an amparo and several months later got a third ruling in our favor.

The process was repeated a fourth time, but this time SIEDO's head, Marisela Morales Ibañez, unbelievably claimed that the government should retain control of the funds because they were "suspicious" the

miners might use the money to buy drugs. This flimsy argument, an absolute embarrassment, was covered in the global media but largely obscured
from the Mexican public. (Three weeks after the release of the Wikileaks
cable calling Attorney General Chávez's suitability into question, Calderón
would pull him out of that role and replace him with Morales Ibañez.
Thanks to her aggressive efforts against the miners, exemplified by this
outrageous accusation, she had won Grupo México's stamp of approval.)

We won a fourth trial against the sequestration, the judges ruling
unanimously in our favor. True to the farcical nature of these proceedings,
another sequestration order was issued. At this point we had no choice
but to present charges against the state and the public officers who were
allowing these spurious proceedings. On September 6, 2011, SIEDO
finally obeyed the courts and canceled the last of its sequestrations without issuing orders for another one. After nearly three years of intense legal
defense, the union had finally regained control of its bank accounts.

With the state charges having been knocked down one by one, the
main legal issue I now faced was the renewed federal charges. In 2009, the
PGR had given the banking fraud charges (which stated that the extinguishment of the $55 million Mining Trust had been illegal) new life when
it hid the banking commission's report and re-filed the case against me
and three other executive committee members. Juan Linares had been
jailed under that arrest warrant. But the same year, the PGR—through
SIEDO—also decided to try its hand once more at money-laundering
charges. Under these, it was declared that every use of the funds resulting from the supposedly illegal extinguishment of the trust were "from an
illicit source," which they claimed constituted money laundering.

SIEDO had previously tried this money-laundering maneuver back
in 2006, but the judge overseeing the matter had denied the arrest warrants and stated that "not only were there no indications of an illegal
source of the assets, but there is clear proof of their legal origin," and "in
any case . . . we can affirm from the documents that the assets belong
to the National Union of Mine, Metal, Steel and Allied Workers of the

Mexican Republic." But in SIEDO's second attempt to work the money-laundering angle, it hid the 2006 resolution from the court and again asked for arrest warrants for me and the others. Contrary to all logic, the federal Ninth District Court agreed and issued the warrants.

In response, we presented an appeal for amparo before the Tenth District Amparo Court in Criminal Matters of the Federal District. Marco del Toro presented the abundant proof of the unconstitutional nature of the warrant. On February 26, 2010, the judge in charge of the trial agreed with him and declared the arrest warrant unconstitutional. SIEDO, of course, filed an appeal, but it was filed by lawyers hired by Grupo México, not SIEDO's own representatives. There is no decent explanation for why this would be—a private firm's legal team has no place working on behalf of SIEDO or anyone else in the attorney general's office.

On December 14, 2010, the judges of the First Collegiate Circuit Court in Criminal Matters of the Third Circuit dismissed SIEDO's appeal, and a month and a half later, the arrest warrant against me was canceled in accordance with the ruling. Notwithstanding this cancellation, once again the PGR appealed—again with the support of the lawyers from Grupo México. It truly is a never-ending story.

The legal headway we were making in Mexico was encouraging but also torturously slow. To get faster recognition of the spuriousness of the accusations, I told Marco del Toro that I wanted to appear directly before the Canadian courts for my supposed crimes. I knew that, there, I could easily display the political persecution of the Mexican government. In accordance with my request, Marco designed a strategy that he said had never been attempted but that he believed was our best hope. As soon as I heard his plan, I gave him the go-ahead.

In order to claim political persecution, I would need the Mexican government to formally attempt to extradite me to face a crime. They supposedly had tried to extradite me back at the beginning of the conflict, in 2006, but they hadn't sent any of the revived charges to Canada as basis for extradition—even though government officials

I presented an amparo against Interpol's involvement in the case, especially since it continued to be in effect after more than two years since the arrest warrants on which it was based were retracted. Despite this, the Mexican authorities have refused to cancel the alert, and it remains in place to this day.

I have come to see that in judicial matters Mexico is a country of lights, shadows, and shades of gray; it is not black and white. There are judges who tremble before any order from Los Pinos, the Department of Labor, or high levels of the PGR. There are other judges who have a taste for the easy money that flows from the pockets of Germán Larrea and his gang. Yet there are some true Mexican judges, upright persons of law who do not crumble under pressure and who cannot be bought. I've met judges who fall into each of these categories. If only we could choose the honest judges to oversee our cases every time, this legal farce might not have dragged on so long.

While I fought my battle against the government's illicit charges, our colleague Juan Linares was still in jail. Since his unlawful arrest, Juan's ongoing imprisonment had caused an international outcry from the labor community and many human rights activists. The United Steelworkers were especially supportive, raising awareness and significant funds to aid Linares by selling "Free Juan Linares" T-shirts and taking up donations from members. I will forever be deeply appreciative to Steve Hunt, director of the USW's District 3, who had this idea, and to all his colleagues and staff, who have been our family during our stay in British Columbia, as well as to Ken Neumann and Leo Gerard, the USW's national director for Canada and the USW's international president, respectively.

Impeding our defense team's efforts on behalf of Juan was Germán Larrea's refusal to testify in court. He had blatantly disregarded the summons to appear, but Judge José Miguel Trujillo had reduced the penalty for his contempt of court from a thirty-six-hour arrest to a mere fine (and a small payment was, of course, no problem for the majority owner of a company like Grupo México). Based on Judge Trujillo's decision, Juan pressed charges against him, arguing that the refusal to arrest the witnesses denied him a fair trial. Trujillo had then recused himself. But in January 2011, the case against Linares was reactivated with a new judge: Jesús Terríquez.

Judge Terríquez reviewed the case and, like his predecessors, ordered the Larrea brothers to present themselves at Mexico City's North Prison. Their deadline was January 18, 2011. But Judge Terríquez also increased the penalty for failure to appear from a fine to a thirty-six-hour arrest, determining that a monetary penalty would do nothing to compel them to appear, given their history. Judge Terríquez did an extraordinary job where Judge Trujillo had failed. Before he announced the summons, he confirmed the addresses of the Larreas' homes and offices, checking driver's license listings and sending judicial requests to the tax authorities, phone companies, electric companies, and the Foreign Relations Department. Grupo México's lawyers and the PGR had both tried to block Larrea's testimony with amparo filings, but Marco had successfully argued against them—this time, there was no way for them to get out of testifying. It finally looked like we were close to having Germán Larrea taken into custody.

January 18 came, but Germán Feliciano Larrea still didn't present himself in court. *La Jornada* faithfully covered his evasion of the court order in an article published on the day of his deadline:

> Businessman Germán Larrea, owner of Grupo México, and his brother, Genaro Federico, have been summoned by judicial authorities 19 times and they have not appeared to provide testimony as witnesses in the trial against Juan Linares Montúfar, secretary of the Vigilance Committee of the Miners' Union. Therefore, the twelfth district judge in federal criminal matters ordered yesterday that they both be arrested if they do not appear today at the West Prison of Mexico City, Federal District.
>
> They were summoned for such day and again undertook actions not to appear in court.

Therefore, such judge having issued a resolution that establishes that the businessmen have set up obstacles through third parties and have even prevented the judicial officer to have access to the real estate of Grupo México, in order to avoid that Germán and Genaro Larrea be summoned, and they have even returned the summons documents, now they will be obliged to do so, or they will face an arrest of 36 hours.

Now that Germán Larrea was subject to arrest and had no further recourse but to show his face before the judge, he realized he had a serious problem. The solution he would employ was characteristically sleazy, but it would give us a golden opportunity to give him a taste of his own medicine.

In January of 2011, shortly after Terríquez issued the arrest warrant for Larrea, Juan Linares began receiving visits in his Mexico City cell from Marco del Toro's former partner, Juan Rivero Legarreta. We had dismissed Rivero as part of our defense team nearly three years earlier for trying to betray us. In my absence, he'd tried to convince my colleagues to give in to Labor Secretary Lozano's demands, and he even seemed to be priming himself to take over the union from me. He was revealed as a pawn of Alonso Ancira, a man who was using his position as our attorney to his own benefit and to the benefit of his corporate backers.

Now, Rivero had resurfaced, acting in a new role—criminal attorney for Grupo México—and he had an unseemly proposition for Juan Linares. In his visits to Juan's cell, Rivero told our colleague that he could be out of prison within fifteen days—on certain conditions. The lawyer said he had "passed the tray around" and taken up a collection from a group of businessmen, and they were ready to offer him $2 million in exchange for a declaration from Juan that I had mishandled the Mining Trust after all. Once Juan had betrayed me, he'd be a free, and rich, man.

When Juan called to tell me about the offer, we immediately got in touch with Marco, who suggested that Juan play along with Rivero's game to learn more about what exactly he wanted. He told us that there was only one way Rivero could get Juan out of jail that quickly: his client, Grupo México, had to be able to convince Elías Morales, Miguel Castilleja, and Martín Perales to sign a pardon before the judge. (Of course this was entirely possible; we'd known from the start that these three were pawns of Grupo México.) Since they were the only three parties listed on the criminal complaint, it would be relatively simple.

Juan took Marco's advice and continued meeting with Rivero. As he got more details of the deal, our suspicions were confirmed. Rivero said that Morales and his two accomplices would fully pardon Linares, as they'd been instructed by the companies who'd put together the $2 million bribe: Grupo México, Grupo Peñoles, and Altos Hornos de Mexico.

After a few more meetings, Rivero presented Juan in jail with a contract that would finalize the deal. It stated that Juan was the provider of a vague service—he was to make a contribution that would "bring peace to the mining sector." Rivero, who is listed on the contract as the party receiving this service, explained to Juan that this phrase referred to his obligation to align with Morales, Castilleja, Perales, Pavón, Zuñiga, and the other traitors and publicly state that I was guilty of misusing the $55 million derived from the Mining Trust. According to the contract, Juan would receive a portion of the $2 million immediately upon his release from prison, while the rest would be disbursed in installments over a two-year period, assuming he joined the others in incriminating me.

Marco del Toro advised Juan to sign it. He knew that because Juan was a victim of bribery and had suffered more than two years of unjust imprisonment, the agreement would clearly be null and void. To successfully get Juan out of jail, we were going to have to fight them on their level and play along with their dishonest games. When Rivero returned, Juan signed the contract.

A few days later, Rivero made another visit to the North Prison with a different document, this one stating that Juan revoked the appointment of Marco del Toro as his defense attorney and appointed Rivero in his place. Juan signed that too, at the urging of both Marco and me.

One week later, on February 23, 2011, Juan received notice in his cell from Rivero that Morales, Castilleja, and Perales would be filing their pardon later that day. Within a few hours, Rivero arrived at the prison and from there walked to the Twelfth District Court in Criminal Matters of Mexico City, Federal District. There, with an attorney from his law firm, he patiently waited for the arrival of the three traitors who would shortly be nullifying their complaint against Juan. What Rivero didn't realize was that Marco—who was away on a work trip to Quebec—had sent two lawyers from his firm to be there as well. For the time being, Marco's men waited outside the court, hidden from sight.

Soon enough, the parade of cowards began: Morales arrived at the courthouse, then Castilleja, and finally Perales. They met up with Rivero and made their way into the court, where they filed their document before the judge. Juan was now pardoned of his nonexistent crime and subject to immediate release. The group of traitors left the building laughing and celebrating, with Rivero seeming especially jovial.

But as soon as they were in their cars, Marco's colleagues rushed into the courtroom with their own document. This one, already signed by Juan Linares, explained to the judge how Rivero had attempted to bribe him, and described in detail the attorney's efforts on behalf of his corporate client to frame me for fraud. The document also stated that the just-completed pardon was a legal procedure that, once ratified, could not be revoked.

Meanwhile, still in his cell, Juan Linares received a call from a smug-sounding Rivero. The attorney said he was on his way to get him out of jail, and that he had the first payment ready. They would leave together to meet the press, the attorney said, where Juan would proclaim my guilt.

But as soon as Rivero finished speaking, Juan said, "I never want to have anything to do with you, ever again." With nothing more, he hung up the phone. Just a couple of hours before, Juan had officially reinstated Marco as his defense lawyer.

It was approximately 2:00 a.m. on February 24, 2011, when Linares left the Mexico City North Prison forever. He had been locked up for more than two years, but the judge had upheld the pardon issued by Morales and his accomplices. Just after the procedure was complete, Juan called me, as we had agreed, and I congratulated him effusively. Outside the prison, a large group of fellow miners had gathered to greet him. Juan Linares left prison with his head high, having proven himself loyal to Los Mineros—and the truth—right to the end.

For his part, Rivero had blatantly broken the law, committing the crime of prevarication under Mexican law. An abundance of evidence— letters, documents, official complaints, and statements—proves the misconduct of this lawyer who cynically turned from defending the union to outright attacks upon it.

The ongoing conflict between the Los Mineros, the mining companies of Mexico, and the country's government has revealed the cowardice and weak character of some—Elías Morales and Carlos Pavón being prime examples—and shown the unflagging loyalty of others. The latter has been the case of Juan Linares, whose commitment to his colleagues helped him bear the dreadful conditions in which he was living for two years, two months, and twenty days in jail. Juan always said that he was willing to spend whatever time was necessary in prison until I was reinstated as general secretary of the union and until this whole conflict was over.

Upon his release, Linares immediately resumed his duties with the Miners' Union, ready to rejoin the struggle for the continued independence of our union. His example stands in contrast to that of many others who have become agents of the ongoing attacks on Los Mineros. With their actions they have demonstrated their cowardice and hypocrisy.

Many of them espouse lofty ideals and claim to respect the workers of Mexico even as they act directly against them. They take bribes from company coffers, which are full of money earned thanks to the sacrifices of the miners. Yet Los Mineros remain thankful for our loyal core, made up of people whose actions back up their ideals and have the courage and commitment to stand up and fight back for justice, respect, and dignity.

NINETEEN

THE EXILE

*No matter how long the storm, the sun always returns
to shine through the clouds.*
—KHALIL GIBRAN

The current state of the mining conflict is far from ideal, but in the six years since it began, we have followed many tragedies and obstacles with hard-won successes. I am proud to have led Los Mineros through this David-and-Goliath struggle against abusive capital, and it heartens me to see so many risking everything to defend their right to dignity, safety, and fair compensation. We have been unbending in our insistence on our members' right to elect their own leaders, without the interference of corporate-backed public officials—and we will not stop until Grupo México and their governmental collaborators are held responsible for Pasta de Conchos. Our fight has taken a toll on each one of the union's members, and several have lost their lives while supporting the cause of their fellow workers—among them Mario Alberto Castillo and Héctor Alvarez Gómez, killed in the attack on Lázaro Cárdenas; Reynaldo Hernández, assassinated at the La Caridad mine in Nacozari; and Juventino Flores Salas, murdered by Carlos Pavón's company-backed gang of traitors at the silver mine in Fresnillo.

The aggression and criminal acts of Grupo México, Grupo Peñoles, Grupo Villacero, and Altos Hornos de México continues up to this day. These corporate entities may be competitors in their field, but they are collaborators against unionism. The situation in Cananea is far from ideal, though the fight continues, as it does in the mines at Taxco and Sombrerete. July 30, 2012, marked the fifth year of the union's strikes in those three union sections—with no solution offered by the company or the government. They have become the longest and strongest strikes in the history of Mexico. The workers in these sections continue their strike, unbending and united in solidarity with the whole of Los Mineros. They know we have honored our commitment to them with honesty and dignity and that neither the union's executive committee nor I personally will ever abandon them. How could we not be inspired by these heroic miners? Each year, on July 30, we hold rallies across Mexico in support of them. Resolving these strikes and forcing Grupo México to recognize its obligations to its employees is our next priority. Cananea will rise again.

Meanwhile, the failure of the impotent company unions has continued. In the few sections that decided—under duress and threats from the companies and the government—to leave the union, abuses have escalated to an unacceptable level. In 2011, six workers were killed in Grupo Peñoles's silver mine in Fresnillo, where workers are represented by Carlos Pavón's sham of a union. Those deaths brought the total number of fatalities in Peñoles operations to twenty for the year. We still hope to reclaim those sections that were intimidated into voting for these completely impotent unions.

Los Mineros has made great strides on behalf of the workers, the vast majority of which have remained in the organization. First and foremost, our union has not collapsed as its enemies so dearly hoped it would. I have had to lead the union from abroad thanks to the real threat of political persecution, but the members have shown ongoing support for the leaders they elected, knowing that to allow the labor department to dictate the union's head would be disastrous. At each one of the annual national conventions of the Miners' Union since the conflict began, I have been unanimously reelected as general secretary six times so far. The last election occurred in May 2012, and there I was appointed president and general secretary. It's clear proof that the workers of the union acknowledge the lies and slander of the government as what they are: the maneuvers of a power structure that is terrified of an unshackled labor union.

In response to the onrush of absurd allegations that began with Morales's "mother claim" against me and five others in 2006, we have decided to take the legal road. Neither I nor any of my colleagues committed any crime, and we cannot allow anyone, especially corrupt businessmen and politicians, to quash an organization that represents thousands upon thousands of workers. We may stand in the way of their ambition and greed, but to us, that is no reason to back down.

Yet, six years after the original accusation, the infamous $55 million is still used to slander opponents of the Mexican right wing. During the run up to the presidential election of 2012, opponents of PRD candidate Andrés Manuel López Obrador tried to discredit him by claiming that his campaign had been funded in part from the extinguished Mining Trust—a lie, of course.

The slow progress of justice does continue, with the help of our outstanding legal counselors. Marco del Toro has proven himself a legal technician of great ability and incorruptible ethics. He and his team have coordinated ably with the office of our labor attorneys, Nestor de Buen and Carlos de Buen, who have done extraordinary work as well. Their reputation for honesty and skill is richly deserved. Our tax lawyers at the José Contreras y José Juan Janeiro law firm and our civil law specialists, Jesús Hernández and his son Juan Carlos, have been protecting us with their professional skills from rigged audits and other abuses of the Mexican government. The members of our Canadian legal team, too—David, Rick, Tamara, Erick Gottardi, Lorne Waldman, and Ryan Rosenberg—who work mainly on matters related to extradition, have been true defenders of justice and ardent believers in our cause. They are firm in their commitment to not allow the corruption of the Mexican justice system to be transferred to Canada. The political cost that the extreme right-wing governments of Vicente Fox and Felipe Calderón are going to pay as a result of their actions will be enormous in the years to come.

In January 2011 our attorneys secured the cancellation of the arrest warrants against me and five other colleagues that had been issued in

2009 during the second wave of money-laundering accusations. It was an enormous legal victory for the Miners' Union. This nullification constituted the total termination of the issue and paved the way for my return to Mexico. In a press release dated Wednesday, February 2, 2011, we confirmed that of eight arrest warrants that existed in the past, seven had been categorically and definitively canceled in different courts. On April 27, 2011, Judge Miguel Angel Aguilar López confirmed once again my complete innocence of the absurd money-laundering charges. And in May of 2012 came two more important rulings: The last fraud charges against me were struck down, and the Supreme Court finally ruled on the lawsuit we had presented against Labor Secretary Lozano, finding that he had acted unlawfully when he denied me the *toma de nota* back in 2008. It took four years, but my legal status as general secretary of Los Mineros was at last restored.

Regardless of our legal victories, I write this book with the absolute serenity of knowing that I am innocent. It is for my ideas that I have been persecuted. It is because I raised my voice at Pasta de Conchos and said that Germán Larrea has hidden the truth with the help of government officials. History will have the last word. This kind of conduct cannot be kept up forever. In the fight he picked with our union, Germán Larrea has paved the way to his Waterloo. Sooner or later his lies will catch up with him, and I'm waiting for him, ready to deliver the final blow.

We have taken the legal road because we cannot stand by while an entire system of corruption and impunity is perpetuated in our country. We are committed to showing that we stand for more than idle talk about principles and progressive values—that we employ honesty and integrity in our public and our private lives. We want Mexico to be a country where the rule of law prevails over hollow and demagogic statements, a country that ensures respect, justice, and equality for the majority of the population.

What these arrogant individuals have done is a shame that will permanently mark their lives. The workers and the people will always call them what they are: criminals. Their violations of human rights occur not only in Mexico but everywhere they operate; many of the most abusive companies, Grupo México included, are transnational, and they exploit workers not only in our country but in others around the world.

My stay in Canada is, nevertheless, a peculiar situation. Though Canadian officials exhaustively reviewed the extradition case sent by Calderón and concluded I was guilty of no crime of any kind, I cannot leave this country, partly because of Interpol's outstanding Red Notice against me. Canada has opened its doors to me, and I have always traveled with complete freedom, but I'm not sure what would happen were I to leave this country and return to Mexico. For my family and me this has been a process of gradually adapting, but we know very well that it is not acceptable to allow corruption and evil to triumph.

My separation from my homeland has been difficult, but the support I have received from Oralia has been incredibly valuable, and she has given greatly to the workers' cause. She abandoned her peaceful and professional life to join us on a journey that has been at times bitter and frustrating. But the members of Los Mineros value, understand, and respect her deeply. Not long ago, women were not accepted in the mines and often were disregarded at possible participants in such a dangerous, manly endeavor. But Oralia's example has contributed to the growing acceptance of women in our field. Now, women are welcomed and encouraged to involve themselves in union activities and leadership. Perhaps, someday, Los Mineros will have its first female general secretary. Oralia recently accepted the honorary presidency of the National Women's Front in Struggle for the Dignity of Workers of Mexico and the World, an organization that began with the solidarity of wives and female workers from the sections on strike in Cananea, Taxco, and Sombrerete. Today, the Front's actions have expanded to the other union sections in the country and to other union organizations, including the members of Mexican Electrical Workers' Union (SME) and the members of Atenco, among many others, including unions in other countries.

Through the sadness over Pasta de Conchos and the anger at the abuses that allowed it and the continuing repression of Los Mineros, international support has buoyed all of our spirits as we persist in our fight. In April 2011, I was humbled to learn that I had been selected to

receive the most important distinction in the labor world: the prestigious International George Meany–Lane Kirkland Human Rights
Award, given to those who struggle for human rights and social justice.
This award is given annually by one of the most important union groups
in the world, the American Federation of Labor–Congress of Industrial
Organizations, AFL-CIO. Then, in May 2011, my colleagues Jyrki Raina,
general secretary of the International Federation of Metalworkers (IMF),
and Manfred Warda, general secretary of the International Federation of
Chemical, Energy, Mine and General Workers' Unions (ICEM), nominated me to receive the prestigious Arthur Svensson Award of Norway,
citing the relentless struggle we have waged for union autonomy and
freedom in Mexico and our commitment to emerge victorious in this
fight against a government that suppresses its people and its workers.
I was also nominated to receive the Edelstam Prize in Sweden, which
is awarded for "outstanding contributions and exceptional courage in
standing up for one's beliefs in the Defence of Human Rights."[3]

Over the past six years, we have been the grateful recipients of the
encouragement and friendship of colleagues throughout the world—
particularly of Leo Gerard and the USW, with whom we continue to
explore a formal unification in defense of workers' rights in Mexico,
Canada, the United States, and the Caribbean. The USW, along with the
IMF, ICEM, and countless other organizations throughout the world,
has flooded the Mexican government with letters on our behalf. More
recently, in June 2012 in Copenhagen, Denmark, I was unanimously
elected by 1,400 delegates to be the first and only Mexican to be on the
executive committee of the world's most powerful labor organization,
IndustriALL Global Union, which represents more than 50 million
workers from 140 countries. Our global colleagues have stood with us
in solidarity. Their support encourages us even more in our efforts to
defend the dignity of workers throughout the world.

Despite the hospitality and justice I have received in Canada and
the kindness of colleagues in many other countries, I still hope to one

---

3   www.edelstamprize.org

day soon return to Mexico, my home. I still keep the baseball I picked up in the union's ballpark in Piedras Negras, Coahuila, the week after Pasta de Conchos, days before I would leave for Texas. I still remember the promise I made, to return to that park one day. I'd hoped that time would come sooner than it has, but I fully intend to keep that promise.

Los Mineros has grown and progressed tremendously during the fight we've been engaged in for the past six years, and adversity has driven us to be stronger than ever before. We strive to be open to change and new ideas. And given the geographically dispersed nature of our organization, we have adopted the use of technology and effective internal communication in a way that many of our peers have not. Aided by the Internet, videoconference tools, cellular phones, and advanced methods of dispensing newsletters, magazines, flyers, banners, press releases, and details on upcoming meetings, marches, and protests, we are proud to be at the vanguard of Mexican unionism.

Abroad, we have built alliances never before seen in Mexico. These relationships form a suit of armor that is almost impenetrable against the aggressions of the Mexican government and the irresponsible companies. Without this umbrella, we likely would have been destroyed. But just as important, these partner organizations give us hope that we are moving toward a truly international workers' movement and solidarity on a scale we couldn't achieve on our own. The governments of every country that supports repression of its workers must learn from this conflict.

In the face of the political persecution of the Miners' Union, we have made it a priority to maintain constructive relationships with the more than seventy companies with whom we have signed agreements. It is our mission that labor unions no longer be seen by Mexican society as corrupt and hostile organizations. In the five years since the conflict began, we have renewed our collective bargaining agreements yearly with overall increases of 14 percent in wages and benefits—four or five times the inflation rate and the wage levels of other unions in Mexico.

These increases are much higher proportionately than the 3.5 percent national average increases that the government authorizes companies to pay, ostensibly to counter inflation. In many cases we have doubled the wages in a matter of five years. These successes indicate that the vast majority of businesses recognize our union, and see that its leadership is serious about defending the interests of workers.

The Miners' Union's recent negotiations with ArcelorMittal—the world's largest private producer of steel—are a good example of the progress we have made. ArcelorMittal is the owner of the steel mill complex in Lázaro Cárdenas, and it had inherited a catastrophically complex management system from the previous owner, Grupo Villacero. In two negotiations, first in March 2010, we developed a "rationality and efficiency" agreement, which stated that one company would absorb the four companies that were previously operating in Lázaro Cárdenas. The new arrangement brought the workers together and vastly improved productivity, and a second negotiation in August 2010 yielded an overall increase of 14 percent in the wages and benefits paid to the union members by ArcelorMittal. These negotiations took place in Canada, led by me, my fellow leaders of the union, and ArcelorMittal Mexico's CEO, William Chisholm, with no involvement on the part of Mexico's labor department.

In February 2011, we also negotiated the termination of an eight-month-long strike at the El Cubo mine in Guanajuato, where the workers of Union Section 142 were demanding that Gammon Gold, the Canadian company that owns the mine, respect their collective bargaining agreement and pay the share of its profits legally due to the miners. We reached a settlement that strengthened the collective bargaining agreement in its entirety, including increasing the share of profits due to the miners, and the company agreed to pay 100 percent of lost wages during the 255-day strike—something most companies would never agree to in Mexico. We also negotiated for three jailed local union leaders to be released; they had been detained under pressure from the company and the authorities, based on false accusations.

The cooperation between the union and companies like ArcelorMittal and Gammon Gold stands as an example of how a group of workers and a company can come to positive, productive agreements that focus both on productivity and the rights of workers, even in the face of stubborn persecution from Mexico's repressive, antiunion government and a small group of despotic businessmen. In these negotiations, my colleagues—both in the executive committee and in the bargaining committees of each of the union's local branches—and I have been the ones who have led discussions with the companies. We have made all this progress without the involvement of the labor department or Javier Lozano, whose dearest but frustrated wish was that the Miners' Union disappear from the labor map of Mexico. The vast majority of collective bargaining agreement renewals were negotiated in Canada with the companies directly, with no invitation sent to Lozano. That hasn't stopped him from trying to prevent settlement being reached, though, as was the case in the El Cubo negotiations. Lozano tried unsuccessfully to take the collective bargaining agreements from members of the Miners' Union—the legitimate owners—and give them to proven traitors like Elías Morales and Carlos Pavón. His efforts failed.

In 2010, Fernando Gómez Mont was forced to leave Calderón's cabinet due to incompetence, like many before him. He sought refuge once again in his law firm, where he continues as a member of the criminal defense team of Germán Feliciano Larrea. His shame will be mirrored by the shame of the others like him in coming years, as the Mexican public comes to understand the deceit and treachery of Presidents Fox and Calderón—presidents who have consistently acted against the interests of the people, always using the justifications that they are advancing freedom and democracy. Having launched their campaign of political persecution against the miners of Mexico, the government officials complicit with Grupo México cannot find a way to end the conflict without revealing their own misdeeds.

Although the PAN routinely accused PRI administrations of cronyism because of a 71-year-long winning streak at the polls, the PAN
has proven itself to be even worse: at least the PRI managed to sustain the political and economic stability of Mexico's image abroad,
something the PAN has utterly destroyed. Polls reveal that few
believe these right-wing lies any longer, as the PAN's reputation with
Mexican citizens has declined steadily in recent years, reaching 20
percent nationwide.

We repeatedly called for Felipe Calderón to resolve the problems
underlying the three ongoing mining strikes and the overarching conflict between our union and the coalition of mining companies and
labor department officials, but the president was stubbornly silent. In
2007, the first year of Calderón's administration, we called at least four
meetings to resolve the conflict, lawfully and with respect for the rights
of the union's workers and their families. In 2008, we called Calderón
three more times, and three more times in 2009. We called twice more in
2010, and have continued to call on him until the present day. We want
no part of the compromises Larrea and his "cat" Javier Lozano propose.
Were we to accept anything less than a full recognition of the negligence
of the labor department and Grupo México, we would tacitly approve
of the unlawful actions of the Fox and Calderón administrations. As we
have always been, we are willing to resolve the conflict within the law.
But we refuse to give them a free pass.

In February 2011, I sent President Calderón a letter and included a
copy of a document I drafted over several months with the help of my
colleagues. Called "A National Plan for Productivity, Job Generation
and Responsible Co-management of the New Mexican Unionism," the
120-page document presents a vision for twenty-first-century Mexican
unionism, and it emphasizes two fundamental and linked concepts:
increased productivity and the creation of jobs, and the role a new free
and independent trade unionism plays in supporting them. This plan
was hand-delivered to Calderón, so I'm absolutely sure he received it.
As we've come to expect, Calderón never acknowledged the document,
much less responded in a meaningful way.

When on February 19, 2011, a group of journalists questioned Javier Lozano on the statements of the respected Bishop Raúl Vera Lopez of Saltillo, who, like the union, bravely and commendably called for the rescue of the sixty-three bodies at Pasta de Conchos, Lozano adamantly refused, saying: "We will not risk more lives only to rescue bodies." I responded publicly to Lozano that his statement was offensive and unworthy of someone holding his office. I questioned whether, if it were his father, son, or brother who were left in the bottom of the mine, would he speak in such a derogatory and insolent manner. He did not answer my question.

A few months before, on October 14, 2010, Raúl Plascencia Villanueva, president of the National Commission for Human Rights (CNDH), publicly responded to a question from the press regarding Grupo México's responsibility for the Pasta de Conchos tragedy. He declared that they are in fact responsible and explained that in his expert opinion the owners of the mine and the public officials belonging to the different departments involved in the supervision of the Pasta de Conchos mine are all to be accountable criminally.

Precisely one day after the interview was published in *El Universal*, Marco del Toro presented a complaint before the CNDH arguing that the PGR had stalled the preliminary investigation into those responsible for the mine disaster, and that their actions constituted a violation of human rights. Although our complaint was consistent with the opinion Plascencia has expressed not twenty-four hours before, the CNDH did nothing to pursue the complaint or compel the PGR to continue the investigation it had abruptly halted in 2007.

A return to the starting point of this aggression and a rescue of the bodies of the sixty-three miners abandoned in the bottom of the Pasta de Conchos mine are the key to resolving the entire conflict. Before 2006, we must look back over a century, to 1889, to find an instance of workers' bodies left in a mine in Mexico—every other time since, the bodies have been recovered. But also, as we have repeated all these years, there must be fair, just, and adequate payment for each of the sixty-five families that lost one of their loved ones in the industrial homicide perpetrated by Grupo México and Vicente Fox's labor

department. That includes, as we have explained in various statements and press releases, that minor children have an education up
through college that is fully funded by the company; that each family
have a dignified and decent household; and that the children and families are guaranteed the right to free health care until the children are
adults. And of course we continue our constant refrain: An investigation must be opened to assign responsibility for the deaths and punish
those responsible. The impunity cannot continue. No one should be
untouchable in Mexico.

For many years the Miners' Union has demanded that Mexico enact
a law that penalizes the irresponsibility and criminal negligence of companies. We have talked with various groups of deputies, senators and
members of different political parties, without any modification of the
law protecting the lives and health of the workers.

For more than seven years, we have sought an end to the mining conflict. How can we resolve an unprecedented siege against a union and its
leadership? How can we best end the series of grave offenses committed against the mineworkers, their families, and the entire population of
Mexico? There is only one way this conflict can be resolved:

- The companies must ensure respect for the safety, freedom, and
  integrity of all the union's members and their families, and of the
  union's leaders. They must see us as active collaborators and treat
  us with respect and dignity. They must acknowledge the value of
  work and see that it is what builds their own wealth.

- The companies must recognize the freely and democratically
  elected leaders of the union, acknowledging that the workers are
  the only ones who can decide who will be their leader.

- The companies must arrange for a legal negotiation of an end
  to the strikes currently in progress. They must fully review the
  proposals and demands of the workers and abide by the commitments they made in the collective bargaining agreements.

- There must be restitution for the moral and material damages caused to the workers, their families, and the executive committee of the union through the tragedy at Pasta de Conchos and the other assaults on our members. The companies must withdraw their false accusations that have served as a pretext for persecuting us and do their best to repair the reputations of all they have slandered, including me.

- The companies and the government must build a relationship of respect with the union, incorporating a "hands off" policy regarding the organization's internal affairs. The union has never tried to insert its members into companies, nor has it ever attempted to impose itself in decisions about a company's plans for growth or investment. We have always been respectful of the autonomy of the companies who employ our members, and it's that same respect that we demand in return. We do not interfere with them and will not allow them to interfere with us.

Despite the brutal war we have been engaged in, I believe that we can build solutions and come to agreements that will benefit all involved. Only after these conditions are met will we be able to build a solution that complies with the law and with the principles of justice. It is a question of political will, of shedding prejudices, and of their ability to view the worker as a vital part of the production process.

This book is my account of our struggle for justice, for respect, and for dignity. It recounts events that should never have happened and must never happen again, neither in Mexico nor in any other part of the world. These events tested the courage and endurance of an important labor union and its leadership. We have faced a backward business sector and a group of self-serving politicians. Absolute power—and its abuse—have corrupted and destroyed the souls of our opponents. In the first twelve years of the twenty-first century, Mexico has lived with the reality of obsolete and pernicious political practices. There have also been viciously demagogic and clumsy deceits that have distorted the reality, not just of the country, but also of the governing politicians themselves and many other persons. These are disagreeable experiences that certainly to a greater or lesser degree are repeated in other nations, since no one in the world is exempt from facing these challenges in life. The important thing is to be prepared and decisive in answering, repelling, and triumphing in each action and decision that we take for our own good and that of our families, but also our dignity and desire to overcome and the ongoing realization that we would all have.

I hope that this book leads its readers to the inescapable and absolutely vital conclusion the we must all struggle constantly for a better world, to rescue what is most valuable about humanity—its principles and fundamental values. I hope that the courageous and steadfast miners of our union become an inspiration to workers around the world. I know they have been to me. When I was first elected, my father was the example of a hero I strove for; now, my example and inspiration is the workers themselves (though I still think of my father often, and know that wherever he is, he looks upon our fight with a smile of satisfaction).

Ours has been a true and extreme test of life, of survival and moral triumph, which will inevitably become a victory in fact, over the moral poverty of those who have opposed the changes in history and who have cared only about their own personal interests, which are those of an infamous minority.

I very much hope that this book becomes an important testimony in the history of the worker movement and the social struggle in Mexico, in this stage of neoliberalism that has been imposed on us against our will. Many arrogant public figures have not had the ability to see this case as a reflection of the failure occurring in many other countries, which today is in full decadent flower in the world. In Mexico, unfortunately a few backward and self-centered minorities persist in maintaining this situation against the will of the enormous majority of the population.

Mexico can—and must—change. Mexicans deserve better than this. We must learn that we all have the capacity and real power to transform organizations, unions, governments, corporations, and companies, to change the mentality of individuals. Above all, we must humanize—to make humane—the politicians and businessmen who flaunt their exploitation of the workers of our country. Our country needs to learn from and follow the model of developed nations, not just on labor issues but also on issues of education, social programs, and economic growth. We cannot, of course, imitate them directly, but we can learn what they have done to make their development possible.

This tragedy and this conflict must serve as an impetus for change. Even after Los Mineros have fully triumphed over our opponents, our struggle will continue. Every one of us has a role to play in the ongoing fight for the dignity and respect of workers, even if all we can do is tell the story of their fight for dignity, respect, and justice.

For a moment, put yourselves in the shoes of a mineworker who each day enters the depths of a pitch-black mine, experiencing intense heat, solitude, insufficient oxygen, choking dust and gases, and the constant threat of imminent danger. Imagine being in these conditions for eight or ten hours, and spending every bit of energy to extract precious minerals from the bowels of the earth—minerals that help your country progress. Imagine looking forward to the moment when you can leave the mine to once again see the light of day and be with your family, who depend on your wages.

In Mexico today, too many miners can't count on exiting their mine alive or on being able to support their family with the pay given them by their employers. We must work together to change the abominable working conditions under which they labor. It has become a disguised form of slavery, through which wealthy company owners reap ever-increasing profits. These conditions are not unique to Mexican miners but extend to working classes throughout the world.

As June Calwood, the outstanding Canadian social activist and writer, said, "If you see an injustice committed, you stop being an observer and you become a participant who cannot help but become part of what is happening in front of you." We must each stand in opposition to the injustices committed against laborers, no matter what industry or country they appear in. The right to liberty and the right to dignity are rights that belong to everyone, without exception—whether a union member, a student, a *campesino*, a contractor, an intellectual, a politician, or a businessman. We must become promoters of these rights wherever we see them denied. It is only through this change that we can progress, as individuals, as countries, and as humanity.

Epilogue

The Future of Unions

In unity there is strength;
strength and solidarity give the power to win.

—A SAYING OF THE UNITED STEELWORKERS
AND LOS MINEROS

At its core, the battle Los Mineros has waged for more than seven years is not about revenge. Instead, it is a reflection of the ongoing class struggle in Mexico and in many other parts of the world. In far too many places, the working class is being abused. Wealth is firmly concentrated at the top of the hierarchy, and the poorest of the world are getting poorer. A large portion of the wealthy disregards the plight of these people, but some—like the heads of the companies who have persecuted us so vilely—are aggressive and greedy in their efforts to keep the status quo.

Every human being has a universal right to find dignified work that provides fair compensation. The purpose of a union is to help ensure that everyone is able to exercise that right. And a union can't be erased just because a company or a government wants it to be. They are the barrier between the worker and outright exploitation.

Despite the way many businesspeople paint them, it is not the purpose of a union to run down the company, and a unionist is not the adversary of the organization. The purpose of a union is to add a crucial counterbalance to the power of the company. And, in fact, a union can empower workers in a way that benefits the goals of the company as well. Workers are in the trenches every day, and they have a hands-on role in production processes that many supervisors, managers, and executives don't have. When the worker is backed by a strong union, he is a partner with the company, not a mere tool. He can therefore be freed to make constructive suggestions—for improvements, efficiencies, expansion, or any other changes that positively impact the workflow and the company's bottom line. The result is a worker who feels necessary and respected, not marginalized, exploited, and frustrated.

When the worker is respected and is treated with dignity, both parties—laborer and company—benefit immensely. That's why we constantly try to implement comprehensive social programs that include access to housing, education, health care, and insurance. Our aim isn't to drain the coffers of executives but to establish the basic rights of workers, a situation that would often benefit the company more than the savings they win oppressing employees and contractors.

Because defense of workers' rights is going to be an ongoing struggle—not just for us but for future generations as well—we also emphasize the need for organizations that build up workers' ability to lead. We have proposed the creation of a Union Training and Leadership Institute that will build up young and aspiring leaders in the workers' movement. We have also created a national political group called National Democratic Change (CADENA), to open up opportunities for workers to participate in the political arena. And we have also encouraged the development of the Women's Front to Struggle for Workers' Dignity in Mexico and the World, which has waged important battles for the dignity of workers. Oralia has been a key organizer in the Women's Front, and it grows every day, in Mexico and internationally.

The fight for the basic principles of trade unionism—unity, loyalty, and solidarity—must extend beyond the programs of our own union, though. In today's world of transnational companies who are eager to exploit labor, it is all the more crucial that we defend them on a global scale. Without them, virtual slavery would prevail, along with mass exploitation and a loss of hope among the lower classes. A robust labor movement is the only way to effectively counterbalance the growing power and resources of global corporations and also the threats to security from organized crime.

Such an arrangement benefits everyone involved, including the people of a country in general. When the greed and arrogance of a few at the top are held in check by a responsible, honest, and supportive union, society as a whole becomes more equitable and stable. When their greed and arrogance are allowed to run rampant, poverty remains and social frustration festers. And when labor leaders and corporate leaders work hand in hand—with mutual respect and a commitment to the agreements made between employer and worker—the company, too, is allowed to flourish.

It is noteworthy that the countries with the greatest rates of unionization (more than 80 percent of workers), such as Sweden, Norway, Finland, and Denmark, also have the highest levels of operating efficiency and productivity in the world. These countries also have the lowest rates of corruption on the planet, which is not an accident. The distribution of wealth, much more evident in Scandinavia than in the rest of the world, is also closely tied to the high rate of labor organization. Thus, unions are not an obstacle to productivity, efficiency, egalitarianism, or social peace. Rather, they are monitors and guardians of the right every citizen has to equality, security, dignity, and hope for the future.

The same can be the case in Mexico, in the United States, in Canada, in Latin America, and throughout the rest of the world. To get there, we need strong unions that encourage a new type of businessperson—one who seeks to collaborate fairly with workers to increase productivity and efficiency, not one who seeks every way possible to abuse workers and lower their wages. In late 2012, Gina Rinehart, Australian mining magnate and the world's richest woman, spoke at the Sydney Mining Club and made a case for drastically lowering miners' wages in her country—so her company could compete with others elsewhere that pay workers $2 a day. Before that, she'd said that if poor people are "jealous" of the wealthy, they should "do something to make more money [themselves]—spend less time drinking or smoking and socializing, and more time working." These absurd and small-minded attacks epitomize the type of business leader the unions need to counterbalance.

Unfortunately, and despite the benefits, the global rate of unionization has decreased. Employers resist making the effort to collaborate; in many places, unionism bears a stigma, and people see it as holding back growth and encouraging corruption; and some union leaders have indeed abused their power and not proven themselves equal to the people who elected them. In cases of the latter, the media magnifies the incident and makes it seem like a fundamental problem with unions, which couldn't be further from the truth.

We face a challenge as we—Los Mineros and workers across the globe—fight for a New Unionism that protects the rights of laborers everywhere. We must build up strong leaders within our organization, leaders who have moral authority and are not afraid to stand up to abuse wherever they find it. We must also promote democracy and transparency within our organizations, so that no one can attack us or paint us as anything but upright and honorable entities. We must educate everyone around us, unionized or not, about the importance of the labor movement, how it protects us from social decay, misery in the lower classes, and corruption in all its forms. And we must never back down when threatened by corporate figures or corrupted governments.

I hope that the heroes who have given so much in this fight will serve as an inspiration of endurance and commitment to the cause. We must all have their tenacity and integrity as we struggle to usher in a new era of unionism that lifts up and dignifies workers—those of Mexico and the rest of the world.

Even after all this struggle against the tyranny of a few, we have not yet seen the flowering of a better and nobler world, where the members of every society can live happily, without the unlimited exploitation that annihilates the most fundamental rights of human beings. But I am convinced that there are many more of us, people with healthy ideas and principles, who will continue fighting until we achieve this highly dignified purpose.

INDEX

A

Abascal, Carlos María, 177, 179–180, 217
  double-talk and double-standards of,
    46
  as enemy of miners, 177
  Gómez Urrutia, Napoleón and, 34–37,
    158
  as Interior Secretary, 34, 37, 40, 42, 171
  as Labor Secretary, 32–34, 40, 115
  support for Larrea Mota Velasco,
    Germán Feliciano, 98, 129
Absolute power, abuse of, 309
  Aceros Planos de México (APM), 146
  auction of, 114
Acosta Azcón, Agustín
  denial of story reported in Milenio,
    258–259
  direction of, from Grupo México, 263
  at Linares, Juan's trial, 254–255
  media appearances of, 254
  son of Acosta Lagunes, Agustín, 253
Acosta Chaparro, Arturo, recruitment
  of, to assinate Gómez Urrutia,
  Napoleón, 223–224, 238
Acosta Lagunes, Agustín
  as former general director of the
    Mexican Mint, 253
  as Grupo México's lawyer, 193
Agencia Federal de Investigacion (AFI),
  46, 260, 289
Agreement 72–73, 87, 159–160
Aguas Blancas, Guerrero, massacre of
  peasants in, 223
Aguilar, Ruben, media campaign of,
  95–96, 103–104
Aguilar López, Miguel Angel (Judge),

confirmation of innocence
  of Gómez Urrutia, Napoleón, 300
Aguilera, Elias, survival of, in mine
  explosion, 89
Alarcón, Javier Lozano (Labor
  Secretary), 248–249
  attention on Cananea strike, 197–198
  bribery of Pavón, Carlos and, 247
  as "cat," 219, 275, 306
  denial of toma de nota, 218–219
  heading of fact-finding commission
    by, 202
  journalists questioning of, 307
  labor progress made without
    involvement of, 305
  as member of PRI, 164–165
  national executive committee in office
    of, 239
  partnership with Gómez Mont,
    Fernando, 249
  as persecutor of miners, 167–169
  pressing of charges against, 219
  resolve to end conflict with union
    members, 215
  Rivero Legarreta, Juan and, 215, 217
Alatorre, Javier, 189
Albor, Mariano, previous criminal
  defense lawyer, 135
Albuquerque, New Mexico, temporary
  relocation of Gómez Urrutia,
  Napoleón to, 108
Alcalde Justiniani, Arturo
  as legal defender of labor, 168
  as outstanding journalist, 191
Allende, 98
Almeida, Jorge, confirmation of, in
  industrial homicide as term, 71

trip to Pasta de Conchos, 56–57

Altos Hornos de México (AHMSA) (steel company), 58, 213
abuse and collaboration in boardrooms of, 142
Ancira Elizondo, Alonso, of, 177
bribery of communications professionals by, 188
criminal acts of, 293, 297
engineers from, 58
government holding company with control of, 267
as largest steel producer, 6, 21, 107
national heritage and, 145
ownership by Mexican government, 227

Alvarez Gómez, Héctor
murder of, 119–120, 124, 297
widow of, 119-120

American Federation of Labor-Congress of Industrial Organizations (AFL-CIO), 302

American Smelting and Refining Company (ASARCO), 257, 262
strike against, 32

Amparo, 135n
filing of, 213
against Interpol's involvement, 290
against JFCA decision, 212
in requesting extradition of Gómez Urrutia, Napoleón, 288–289
against SIEDO's actions, 285–286

Ancira Elizondo, Alonso, 145, 208
accusations against, 107
anti-mining stance with, 164
bribery attempt by, 234–235, 247
as CEO of Altos Hornos de México, 227
as enemy of miners, 177
filing of complaint against Pavón, Carlos and Linares, Juan and Barajas, José, 243
Gómez Urrutia, Napoleón, and, 130, 175, 228–234
prop up of union leaders and then persecution of, 227–228
Rivero and, 213, 214, 215–216, 292

ties to Fox and Calderón, 228
union relationship with, 214

Ancira Elizondo, Deacero, accusations against, 107

ArcelorMittal Steelworks, 6, 124
Miners' Union and, 304, 305

Aristegui, Carmen, as upstanding journalist from MVS Radio, 190

Arizona Rangers, 212

Armenta, Manny, 109
as representative of United Steelworkers Union (USW), 108

Arthur Svensson International Prize for Trade Union Rights, Gómez Urrutia, Napoleón as recipient of, 302

Aspe, Pedro
as president of board of governors of the Mint, 8
relationship between Bailleres, Alberto, 146
as treasury secretary, 8

Atacama desert, xv

Atenco, members of, 301

Atracciones y Emociones Vallarta (gaming company), 249

Autlán Mining Company, Gómez, Napoleón as general director of, 12

Autonomous University of Nuevo León (UANL), 7

Autrey, Xavier, 145

Avcenscio Romero Hernández, Victor, ruling on continuation of strike, 279

Aviation Workers' Union, 163, 179

Azcárraga, Emilio, of Televisa, 163

Azcárraga, Gastón, protection of, 162

B

Bachoco (agro-industrial company), 204

Bailleres, Alberto, 208
aggression against Miners' Union, 267
disloyalty of, 268
donation of money to Calderón, 231–232
fear of angering, 272
opposition to workers, 227
Pavón, Carlos and, 247–248

Bailleres, Raul, 267–268
clandestine trafficking and, 268
mining of mercury by, 267

Bailleres Gonzáles, Alberto
   concern over, 36
   education of workers and, 27
   as enemy of the miners, 177
   as member of board of Televisa, 183
   opposition to Gómez Urrutia,
      Napoleón's run for Senate, 175
   priorities of, 184
   relationship between Aspe, Pedro and,
      146
   wealth of, 163
Banamex, 25
Banking fraud charges
   categorizaton of, as serious, 242
   Mexican banking commission
      investigation of, 241
Bank of Mexico, 164
Banorte, 10
Barajas, José, 118
   Ancira, Alonso's charges against, 244
   avoidance of capture, 251
Barragán, Marisol, 257
"Behind the News" broadcasts, 190–191
Bejarano, René, 253–254
Bello, Marco Antonio (Judge), 275
Beltrán, Sergio, as loyal union member,
   274
Berney, Horwath
   hiring of, by International
      Metalworkers' Federation (IMF),
      192
   union finances and, 193–194
BHP Billiton, common strategies to
   defend their interests, 155
Black Mexico, 47
Bonds, Terry, 109
   as representative of United
      Steelworkers Union (USW), 108
Boot Summit, 110
Bours Castelo, Eduardo, 201
   lies of, 203–205
   on takeover of La Caridad mine,
      204–205
Brando, Marlon, 103
British-Australian Rio Tinto, common
   strategies to defend their interests,
   155
British Council, grant to Gómez,
   Napoleón, 5

Brown, Garret, 201
Bush, George W., 109
Bustillos, Juan, as upstanding journalist of
   Impacto magazine, 190

C

Cabeza de Vaca, Daniel, Larrea Mota
   Velasco, Germán Feliciano payments
   and gifts to, 130
Calderón Hinojosa, Felipe (President)
   appointment of Chávez as attorney
      general, 283
   deceit and treachery of, 305
   government of, 139, 144, 159, 163–
      164, 281, 299
   hostility to Miners' Union, 163–164
   Los Mineros request for audience
      with, 158
   opposition to union leadership, xix
   political prisoners of, 243
   as religious fundamentalist, xix
   resolution of problems with mining
      stikes, 306
   as secretary of energy, 161
   support of business interests, 162–163
   war against organized crime by, 154
   war on drugs, 237
Calwood, June, 311
Camarillo, Pedro, 65
   responsibility for mining inspections, 87
Camilo Mouriño, Juan (Interior
   Secretary), 223–224
   as controversial figure, 238
   death of, in plane crash, 237
   as no friend to miners, 238
   war on drugs and, 237
Campesinos, distributing land to, 120
Camp Hope, xv
Campos Miranda, Jorge, 71
   International Metalworkers'
      Federation's Latin America
      representative, 193
   trip to Pasta de Conchos, 56–57
Camus, Albert, quote from, 125
Canada
   Gómez Urrutia, Napoleón stay in,
      109–110, 301
   yellow unions in, 28
   See also Vancouver

Canales Clariond, Bernardo
    as enemy of miners, 177
    offering of professional services by,
        131–132
Canales Clariond, Fernando, 177
Cananea, Sonora copper mine, 195
    closure of, by Salinas, Carlos, 197
    closure of Workers Clinic at, 198
    conditions at, 196, 199–202
    injury of miners of, 278
    inspection at, 199
    payments to workers of, 31
    privatization of, 145–146
    request for study of, 199–202
    resistance of workers at, 211
    strikes at, 1, 197–198, 210, 217, 240,
        247, 277, 301
Canary, use of, in assessing dangers in
    mines, 78–79
Canavati Tafich, Ricardo, 10
    Serna, Napoleón Cantú's replacement
        of, 10
Cantú Serna, Napoleón, replacement of
    Tafich, Ricardo Canavati by, 10
Capitalism, impact of, 3
Carbon monoxide, exposure to, in mines,
    78–79
Cárdenas Batel, Lázaro (governor of
    Michoacán), 120, 206–207
    demand for compensation of families
        of slain men, 121
    Fox, Vicente, tour with, 129
    Gómez Urrutia, Napoleón's protests
        to, 122–123
Cárdenas Limón, Adrián, 92
Cárdenas Solórzano, Cuauhtémoc
    (presidential candidate), 121
    nomination of, 24
Carrasco, Silvia (Judge), 252, 255, 256,
    259
Carta Minera (Miners' Letter),
    publication of, 13
Casa de Moneda de Mexico (Mexican
    Mint), Gómez, Napoleón at, 6–7
Case 2478, 219–220
Castilleja Mendiola, Miguel
    charges brought by, 252
    as Grupo México lackey, 241
    lies spread to press by, 106

signing of pardons by, 293, 294
Castillo, Mario Alberto
    murder of, 119, 123, 297
    voice of father of, 119
Castro Estrada, Álvaro (Labor
    Undersecretary), 167, 201
Catholic Church, recognition of value of
    work, 36–37
Cedillo, Juan Alberto, 268
Center for Labor Action and Reflection,
    208
Central Light and Power Company, 2009
    shutdown of, 169
Cervantes Calderón, José, 48
Chávez, Luis, 246
    as attorney for Pavón, Carlos, 245–246
Chávez Chávez, Arturo, appointment of,
    as attorney general, 283
Chihuahua, 208
    visits to mines in, 77
Chile, conservative government in, 279
Chisholm, William, 304
CISEN, 97
Ciudad Juarez, investigation of mass
    murders of women in, 283
Clariond, Santiago, as enemy of miners, 177
Clariond family, as enemy of miners, 177
Coahuila, 98, 208
    coal production in, 21, 78
    Gómez Urrutia, Napoleón, visits to, 77
    visits to mines in, 77
COFETEL, 164, 166
Collective Bargaining Agreement (2005),
    90, 93
Collective bargaining agreements,
    disaster-prevention measures in,
    92–93
Colosio, Luis Donaldo (president of PRI
    party), 8, 9
    assassination of, 12
    Gómez, Napoleón's meeting with, 8,
        9, 10
    on selection of candidate for governor,
        10–11
Committee on Freedom of Association
    of International Labor Organization
    (ILO), 218–219, 219–220
Communications media
    abuse by companies, 189

Mexican government's control over, 187

Compañía Mexicana de Cananea
acquisition of, by Larrea Ortega, Jorge, 25
privatization of, 26, 31

Compañía Mexicana de Cobre
acquisition of, by Larrea Ortega, Jorge, 25
privatization of, 26, 31, 145

Confederation of Mexican Workers (CTM), 41–42

Contreras, José, as member of defense team, 137

COPARMEX (Confederación Patronal Mexicana), Abascal, Carlos María as president of, 34

Copiapó, xv

Correa, Roberto, 249

Cristeros movement, 34
Virgin of Guadalupe as emblem of, 40

Croce, Benedetto, 39

Cronyism, National Action Party (PAN) accusation of PRI administration of, 306

Cuban Revolution, 3

D

Darlinda (Oralia's sister)
arrival at Coahuila, 63
nocturnal departure from Mexico, 102

Day of Global Solidarity, announcement of, with Miners' Union, 157–158

Dean, James, 103

De Balzac, Honore, quote of, 171

De Buen, Carlos, 275, 299
as lawyer of Gómez Urrutia, Napoleón, 131
as outstanding journalist, 190–191
supposed intention to negotiate fairly, 159

De Buen, Néstor, 275, 299
as labor lawyer, 168, 215
as lawyer of Gómez Urrutia, Napoleón, 131
as outstanding journalist, 190–191
supposed intention to negotiate fairly, 159

Defence of Human Rights, 302

De Gaulle, Charles, visit to Mexico of, 3

De Hulla, General, 54
de la Fuente, Javier, as head of, 62–63
ordering of miners to use blowtorchs in depth of mine, 81
responsibilities of, for mine conditions, 79, 85
as subcontractor at Pasta de Conchos, 83
threats from, 65
treatment of non-union contractors, 88

De la Fuente, Javier
miners complaints on, 62
request for not taking legal actions, 62
threats from, 65

De los Santos, Marcelo (Governor), 209

Del Toro, Marco Antonio
approval to cancel banking fraud charges against Gómez Urrutia, Napoleón, 284
arguments between Morales, Elias' lawyer and, 253
communication with, 252
decision not to cross-examine Larrea, Genaro, 264
as defense attorney, 213–217, 239, 245, 260
desire of Gómez Urrutia, Napoleón to appear in Canadian courts and, 288
desire to have Larrea Mota Velasco, Germán Feliciano, in courtroom, 255–256
as former partner of Rivero Legarreta, 223
Linares Montúfar, Juan's visits from, 293–294, 295
preparation of defense by, 135, 137
presentation of complaint before National Commission for Human Rights, 307
presentation of complaints on behalf on Zuñiga, 134
receiving of writ by Judge Trujillo, 262
relationship between Garcia and Acosta and, 255
research on Barragán, 257
as supporter of Gómez Urrutia, Napoleón, 131
on unconstitutionality of warrant on money-laundering charges, 286–287

verification of story and, 258–259
visiting of Linares, Juan in jail, 248
Dia del Amory la Amistad ("Friendship
and Love Day"), 41
Díaz, Francisco Gil, Larrea Mota Velasco,
Germán Feliciano payments and gifts
to, 129–130
Díaz, Porfirio, mining conditions in
regime of, 212
Dirty War, detainees and casualties of,
223–24
Durango, 14
Dylan, Bob, 103

E

Ebrard, Marcelo, as elected governor of
Mexico City, 166
Echeverría, Luis, 164
Economics Sciences, University of
(Berlin), 5
Economic Studies Department of Banco
de Mexico, Gómez, Napoleón, as
analyst at, 3
Edelstam Prize, Gómez Urrutia,
Napoleón as recipient of, 302, 347
"Educated Miner," 26–27
El Cubo mine (Guanajuato)
negotations of, 305
strike at, 304
Electrical Workers' Union, 163
Elizalde, Benito Ortiz, expel of, from
national convention of Miners'
Union, 18
El Palacio del Hierro (department store
chain), 146, 268
El Universal (paper), antiunion articles
in, 185–186
El Yunque ("The Anvil"), 39–40
Escudero, Ruben, as mine manager, 66
Escuela Libre de Derecho, 164
Esponda, Julio, 238–239, 249–250
Estrada, Castro, pressing of charges
against, 219
Estrella, Héctor Félix, 241
accusations against, 107
arrest warrant for, 134
government authorization of searches
of, 132
as union's secretary treasurer, 52, 55

Eureka Committee, Nájera, Andrés as
president of, 224
European Organization of Economic
Development, studies conducted by, 33
Extradition, 287
Extraordinary National Convention
(April, 2007), 179
Extraordinary National Convention
(March 16 and 17, 2006), 109

F

Fabio Beltrones, Manlio, 225
Faculty of Economics at the National
Autonomous University of Mexico
(UNAM), 3–4
Institute of Juridical Research of, 194
The Fallen (documentary), 90
Familiar, Marcelo, leaving of Mexico, 101
Faux, Jeff, 142
Federal Labor Law, article 132, Section
XVII of, 90
Federal Mediation and Arbitration Board,
192
Federal Preventive Police, 118
Fernández-Vega, Carlos, 149
as upstanding journalist of La Jornada,
190
Fernando Salazar, Martín, prison
detainment of, 278
Ferriz, Pedro, professional fees of, 186
Ferrocarril Endige (company), 249–250
Financial Intelligence Unit, seizures of
personal assets and, 126
Flores, Victor
efforts to reelect as president, 42–43
Labor Congress and, 41, 42, 43–44
labor department support of, 54
reelection of, 62
throwing their lot in with Fox, 176
Flores de la Peña, Horacio, 6
as economist, 3–4
Flores Salas, Juventino, murder of, 269,
270, 272, 297
Forbes, ranking of wealthiest individuals, 163
Fourth Collegiate Tribunal for Labor
Matters of the First Circuit,
declaration of Gómez Urrutia,
Napoleón as legitimate leader of the
Miners' Union, 180

Fox, Vicente (Mexican president)
administration of, xviii, 32, 43, 44, 71,
139, 144, 145, 158, 163, 280, 299
appointment of Abascal, Carlos María
as secretary of the interior, 40
deceit and treachery of, 305
double-talk and double-standards of, 46
guilt over explosion of mine at Pasta
de Conchos, 70
imposition of Flores on Labor
Congress, 43–44
interests in businessmen, 33
labor department of, as antiunion, xvii
lies and slander of, 124
Moreira, Humberto's, public
allegations against,
171–173, 179
neglect in visiting scene, xvi
non-appearance of, at mine, 67
opposition to union leadership, xix
partnering with Grupo México and
Grupo Villacero in carrying out
intimidation and repression, 115
as pendejo, 168
private companies and, 146–147
smear campaign of, against Gómez
Urrutia, Napoleón, 95–97
stepping down from presidency, 159
Franco, Francisco, 49
Fresnillo PLC, suspension of work at, 268
Fresnillo worksite, set up of Miners'
Union at, 268
Fuentes, Manuel, as legal defender of
labor, 168
Fundidora Monterrey (quasi-
governmental iron and steel
company), 6, 113
bankruptcy and dissolution of, 114

G

Gamboa Patrón, Emilio, 225
Gammon Gold
collective bargaining agreement of,
304–305
cooperation with Miners' Union and,
305
Gandhi, Mahatma, quote of, 113
Garcia, Javier, 85
García, Mario, 117

Garcia, Roberto, 263
García Cisneros Group, 268
García de Quevedo, Xavier, 62, 261, 280
as enemy of miners, 177
flight of, 95
as president of Industrial Minera, 58
public statement made by, 130
García Medina, Amalia (Governor), 270,
271
Garcia Ortiz, Maria, 205–207
Garcia Ortiz, Mario, 205–207
Garcia Ortiz, Miguel, 206
García Puebla, Eduardo, owner of Garcia
Puebla Consultores, 185
Garcia Puebla Consultores
Grupo México's hiring of, 185
publicity produced by, 185–186
Garza, Ramón Alberto, as upstanding
journalist of Reporte Índigo, 190
General Mines Director, 286–287
Gerard, Leo W., 290, 302
Gómez Urrutia, Napoleón and, 98–99,
102, 108, 118
as International President of United
Steelworkers Union (USW), 31, 55
Gibran, Khalil, quote of, 297
The Global Class War (Faux), 142
Globalized companies, working
conditions in, 155
Goebbels, Joseph, 187
Gómez, Alejandro (son)
leaving of Mexico with family, 102
return to Texas, 110
Gómez, Ernesto (son), 111
murder of men at Sicartsa mill and
grief of, 119
Gómez, Napoleón (son)
relocation of, to Vancouver, 111
reluctance of leaving Mexico, 101
threats delivered to, 97
Gómez Mont, Fernando, 249
assurance on ending of conflict, 248
as defender for Larrea Mota Velasco,
Germán Feliciano, 239
desire to be communication bridge,
240, 241, 242, 248
incompetence of, 305
as Interior Secretary, 239–240, 278
partnership with Lozano, Javier, 249

seizure of bank accounts and, 241–242, 243

validation of doubts, 240

Zinser, Alberto's meeting with, 239–240

Gómez Sada, Eloisa (mother), 2

death of, 18

move to Mexico City, 2–3

Gómez Sada, Napoleón (father)

death of, 18–19

decline of health, 15

as general secretary of Miners' Union, 2, 75

involvement of, in National Union of Mine, Metal, and Steel Workers, 1

as leader of Local 64, 2, 13

lifestyle of, 2

move to Mexico City, 2–3

as president of Labor Congress, 13

quote from, 51

relationship with son, 14

as figure in Mexico's labor movement, 13

as smelter, 1, 2, 15

visits to Chihuahua, 77

visits to Coahuila, 77

visits to San Francisco del Oro, 77

visits to Santa Barbara, 77

visit to Real del Monte y Pachuca silver and gold mine, 75–77

visit to steel facility in Lázaro Cárdenas, 15

Gómez Sada, Roberto (brother), move to Mexico City, 2–3

Gómez Urrutia, Alejandro (son), birth of, 5

Gómez Urrutia, Ernesto (son)

birth of, 5

seizure of property belonging to, 222

Gómez Urrutia, Napoleón

Abascal, Carlos María and, 34–37, 158

accusations against, 106–107, 193

Acosta Chaparro, Arturo's recruitment of, to assinate, 238

acquittal of, by Ninth Criminal Chamber of the High Court of Justice of the Federal District, 284–285

action of Interpol against, 289–290

Ancira, Alonso's attempt to convince,

to abandon union leadership, 228–234

Angel Aguilar López, Miguel's confirmation of innocence of, 300

appointment as alternate general secretary, 16–17

arrest warrant for, 134, 267

assassination plot against, 225–226

as Assistant Director for Planning in Department of Planning and Budget at Sidermex, 6

attendance of conference at Autonomous University of Nuevo León (UANL), 7

base of, in union headquarters in Mexico City, 23

birth of children, 5

brush with politics and, 7

calls from Los Mineros to step down, 130

cancellation of arrest warrant against, 287

childhood of, 1

claims of political persecution, 298

as consultant, 13–14

contact between Gerard, Leo W. and, 102

contact between United Steelworkers Union (USW) and, 102

decision to leave Mexico, 99–100

del Toro, Marco, as steadfast supporter of, 131

denial of toma de nota, 218–219

desire to appear in Canadian courts for supposed crimes, 288

as economist, 3, 5–6, 35

education of, 1, 3, 4, 5–6, 347

efforts to charge, 171–172

election as first vice president of Labor Congress, 43

election as interim general secretary of union, 19

filing of amparo, in requesting extradition of, 288–289

at fortieth anniversary celebration of Labor Congress, 50

as general director of Autlán Mining Company, 12

as general secretary of the union, 17–18, 19, 22–24, 27, 71, 182, 347

González Uyeda, Abraham, meeting with, 161
granting of permanent residence status to, 288, 289
grief at death of father, 21
Grupo México and Grupo Villacero challenge to leadership of, 22
Grupo México's support for prosecution of, 181
as head of Miners' Union, 21
implementation of "Educated Miner," 26–27
interest in becoming governor of Nuevo León (town), 8–9
interview with Granados Chapa, Miguel Ángel, 54–55
issuance of humanitarian visa to, 288
job in Department of National Heritage, 6
Larrea, Germán Feliciano, publicizing of bogus charges against, xviii, 125
Larrea Mota Velasco, Germán Feliciano, and, 129
leaving of Mexico by, 100–106
Los Mineros's protests against removal of, 126
meetings with Larrea Mota Velasco, Germán Feliciano and, 29–31
meeting with Salinas, Carlos and, 8–9
as member of IndustriALL Global Union, 347
Morales, Elías's "mother claim" against, 115, 126, 299
"Napoleón for Nuevo León" groups and, 8
offering of support from United Steelworkers Union (USW) and Gerard, Leo W., 98–99
opposition to run for Senate, 175
passion for baseball, 100
passion for transforming Mexico, 104–105
PGR desire for Red Notice against, 289
philosophy of, xviii–xix
presentation of International George Meany-Lane Kirkland Human Rights Award to, 301–302, 347
as president of World Mint Directors Organization, 12

press interviews of, 45–47
protest to Cárdenas Batel, Lázaro (governor of Michoacán), 121
reassessment of, on Miners' Union, 104–105
as recipient of Arthur Svensson International Prize for Trade Union Rights, 302, 347
as recipient of Edelstam Prize, 302, 347
as recipient of International Meany-Kirkland Human Rights Award, 301–302, 347
refusal of state officials in San Luis Potosí to issue arrest warrants against, 284
renewed federal charges against, 286–287
resignation from Mint, 12
return to job at Mint, 12
return to Mexico, 6
Rivero's attempts to get, to step down, 215–216
running for governor, 7
seizure of home in Mexico City, 223
SIEDO charges of money laundering against, 136–137
smear campaign against, 95–97
as Special Delegate to National Executives Committee in Section 120 of La Cienega de Nuestra Señora, 14
stay in Canada, 301–302
struggle for union democracy, 316
support of miners for, 71
toma de nota denial of, for, 300
tour of mines and steel plants by, 21–22
tours of Nuevo León (town) by, 8–9
as union member, 14
in Vancouver, 109–111, 130–131, 137–139
Villarreal Brothers and, 129–130
violent campaign against Los Mineros and, 72–73
visiting with survivors of mine explosion, 63–64
visits to Chihuahua, 77
visits to Coahuila, 77

visit to Real del Monte y Pachuca
   silver and gold mine, 75–77
work of, with executive committee,
   23–24
Gómez Urrutia, Napoleón (son)
   arrival at Coahuila, 63
   birth of, 7
Gómez Urrutia, Oralia (wife), 14, 32–33,
   57
   birthday celebration of, 233–234, 235
   birth of children, 5
   completion of art school, 4
   desire to go abroad, 16
   foreign studies of, 4–5
   as honorary president of National
      Women's Front in Struggle for the
      Dignity of Workers of Mexico and
      the World, 301
   impact of events on, 108–109
   as key organizer, 314–315
   leaving of Mexico by, 100–106
   life in Oxford, 5
   murder of men at Sicartsa mill and
      grief of, 119
   nocturnal departure from Mexico,
      101–102
   planning of special day for, 229
   recommendation of divorce to, 214
   return to Mexico, 5
   return to Texas, 110–111
   sensing of danger and, 71
   at site of mine explosion, 52, 62
   support of miners for, 71
   trip to Pasta de Conchos, 56–57
Gómez Zalce, Marcela, as upstanding
   journalist of Milenio, 190
González Barrera, Roberto, 10
González Blanco, Salomón, 164
González Cuevas, Isaías
   election as president of Labor
      Congress, 42–43
   at 2006 meeting, 41
González Uyeda, Abraham, meeting
   with Gómez Urrutia, Napoleón and,
   161–162
Gordillo, Elba Esther, 226
Gottardi, Erick, as member of Canadian
   legal team, 299
Granados Chapa, Miguel Ángel

interview with Gómez Urrutia,
   Napoleón, 54–55
as upstanding journalist of Reforma
   and Proceso, 190
The Grapes of Wrath (Steinbeck), 103
Grupo Bal
   Bailleres, Alberto, as owner of, 146
   as holding company, 163
Grupo IMSA, as enemy of miners, 177
Grupo Maseca, 10
Grupo México, xviii 18, 29–31, 62
   abuse and collaboration in
      boardrooms of, 142
   accusation of misuse of Mining Trust
      and, 45
   approach to the rescue, 68–71
   articles written about abuses of, and
      their corporate colleagues, 191
   assets owed to union, 39
   attempt to place Morales, Elías at head
      of Los Mineros, 52
   banking law violation invented by,
      107–108
   bankruptcy of, 128
   battle against union by, 106–107
   botching of recovery efforts, 89
   bribery and, 188, 293
   challenge to Gómez Urrutia,
      Napoleón's leadership, 22
   charges of industrial homicide against,
      55, 71–72, 90, 93, 97, 102, 127,
      178–179, 181, 182, 280
   closing of mine after explosion, 69–70
   common strategies to defend their
      interests, 155
   concessions won by, 144–145
   creation of new businesses, 145
   criminal acts of, 292–293, 297
   debt of, to union, 31
   disappearance of evidence against, 134
   efforts to cover criminal negligence
      of, 67
   efforts to provide safe work
      conditions, 55
   efforts to undermine union
      organization, 207–208
   financial interests of, 91–92
   financing of, 48
   force majeure maneuver of, 275–277

government support of, 162
high earnings of, 92
hiring of Garcia Puebla Consultores, 185
hiring of General de Hulla to run mine, 53–54
incompetence of rescue effort, xvi, xvii, 64, 69
interests of, 40–41
investment on publicity campaign against unions, 183–184
lack of effort in meeting needs of demand of miners, 197
lack of investment in safety of coal mines, 92
Larrea Mota Velasco, Germán Feliciano's position at, 29–30
leadership of, 26
Mexican railroads sale to, 41
mines operated by, 25, 26, 163
mining conditions and, 79–80, 85
need of, to recognize obligations to employees, 298
negligence of, 51–52, 90
on not building another exit, 82–83
ownership of Mine 8 of Pasta de Conchos by, 51–52
partnering with Grupo Villacero and Fox, Vicente in carrying out intimidation and repression, 115
persecution of Gómez, Napoleón, 195
PGR coverage for, 262
presentation of false evidence, 273
pressure of strikes on, 197
profits of, 143
publicity campaign against leaders of Miners' Union, 182
refusal to review mine safety conditions, 196
responsibility of, for Pasta de Conchos, 71, 96, 105–106, 115, 141–142, 297
Rivero as criminal attorney for, 292–293
shutdown of Workers' Clinic, 274
smear campaign against Gómez Urrutia, Napoleón, 96
special proceeding of, before JFCA, 276–277

strikes against, 92–93
support for Chávez Chávez, Arturo, 283
support for prosecution of Gómez Urrutia, Napoleón, 181–182
use of de Hulla, General as subcontractor at Pasta de Conchos, 83
violation of collective bargaining agreement with union, 274
worksite conditions of, 195
Zuñiga bought off by, 134
Grupo Peñoles (metal company), 25, 26, 100, 247, 269
Bailleres Gonzáles, Alberto of, 177
bribery of communications professionals by, 188
criminal acts of, 267, 293, 297–298
employment of Gómez, Napoleón by, 14
Grupo Bal control of, 146, 163
Mexican railroads sale to, 41
privatization and, 267
workers killed at silver mine in, 298
Grupo Protexa of Monterrey
purchase of mines, 25
as winning bidder for Compañía Mexicana de Cananea, 25
Grupo Villacero
abuse and collaboration in boardrooms of, 142
aggression and criminal acts of, 297–298
aid to Morales, Elías, 115
battle against union by, 106–107
brutal tactics used by, 124
challenge to Gómez Urrutia, Napoleón's leadership, 22
coffers of, 113
criminal arrangements and, 114
fraud and, 113–114
government support of, 162
influence with Fox, Vicente (Mexican president), 117
Las Truchas steel mill and, 145–146
partnering with Grupo México and Fox, Vicente in carrying out intimidation and repression, 115
purchase of Sicartsa, 114

Villarreal Guajardo, Julio, as leader of, 177
Guajardo, Villarreal, concern over, 36
Gutiérrez, Raúl, accusations against, 107
Gutiérrez, Sergio, accusations against, 107
Gutiérrez Vivó, José, as upstanding journalist, 190

H

Healthy Miners, 27
Hermosillo, 274
Hernández, Jesús, 299
  as member of defense team, 137
Hernández, Juan Carlos, 299
  as member of defense team, 137
Hernández, Raúl, 18
Hernández Gámez, Francisco, 208
Hernández González, Reynaldo, murder of, 203, 204–205, 209, 220, 297
Hernández Juárez, Francisco, 217
Hernández Puente, José Angel, 118
  on explosion of Mine 8 of Pasta de Conchos Unit, 51–52
  return to San Antonio, 102–103
  trip to Pasta de Conchos, 56
Hidalgo, 55
Hipódromo de Las Américas, 29
Horwath, Crowe, audit of union by, 192
Hugo, Victor, 283
Human beings, universal right of, to work, 313–314
Human rights and human dignity, fight for, xx
Humberto Calvillo Fernández, César, as member of rescue team, 67–68
Hunt, Steve, 111
Hylsa (Mexican steel mill), 113

I

Ibero-American University, law school at, 194
Impacto magazine, 190
Industrial homicide, charges of, 55, 71–72, 90, 93, 97, 102, 127, 178–179, 179, 181, 182, 280
IndustriALL Global Union, 302
  creation of, 155
  Gómez Urrutia, Napoleón as member of, 155
"Industrial Minera México" (sign), 57

Institutional Revolutionary Party (PRI), Labor Congress's tie to, 40
Instituto Mexicano de Televisión, Imevisión, 96
International Federation of Chemical, Energy, Mine and General Workers' Unions (ICEM), 302
  studies conducted by, 33–34
International Federation of Metalworkers (IMF), 302
International George Meany-Lane Kirkland Human Rights Award, presentation to Gómez Urrutia, Napoleón, 302
International Labor Organization (ILO), 55, 72
  Committee on Freedom of Association of, 218–219, 219
  Convention 87 of, 209, 218
  investigation of explosion, 91
  Malentacchi, Marcello, as speaker at Geneva conference, 220
  Mexican ratification of, 160
  principles set forth by, 218
  studies conducted by, 33–34
  vindication from, 221–225
International Metalworkers' Federation (IMF), 31
  hiring of Berney, Horwath, 192
  studies conducted by, 33–34
  2006 press conference of, 157–158
International Steelworkers Convention (Las Vegas, May, 2005), 32
International Tribunal on Trade Union Rights, 277
Interpol, action of, against Gómez Urrutia, Napoleón, 289–290
Iztapalapa, 46

J

Jalisco, 161
Janeiro, José Juan, as member of defense team, 137
Javier Lozano & Associates, 165
Javier Salazar, Francisco
  blaming of victims by, 89–90
  calling off of rescue efforts and, 69, 91
  claims of, on inspections prior to explosion, 86

closure of mine after explosion and, 69–70
code name in El Yunque, 40
companies covering for lack of inspections by, 65
declaration of illegal strike, 118
efforts to prosecute for forgery, 133
as enemy of miners, 177
focus of, on financial interests of Grupo México, 91–92
impact of granting of toma de nota, 72
industrial homicide leveled against, 93, 181
as Labor Secretary, 39–40, 58, 171
lack of call for direct legal action against, 142
Larrea Mota Velasco, Germán Feliciano, payments and gifts to, 129–130
Morales, Elías's granting of toma de nota by, 176
opposition to union, 88
as religious fundamentalist, 39–40
removal of Gómez Urrutia, Napoleón as general secretary of Miners' Union, 71
support for Larrea Mota Velasco, Germán Feliciano, 98
Joint Health and Safety Commission, 86
complaints from, 64
at Pasta de Conchos, 54
reports issued by, 84–85, 93
Jonson, Ben, 267
Joplin, Janis, 103
José Contreras y José Juan Janeiro law firm, 299
Juegos de Entretenimiento y Video de Cadereyta (company), 249–250
Junta Federal de Conciliación y Arbitraje (JFCA), 126
call for union preferences, 208
declarations of, on strikes, 198, 211–212, 273–274, 275
Grupo México special proceeding of, before, 276
issuance of resolution against workers at Cananea, 211
Justice, slow progress of, 299

K
Kansas City Southern Railways, 41
Kennedy, John F., assassination of, 3
King, Martin Luther, Jr., 237
Kirchner, Nestor, 110
Kolteniuk, Moises, tried convincing Gómez Urrutia, Napoleón to surrender the fight, 130

L
Labor, Department of
issuance of mining permits by, 84
lack of regulation enforcement, 90–91
mining inspections by, 84
negligence of, 90
Labor Congress
celebration of fortieth anniversary, 50
election of new presidents, 40
founding of, in 1966, 40
Gómez Sada, Napoleón (father) as president of, 13
González Cuevas, Isaías's, election as president of, 42–43
meeting of, in February 2006, 40
tie to PRI, 40
Labor movement, importance of, in Mexico, 32
La Caridad copper mine
labor-related violence at, 202–205
polling at, 209
strike in, 243
La Ciénega mine, 14
Gómez, Napoleón's resignation from, 18
Lagunes, Acosta, efforts to use power to repress peasants, 253
La Jornada (daily paper), 134, 190–191
objective reporting in, 191
story in, on Moreira and Fox, 172
Landry, Carol, 111
Larrea Mota Velasco, Genaro Federico, 261
arrest warrants for, 264, 291–292
efforts to block testimony of, 291
evasion of the court order, 291
as not cross-examined by del Toro, Marco Antonio, 264
order for appearance at Mexico City's North Prison, 291

Larrea Mota Velasco, Germán Feliciano,
33, 71, 162–163, 215, 264, 280
Alarcón, Javier Lozano, as "cat," 168,
219, 275, 306
anti-mining stance with, 163
arrest warrants for, 264, 292
assumptions of, on unions, 152
attention on Cananea strike, 197
avoidance of scene by, xvi
Bours and, 204
bribery and, 247, 290
as client of Rivero, 216
concern over, 36
concessions gained by, 146
creation of new businesses, 145
creativity of, 275
criminal defense team of, 305
del Toro's desire to have, in
courtroom, 255
desire for end of Cananea strike, 205
donation of money to Calderón,
231–232
economic power of, 134
efforts to block testimony of, 291
efforts to prevent court appearance
of, 256
efforts to protect profits, 98
as enemy of miners, 177
evasion of the court order, 291
Gómez Mont, Fernando as
professional defender for, 238–239
greed of, in not preventing disaster,
143
industrial homicide leveled against,
181
Javier Salazar, Francisco's reason for
defending, 39–40
lack of call for direct legal action
against, 142
leadership of, 26, 115
as legal representative of Mexicana de
Cananea, 128
lies of, 300
lobby for natural gas concession, 144
meetings with Gómez Urrutia,
Napoleón, 29–31
as member of board of Televisa, 183
national media blitz of, 184
not afraid of losing fortune in fight

against the Miners' Union, 183
opposition to Gómez Urrutia,
Napoleón's run for Senate, 175
opposition to workers, 227
order for appearance at Mexico City's
North Prison, 291
payment by, for slanderous articles,
95–96
payments and gifts to Abascal, Carlos
María, 129–130
payments and gifts to Cabeza de Vaca,
Daniel, 129–130
payments and gifts to Díaz, Francisco
Gil, 129–130
payments and gifts to Javier Salazar,
Francisco, 129–130
payments and gifts to Muñoz, Ramón,
129–130
position at Grupo México, 30
powerful friends of, 275
priorities of, 184
private meeting of, with Quintero,
Alexjandro, 130
publicizing of bogus charges against
Napoleón, Gómez, xviii
reckless company of, 54
refusal of, to enter own mines, 90
relationship with Lozano, Javier, 306
requesting of documents regarding
audit by International
Metalworkers' Federation (IMF), 194
responsibility for mine disaster and, 67
spending of money toward the cause,
183
statements made by, 127–130
strategy of, against Gómez Urrutia,
Napoleón, 101–102, 125, 129–130
threat of Miners' Union to, 34
wealth of, 25, 163
Larrea Ortega, Jorge, acquisition of
Compañía Mexicana de Cobre and
Compañía Mexicana de Cananea by, 25
Las Palmas, 161
Las Truchas steel mill, 145–146
Latinoamericana de Productos Químicos,
39
LaVenture, Robert, as representative of
United Steelworkers Union (USW),
108

Layton, Jack, 158
  meeting with Lozano, Javier, 169
Lázaro Cárdenas
  armed attack on workers at, 125
  failed eviction at, 130
  invasion of, 122
  meeting of Fox, Vicente's security
    cabinet prior to invasion of, 122
  Michoacán branch of, 117
    assault on strikers at, 117–120
    industrial port of, 114
    news reports from, 120
    protesting of attempted
      imposition of Union Local 271
      from, 115
    Sicartsa mill complex in, 114
    situation at, 115
  ultimate victory of workers at, 123
Lázaro Cárdenas-Las Truchas (currently
  Arcelor Mittal) Steelworks, 6, 15
Lázaro Cárdenas Sicartsa mill, strike at,
  123
L'Ecole des Hautes Études (Paris), 4
Leipen Garay, Jorge, 267–268
  former undersecretary of Energy and
    Mines, 114
Lepanto (hotel), 42
Limón, Leonardo, 7
Linares Montúfar, Juan, 118, 241
  accusations against, 107
  Ancira, Alonso's charges against,
    243–244
  arrests of, 268, 290
  arrest warrant for, 134, 267
  attempted bribery of, 295
  call from Rivero and, 295
  disadvantage of, 264
  fending off of charges against, 251–252
  government authorization of searches
    of, 132
  jailing of, 248, 273, 283–284, 286, 290
  limited protection for, 136
  offering of freedom to, for betrayal of
    Los Mineros, 251–252
  persecution of, 255
  release from jail, 294–295
  Rivero Legarreta proposal for,
    292–294
  as secretary of union's Safety and

Justice Council, 242–243
  taking care of Miners' Union's
    business, 55
  trial of, 254–255, 257–258, 291–292
Lira, Carmen, as upstanding journalist, 190
Local 64, Gómez Sada, Napoleón, as head
  of, 1, 13
Lomelín, Jaime
  CEO of Grupo Peñoles, 272
  education of workers and, 26
  as enemy of miners, 177
London School of Economics, 4
Lopez Mateos, Adolfo
  government of, 143
  as secretary of labor, 164
López Mayrén, Joel, 41
López Obrador, Andrés Manuel, claims
  on election win as fraud, 173
Lopez Portillo, José, 253
Los Mineros, 13, 126, 208
  anger of members of, over
    identification of leader, 72–73
  biannual convention of, 217–221
  calls for Gómez Urrutia, Napoleón to
    step down, 130
  compromising democracy and
    autonomy of, 102
  convention of, in May 2000, 18
  dislike of Morales, Elías, 49
  Gómez, Napoleón's tenure as general
    secretary of, 17–18
  Gómez Sada, Napoleón (father), as
    leader of Local 64 of, 1, 13
  government's oppression of, 169
  growth and progress of, 303
  Grupo México's attempt to place
    Morales, Elías at head of, 52
  international support for, 205–207
  leaders of, 115
  loyalty of Linares Montúfar, Juan to,
    295
  loyalty to Gómez Urrutia, Napoleón,
    109
  Morales, Elías and, 48
  negotiation of wage and benefit
    increases for, 28–29
  negotiations with ArcelorMittal, 304
  offering of freedom to Linares and
    Pavon for betrayal of, 251–252

open aggression toward, 115
opposition to Fox, Vicente's proposed changes in labor laws, 48
protests against removal of Gómez Urrutia, Napoleón, 126
recent developments in campaign against, 111
reliance on legal advisors, 213–217
request for law that penalizes irresponsibility and criminal negligence, 308–309
story of, xx
strides of, on behalf of workers, 298–299
strike by, 116
struggle to secure safe working conditions, 55
support for, 158
violent campaign against Gómez Urrutia, Napoleón and, 72
Los Pinos, 154
Lozano, Javier
in defense of interests of Grupo México, 167
Gómez Urrutia, Napoleón's challenge to public debate, 189
as labor secretary, 166–168
Lozano Alarcón, Felipe, as secretary of labor, 159
Lula da Silva, Luiz Ignacio, 110
Luz y Fuerza del Centro (Central Power and Light), demise of, 249

M

Macroeconomics, 6
Madrazo, Roberto, 174–175
Malentacchi, Marcello, 157
International Metalworkers' Federation's general secretary, 194
as speaker at International Labor Organization (ILO) conference in Geneva, 220
Manuel López Obrador, Andrés, efforts to discredit, 299
Maquiladora Health & Safety Support Network (MHSSN), study of mine, 192–202
Maquiladoras, workplace hazards in, 199
Marti, José, 21

Martin, David J., 288, 299
Martinez, Mario, testimony of, 260
Martínez Molina, Armando, expel of, from national convention of Miners' Union, 18
Martín Perales, José, lies spread to press by, 106
Matamoros, Tamaulipas, 113
Methane gas
exposure to, in mines, 78
gas meters for measuring, as defective, 80
Mexicana Airlines, bankruptcy of, 162
Mexicana de Cananea
Larrea Mota Velasco, Germán Feliciano as legal representative of, 128
privatization of, 127, 145
Mexicana de Cobre de Nacozari, privatization of, 127
Mexican banking commission (CNBV), on banking-fraud investigation, 241
Mexican baseball, 100
Mexican Constitution, 84–85
company responsibility in, 79
subsoil mineral resources in, 143
Mexican Credit Institutions Act, Article 113 bis of, 108
Mexican Electrical Workers' Union (SME)
aggressive actions taken against, 179
agreement not to attend Labor Congress, 44
Alarcón, Lozano's clash with, 168
Calderón's administrations maneuver to destroy, 249
solidarity with National Women's Front, 301
Mexican left, loss of opportunity to create change, 24
Mexican manual labor, exploitation and discrimination against, 148
Mexican Mediation and Arbitration Board, 126
Mexican Mint. See Casa de Moneda de Mexico (Mexican Mint)
Mexican Revolution (1910–1920), 1, 212
Mexico
abuses of law that could be practiced in, 97

capital deficit in, 150
capital flight from, to foreign
    countries, 150
class struggle in, 313
Department of Treasury in, 164
desire for rule of law in, 300
legal, economic, and political structure
    of, 153–154
mining industry in, 311
money to be made off of resources, 147
need for change in, 310
need for new ownership culture, 152
types of offenses in, 242
Mexico City North Prison, 252
Microeconomics, 6
Mier y de la Barrera, Jorge, 167
Miguel Trujillo, José, 253
Milenio (publication), 185, 190
Mine 8, lack of alternative exit tunnel in,
    82–83
Minero magazine, publication of, 13
Miners, education of, 26–27
Miners' Insurance, 27
Miners Union
    announcement of Day of Global
        Solidarity with, 157
    bylaws of, 72
    Calderón, Felipe's persecution of, 163
    creation of opportunities for member
        participation in politics, 27
    election of Gómez Urrutia, Napoleón,
        as general secretary of, 21, 27
    founding of, 55
    Grupo México's publicity campaign
        against leaders of, 182
    Morales, Elías's efforts to destroy
        autonomy of, 96
    prevention of explosion and, 92
    selection of Joint Health and Safety
        Commission at each work site, 84
    signing of collective contracts by, 28
    slander campaign against, 98
    solidarity with United Steelworkers
        Union (USW), 31
    Strategic Solidarity Alliance between
        United Steelworkers Union (USW)
        and, 32
    struggle for better wages and benefits,
        147

taking care of business of, 55
    See also Los Mineros
Miners with Homes, 27
Mines, working conditions in, 76–77
Mining conflict, current state of, 297
Mining Trust
    accusation of fraud involving, 45, 107
    assets from, 192–193
    bank fees for administration of, 193
    creation of, 31
    defending union leaders against
        allegations of mishandling of, 45
    money in, 127
    need for hard proof that money was
        not missing from, 192
    1990 creation of, 202
    ownership of contents of, 128–129
    termination of, 194
Monclova, Coahuila, planning of national
    convention in, 73
Money-laundering charges, SIEDO and,
    286–287
Monterrey, Nuevo León (city), 1
Monterrey Institute of Technology and
    Higher Education, alliance with
    union, 26
Montesquieu, 195
Montúfar, Juan Linares, as secretary of
    the union's Security and Justice
    Council, 52–53
Morales, Elías, 18, 125
    accusations of, 241, 252
    aid from Grupo Villacero to, 115
    ambitions of, 16–17
    charges against Gómez Urrutia,
        Napoleón on inappropriate use of
        Mining Trust, 95–96
    claim of, as leader of miners, 44
    claims of, on money belonging to
        Miners' Union, 127–128
    company-backed takeover attempt,
        95–96
    damage done by, 52
    declaration of workers of Lázaro
        Cárdenas, Michoacán, as terrorists,
        117
    dirty interests of, 22
    dislike of, by Los Mineros, 48–49
    as double-crosser, 24

efforts to declare strike illegal, 117
efforts to destroy autonomy of Miners'
    Union, 96–97
efforts to prosecute for forgery, 133
as enemy of miners, 177
expel of, from national convention of
    Miners' Union, 18
expulsion from union, 22, 45
freezing of bank accounts of
    individuals charged in complaint
    of, 125
as general secretary of the Miners'
    Union, 71
granting of toma de nota by Salazar, 176
as Grupo México lackey, 241
Grupo México's attempt to place, at
    head of Los Mineros, 52
interest in position of general
    secretary, 16–17
labor department support of, 54
lies of, 109
"mother claim" against Gómez
    Urrutia, Napoleón, 115, 126, 299
presentation of toma de nota
    designating him as leader of
    Miners' Union, 47
reputation of, 15
signing of pardons by, 293–294
stripping of official title of, 108
stripping of title as general secretary,
    180
toma de nota of, 62
as traitor, 305
Morales, Melquiades, 165
Morales Ibañez, Marisela, on retention of
    funds, 286
Moreira, Humberto (Governor)
    Abascal, Carlos María's warning at
        inauguration of, 174
    handling of catastrophe at Pasta de
        Conchos and, 62
    inauguration of, 40
    public allegations against Fox, Vicente,
        171–174, 179
    suppression of workers and, 228
Mother claim, 107, 115, 126
Muñoz, David Ibarra (Secretary of the
    Treasury and Public Credit), offering
    of job to Gómez, Napoleón, 6

Muñoz, Ramón, Larrea Mota Velasco,
    Germán Feliciano payments and gifts
    to, 130
Muñoz Ledo, Porfirio, 164
Mussolini, Benito, 49
Múzquiz, 57
MVS Radio, 190
MX (magazine), 187

N

Nacozari mine
    payments to workers of, 31
    privatization of, 146
Nájera, Andrés, as president of Eureka
    Committee, 224
Nájera, Celso, 131
    representation of union by, 106–107
Napistas, 185
Napoleón, Don, 77
"Napoleón for Nuevo León" project, 7–8
National Action Party (PAN)
    accusation of PRI administrations of
        cronyism, 306
    policy toward mines, xvii
National Banking and Securities
    Commission (CNBV)
    formal opinion of, 125
    opinion from, 129
    review of charges by, 108
    ruling on, 126
National Commission for Human Rights
    (CNDH), 307
    del Toro, Marco Antonio's
        presentation of complaint before,
        307
National Commission on Human Rights,
    141
National Democratic Change ("Cambio
    Democratico Nacional" in Spanish)
    (CADENA), creation of, 27, 314
National Energy Regulatory Commission,
    145
National Executives Committee in
    Section 120 of La Cienega de Nuestra
    Señora, 14
National Financial Authority, 127
National Heritage, Department of,
    Gómez, Napoleón, as analyst and
    researcher, 3

National Miners' Union
  insistence on fair treatment for
    laborers, 154
  political persecution against, 153
National Mining and Metal Workers
    Union, 217
  Gómez Urrutia, Napoleón as general
    secretary of, 17, 19, 316
  May 1960 convention of, 2
"A National Plan for Productivity, Job
    Generation and Responsible Co-
    management of the New Mexican
    Unionism," 306
National Teachers' Union, 226, 228
National Union of Mine, Metal, Steel
    and Allied Workers of the Mexican
    Republic, xvii, 286–287
  aggression against, xx
  founding of, 1
  Gómez Sada, Napoleón, involvement
    of, in, 1
National Union of Workers in the
    Exploration, Exploitation, and
    Benefit of Mines (SUTEEBM),
    208–210, 247
  members of, at mercy of company's
    whims, 210
National University Workers Unions
    (STUNAM), agreement not to
    attend Labor Congress, 44
National Women's Front in Struggle for
    the Dignity of Workers of Mexico
    and the World, Gómez Urrutia,
    Oralia as honorary president of, 301
National Workers Union (UNT), 168, 179
  agreement not to attend Labor
    Congress, 44
Nava, 98
Navarro, David, 269
  complaint against, 272
The Nazis in Mexico (Cedillo), 268
Neoliberal economic model, 149
Neoliberalism, 310
Neoliberal technocrats, invasion of, 153
Neumann, Ken, 108, 118, 142, 290
  as national director for Canada United
    Steelworkers Union (USW), 55
New Democratic Party (NDP), 158, 169
Newman, Paul, 103

NINI, 154
Ninth District Court on Federal Criminal
    Procedures, denial of money-
    laundering charges, 136–137
North American Free Trade Agreement
    (NAFTA), 238
Notimex (news agency), 187
Nueva Rosita, Coahuila, xvi, 62, 98
Nuevo León (town), 126
  disappointment in leaders, 8
  Gómez, Napoleón's interest in
    becoming governor of, 9–10
  Gómez, Napoleón's tours of, 8
  invalidation of arrest warrants issued
    in, 284
  political situation in, 7
  state appeals to, 173

O

Obama, Barack
  election of, 238
  visiting site of mine accidents, 280
O'Farrill, Antonio, 106
  efforts to discredit, 115
O'Farrill, Patricio, efforts to discredit, 115
Operation San Lorenzo, xv–xvi
Ordinary General Miners' Convention
    (May, 2008), 180
Organized crime, Calderón, Felipe's war
    against, 154
Ortega, Armando, 263
Ortiz Elizalde, Benito
  as enemy of miners, 177
  expulsion from union, 22
Orwell, George, quote from, 75
Ospina P., Olga, 123
Oxford University, 10
  Ruskin School of Drawing and Fine
    Arts, 5
  studies at, 5

P

Palacio de Hierro (department store
    chain), 163
Paleta, Cuauhtémoc, 41
  election of, as second vice president, 43
Partido Acción Nacional (or National
    Action Party) (PAN), 25, 179
  threat of Miners' Union to, 34

Partido de la Revolución Democrática
(Democratic Revolutionary Party)
(PRD), 24, 120
Pasta de Conchos (coal mine)
approach to rescue at, 68–69
bodies abandoned at bottom of, xvi,
130, 307
calling off, of rescue efforts, 95
collapse of, 53
conditions inside of, xvii, 51, 58, 61,
65–66, 77–78, 80–83, 87–88
creation of commission to investigate
cause of explosion, 141
dead miners at, 78–79, 142
destruction of railway in, 60–61
discovery of bodies in, 106
entrance through inclined tunnel to
Mine 8 at, 80
explosion at, 51, 53, 55, 82, 131, 144
Grupo México as accountable for, 70,
96, 115, 297
guilt of Fox, Vicente, after disaster at
mine, 70
industrial homicide at, 127
inspections of, 84–87
insufficiency of ventilation system of,
80
Joint Health and Safety Commission
at, 54
landscape around, xvi–xvii
media's coverage of, xix, 70, 96
methane gas in, xvi, 80
mismanagement of work site, xviii
missing miners at, 53
reason for Javier Salazar, Francisco, at,
66–67
reinforcement of tunnels in, 82
safety deficiencies at, 91
shift work in, 89
survivors of explosion, 88–89
tragedy at, 145
union complaint for crimes committed
at, 181
union members at, xvii
verification visit to, 87
years since, 217
Pavón, Carlos, 244–245, 268, 297
acquittal of, 248
arrests of, 268–269

betrayal of, 273
bribery of, 247
complaint against, 272
establishment of useless company
union and, 269
filing of robbery charges against,
248
offering of freedom to, for betrayal of
Los Mineros, 251
as pawn, 267
release from prison, 245–246
as traitor, 268
Pavón, Héctor, 269
complaint against, 269
Peck, Richard C. C., 288
Pendejo, Fox, Vicente (Mexican
president) as, 167–169
Peñoles Miners, 100
Perales, Martín
charges brought by, 252
as Grupo México lackey, 241
signing of pardons by, 293–294
Perez, Francisco, decision not to report
to mine on February 18, 2006,
87
Pérez Romo, Gregorio
accusations against, 107
arrest warrant for, 134
Petroleum Workers' Union, 226
Pichardo, Carolina (Judge), 275
Piedras Negras, 98–101, 103
leaving border town of, 101
Piñera, Sebastián (President)
firing of mine officials, xvii–xviii
visit of, to disaster scene, xvi
Plascencia Villanueva, Raúl, 307
Political Constitution of the United
Mexican States, violation of Article
123 of, 91
Political Coordination Board, 277
Political landscape, changes in 2000,
24–25
Pomar, Julio, 224
Portillo, José López (President), 6
Poverty line, citizens living below, 144
Presley, Elvis, 103
Presumption of innocence, nonexistence
of, in Mexico, 97
Privatization

of Compañía Mexicana de Cananea, 26, 31

of Compañía Mexicana de Cobre, 26, 31

policy of, 144

role of family relations and friendships, 146

Proceso magazine, 55, 190

exposure of complicities and aggressions against Miners' Union and its members, 191

Procuraduria General de la República (PGR)

appointment of Chávez as attorney general, 283

coverage of Grupo México, 262–263

desire for Red Notice against Gómez Urrutia, Napoleón, 289

neglect in investigating complaint on crimes committed at Pasta de Conchos, 181

politicians rise of, 125

Productos Químicos de San Luis, 39

Protection contracts, 28

Q

Quintero, Alexjandro, Larrea Mota Velasco, Germán Feliciano's private meeting with, 130

R

Raina, Jyrki, 302

Ramírez, Ulises, 223–224

Rat unions, 28

Real del Monte y Pachuca (silver and gold mine)

Gómez Sada, Napoleón (father) visit to, 75–77

levels in, 76

working conditions within, 76

Rebolledo Gout, Juan

claims on safety conditions in mine, 66

as Grupo México's official spokesman, 66

Red Notice, desire for, against Gómez Urrutia, Napoleón, 289

Reforma newspaper, 55, 190

Regional Conference of IMF of Latin America and the Caribbean, global solidarity resolutions of, 205

Regional Mexican Workers Confederation (CROM), 43

Paleta, Cuauhtémoc of, 43

Registry of Associations of the Labor Ministry, 48

Regulation to the Mining Act, 276

Reporte Índigo, 190

Revolutionary Confederation of Workers and Peasants (CROC), 41–42

Revolutionary Workers Confederation (COR), 41

Rico, Sergio, assurances from, on plans to improve Mine 8, 86

Right-wing politicians, loss of moral compass by, 153

Rinehart, Gina, 316

Rio Tinto Alcan, common strategies to defend their interests, 155

Rivera, Genaro (Judge), 275

Rivera, Miguel Ángel, as upstanding journalist of La Jornada, 190

Rivero Legarreta, Juan, 223

Ancira, Alonso as client of, 216

attempts to get Gómez, Napoleón to step down, 215–216

call from, to Linares Montúfar, Juan, 295

Larrea Mota Velasco, Germán Feliciano as client of, 217

Lozano, Javier as client of, 217

pardoning of, 294

preparation of defense by, 135

Rizzo, Socrates (mayor of Monterrey)

bias toward, 11

as governor of Nuevo León (town), 11–12

lack of businessmen's faith in, 12

relation with Salinas, Carlos, 10

Rocha, Ricardo, as upstanding journalist of "Behind the News" broadcasts, 190

Rocha, Salvador, 254

Rocha Pérez, José Angel

accusations against, 106–107

arrest warrant for, 134

as defendant in mine tragedy, 241

Rodarte, Héctor, leaving of Mexico, 101

Rodríguez, Francisco, as upstanding journalist, 190

Romero, Constantino, as union's
    Secretary of Acts, 17
Romero, Gilberto (Judge), 288
Romero Deschamps, Carlos, 226
Ronquillo Hospital, 198
    meeting with personnel of, 274
Rosenberg, Ryan, member of Canadian
    legal team, 299
Route 66, drive along, 103
Royal Canadian Mounted Police, 224
Ruiz Cortines, Adolfo, 164
Ruiz Sacristán, Carlos, 164

S

Safety and Hygiene Commission,
    repeated warnings of, 63
Safety and Justice Council, 270
Sahagún Fox, Marta, 32–34, 163
    support for Larrea Mota Velasco,
        Germán Feliciano, 99
    support from business sector, 24
    Vamos Mexico Foundation run by,
        146, 228
Salazar Diez de Sollano, Francisco Xavier,
    145
Salinas de Gortari, Carlos
    closure of Cananea mine by, 197–198
    economics studies of, 8
    election of, 24
    government of, 143
    meeting with Gómez, Napoleón and, 8
    privatization of Televisión Azteca by,
        96
    privatization under, 24, 146, 227
    Rebolledo Gout, Juan as former
        personal secretary of, 66
    relation with Rizzo, Socrates, 10
    Sicartsa bought during presidency of,
        114
    simulation of democracy and, 8
Salinas Pliego, Guillermo, 131–132
    as brother of president of TV Azteca,
        132
Salinas Pliego, Ricardo, 164–165
    Larrea Mota Velasco, Germán
        Feliciano's close friend, 189
    of TV Azteca, 163
San Esteban Mining Company
    failure to equip mine with safety
        ladders, xvii
    financial problems of, xviii
San Francisco del Oro
    Gómez Urrutia, Napoleón visits to
        mines in, 76
San José de Atacama mine
    collapse of roof of, xv
    complaints about safety at, xvii
    explosion in, 279
    rescue of miners from, xv–xvi, 279
San Juan de Sabinas, 98
    Gómez Urrutia, Napoleón and others
        to visit, 52–53
San Luis Potosí, 126, 208
    conservative state of, 40
    invalidation of arrest warrants issued
        in, 284
    state appeals to, 173
Santa Barbara, Gómez Urrutia, Napoleón
    visits to, 77
Santiago Papasquiaro (town), 14
Santiago Vasconcelos, José Luis
    death of, in plane crash, 237–238
    as figure in war on drugs, 237
Scotiabank
    acquittal of, 136
    charges against, 136
Sequestered bank accounts, progress in
    matter of, 285
Sicartsa steel mill, 116
    deployment of armed forces against
        strikers at, 283–284
    government investment in, 114
    government's aggressive tactics at,
        119–120
    Grupo Villacero purchase of, 114
    management to keep control of mine
        and plants for five months, 123
Sidermex, 6, 114, 267
Silicosis, 200
Sixth Collegiate Tribunal in Labor
    Matters of the First Circuit, 275
Slim, Carlos, Lozano's aggression against,
    166
Smear campaing, Grupo México's against
    Gómez Urrutia, Napoleón, 95–96
Sobrevilla, José, 165
Socialism, impact of, 3
Social Security Union (SNTSS),

agreement not to attend Labor
Congress, 44
Sojo Aldape, Eduardo, as chief economic
advisor, 32
Solidarity, 179
Solórzano, Javier, 288
as upstanding journalist, 190
Sombrerete, Zacatecas (multi-mineral
mine), 196
conditions at, 196
strikes at, 210, 217, 240, 247, 301
Sonora, 126
invalidation of arrest warrants issued
in, 284
state appeals to, 173
Special Unit of Investigationfor the
Prosecution of Criminal Offenses
Committed by Public Servants,
complaint against the crimes
committed at Pasta de Conchos,
181–182
Stabilizer development, 143
Steelworkers, encouragement of
relocation to Canada, 109–110
Steinbeck, John, 103
Strike, right to, 116
Strikers, assault on, Lázaro Cárdenas,
Michoacán, 117–119
Suárez, Mario, 41
as leader of Workers Revolutionary
Confederation, 49
Subprocuraduria de Investigación
Especializada en Delincuencia
Organizada (SIEDO), 241
amparo against action of, 285
charges of money laundering against
Gómez Urrutia, Napoleón, 136–
137
compliance with ruling on sequestered
bank accounts, 285–286
money-laundering charges and, 286
Sydney Mining Club, 316

T

Tagore, Rabindranath, quote of, 181
Taxco, Guerrero silver mine, 19, 196
conditions at, 196
strikes at, 210, 217, 240, 247, 301
Telecommunications Law Institute, 165

Telephone Workers' Union, 179, 217
Televisa, 102, 130, 146, 166, 218
ads against unions on, 183
Azcárraga, Emilio, of, 163
Larrea Mota Velasco, Germán
Feliciano on board of, 96
ownership of, 188
Televisión Azteca, 96
ads against unions on, 183
Telmex, 166
Ternium, 113
Terríquez, Jesús, 291
issuance of arrest warrant for Larrea
Mota Velasco, Germán Feliciano,
292
Tomada, Carlos, Minister of Labor, 110
Toma de nota, 42, 44, 47–49, 62
Gómez Urrutia, Napoleón denial of,
218
as instrument of political control, 49
Lozano's recent denial of, 240–241
Morales, Elías's presentation of,
designating himself as leader of
Miners' Union, 47
Trade unionism, fight for basic principles
of, 315
Trouyet, Carlos, 268
Trujillo Matamoros, Victor Alberto
(Brozo the Clown), 253
Trujillo Salcedo, José Miguel (Judge)
Acosta Azcón, Agustín's case
suspended by, 259–260
Agencia Federal de Investigacion
(AFI)'s failed searches and, 262
filing of criminal complaint against,
264
issuing of arrest warrant for Larrea
brothers, 264
lack of profesionalism of, 260
recusal of, 291
testimony of Larrea Mota Velasco,
Germán Feliciano before, 256
Trumka, Richard, 319
TV Azteca, 102, 166, 218
Alatorre, Javier, as news director of, 189
ownership of, 188
portrayal of unarmed workers as fault
of violence, 120
Salinas Pliego, Ricardo of, 163

U

Unefon, 164
Union of Miner, Steel, and Related
    Workers of the Mexican Republic,
    assets of, 137
Union Pacific, 41
Unions
    correlation with operating efficiency
        and productivity, 314
    decline in global rate of, 316
    future of, 313–317
    purpose of, 313–314
Union Training and Leadership Institute,
    proposed creation of, 314
United Steelworkers Union (USW), 31, 290
    contact between Gómez Urrutia,
        Napoleón, and, 98–99, 102
    Gerard, Leo, as international president
        of, 31, 55
    Neumann, Ken, as national director
        for Canada, 55
    Strategic Solidarity Alliance between
        Miners' Union and, 32
Uruapan (city), 122

V

Valadez, Blanca, writings of, 258
Valdés, Humberto Moreira, inauguration
    of, 35
Vale, common strategies to defend their
    interests, 155
Valentine's Day, 41
Value-added taxes (VATs), 151
Vamos Mexico Foundation, 146
    Grupo Villacero's contribution to, 122
Vancouver, Gómez Urrutia, Napoleón's
    stay in, 109–111, 130–131, 137–139
Vega Morales, Alejandro, 269
Velásquez, Juan, 108
Vera Lopez of Saltillo, Raúl (Bishop), 307
Veta de Plata, 252
Villarreal Guajardo, Julio
    attorneys borrowed from, 106–107
    inheritance of scrap steel business
        from father, 113
    as leader of Grupo Villacero, 177
    opposition to Gómez Urrutia,
        Napoleón's run for Senate, 175

Villarreal Guajardo, Pablo, inheritance of
    scrap steel business from father, 113
Villarreal Guajardo, Sergio, inheritance of
    scrap steel business from father, 133
Villarreal Guajardo brothers
    donation of money to Calderón,
        231–232
    as enemy of miners, 175
    opposition to workers, 227
    strategy of, against Gómez Urrutia,
        Napoleón, 101–102, 129–130
Virgin of Guadalupe, as emblem of
    Cristeros movement, 40
Vives, Emilio Gómez
    as enemy of miners, 175
    industrial homicide charges leveled
        against, 181
    as Undersecretary, 48
Volkswagen Workers Union, 231
Von Goethe, Johann Wolfgang, quote of,
    141

W

Wage-control policies, 36
Waldman, Lorne, as member of Canadian
    legal team, 299
Warda, Manfred, 302
West Virginia, death of workers in
    accident at coal mine in, 280
"White Cape," 40
Women's Front to Struggle for Workers'
    Dignity in Mexico and the World,
    314–315
Workers Revolutionary Confederation
    (CRT), 41–42, 49
Workers' rights, defense of, 314
Working conditions in globalized
    companies, 155
World Congress of Vienna, Austria,
    election of Gómez Urrutia, Napoleón
    as member of Global Executive
    Committee, 31
World Mint Directors Organization,
    Gómez, Napoleón, as president of,
    12

Y

Yellow unions, 28

Z

Zabludovsky, Abraham, as upstanding
  journalist, 190
Zabludovsky, Jacobo
  radio interview with Moreira, 171, 173
  as upstanding journalist, 190
Zacatecas, 270
Zavala, Juan Ignacio, 165
Zedillo, Ernesto, 164
  government of, 143
Zhenli Ye Gon, 167

Zinser, Alberto, 249–250
  meeting with Gómez Mont, Fernando,
  239–240
Zuñiga, Javier, as loyal union member,
  274
Zúñiga Velázquez, Juan Luis, 295–296
  del Toro, Marco Antonio's
  presentation of complaints on
  behalf on, 134
  forgery of signature of, 133
Zweig, Stefan, quote from, 95

About the Author

Napoleón Gómez Urrutia's struggle for union democracy and for the respect and dignity of workers is well known worldwide. He has served as general secretary of the National Mining and Metal Workers Union since his unanimous election in 2002, and was reelected unanimously for a new six-year term in 2008 in addition to being elected president of the union in 2012. An Oxford-educated economist, Gómez also graduated with honors from the Department of Economics at the National Autonomous University of Mexico. For twelve years, he served as director of the Mexican Mint, and is the only Mexican to serve as international president of the Mint Directors Conference, a position he held for two years.

Gómez was the 2011 recipient of the AFL-CIO's prestigious International Meany-Kirkland Human Rights Award, and in the same year, he was nominated for the Edelstam Prize and the Arthur Svensson International Prize for Trade Union Rights. He is also a member of the executive committee of IndustriALL Global Union, the world's most powerful union organization. He works closely with leaders of unions around the world, including the United Steelworkers Union of North America.

Napoleón is a hero, because every day he fights for the lives and welfare of the Mexican workers and their families.

—RICHARD TRUMKA, PRESIDENT OF THE AFL-CIO